MW00806043

Many thanks, Joe,
for the kind words —

I know they will help
Fritz immensely —

All best,

[signature] Vonnie

September 15, 1995

I Finally get to sign
A Book For you —

Counterfeit Hero

Art Ronnie

Counterfeit Hero

Fritz Duquesne, Adventurer and Spy

Naval Institute Press
Annapolis, Maryland

For Franz Christian Ronnie,
my grandson and staunch comrade in adventure

And for my sons and their wives,
Christopher Patrick and Elizabeth *Liz*
Matthew Brian and Bridget *Bridget*

And, again, for Sharon *Sharon*

© 1995 by Art Ronnie
All rights reserved. No part of this book may be reproduced without
written permission from the publisher.

Library of Congress Cataloging-in-Publication Data
Ronnie, Art.
   Counterfeit hero : Fritz Duquesne, adventurer and spy / Art Ronnie
        p.   cm.
   Includes bibliographical references and index.
   ISBN 1-55750-733-3 (acid-free paper)
   1. Duquesne, Fritz Joubert, b. 1879.   2. Spies—Germany—
Biography.   3. Spies—United States—Biography.   4. World War,
1939–1945—Secret service—Germany.   I. Title.
D810.S8D857   1995
940.54'8743—dc20   95-12401

Printed in the United States of America on acid-free paper ∞
02 01 00 99 98 97 96 95   9 8 7 6 5 4 3 2
First printing

The world's greatest adventurer is Fritz Duquesne.
　　—*Arthur Sullivant Hoffman,* Adventure *magazine*
　　　managing editor, Adventurers Club founder

He was the most adventurous man on earth in the nineteenth and twentieth centuries. He may have been the most adventurous man who ever lived.
　　—*Clement Wood, Fritz Duquesne biographer*

Fritz Duquesne, man of tragedy and sin that he is, is the best company in the world.
　　—*Arthur Pound,* Akron Beacon Journal *managing editor*

You couldn't believe anything Fritz said. But he said it all so perfectly, you thought it was all true.
　　—*Mildred Wortley, sister-in-law*

I believe this man to be one of the most dangerous criminals in the United States.
　　—*George H. McCullough Jr.,*
　　　Leavenworth Penitentiary official

It is known that Duquesne for a period of years resided with women of questionable character and to a degree secured his livelihood from them; and from persons who knew him over a period of years, none have ever stated that he ever pursued a legitimate business for any length of time.
　　—*Federal Bureau of Investigation*

If you want a little advice, never take your shoes off when you're being hunted. A man can't run or fight unless there's leather under him.
　　—*Fritz Duquesne, certified lunatic*

Contents

Author's Note

As in the case of all adventurers, accounts of Duquesne's exploits differ, a certain amount of romance doubtless embellishing all of them.

From New York Times *obituary for 27 April 1916, erroneously reporting the death of Fritz Duquesne in battle with Bolivian Indians*

The *Times* knew its man. Frederick (Fritz) Joubert Duquesne embellished many of his exploits with a certain amount of romance. The embellishment and romance effectively clouded facets in the history of this man who lived the life of a professional spy for more than forty years. Although much is known of his life, some of the truth may never be revealed.

This narrative is the truest account possible. It is gleaned from newspaper and magazine stories, espionage histories, and primary sources, including interviews with his friends, his prison records in South Africa, Bermuda, and America, his personal letters, interviews with Federal Bureau of Investigation special agents who investigated Duquesne, and information from the files of the FBI.

Fritz Duquesne used at least forty aliases, thus confusing his history even more. There was even confusion over his family name. Prison records in South Africa and Bermuda and even his own letters offered several different versions. He was variously identified as Fritz Jean du Quesne, Fritz Jean Duquenne, Fritz Jean du Quenne, Fritz Duquenne, Fritz Joubert du Quenne, and, of course, Fritz Joubert Duquesne. For the purposes of this biography and to avoid confusion, except when quoting a source the accepted spelling will be used: Frederick, or Fritz, Joubert Duquesne.

Acknowledgments

Researching and writing a biography of Fritz Duquesne—a professional rascal who left behind a litter of lies rather than a trail of truth—would have been impossible without the help of many people and organizations too numerous to mention. Here are those who must be mentioned and who helped make believable those few of Fritz's statements that were truthful. (Or were they?)

Altadena Public Library, California. Librarian William J. Tema and his staff, particularly Melloney Bailey, Susan Cahill, Pauli Dutton, Victoria Escobar, Jackie Freeman, Martin Funches, Michelle Hoskins, Laureen McCoy, Jane Mooney, Leone Probst, Joyce Salter, and Connie Shair.

Colin H. Benbow, M.A., assistant professor of history for the Off-Campus Division of the University of Maryland, Warwick. For his invaluable book, *Boer Prisoners of War in Bermuda,* and for a guided tour by motor bike and motorboat of the Bermuda islands on which Fritz Duquesne was imprisoned.

Walter and Roberta Berg. For expert editorial advice.

Andrew Bermingham, retired superintendent, Bermuda Police, Hamilton. For a guided tour of Bermuda's former Boer POW camps.

Robert Brosio, chief assistant U.S. attorney, Los Angeles. For obtaining Fritz's "mug shots."

Jerry Buck. For invaluable editorial advice and for suggesting the title of this book.

Norman A. Carlson, director, United States Department of Justice, Bureau of Prisons.

Rosemarie Close. For Duquesne information.

Kirk Cromer, analyst, Federal Bureau of Investigation.

Wallace Finley Dailey, curator, Theodore Roosevelt Collection, Harvard College Library.

Jerry Devine, producer-director of the radio show *This Is Your FBI*.

John P. Eaton, president, Titanic Historical Society, New York City.

James H. Farmer. For editorial advice.

Kerriann Flanagan-Brosky. For playing Nancy Drew and finding the Centerport spy cottage.

Dr. John A. Gable, executive director, Theodore Roosevelt Association, Oyster Bay, Long Island.

John and Larry Gassman, SPERDVAC, Whittier, California.

Ted Heithecker, president, Old Old Timers Club (Amateur Radio), Irving, Texas.

The House on 92nd Street cast: Leo G. Carroll, Signe Hasso, Lloyd Nolan.

Robert Howard, historian, Beta Theta Pi, Oxford, Ohio.

David Kahn. For research advice.

Rocco Lombardo, supervisor, Reprographic Services, New York Public Library.

Rose Mandelsberg, editor-in-chief, *True Detective*, New York City.

Georgianna McAdam. For Duquesne information.

Jack Nicholas. For his Boer War knowledge.

Tom Owen, Los Angeles Public Library.

Kevin Reeves, of the Bermuda Police, Hamilton.

Guy St. Clair, Alpha Delta Phi Club, New York City.

Don Shump. For his patience and computer skills in preparing the manuscript of *Counterfeit Hero*.

Translators: Afrikaans—Sonny Ismond, Rayno Seegers. Flemish—Henri Bollinger. French—M. Olivier. German—Christle Balvin, Claude A. Molveau, Ernest Semler, Raymond Semler, Franz Vote. Spanish—Elizabeth Ronnie.

Transvaal Archives Depot, Department of National Education, Government Archives, Republic of South Africa. G. J. Reynecke, former chief. J. H. Snyman, chief.

University Club, New York City. Teresa Janiello, secretary. Stephen Joy, former secretary.

P.M.E. van Zyl, city librarian, Durban, South Africa.

Mary V. Yates. For being an exceptional editor and for never having the courtesy to be wrong.

Counterfeit Hero

Prologue

Pride forced the old man to push one foot after the other on his tortured walk through the sweltering streets of New York City.

Age, a stroke, and almost thirteen years in a federal penitentiary had robbed the once robust and athletic figure of its strength and military bearing. Now the man was bent and limping. The pleasant and resonant voice that had once enchanted audiences, and that for a lifetime had affected a clipped English accent, was now a halting and slurred whisper.

A long, aimless ride on the subway, and now this rambling walk through the streets of the city he once knew so well, had put him on the verge of collapse. He would have fallen hours ago, but memories of past glories and family pride propelled him.

It was eleven o'clock at night now, and the evening hours had brought some cooling comfort, but he knew there would be no comfort back at the London Arms Nursing Home in his airless room with its awful stench from the festering bowels of the other patients. It would be maddening.

Stumbling along West Twenty-second Street, he at last found the brick-facade home at number 443. The physical relief did more than momentarily ease his pain. It also lifted a burden of mental anguish. He had violated his parole by going uptown without permission. But the possibility of work and of a movie deal—a movie based on his life—was too much of an incentive to risk his parole officer forbidding the journey uptown.

Grasping the iron railing to the steps leading below street level, he agonizingly made his way down the stairs, relieved that he could now stop proving he wasn't an invalid. Despite the stench and the heat of his unventilated room, he could lie down and rest.

What were the thoughts of the seventy-eight-year-old man as he lay back in the uncomfortable bed seeking relief from the pain and misery of his present condition, a handkerchief across his face to filter the fetid air?

The date was 13 July 1955. But was it really so long ago that the old man had lived so elegantly in New York? It must have seemed so as he lay there between soiled sheets, surrounded by rotting patients.

An obsessed Anglophobe, he had spent more than forty years of his life as a spy, attempting single-handedly to destroy the British Empire. It all came to an abrupt halt in 1941 when he and thirty-two other German espionage agents were arrested by the FBI in what director J. Edgar Hoover called "the greatest spy roundup in U.S. history."

But during those four decades preceding the nadir of his career, he was often called the world's greatest adventurer. In those action-crowded years he was a soldier of fortune, Boer prisoner of war, escaper several times over, pimp, explorer, lecturer, animal conservationist, environmentalist, presidential adviser, inventor, newspaper reporter and editor, novelist, playwright, movie publicist, WPA inspector, stockbroker, womanizer, poseur, fraud, liar, spy, saboteur, murderer, traitor, and certified lunatic.

His mystique was so great that in 1942 at the age of sixty-five, while serving a term of eighteen years for espionage and confined to a maximum-security cell in Leavenworth Federal Penitentiary, a prison official said of the old and ailing spy who would never again go out in the cold, "I believe this man to be one of the most dangerous criminals in the United States."

He was no hero, but his was an incredible life encompassing bizarre exploits of drama, danger, and adventure few people are privileged to live.

That life was led by Frederick Joubert Duquesne—Fritz, the counterfeit hero.

CHAPTER 1

Huguenots and Boers

W HEN LOUIS XIV, the Sun King of France, repealed the Edict of Nantes in 1685, thus restricting freedom of worship to Catholics, stubborn Huguenots, who had fought a civil war for sixty years and had enjoyed religious freedom for another eighty years as a result of that war, packed what few possessions they could carry and went to England, Denmark, Switzerland, and the Netherlands. Of the fifty thousand refugee families, many went to Holland, where fellow Calvinists welcomed them. French names like du Toit, Malan, Joubert, and Duquesne infused the country.

The Dutch East India Company, ever watchful for immigrants, was particularly delighted with the prospects of settling the Huguenot hordes on territory awarded the company by the Netherlands government. That territory included all the land west of the Strait of Magellan in South America to the Cape of Good Hope at the southernmost tip of Africa. When the first permanent settlement was made at the Cape in 1652, the company was authorized to set up trading centers, to raise taxes, to pass sentences of death, and to make war. Freedom to practice any religion was an additional inducement that persuaded thousands of Huguenots to sail for South Africa in December 1687. Though they became absorbed through the centuries into the Dutch way of life in Africa, their names, culture, and agriculture remained obstinately independent of the Afrikaners.

Among these new Afrikaners were the Duquesnes and Jouberts, the Duquesnes being relatives of the great French naval commander Abraham Marquis du Quesne, who, ironically, had served nobly under that same Sun King who forced the Huguenots into exile.[1] Du Quesne, a staunch Calvinist, had distinguished himself in the Thirty Years War. His greatest exploit was decisively defeating the combined fleets of the Dutch and Spanish in 1678. In 1681 he received the title of marquis, his Protestantism precluding his ever being made an admiral. Despite the revocation of the Edict of Nantes, his reputation protected him, and he was allowed to retire in peace. Too great to yield his religion and too old to leave his country, Marquis du Quesne did help outfit some of the ships that took fellow Calvinists and members of his family to South Africa.

The descendants of the great French sailor settled, along with many other Huguenots, in Pondoland, Cape Province, a territory along the coast of the Indian Ocean. In 1875 Abraham Duquenne—Fritz did not adopt the familiar spelling until he came to America in 1902—married Minna Joubert. She was a sister, Fritz always claimed, of Piet Joubert, the Boer patriot who ran unsuccessfully several times for the presidency of the Republic of Transvaal and who was commandant general of the country's army during the Second Anglo-Boer War. Even though "Clever" Piet was noted for possessing innumerable relatives, there is no evidence, either in Joubert family records or in historical records, that Fritz was related to the general.

The Duquennes settled in East London, a port city on the mouth of the Buffalo River. Following the Crimean War many Germans who had fought with Britain in the Crimea settled there. Fritz would have his first contact with Germans among these immigrants, a people who would greatly influence his adult life.

Frederick L'Huguenot Joubert Duquenne, or Fritz, as he was more familiarly known, was born to Abraham and Minna on 21 December 1877, in a little upper chamber of a house on Oxford Street just above the Buffalo River.[2] A sister, Elsbet, and a brother, Pedro, would follow. Fritz Duquesne always rejected this rather prosaic account of his beginnings, preferring a more dramatic nativity that had his parents on a trek across country with a party of Boers. At the moment of his birth an attacking party of Kaffirs were being beaten off, so the first sound this future soldier of fortune heard was the rattle of musketry. Most of his stories of his early life are as fanciful and changeable as that of his birth. The details of his youth as related here are largely drawn from Clement Wood's 1932 biography, *The Man Who Killed Kitchener*, and verified when possible.

Embellishment of the truth became one of his most conspicuous attributes as he matured, and his consummate skill as a liar often confused even himself as throughout his long life he continually reinvented the persona of Fritz Duquesne. His claims sometimes reached heroic proportions, and he found it easier and more romantic to believe his own accounts than to believe the truth, even though the two were often in conflict.

For this reason it is difficult to separate fact from fiction in Fritz's early years. Captain Franz von Papen, Germany's saboteur-diplomat and military attaché to the United States, described spies and their stories in his 1953 *Memoirs:* "In all spy stories [the author] seeks to bolster up some of his genuine successes with a certain amount of fantastic overelaboration."[3] Franz must have had Fritz in mind.

One such elaboration was his account of being captured as a teenager by a band of Kaffirs. (Kaffirs were members of a Bantu-speaking tribe, but the term became one of opprobrium, and the Boers used it to describe any African black.) He escaped torture and death only by making love to the buxom daughter of his captors' chieftain. It could have happened, though most of his teen years were spent in England. It was also the kind of story that bolstered, he believed, his appeal to women. In this there was some truth: Fritz never lacked for feminine companionship.

Abraham Duquenne was a hunter and trader who roamed all over South Africa, bartering animal skins, tusks, and horns. When he was away, which was often, his place was taken by old, blind great-uncle Jan Duquenne. Uncle Jan had once been a hunter too, but years earlier an elephant gun had exploded during a hunt, blowing away his eyes and much of his face.

The family fortunes grew, and a farm was purchased near Nylstroom, a village in the northern Transvaal. Trekkers at one time believed that the Nyl River, flowing nearby, was the source of the Nile. Nylstroom was more like an African village than a white man's farm. There were two large houses for the white people and thatched huts for the servants and native workers in the kraal. Stables and a trading room completed the complex. There wasn't another farm for two miles. An old Kaffir grandma nursed Fritz, and Kaffirs taught the boy how to whittle the iron-hard wood from the *bolkenhout* tree into fantastic shapes, how to shear sheep, milk cows, and wring the neck of a chicken, and—most important to young Fritz—how to use a Zulu assegai. There was the hurling assegai and the unique short spear designed for use as a thrusting weapon in close combat.

Expert with both, Fritz used one in a fatal encounter before he was a teenager. A Zulu had stopped at the farm to trade a sack of peas for goods. Not satisfied with the beads, cloth, and liquor Fritz's mother offered in exchange, and knowing that the only man in the house was old and blind Uncle Jan, the Zulu advanced threateningly. He ignored the small boy watching in fear. Unseen, Fritz picked up the Zulu's stabbing assegai where it had been laid aside, and at the moment the African leaped at his mother, Fritz made his move. The Zulu never saw him. He only felt the spear enter his stomach midway in his leap. Screaming as he fell and thrashing in agony, he pulled at the assegai where it had snapped in two from the force of the thrust.

"You've killed him!" screamed Fritz's mother, stunned.

"He was a dog. It's what niggers are for," said the young Fritz, trying to hold back the tears. Then with a sudden tumult of tears, he cried, "Oh, mother!" and buried his head in the folds of her skirt. "I wasn't frightened a bit. But I did feel funny."

A peaceful and religious society, the Boers nevertheless were prepared to fight for their principles, and they trained from youth to ride and shoot. Their commando system, perfected over the years, allowed them to become fully mobilized at a moment's notice to repel the hostile natives who often attacked farms and populated areas without warning. All burghers aged sixteen to sixty were eligible for military service, but commandos often contained members who were younger or older.

Fritz encountered his first warring natives when he was twelve, fighting for his life with his parents and relatives in a laager (camp).[4] It all started at noon one day at the Nylstroom farm when a cloud of dust, created by a hard-riding horseman, could be seen moving swiftly along the road toward the farm. Knowing that only bad news traveled so fast on a day like this, Abraham Duquenne was prepared for the worst when his son called him out to the farmyard. "The impis are on the warpath!" shouted the horseman as he reined up. "They're swarming across the countryside! Take your women and children to the laager at Sand River. And get me another horse so I can ride to the next farm!"

While a Kaffir rushed to get a fresh horse, Duquenne scattered the others with orders to inspan (harness) the oxen and round up the cattle. Wagons, each drawn by sixteen oxen, were hastily loaded with biltong (jerked meat) and other food, cooking utensils, clothing, and specially prized articles. Members of the family and the servants took their seats, Fritz's mother clutching the big family Bible to her breast.

The wagons lumbered across the veld. Silhouetted against the setting sun were neighboring farmers Piet van Reenan and Fritz's Uncle Koos and his family. Before midnight half a dozen more trains joined them. The men scouted on the flanks, wary of a Kaffir ambush while the daring Oom Koos rode far ahead. Suddenly one came galloping back. "Laager! Laager!" he cried. "The Kaffirs are in the grass!"

Quickly the wagons were formed into a square, enclosing the oxen and horses. Heavy baggage was piled in strategic places, along with whatever else would present a shield. The children's hands were filled with bullets to pass to those loading the rifles while a number of men stood guard about two hundred yards from the wagon.

The attack came in the morning, interrupting the prayers of the families gathered in the camp's open ground. A guard fired a warning shot when he caught sight of the ostrich plumes worn as headdresses by the Kaffirs moving silently through the tall grass. The guards came running in, and without orders the men, women, and children grimly took their places. Fritz, already an expert shot, manned a position by the wagon tongues.

Then with screams meant to bring terror to the defenders, the Kaffirs rose and charged the laager, holding their shields outstretched and hurling their assegais as soon as they were within range. Some were armed with English rifles and gave support to the charge from behind distant rocks.

The screaming natives were almost upon the camp before a thunderous defending volley piled up the first ranks in heaps of dead and wounded. But the mass behind plunged madly on until the charge was checked at the wheels of the wagons by the murderous gunfire unleashed as rapidly as the Boers could pull a trigger and replace empty weapons with loaded guns hastily handed to them by the women and children not in the firing line.

Still the Kaffirs charged, many of them close enough to use their stabbing assegais. Much of the combat now was hand to hand, empty guns being used for clubs, while rifles too hot to be held from the incessant firing were gripped with wet cloths. So desperate were the Kaffirs to break the square that they grasped bodies of their own dead and used them for shields as they pressed forward. Women grabbed handfuls of mixed pepper and sand and threw the stinging particles into the faces of the attackers until they fell back, painfully blinded.

After hours of desperate fighting and unable to pierce the defenses of the laager, the Kaffirs withdrew to try another form of attack. They set fire to the grass. Soon it was burning in a great circle around the camp. As the flames came nearer to the wagons, some of the defenders tore up the grass inside the laager while others sallied out to clear the grass away and pile bodies of the dead Kaffirs in a circle to break the fire. But the flames and the assegais hurled at them drove the men back in.

Aware that the Kaffirs did not know how greatly they had been weakened, the Boers gambled on a desperate effort to stop the attack by sortieing out into their midst with a bold charge. Two-thirds of the remaining men mounted their horses and dashed out of the laager, cut through the attacking lines, and wheeling instantly, fell upon the Kaffirs from the rear. The Kaffir center was shattered, and the divided wings fled in wild disorder. But the Boers kept up a running fight for miles and did not return until they were sure they had thoroughly broken the will of the raiders. Uncle Koos, his wife, and their baby were lost in the attack along the Sand River.

Hunting was as much a way of life for the Boer as fighting was. Fritz became a fine hunter. It would have been difficult to avoid the pursuit, considering his environment. His hunting skills proved of inestimable value to him as an adult, when he made a comfortable income writing about big-game hunting for American newspapers and magazines.

As a youth Fritz became attracted to the beauty and litheness of the panther, an attraction that during the Boer War earned him the soubriquet the Black Panther of the Veld. Throughout his life he liked to tell the story of how he first observed one of the ebony felines. His father had taken him at age eleven along with a hunting party into Mozambique, a territory of Portuguese East Africa. When the hunters split up to seek different quarry, Fritz was told to wait with his rifle beside a tree near a water hole. Throughout the day Fritz watched the cautious animals drink their fill. When a Cape buffalo dipped its great head to the water, Fritz caught a slight movement in a tree a few feet above. It was a panther, tensed and motionless, ready to spring. Suddenly aware of its danger, the buffalo bolted. The panther remained still. There would be another day.

Fritz was impressed by the attitude of the sleek cat. Obviously not one to waste an attack, it would wait until its prey was at a maximum disadvantage, then strike without warning or quarter. It became his own hunting style. In later life the parallel was obvious. Fritz was the black panther waiting to pounce. England was his prey.

Enhancing his affinity for the panther was the Kaffir belief that every human at the time of birth is associated in some way with the animal world, and that his nature is controlled and motivated by some animal's characteristics.[5] That animal is the human's totem. One must never slay the totem or eat its flesh. The black panther was a sinister totem that the Kaffir believed would work relentless evil in the spirit of a man until he died. It was a symbol of black, undying hatred. For Fritz it symbolized his own passions toward England as a young adult during and after the Boer War.

It surely did not go unnoticed by Fritz that two black, snarling panthers on the attack were represented in the coat of arms of the Duquesne family. It was a neat contrivance. During his spy activities prior to America's entry into World War II, Fritz continued his association with the panther by stamping all his communiqués to Germany with the figure of a cat, its back arched and fur raised in anger. He called it a "cat's paw"; he was that cat, poised in anger and always ready to strike.[6]

Life for the Boer in South Africa was not as idyllic as it might seem. A long-smoldering condition that would shape the thinking and life of Fritz Duquesne was the fact that since 1877 the Boers had been under the unyielding thumb of Queen Victoria. It was an intolerable situation for the freedom-loving Boers, whose ancestors had escaped the yoke of a French king. It was unthinkable that their descendants should be restrained by the yoke of a British queen.

The yoke became so heavy in 1877 that Sir Theophilus Shepstone, secretary for native affairs in Natal, declared the Transvaal a British possession.[7] Otherwise, he believed, the country would only fall into anarchy because of the constant hostility of the Zulus, troubles with the Pedi led by Sekhukhune in the northern Transvaal, and the near bankruptcy of the Boer government. The British used the proclamation as a ploy to occupy the country with troops. The result was an administration more satisfactory to the British, but hardly so to the Boers.

Benjamin Disraeli was led to believe that the Boers approved of annexation. But in June 1880 the *London Times* editorialized, "English-

men will find it difficult to reconcile themselves to the forcible occupation of a country whose people declare that they never have been
and do not wish to be Her Majesty's subjects."[8] Even more difficult for
Englishmen to reconcile themselves to was defeat by a "bunch of farmers" when the Boers in 1881, impatient with British domination, fought
the First Boer War and decisively beat English troops at Majuba Hill.
Prime Minister William Gladstone restored the Boers' independence,
with Britain retaining suzerainty only over the South African Republic's foreign relations.

The Boers lived with this quasi-independence until 1886, when the
world's richest gold fields were discovered at Witwatersrand—the
Rand—in the southern Transvaal. Overnight the city of Johannesburg
grew up in the center of the Rand, which quickly became a magnet for
an international gold rush.

The Boers were appalled by the rabble of foreigners—they called
them Uitlanders (Outlanders)—who poured into their republic, attracted by the lure of quick riches in the gold fields. Most repugnant
was that the greatest number of those people were British, which immediately created new problems. President Oom Paul Kruger of the
Transvaal and his almost dictatorial powers disallowed the Uitlanders
a franchise. Though they were becoming wealthy, the British wanted
the right to vote and representation in the Volksraad, the republic's
parliament. But Kruger, aware that the Uitlanders would soon out-
number his burghers, denied them the franchise that could well mean
the end of the Boer republic.

It was a seething cauldron, a situation both sides believed could be
settled only by war.

It was in this climate of hate that young Fritz was weaned, but it was
in England that he received his education. There he developed the
clipped British accent he used throughout his life. Despite his hatred
of the British, their style of speech best fitted his character, drawing attention to himself and lending an aura of romance to the figure of history and intrigue he believed he was creating.[9]

The spurious Uncle Piet Joubert was responsible for sending him
and other promising boys to hated England for schooling. Uncle Piet
lectured them on their duty to their country:

It is from our young men that the salvation of the Republic tomorrow, the
preservation of its liberty, the achievement of its success and infinite wealth
and eternal independence is to come. All that is what you are being trained
for. England for a little while; then to school on the continent where you can

fit yourself for our diplomatic service, speaking like a diplomat as well as like a burgher. We must have leaders!

So it was a forlorn boy, just thirteen, who one day in 1890 boarded the German steamer *Kamerun* at the foot of Jetty Street in Port Elizabeth. Despite the prospect of a great future, it wasn't easy for him to leave his mother and his beloved South Africa. But as a patriot and the son of a prominent farmer and businessman in the republic, he reconciled himself to his duty. The sea voyage ended at Hamburg, and within a week he was settled in an expensive private school in central England.

Physically well developed, Fritz excelled in the unfamiliar sports played in England: rugby, cricket, wrestling, and boxing. Because he at first refused to mix with the English boys, he found it a defense to surpass them in their own games. A fine student, and convinced that he was a man of destiny in South Africa, he realized that he must have the knowledge necessary for the position. Two years later he returned home for a vacation, then it was back to the English school for another two years.

It was during his last term at school that he experienced his first affair, if the incident with the Kaffir chieftain's buxom daughter can be discounted. The romance with Elspeth, the daughter of Dr. Helton, the vicar, lasted the rest of the term. Fritz used women to his advantage all his life, discarding them when they were no longer of any use to him. An exceptionally handsome man throughout his life, he never experienced difficulty in acquiring feminine companionship.

Fritz completed a year at Oxford and then, in accord with the wishes of Uncle Joubert, who wished his South African boys to be thoroughly educated in the arts, sciences, and the military, Fritz was enrolled at the Ecole Militaire, the Belgian West Point in Brussels. In addition, he spent a short time at the French military academy St. Cyr, and at Napoleon's artillery school, La Fère.

It was at the Ecole, according to Clement Wood, that Fritz acquired his great knowledge of explosives, military engineering, and artillery. He also trained under the celebrated fencing master Julian Mercks. Fritz became so skilled that in two years he was the champion swordsman of all Europe, winning the International Tournament in foils, rapier, and sabre. (He was careful never to mention in which year he demonstrated this dazzling display of sword work.) He also made enemies. His arrogance and womanizing resulted in eight duels, in three of which he killed his man.

Frederick Joubert Duquesne at age twenty. "The handsomest man and deadliest swordsman in Europe!" according to The Man Who Killed Kitchener. *So young to have so many medals. From the credit on the photo, it appears to have been taken in Vienna. (Author's collection)*

There is in fact no trace of Fritz's attendance in the records at Oxford, St. Cyr, La Fère, or the Ecole Militaire.[10] The following story told by him, although less dashing and romantic, is probably closer to the truth.[11] Following a vacation in Africa after completing his English schooling, Fritz was sent to Europe to study military engineering. But aboard the ship he met an elderly tutor, Christian de Vries, who persuaded him to use his school money for a trip around the world.[12] He subsequently learned that de Vries was really an absconding bank cashier who had already squandered the large sums of money he had embezzled. De Vries was now determined to squander, with Fritz's assistance, Abraham Duquenne's money.

"So we started off," recounted Fritz. "I paid the tutor's way. He was always thirsty—extremely so—for at each port he would go ashore and fill up on 'stagga juice.' Thus matters ran along for six months or so until my father overtook us in Singapore. He had a heavy sjambok with him and both the tutor and myself got a painful taste of that whip."

There is no authentic record of what Fritz did for the next three years. But in all probability he knocked about Europe pursuing some form of education in addition to his playboy activities. Sporadically, he returned home for hunting safaris.

But whatever his activities were, it was now 1899. Fritz was twenty-two, and differences between the Boers and British in South Africa had reached a point where war seemed the only solution. Matters had been precipitated by the fiasco of the Jameson Raid, a quasi-military venture arranged by financial magnate Cecil Rhodes, who had made his fortune in the Kimberley diamond mines. He was managing director of the British South African Company, prime minister of Cape Colony, and a determined empire builder. Leader of the raid was Dr. Leander Starr Jameson, a good friend of Rhodes's with a nihilist turn of mind.

It had been rumored that a group of Uitlanders in Johannesburg, calling themselves the Reformers, were plotting rebellion against the Kruger government. Rhodes decided to support them. When the rebellion broke out, Jameson would ride in with his troops and add to their strength. But indecision on the part of the Reformers caused Rhodes to withdraw his support. Undaunted, James rode across the Transvaal in the last part of December 1895 to precipitate the rebellion. But there was no rising of the Uitlanders, and Jameson was ignominiously captured a few days later on 2 January 1896.

After this military muddle there was only a semblance of relations between England and the Transvaal. Then in 1897 Sir Hercules Robinson, high commissioner of South Africa, was replaced by Sir Alfred Milner, who was dedicated to maintaining British supremacy in South Africa. Even if it meant "working up a crisis," Milner would demand the franchise and other civic rights for the Uitlanders. But Kruger regarded compromise on any issue as detrimental to Boer independence. At the Bloemfontein Conference in June 1899, negotiations broke down completely between Milner and Kruger over the question of the Uitlander franchise. Joseph Chamberlain, the colonial secretary in England, now championed the cause of the Uitlanders.

It was about this time that Fritz received a letter from his father urging him to return home because of the imminence of war:

So you see why the diplomat must wait until the soldier has finished his job [wrote Abraham Duquenne]. Your uncle, the general, and I agree that with your knowledge of the hinterland and your new found skills you should be with our scouts. A commission awaits you on your return. You are to close up your affairs with the utmost haste and proceed to Hamburg. Do not delay. Time is precious if we are to give the Rooineks the blood bath they would wish on us. Hurry.[13]

According to Clement Wood, Fritz's father was already dead at the time of this letter.[14] But as with all of Fritz's family—except for his mother—his father, brother, and sister seemed immortal and were resurrected at Fritz's convenience.

While Fritz was on his way home, events in South Africa were moving rapidly toward hostilities and the Second Anglo-Boer War (or, as the Boers called it, the Second War of Independence). Great Britain and the South African Republic were gripped by war fever. Britain sent reinforcements from England and mobilized what few troops it had in South Africa while Boer commandos were mustering across the veld. The Orange Free State, resolved to support its neighboring republic, joined the Transvaal in issuing an ultimatum to Milner on 9 October 1899. Drafted by Jan Smuts, the young state attorney—a brilliant commando leader in the coming war and prime minister of the Union of South Africa from 1919 to 1924—it demanded the withdrawal of British troops from their frontiers and the dispersal of all reinforcements. The ultimatum expired on 11 October. Britain did not comply, and war was declared on 12 October.

Britain moved immediately to close all ports into South Africa and deny the Boers lines of supply to the outside world. The only link to this outside world for the Boers was the railway line from Pretoria, the Transvaal capital, east across the high veld to Komati Poort on the border of Portuguese East Africa (now Mozambique), then diagonally south to Lourenço Marques, the colony's capital on Delagoa Bay in the Indian Ocean. It was the only way the Boers could be supplied, and it was the only way they could escape when blockaded by British men-of-war in December 1899 and the following January.

Fritz arrived in Lourenço Marques before the month was out.

Life would never again be the same for him. The fate of his country and of his family would breed in him an all-consuming hatred of England—would turn him into what Clement Wood called a "walking living breathing searing killing destroying torch of hate."[15] In a few months he would be launched on a forty-year career as a professional spy and a counterfeit hero—a man who would constantly reinvent himself to suit the needs of the moment.

CHAPTER 2

The Black Panther of the Veld

FRITZ DUQUESNE was not yet twenty-two years old when he boarded the Delagoa Bay Railway for Boer headquarters in Pretoria, where he was given a lieutenant's commission, the first of his military ranks; colonel would be his last. Fritz was attached to the staff of the commandant general and the man he claimed was his uncle, the elderly Slim Piet Joubert.

The war was going well for the upstart bearded farmers whose strange garb of broad-brimmed hats, long coats, and corduroy trousers was abhorrent to the spit-and-polish soldiers of the queen who confidently expected to sweep through South Africa in a rush. Their only concern was that these odd fellows who sang hymns and prayed aloud for guidance and victory before every battle wouldn't put up much of a struggle. Someone must have been listening to the prayers of "Johnny Boer," because it was not the rout expected by the watching world and the jingoist Brits at home. These shaggy men on their shaggy horses were fighters and supreme marksmen who taught new tactics to an army mired in tradition that still had lessons to learn in modern warfare and particularly in guerrilla tactics.

In a rare tribute to a vanquished but unrelentingly aggressive foe, Arthur Conan Doyle described the farmer-fighter best in his history of that conflict, *The Great Boer War:*

Take a community of Dutchmen of the type of those who defended themselves for fifty years against all the power of Spain at a time when Spain was the greatest power in the world. Intermix with them a strain of those inflexible French Huguenots who gave up home and fortune and left their country forever at the time of the revocation of the Edict of Nantes. The product must obviously be one of the most rugged, virile, unconquerable races ever seen upon earth. Take this formidable people and train them for seven generations in constant warfare against savage men and ferocious beasts, in circumstances under which no weakling could survive, place them so that they acquire exceptional skill with weapons and in horsemanship, give them a country which is eminently suited to the tactics of the huntsman, the marksman, and the rider. Then, finally, put a finer temper upon their military qualities by a dour fatalistic Old Testament religion and an ardent and consuming patriotism. Combine all these qualities and all these impulses in one individual, and you have the modern Boer—the most formidable antagonist who ever crossed the path of Imperial Britain.[1]

That formidable antagonist lay siege to Mafeking in northwestern Cape Colony for seven months beginning 14 October 1899.[2] The invested British soldiers and civilians became a patriotic rallying point back in their island home where surprised and discouraged Victorian England, used to quick victories by the empire, was now becoming concerned about those disheveled farmers. British khakis (or kakis), as the Boers called all British soldiers because of their dust-colored uniforms, won the battle of Talana Hill, but at great cost; and they won a decisive victory at Elandslaagte, which avenged the army's loss at Majuba Hill in the First Anglo-Boer War in 1881.

The kakis appeared to be on a roll until they suffered a humiliating defeat in a mountain pass called Nicholson's Nek. It was the first of three devastating defeats for the English army in a single day. The date was 20 October and was set down in British military history as Mournful Monday.

Then the boorish Boers won a decisive victory a second time at Lombard's Kop, where Fritz was first blooded in battle. Lieutenant General Sir George White, in command of the British army in Natal, had hoped to use his entire force of thirteen thousand troops to outflank the Boers at Lombard's Kop, east of Ladysmith and one of several hills surrounding the town soon to become famous throughout the world. Leading White's cavalry was Major General John French, who in fifteen years, during the coming Great War, would be appointed commander-in-chief of the British expeditionary force to France. His chief of staff was Major Douglas Haig, later a field marshal who would succeed French as commander-in-chief in France.

But neither French's cavalry nor the numerical superiority of White's forces could break through the Boer defenses and the havoc created by their accurate rifle fire and artillery. The British were forced to fall back in "extreme confusion"—a euphemism for a rout—to Ladysmith, where they remained besieged by the hymn singers until February 1900. It was the third defeat that day for British arms and, indeed, a Mournful Monday. It was Majuba all over again.

And how had Lieutenant Fritz Duquesne fared?

He received a bullet through his right shoulder.[3] It was a wound he wore in triumph for the rest of his life, not being shy to show it at the right opportunity, and of course not being shy about embroidering with exquisite braggadocio the tale of how he had received it.

Six months later, on 15 December, General Redvers Buller, V.C., commander-in-chief of all British forces in South Africa, determined to relieve Ladysmith by advancing through the small village of Colenso twelve miles south, cross the Tugela River, and then march uphill through the defending Boers, who at that time, it was planned, would be under attack from the rear by the besieged General White's troopers sortieing out from Ladysmith. Buller would then continue marching victoriously through the Orange Free State and into the Transvaal.

It was a good plan but failed miserably despite the overwhelming British force of twenty-one thousand men, including sixteen thousand infantry and upwards of four thousand cavalry and mounted infantry supported by artillery and naval guns in great strength. Facing what was considered to be the largest body of men ever put into the field in modern warfare by the British was a relatively small force of Boers numbering about six thousand men. (All of these figures vary by a few thousand in the many accounts of the battle.)

England had suffered Mournful Monday and was now to agonize through Black Week, when from 10 to 17 December the empire's military endured the trauma of staggering defeats at Stormberg, Magersfontein, and Colenso.

British naval guns in the field opened the engagement at Colenso a little after five in the morning under a clear blue sky on a day that developed into an unrelenting fury of seething heat. Shells fell into the seven miles of kopjes (hills) where the Boers were entrenched north of the Tugela River. They did not respond but waited patiently for the advancing infantry.

Fritz Duquesne was dug in with the Boers, who were so well protected and hidden from sight in their trenches gouged out of the hillsides that it was reported by the majority of the kakis that they never even saw a Boer during the one-sided battle. With the British so close, the Boers could not miss. They poured down a hailstorm of bullets into the closely grouped ranks. Their vaunted marksmanship was not needed. They didn't even have to take aim.

It was the first battle for the burghers under the command of Louis Botha, who had taken charge of the Boer armies when the sixty-eight-year-old Piet Joubert was thrown from his horse and severely injured. Inexperienced, unschooled but brilliant, and a natural politician, Botha proved to be a master strategist and a fine tactician. In 1910 he would become the first prime minister of the newly formed Union of South Africa.

It was this charismatic amateur who put to flight General Buller, who had distinguished himself in wars against the Chinese and the Zulus, winning a Victoria Cross for bravery in 1879. He had also taken part in the Gordon Relief Expedition in an attempt to save that ill-fated general at Khartoum. Despite his great experience and skills in battle, Buller was an amateur when it came to conception and execution of an overall campaign. He had never done either.

His command was to suffer one of the great humiliations in British military history shortly after the battle began. Outracing the infantry, and thus losing its protection, were twelve Royal Artillery guns under the command of Colonel Charles Young, who placed the heavy weapons in parade drill order only seven hundred yards from the Boer front line of defense. Young's gunners and horses suffered heavy losses from the withering fire of the farmers.

More men were lost attempting to retrieve the guns, the loss of which remained for years an ignominious disgrace to British arms. Only two were recovered. Among those killed in the attempt was Lieutenant Frederick Roberts, the only son of Field Marshal Lord Frederick S. Roberts, V.C., of Kandahār (soon to replace Buller).

Unable to accept the continuing slaughter of his troops, Buller ordered a withdrawal before twelve noon. Fritz, now a captain of artillery, was placed in charge of the remaining ten guns.[4] The Boers offered prayers of thanks for their victory, and Fritz no doubt gloried in the task he had been given.

Then the "body snatchers" began the gruesome and wearisome chore of collecting the bodies of dead and wounded British soldiers. They were the South African Indian Ambulance Corps under the leadership of a young barrister named Mohandas Gandhi, later to be called the Mahatma. Their grim assignment would continue throughout the following evening, in the penumbra of a full eclipse of the moon.

The Boers followed up their stunning victory at Colenso with an aggressive and energetic propaganda war on the continent directed by the former state secretary of the Transvaal and now minister of the republic, Dr. Willem J. Leyds. As official representative of the South African Republic in Brussels, this talented, intriguing, and sometimes unpopular man fed the flames of Anglophobia and was responsible for the propaganda that accused the British of unspeakable atrocities.[5] Leyds would aid Fritz almost a year later in returning him to South Africa and the war after a prison escape.

On 18 December, only three days after Colenso, the British government replaced Buller with Lord Roberts—affectionately known as "Bobs" to his troopers—as commander-in-chief, although Buller retained command of forces in the field. Because of Roberts's sixty-seven years, a younger man and one who had distinguished himself in the Sudan was named his chief of staff. For Fritz Duquesne it was a fateful appointment and one that would have a profound role in shaping the rest of his life.

The forty-nine-year-old chief of staff was Major General Lord Horatio Herbert Kitchener of Khartoum and Aspall. The cold and ruthless Kitchener would eventually succeed Roberts as commander-in-chief and, because of questionable tactics used to end the war, would become the object of Duquesne's hatred and the rationale for his lifelong determination, however illogical, to destroy the British Empire.

Meanwhile, a new century had begun. It was 1900, and the war persisted. But no longer were the Boers favored by a string of surprising victories. The Roberts-Kitchener team had turned the tide, and the inevitable defeat of the burghers was marching steadily closer. The farmers won a questionable victory in the bloody horror of Spion Kop. General Piet Cronje surrendered his army at Paardeberg, and Buller finally relieved Ladysmith. Mafeking was also relieved, General Joubert died, the British won at Driefontein and Bloemfontein, the Orange

Lord Horatio Kitchener, Fritz's raison d'être, *the cause for his raging hatred against England. (Imperial War Museum, London)*

Free State was annexed, and Johannesburg, the Transvaal's largest town with its treasured Rand gold fields, was captured, as was Pretoria, the capital.

The Boer government fled the fallen capital, and President Kruger began his long flight from May to October to Lourenço Marques and to exile in Europe. To keep the Boer treasury from the British, Kruger ordered over a million pounds—or five million, depending on the story's source—of gold bullion from the Johannesburg mines and state treasury to be placed aboard the Delagoa Bay Railway for transfer to Lourenço Marques and to eventual safety in Europe. But fearful that the rail line could fall to the kakis at any time, it was decided to transport the bullion by thirty ox-drawn wagons rather than by train to the coast.

This was the setting for another Fritz Duquesne myth, one that earned him another soubriquet: the Man Who Hid the Kruger Millions. It may have been simply one more romantic story created and circulated by Fritz. Nevertheless, it persists.[6]

The wagons were loaded in secret. Some contained state papers; the others held the bullion. They were sent out at different times in different directions under the command of picked men with instructions to rendezvous at a location in the eastern Transvaal. There, other men bearing credentials from Kruger would take over.

But the plan took a different course following the rendezvous. After trekking a few miles they were met by Duquesne, who showed them what was purported to be a letter from President Kruger giving him supreme command of all the wagons. After carefully examining the wagons, he sent fifteen on to Lourenço Marques and set out into the bush with the remaining fifteen wagons holding the gold. The trekkers with Fritz included four white men and a number of Kaffirs.

During the next two weeks as they trekked deeper into the bush, the white men learned of the gold and decided to get rid of Duquesne and keep the spoils. Their plan was to knife him while he slept and take control of the convoy. But the Black Panther of the Veld was not easily fooled. A bullet entered the head of the assassin before his knife could plunge into a blanket roll stuffed with clothing. Then Fritz fired three more times from concealment, and Kruger's millions were his.

Fritz turned the convoy south to the Drakensberg Mountains, where he ordered the Kaffirs to carry the gold by hand into the Caves of the Leopards. A hostile native kraal nearby objected to the behavior of Duquesne's men, who were making advances to their women. Fritz saw the advantage of this hostility and figured that if his men were killed there would be no witnesses to where the gold was hidden. Fritz visited the chieftain. What transpired is not known, but Fritz was always persuasive. Two nights later the natives attacked the Duquesne camp, and all his followers were killed. The wagons were burned, and the assassins were given all the oxen but one as a reward. Triumphant, the Man Who Hid the Kruger Millions rode away on the ox.

The story, which varies in details, never reveals whether Fritz wanted the gold for himself or for his country after the war ended. Fritz the patriot, of course, would have preferred the former suggestion. But then there was always Fritz the fraud. Chronologically, it could have happened. Fritz was roaming the veld during the time the bullion was presumably sent on its journey. But it never happened.

Or did it?

The last set-piece battle of the war was fought on 11 and 12 June 1900 at Diamond Hill, where Lord Roberts commanded sixteen thousand troops who carried the attack against Botha, Jacobus de la Rey, and Ben Viljoen and their four thousand burghers. After two days of fighting it appeared to be a stalemate, and the British planned a final assault, only to learn that the Boers had stolen away in the night. Limping along with them was Fritz Duquesne, who had been wounded in the foot by a British lancer, indicating that he had been engaged in close combat.[7] Perhaps he had come up against Colonel Ian Hamilton's Twelfth Lancers when a body of mounted Boers attempted to capture a battery of guns but were driven off in one of the battle's recorded incidents. In Fritz's account, "British lancers charged on surrendered and wounded men. I got a thrust through my foot, the only part of me showing from under the horse. When night fell I was dragged from under my horse by some English girls who were doing the nurse business and before morning I managed, with a broken arm, a numbed body, and a split foot, to reach the Boer commander."[8]

The flight from Diamond Hill also marked the beginning of a new kind of war: a guerrilla style of war better suited to the undisciplined Boers, who were fighting against an army still rigid in the old ways and not accustomed to the mobile hit-and-flee tactics of the guerrilla. Fritz gave an account of his exploits at this time in *Adventure* magazine. Claiming a "vast knowledge of the destructiveness of high explosives," he destroyed armored trains in Natal and British retreats:

I had a squad of dare-devil boys who used to ride around with from twenty to fifty pounds of dynamite caps and fuse to match in their saddle bags. At Dundee I fought a duel with an English Zulu while I was carrying despatches from Buffalo River to Eland's Laagte. He shot my horse under me. I killed him. A shell killed my second horse at Eland's Laagte and it rolled over me, breaking my arm. Had my arm broken a second time in a hand-to-hand fight at O'Neal's farm. I fought the other fellow, a Natal carbineer, with my teeth. He is dead. . . . [G]athered a number of kindred spirits, we scouted and sniped the Britishers. I had charge of an expedition against Stenacker's Horse in Lebombo. I kept them awake for three weeks, killing a few when the windage and light were good. The British now started to take notice of me and I was sentenced to be shot on sight.[9]

And so it continued. Fritz was certainly a busy Boer.

Constantly on the run, and fighting their way across the Transvaal against the steady advance of "Bobs" and his boys, the Boers fought in individual commandos under no central command. Fritz, no longer attached to a specific commando, soon found himself in Barberton, further east of Pretoria and strategically important because it was a Boer commissariat depot, ripe with gold stores and railroad rolling stock including forty locomotives.[10]

He was on the run, a fugitive in his own land. He could not fight. He could only hide. Fear of capture was constant. There was no longer the security of a commando or regular military unit. He had not been in this situation before. But now he would have to get used to it, because it would soon become a way of life for him in a country rapidly being overrun by the kakis. The running at last came to an end in Barberton.

Fritz was made a prisoner of war for the first time. It was another way of life he would have to get used to. But while being marched with several others to a prisoner-of-war camp by a single guard, Fritz grabbed the man's pistol and shot him in the head. Twelve days later he was in Komatipoort. But the British had entered the Boer town on the border of Portuguese East Africa just two days earlier to find it destroyed and deserted. Fritz fled quickly and worked his way south, hoping to join a marauding commando.

He managed to find a small troop a little south of Newcastle, but his freedom was short-lived. At Muller's Pass the roving burghers stumbled on a superior kakis force that made short work of them. Fritz was hit a glancing blow on the forehead by a bullet, lost consciousness, and upon recovery found himself a prisoner again. Bloody forehead bandaged and hands bound in front of him with rope, Fritz straggled behind the small column of prisoners as they marched slowly north toward Vrede in northeast Orange Free State.

Realizing that he would soon be in a prison camp and possibly transported to India, Ceylon, Bermuda, or St. Helena where the British were sending POWs, Fritz deliberately lagged behind, engaging in idle chatter with the English trooper bringing up the rear. Although fierce in battle, both sides were generally amicable when the fighting was over. It was why the Boer War was often called "the last war between gentlemen." But amicability was not Fritz's concern. If he was going to escape, he wanted the soldier off guard.

His chance came in that moment before darkness at dusk while crossing a wooden bridge over the Klip River.[11] Alone at the rear of the strung-out column, Fritz raised his arms in one quick movement and brought them down with great force on the head of his guard. Stunned, the soldier fell to the wooden planks. Fritz sprang to the handrail and without hesitation leaped over the side into the swirling waters below. He had formed a plan even before jumping. Sinking to the bottom, Fritz crawled along as far as he could, coming up near the far bank. Lying on his side and using a double-sided stroke because of his tied hands, he swam desperately for a mass of overhanging shrubs. Only when under its shelter did he look back. He could hear shouts and see dark figures hanging over the bridge looking for him.

There was one shot. Then they were gone.

Remaining still, he shivered in the cold water for another half-hour before daring to wade out. He loosened the rope around his hands by rubbing it laboriously against a jagged rock. The Black Panther of the Veld had no weapons and knew that British troops commanded every pass and town, every railway and road. He would strike north, hoping again to run into a roaming commando.

As Fritz passed Amersfoort, Rolfontein, Dreifontein, and eventually Ermelo, he saw the devastation of war everywhere. Kitchener's new scorched-earth policy of burning farms to deny commandos their sources of food, ammunition, and intelligence was leaving its visible mark. At night there was the red glow of the flaming homesteads; during the day there were towering pillars of smoke. Fritz did not lack long for food and weapons. He would often come across a laager of women and children fleeing the destruction, who would give him what he needed, including arms.

Frequently too he came across herds of wild horses shot and machine-gunned by the British to prevent commandos from obtaining fresh mounts. Crops were trampled or burned, herds of sheep and cattle shot, clubbed, or bayonetted to death. Wild game abounded, but domestic animals had ceased to exist. Fritz's South Africa had become a wasteland devoid of people. Except for the occasional laagers, he saw no one. The desolation served to harden his hatred and anger against everything English.

Striking east from Ermelo, Fritz made for Swaziland, a tiny country north of the Transvaal and west of Mozambique. The Swazis were friendly to the British, which made it a dangerous move, but it was the quickest way to Lourenço Marques. He might be able to get a ship there, land somewhere further down the coast, and rejoin the fighting.

Fritz didn't know it, but his fighting days were over. He was arrested in a small village by two Portuguese colonials for being a combatant on neutral soil.[12]

His hands were bound again, and after a forty-mile train ride to Lourenço Marques, Fritz was tossed into a vermin-infested prison cell close by an open sewer, which meant that he shared his cell with the stench and filth and crawling visitors to be expected of such foulness. But already the escaper's mind was racing. There had to be a way out!

He found it in a barred, wooden ventilating space in the ceiling. In the quiet hours of the morning he pushed his cot under the ventilator. Then he placed a chair on the cot and a stool atop the chair. It was a perilous support, but Fritz climbed gingerly to the stool, pushed against the ventilator until it gave way, then pulled himself through the opening. He was now in the dark space between the roof and the ceiling, where he padded quietly across the whole length of the jail to a window at the far end. The window was barred. Desperation gave way to elation when the rusted bars crumbled in his hands.

But there was no escape. A guard paced directly below. Looking desperately around, Fritz found another ventilator space leading to a room on the other side of the jail. He had no sooner slipped through into the empty room than several guards entered the room and he was arrested again.

Lisbon and a more secure jail, it was decided, would be the best place for this restless prisoner. Fortunately for Fritz, prison in Portugal was not an unpleasant experience. His warden was a jailer who could not understand why a gentleman like Captain Duquesne should be shackled and put behind bars. Fritz was given the freedom of his jailer's prison and home—and, unwittingly, the freedom of his jailer's daughter, Donna Joanna. The liaison lasted until Fritz managed to escape and sail for Cadiz, then Paris, and finally Brussels, where he immediately contacted Dr. Leyds, the Transvaal representative. Ever since the battle of Colenso and his arrival in Brussels, Leyds had been unsuccessfully striving to induce Germany, Russia, and France to band together in a common cause against Great Britain.[13] But his only success was to persuade a few hundred adventurers to fight on the side of the burghers and to obtain only sympathetic support in several countries, including England.

Since Fritz was so intent on returning to the war, Leyds advised him to join the British army as a Boer defector at Aldershot, the country's main military encampment.[14] The army would return him to South Africa to fight against his countrymen. It would then be up to Fritz to desert and find a fighting commando. The efficient and well-financed Boer espionage system would assist Fritz by supplying him with the proper papers for joining the kakis.

Some reports say Duquesne was given new identity papers and entered Cape Town as a war correspondent for the Belgian newspaper *Le Petit Bleu du Matin*.[15] He was also purportedly given plans for the destruction of Cape Town. In any case, within two weeks of arriving at Aldershot, Fritz had been given a lieutenant's commission and was aboard ship for the seventeen-day voyage to Cape Town along with hundreds of other troops, turncoats, and officers.[16]

It was not unusual for a Boer to change sides.[17] Many of the fighting farmers had become disenchanted with their cause and wanted only to return home to the land. Perhaps they were even fighting and killing their countrymen, serving the crown at 5 shillings a day. They really didn't care anymore who won the war, just as long as it ended soon. They were called Judas Boers, the "sweepings" and scum of Africa, so hated by their former comrades that if captured they were instantly executed and their fates publicized. A few months later Kitchener formally organized them into a division called the National Scouts or Colonials. It was a successful policy he had used in the Sudan, pitting countryman against countryman. It was a cheap way to fight a war, and it saved British lives.

Fritz ran the risk of death at the hands of his countrymen, but he had no choice, since there was no other way to enter South Africa. Among his shipboard companions would have been the last remnants of those daring young men of the British aristocracy who, as fledgling army officers, felt duty bound to participate in the war and see what they called "the fun."[18] What did it matter if some of them were killed? They saw some of the fun, didn't they? "The fun" for Fritz was to see these young men in their pajamas early every morning running circuits around the deck to keep in prime physical condition, suffering a cold bath, and then returning to their companions on the deck in neatly cut flannels. They fully intended to have fun on their way to "the fun."

In Cape Town Fritz was assigned to a flying column of light cavalry commanded by Colonel George E. Benson of the Royal Artillery, a gadfly whose daring attacks kept the Boer commandos off guard. Fritz rode with them until he had an opportunity to strike out on his own.[19]

The Black Panther of the Veld was loose again.

It was a different South Africa Fritz Duquesne returned to. The war still dragged on, even though President Kruger had sailed for France and exile, never to return. Roberts was reassigned to England, and Kitchener was handed the Boer War as the new commander-in-chief in South Africa. Kitchener would substitute a steel fist for the often criticized velvet-glove approach of Roberts.

The devastation created by farm burning had been going on since the previous July. It was now March 1901, and an unforeseen problem had been created: thousands of women and children had been left homeless and were forced to wander the veld. In what was meant to be a humanitarian gesture but turned into another shocking horror of war, the British set up at military posts what were at first called refugee camps, and then concentration camps. The plan was to provide food, shelter, and medical care for the displaced women and children and some men in the tented camps. Otherwise they faced certain death in the open on the veld, not only from exposure and lack of food but also from possible attacks by marauding natives. But their British captors were soon overwhelmed by the sheer number of families driven from their homes and were unable to cope with their needs. Overcrowding, poor hygienic facilities, and a lack of food, medical supplies, and aid resulted in epidemics and starvation that contributed to staggering mortality rates in the camps as long as they were in operation. To the Boers, it was calculated genocide.

Two months later Kitchener ordered the crisscrossing of South Africa with an immense system of barbed-wire fences interspersed with tin and stone blockhouses within rifle range of each other. It was an enormous task designed to draw the remaining Boer commandos into a net from which there was no escape. Eventually these methods—considered barbarous by the Boers and even by many British citizens and politicians opposed to the war at home—proved effective.

But meanwhile the Black Panther was roaming the veld, earning still another soubriquet: the Boy Scout of the Boer War.[20] Incongruous as it sounded, he had been appointed a courier between the many isolated commandos that had managed to evade not the queen's troops but the king's. After a reign of sixty-four years, the longest of any British monarch in history, Queen Victoria had died in January. Albert Edward, the fifty-nine-year-old prince of Wales and assuredly the most patient son in royal history, ascended to the throne and was now King Edward VII.

During this time Fritz often ran across the trail of Major Frederick R. Burnham, an American explorer and adventurer who was serving as chief of scouts for the British army. In a 1951 letter from a federal prison in Springfield, Missouri, where he was serving time for espionage, Fritz wrote his longtime lady friend, Lillian Linding, "Sir Fred. Russell Burnham chief of scouts for Lord Kitchener named me the Black Panther after I knocked hell out of his command with a lot of kids. I attacked him at night, the same as Korean's are doing to UN troops now, until I wiped him out. There's nothing a sleepy man hates so much as being shot at at 1:30 in the morning."[21]

In a 1953 letter to Lillian Fritz accused Burnham of murdering his fourteen-year-old brother outside Johannesburg.[22] Despite the accusation, Fritz and Burnham still had respect for each other. In his 1944 autobiography, *Taking Chances*, Burnham recalled that "there were only two men on the veld I feared, and one was Duquesne."[23] He didn't say who the other was. Burnham added:

Much has been written about Duquesne, most of it rubbish. Yet his real accomplishments were so terrible and amazing that they make the yellow-journal thrillers about him seem as mild as radio bedtime stories. Duquesne and I were enemies in the Boer War, but by some strange fate we escaped a personal clash, although each of us had been given special orders by our respective governments to kill or capture the other,—he, under order of the Boers: I, under order of the British, and I have in my possession a signed letter received by him during the Boer War craving the high honor of killing me.

Fritz and Burnham obviously never had the opportunity to kill each other, but they would meet less than ten years later in Washington, D.C., under circumstances brought about by President Theodore Roosevelt.

Always evading British patrols and warily making his way through the blockhouse system, Fritz slowly trekked to the Duquesne family farm at Nylstroom, north of Pretoria. He had heard nothing of his mother, his sister Elsbet, or Uncle Jan since the beginning of the war. Surely they were safe. Who would have any reason to harm a middle-aged woman, a girl not yet twenty years old, and an elderly blind man? But denial of what might be could not change what had happened. Fritz's shattered expectations were described by Clement Wood in *The Man Who Killed Kitchener:*[24]

Just beyond the next rise, just a few miles further on, just a few rods further on, it must be as it had always been—the cheery house, the briskly painted outhouses, the lowing cattle, the green plantings spearing the rich veldt soil, the mother and the blind old great-uncle coming forward to greet him, with tears of joy in their eyes because he was returning to them at last, their own, who had been away so grievously long, but longing all those weary months for the touch of them and the glow of hearing their voices and sitting quietly down with them to watch the slow sun sink, and the sweet-scented night rain over them.

But it was not to be and would never be again:

Only when his horse, somehow wiser than he, stopped before an irregular little rand of blackened, plastered stone, and he dismounted and touched with an appalled foot what had been the corner of the foundations of the front porch of his house, did a little of it come over his soul.

It was all gone.

Hatred for the English was building as he picked his way through what was left of the Duquesne farm. He did not have to see everything, nor did he want to. The sweet scent of death, mingled with the acrid odor of fire-blackened ruins, told him of the slaughtered livestock, of the burned farmhouse, kraals, and crops. But what of his family?

He learned what had occurred from old Kanya, the Mponda who had worked for the Duquesne family since Fritz was a boy. Bent and stooped now, Kanya had remained on the farm, digging out a shelter for himself in the ruins, waiting for the young master he knew would return one day.

The horror was worse than anything Fritz might have expected. Despite the policy of farm burning and concentration camps, the British and Boers had fought the war as, paradoxically, gentlemen. Each side had grudging respect for the other, and combatants and noncombatants were generally treated humanely by both. But there was always that rare occasion when troopers went beyond their orders. Especially now, the frustration of a protracted guerrilla war was resulting in brutality on both sides.

Kanya told Fritz that old Uncle Jan had been hanged from a telegraph pole with a cow rope, and as his face turned black, the soldiers "stuck him with the shiny knives on the ends of their guns." It was worse for Elsbet, Fritz learned from Kanya:

Three of them hold her down, and two stood by and made the laughing noise, and one of the three did what it is not lawful for man to do to maid unless he marries her, and she cried out very loud, even while they made the laughing noise. . . . And then, when he had finished, the first man, the second, and then the third. And she cried a great deal, but when they let her up and she started to run away and would not stop, it was one of those who made the laughing noise who . . . shot her.

"And what of my mother?" Fritz asked.

I do not know where the mother missis is. She was led away with them. I did not even see what they did to her, it was behind the house where she had run toward the stable. But I heard her, too, crying out very loud, and when they brought her back there was no skirt left on her, and her underskirt was very dirtied, and she was crying but not very loud now, and her hands were tied. They led her away with them.

Fritz was blinded by the hate now. It would consume him for the rest of his long life. When he died fifty-five years later in 1956, he was still talking of his hatred for everything English.

Fritz could only assume that his mother had been taken to a concentration camp. The nearest one was several days away at Germiston, nine miles east of Johannesburg.[25] Once again in his lieutenant's uniform, he requested of the commandant to have a word with an old Boer woman named Duquesne. It was rumored that she had valuable information. He was led through rows of white tents, their military preciseness belying the tragedy they represented. Numbed and diseased women and children watched silently as he passed.

Fritz wasn't prepared for what he found. His mother was in a barbed-wire kraal, starving and dying from syphilis and holding a seven-month-old baby boy in her arms. There was nothing he could do. They would both die. He didn't care about the British bastard. Let it die. But he told his mother quietly, "As long as I live I will never draw one breath but to pay back the English for what they have done. Most of all, Kitchener, who had done it, who had ordered it, who had planned it. I pledge my soul that for every drop of rotten, poisoned blood in your body I will kill 100 Englishmen."[26]

Fritz turned and left her, knowing he would never see her again. He passed again through the crowded camp to his horse. A few miles past Germiston he passed an English captain and one of the hated Colonials, another captain. They saluted each other in passing, then Fritz turned and shot both soldiers in the back. Walking over to the dead men, he kicked each in the face, then smashed their bodies with the butt of his rifle. He felt better for it, but it didn't lessen the hate.

As Clement Wood wrote, "Something happened inside of him that had fused him into a unit, a unit of hate, at last. He would never alter from this as long as he lived."[27]

He never did.

CHAPTER 3

The Cape Town Plot and Capture

CAPE TOWN was a city at war but curiously devoid of the ravages of conflict. Its large harbor made it the base for British supplies, which poured out of the city by rail to the ever more victorious army of the crown fighting the guerrilla war with the stubborn Boer farmers throughout South Africa.

Thousands of British soldiers were garrisoned there, waiting in reserve to bolster weakened forces when needed. To a less determined foe their presence and the apparently never-ending supply of men and weapons of war would have been disheartening. Even this far south, ever fearful of raids by marauding Boer commandos led by Jan Smuts and Christian De Wet, the troops were always at the ready. Thousands of refugees had swelled the city's population to more than three hundred thousand, almost twice its normal number.

Cape Town was not a city possessing a friendly attitude toward the Boer. The refugees were seeking asylum from the war and were hoping the conflict would soon come to an end with the British victorious. There were many Boer sympathizers in the Cape, and the guerrillas optimistically hoped they would rise and declare their independence from the British crown. But it did not happen. Boer commando raids early in 1901 in Natal and Cape Colony did not inspire an uprising of the Dutch. There were too many reasons against a mass revolt.

In the century that the Cape Dutch had been British subjects, they had never formed an independent republic as had their compatriots in the Orange Free State and the South African Republic.[1] The Cape Colony Afrikaners respected the law, but their government offered them no leadership in breaking from British rule. Additionally, Prime Minister William Schreiner did not resign from office, even though he knew he would be powerless to prevent the Cape from being used as a troops and arms base against the republics and that they would not be able to remain neutral.

It was the easy way to go because Sir Alfred Milner, high commissioner of South Africa, had promised that there would be no conscription in the Cape and that the Cape Police and Cape Mounted Rifles would serve only in the Cape Colony. Despite the apparently compliant attitude of the Cape Dutch, Kitchener had long been trying to induce the Cape government to declare martial law. He was finally successful in early October, and now all of South Africa was under "Martie Louw."[2] Kitchener did not consider the Boers to be a civilized race and firmly believed they could never be an asset to the British Empire.[3] "They are uncivilized Afrikaner savages with a thin white veneer," he wrote in a letter to St. John Brodrick, secretary for war. "The Boer woman in the refugee camps who slaps her protruding belly at you, and shouts, 'When all our men are gone, these little khakis will fight you,' is a type of the savage produced by generations of wild lonely life. The leaders and townspeople are sufficiently educated and civilized. I only refer to the bulk of the population."[4]

But the result was only to fan Dutch hatred of the increased British authority, particularly since the military bungled in administering the new laws.[5] Afrikaners objected to the humiliation of being detained on suspicion, to the compelling of natives to work for the military and at higher wages, and especially to the acceptance of a native's word against that of an Afrikaner suspected of subversion.

Kitchener also urged the British cabinet to be realistic and to authorize the forcible and permanent banishment of all Boers who had at any time borne arms against the British, together with their families and dependents. But Brodrick pointed out that if such drastic measures still failed to break the Boer spirit, "Europe would be needlessly scandalized."[6] Nevertheless, Lord Kitchener had his way, and on 15 September 1901 he proclaimed a law that any burgher found bearing arms after that date would be permanently banished from South Africa. The harsh measure, called "the paper bomb," failed to make an impact and was derided everywhere.[7]

Martial law, the refugees, and the omnipresence of British soldiers made Cape Town a city at war. But Cape Towners continued to lead as normal a life as possible, even though refugees outnumbered them everywhere, lining the pavements and blocking shop doors. If there was an open space, it was sure to be occupied by drilling volunteers. With nothing else to do, refugees would stand gaping at them for hours. There were so many people crowding the streets that pedestrians were not allowed to loiter, which made life even more difficult. One could not wait for a tram car, nor could friends shake hands without being ordered to move on. But soon even the most zealous policeman realized the inevitable and ignored these misdemeanors.[8]

It seemed that most of the refugees were men. The women were kept at home caring for the children. The men, among whom were Americans, Australians, and Englishmen, were mostly young miners from Johannesburg.[9]

And in the better hotels were the rich refugees bemoaning the fact that they would lose all they had if the British did not soon take the Transvaal and prevent the destruction of Johannesburg by the Boers.[10] The Mount Nelson, the Queen's Hotel, and the Grand Hotel were filled with merchants and millionaires, idle during the day and busy at night discussing what percentage of their losses they would recover from the British government in a postwar South Africa. There were so few vacancies at the Nelson that General French and Major Haig once had to share a room when passing through Cape Town.[11] Nevertheless, during the war the hotel became noted as the city's social center, and it attracted other distinguished visitors such as a young war correspondent named Winston Churchill, who not untypically complained about the service.

It was different in the evenings. Then life in Cape Town was all gaiety for the refugees.[12] Talk was of the opera and the theater as the millionaires and the mining magnates, splendid in their evening dress, gathered at the great dining halls of the hotels with their wives and their mistresses. The ladies would be ultrafashionable in the latest styles, resplendent in décolletage and flashing gems, a startling contrast to the wives of the battling burghers starving on the veld or in concentration camps. At the Queen's, couples would stroll along paths where the grass met the sea. At the Mount Nelson, Swiss waiters would serve delicacies from the London market, thanks to the miracle of refrigeration aboard ships of the Castle Line.

And so life went on in Cape Town. Except for drilling soldiers, a preponderance of uniforms, and a few inconveniences, it was hard to believe that men were killing each other in a war that was becoming increasingly unpopular in England.

In the Boers' favor was English public opinion, which, used to victory abroad in all of England's little wars, was tiring of the loss of men and the drain on the treasury. The Boer War had become "Chamberlain's war." A Welsh radical named David Lloyd George was beginning to make a name for himself at this time with the passion and fierceness of his expressions of sympathy for the Boers. "I say it is time to stop the slaughter in the African sand of brave soldiers on either side," was George's cry.[13]

But the election decided the issue, and the Unionist-Conservatives won by a vast majority over the Liberals. Chamberlain was free to carry the war to a successful conclusion, however destructive to both sides.

This was the political and social climate in Cape Town in October 1901, when Fritz Duquesne, attired in the uniform of a British soldier, slipped into the city to carry out a destructive plan that he was sure would cripple Kitchener's troops and result in victory for the Boers. With a group of twenty Boer sympathizers he had selected carefully from the many in Cape Town, Fritz laid out a plan of terror and destruction that would cripple the British war machine and, if not bring victory to the Boers, at least create a draw.[14]

Passionately, he poured out the Boer situation to his accomplices, promising that they would treat Cape Town, the heart of England in South Africa, as the British treated the Transvaal and the Free State. Kitchener's scorched-earth policy had virtually wiped out the farmlands and homes of the Boers. The English would suffer as greatly.

Explosive bombs would be placed at all enemy vantage points. Barracks, wharves, depots, munition dumps, warehouses, public buildings, power plants, rail yards, and bridges would be mined and the explosives set off on a certain date. This would include Simon's Town docks and the railway tunnels in the Hex River Mountains. Should some of the conspirators fail their appointed tasks, Fritz had devised the ultimate solution. He had delegated to himself the pleasure of destroying the water pipe leading from Molteno Reservoir atop Table Mountain, rising 3,549 feet behind Cape Town. He would be unleashing forty-three million gallons of liquid destruction on the city.

Fritz selected the night of Friday, 11 October, for carrying out the

Cape Town Plot, an evening when city officials and army officers would be preoccupied at Somerset House with a fete honoring Sir Walter Hely-Hutchinson, governor of Cape Colony. Explosives would be placed by midnight and detonated at four the next morning.

Pleasing his own saturnine sense of humor, Fritz attended the dinner for the governor in full dress uniform and savored the information only he possessed   that few of the hated English enjoying themselves that night at the dinner would be alive in the morning. As dinner progressed, Fritz gave little attention to the feasting about him, or to the beautiful women so easily available.[15] His thoughts were on the confusion and terror that would soon be gripping Cape Town. The Customs House would be burning on Adderly Street, along with the railroad station, Parliament House, Government House, and the law courts on Queen Victoria Street. The flimsy buildings housing the British press on St. George's would be a shambles, and the warehouses near Riebeck Square where the old slave market was would be smoking ruins. The munitions warehouse near the old opera house would go up in a shattering explosion. And finally there would be the deluge of millions of gallons of water pouring down from Table Mountain and destroying all that was left in Cape Town.

But it was not to be. While Fritz was still reveling in anticipatory pleasure, the plot was being betrayed by one of the twenty, a Cape Town Boer long faithful to the cause. But now, realizing that his own property would be destroyed by the fire and flood he was instigating, he decided the Boer cause was not all that important. He revealed the scheme to British authorities.

At nine o'clock an orderly handed a note to the governor. He read it, excused himself to his wife, and left the room, a slight smile masking his concern. A few minutes later the orderly returned and asked Lieutenant Duquesne to excuse himself for a moment. Immediately on his guard, Fritz was suspicious, but there was nothing he could do but obey.

Outside the banquet room the grim-faced governor was waiting with a colonel. The colonel told Fritz, "You're under arrest, Lieutenant."

"For what?" Fritz asked, continuing the charade.

"For conspiracy against the British government and espionage," the colonel replied brusquely.

It was a shock to Governor Hely-Hutchinson, who was aware of Duquesne's loyal service to the crown as a Boer defector.

"It must be a mistake, Colonel," said the agitated governor. "Lieutenant Duquesne has had the highest recommendations, he is in line for a decoration and I doubt if there is anyone more faithful in His Majesty's service."

Fritz merely shrugged and was marched off to Cape Castle, where he would be jailed and held for trial.

Cape Castle was a giant pentagonal fortification near the shore of Table Bay looking out to sea. The Dutch had laid the first stone for its construction in 1666, but it was many years before the pile of high bastions and deep dungeons, with walls varying in thickness from two to fourteen feet, was completed. Fritz must have felt a twinge of irony when he was marched through the main entrance of the castle. Above the archway was the figure of a cat in bas relief, much like the feline in his family crest.

Fritz was placed in one of the cells with a view of the sea where he could look out over the palm-lined bay and the ocean beyond. No time was wasted by the outraged British. Trial was set for the next day. Fritz and his nineteen fellow conspirators would serve as an example to any other Cape Boers who might have thoughts of rebelling against English rule.

Actually, more than fifty arrests had been made of alleged members of the Boer spy system in Pretoria and Johannesburg. These spies had also apparently been pro-British. Most had given their parole, taken the oath of neutrality, or even been employed by the British. They were put on trial also.

As an officer in the British army, Fritz was to be court-martialed. His trial and that of his nineteen co-conspirators was held in a Cape Castle room. A major was assigned to defend him. The turncoat was placed on the stand and fearfully told his story of the Cape Town Plot. He had revealed the plan because he feared for his property. Now he feared for his life at the hands of the Cape Boers and asked to be sent to England.

It was a short trial.[16] Did Fritz or the prisoners have anything to say in self-defense? One by one the nineteen all shook their heads. "You were wearing a British uniform, Lieutenant," the presiding general addressed Fritz. "You must have something to say in your own defense. If this is libel, if it is untrue, it is your duty to tell the court so."

Still the soldier, though he despised the uniform, Fritz stood at attention and said quietly, "It is all true. That, and much more."

"About all of these prisoners, you mean?" asked the prosecuting advocate, leaning forward in his eagerness.

"As to myself only, I mean," replied Fritz. "I never saw these other men before, except this one man who has just testified. There were nineteen others with me, but they are not these defendants. And I was responsible for more than just a plot to blow up Cape Town."

"Do you mean you are a traitor, a soldier of His Majesty's army?" queried the general.

"That's a lie! I am not a traitor!"

"But you are wearing the British uniform—"

"General," replied Duquesne quietly, "I am a Boer, not a Britisher."

Fritz then explained patiently how the Boers came to Africa seeking freedom and how the British took it from them, and why he believed he was a patriot and not a traitor. "You have made it clear you are a Boer," the general interrupted, "but your conduct in our army has been exemplary and worthy of the highest praise."

"So exemplary, so worthy of praise," said Fritz, with some dramatic flair, "that I have not failed one day in this uniform to send out word to my own people of what the British were doing and planning to the last detail. If we have won during this time, give me a little of the credit. Traitor? I have been the most faithful Boer subject in all Africa.

"But I have not begun to tell you yet why I have done as I have, why I am proud of all I have done. The vilest bastard spawned in hell, the blackest, most poisonous soul that ever befouled the earth, your commander-in-chief, General—"

The soldiers in the room leaped to their feet amidst cries of "By god, he won't go on!" and "I'll stop his bloody mouth for him!"

The general was also on his feet, his heavy fist pounding down the tumult. "Gentlemen! Prisoners! This is all unbecoming! Lieutenant Duquesne, control your tongue. Have you anything further to say?"

Fritz was white-hot now, choosing his words carefully.

"Your commanding general has swept my land clean of cattle, property, fodder; he has burned all the fields, all the houses, my own among them. He has driven helpless noncombatants into his concentration camps. At Kitchener's order my young sister was assaulted by three British soldiers and raped and killed."

"It's a lie," shouted a captain.

The general quieted him with a trembling hand.

"My blind great-uncle, who had never harmed man or beast in his life," Duquesne went on, "was hung by jeering soldiers. My mother was raped. She became pregnant and was given syphilis. She is nursing the bastard now in a concentration camp. Do you wonder, sir, that the little I have done is nothing to what I will do to England before I am through?"

There was a strained silence.

Fritz stepped closer to the general seated at the center of the long table, flanked by angry officers.

"For what England did to my mother," he vowed, "I will wreck that bastard land, that bastard empire, to the last foul inch of its stolen possessions. For my mother's violated and defiled body I will send your daughters to the stews, your foul sons to torture and death. For that fiend Kitchener—"

Duquesne never finished. An angry soldier struck him with his fist and sent him staggering back.

The general and his officers didn't even leave the room to discuss the verdict of the twenty potential saboteurs. After a few moments the general gave the results of their deliberation: "The sentence of the court on these nineteen is that they be shot at sunrise. The sentence of the court on Fritz Duquesne is that he be given a dishonorable discharge from His Majesty's forces and that he be shot at sunrise after seeing his accomplices shot. And may God have mercy on the souls of all of them."

Fritz and the others were returned to their cells under armed guard early that evening. In thirteen hours they would be dead.

Late that evening Fritz was surprised when the general came to his cell door with two armed soldiers. "May I talk to you a little while?" the general asked in a tone that suggested a command rather than a question. Ordering his men to the end of the corridor, the general stepped closer to the dark cell and said quietly, "You do not have to die."

When Fritz did not answer, the general continued: "I have come to show you how you need not die. You say you have been in touch with the Boers during all your service with us. You know, of course, that coded messages fall into our hands. You must know these codes. If you die at sunrise, where will your plans for vengeance be? How can you aid the Boer cause dead?"

Still Fritz did not reply, turning over in his mind what the general was suggesting. Perhaps there was a way out and he could continue his fight against the hated English. At last he said tonelessly, "I will not die at sunrise."

"Good. I knew you would be sensible."

"What do you expect from me?"

"The complete Boer codes. That for your life. Tell us the codes and I give you my word for a commutation. Nothing worse than life imprisonment anyhow."

"That is no gain," said Fritz.

"Tell us the codes and at least you stay alive."

"You want to make a traitor out of me."

"If saving your life for your country is being a traitor, yes."

"Very well," Fritz said reluctantly. "I accept."

Fritz was given until dawn to prove his word. By that time he was expected to turn over Boer secret codes in exchange for his life. For the rest of his life he swore he never betrayed the Boer cause but actually created new codes that would mislead the British, giving him precious time to escape before the ruse was discovered.

At dawn Fritz was led out to watch the execution by firing squad of his nineteen comrades. Then he was brought to the commandant's office, where he was ordered to translate several Boer dispatches. He was placed in a cell looking out to sea and told he would spend the rest of his life there.

On 17 October, just six days after being arrested, Fritz wrote the first of many letters he would write over the next fifty years during periods of confinement. They reflected the tone of a natural complainer, and invariably they had an ingratiating theme intended to solicit favor from his captors. This one also showed that he had not yet mastered the English language even though, inexplicably, he had listed his nationality as American on his arrest record:[17]

To the Staff Officer
Prisoners of War
Cape Town

Sir: Herewith I make complaint against the treatment receive at the hands of the Prison Authorities. In the first place the food is of a very poor quality. And consists of, for three days out of four, bread and black tea for two meals and beef? and potatoes for one. On the other day of the four I receive a pound of jam. Considering my close confinement I think you will agree that the fare is not likely to be conducive to one's health. As I suffer from constipation which generally brings on other evils. I should be much obliged if you give this the complaint a little of your attention. Again the night of my arrest I was taken to the *civil* prison and placed amongst common thieves, drunkards, etc. The warders who placed me in the cell, some of whom were drunk, on not being answered some most impertinent questions, grossly insulted me, making use of such expressions as, bastard, bloody son of a bitch, go to fuckin' hell, etc. This is not likely to do any good and hurts the feelings of a prisoner. Anyway I let you know to save the feelings of others who are placed in the position in which I was.

Yours respectfully,
Fritz Duquenne
Prisoner of war

A Captain M. A. Trevor wrote across the bottom of the complaint, "Forwarded for any action you may think necessary with regard to that portion of the complaint which refers to the treatment received by this man at the civil prison. The food he receives here is the ordinary Field Service Ration issued to British troops I believe."

The reply to this note agreed about the quality of food served in the prison but also noted that Duquesne was troublesome and dangerous, a trait not to be overlooked by future jailers: "This man receives same food as most in country who are interned. He is reported as troublesome and dangerous."

Dangerous he was. Fritz was not about to accept the fate of spending the rest of his life looking at the South Atlantic Ocean from the narrow confines of a cell. He immediately set about planning his escape, the first of three he would make during the next twenty years from as many prisons. During these bids for freedom Fritz showed great courage, cunning, resourcefulness, and a singleness of purpose that he never demonstrated in any other phase of his long life. If he had, the whole direction of his life might have taken another turn.

Fritz began his preparations by moving his cot under the window, explaining to the guards that he would get more cool sea breezes from that position.[18] Then every night for weeks, emulating the escape of Edmond Dantes from the Château d'If in *The Count of Monte Cristo*, Fritz used a dinner spoon to scrape away at the mortar binding together the large stones brought down from Table Mountain. Before the morning sun came streaming through his window and lighting the cell, he would sift the cement dust through the barred window and let it blow away in the wind.

After weeks of grubbing work, one stone was loosened. Then the next. Finally came the day when Fritz knew he would be able to escape through the walls and to freedom. At night he pushed away the first stone at the base of his cell wall and listened in suspense, fearful that a guard would hear its muffled tumble down the slopes to the shore below. Nothing. Then he pushed away another stone, and another, and another. At last there was room to squirm through on his back. But disaster struck when he was partway through. A large stone above, loosened by the removal of the others, slipped suddenly down on his chest, pinning him to the ground. Fritz found it almost impossible to breathe with the crushing weight across his chest. Soon he lost consciousness.

They dug him out in the morning. Brought before the commandant of the castle, Fritz learned that he was now considered an incorrigible and was no longer wanted as a guest at the castle. "You ought to be shot for jailbreaking," he was told. "Instead, you'll be put in solitary in an inside cell at once. Then it's to the Bermudas for you. We've no time for jailbreakers here. The *Harlech Castle* sails for Bermuda next Saturday and you'll be aboard. Under order of the banishment proclamation of 15 September, you are to be perpetually excluded from South Africa. Under no circumstances will you ever be allowed to return."

"Thank you," said Fritz quietly.

He could not help but be concerned about the banishment decree, but he was also grateful. Any change meant another opportunity for escape.

Fritz was immediately placed in irons that would not be removed until he was safely locked up in the penal colony in Bermuda. The chains were so heavy that they cut into his wrists and ankles, leaving scars that remained with him the rest of his life. A further indignity was added when prison guards cropped his lengthening hair close to his skull. In a moment of anger, Fritz had unwisely admitted to his captors that he had vowed never to cut his hair until the Boers had their freedom.

On Saturday morning, 7 November 1901, Fritz Duquesne and 339 other Boer prisoners of war were marched through the streets of Cape Town to the docks and the Castle Line's waiting ship. Dragging himself alongside Fritz was Baron von Kaynach, a Boer officer also in chains for his escaping proclivities.

As the *Harlech Castle* steamed slowly out of Table Bay, Fritz took one last look at his beloved South Africa as he was hustled below in the crush of prisoners.

He would never see his country again.

CHAPTER 4

POW in the Enchanted Isles

T HE FORTY-FOUR-DAY VOYAGE from Cape Town to the "Enchanted Isles" of Bermuda was no luxury cruise for the 340 Boer POWs crammed into hammocks and cells below decks. To keep their spirits up, the Boer national anthem and other patriotic songs had been sung as they sailed out of the harbor and Table Mountain passed from view. But not even patriotism could relieve the depressing routine of life on a prisoner-of-war ship.

Compounding the misery of rough seas, short rations included weak black tea and one two-ounce bun daily. Breakfast consisted of absolutely raw oats, the bun, and a cup of dirty water that passed for either tea or coffee. The same oats were served up for dinner boiled into soup. Those who had a few shillings bought extra rations from ship's stores. Occasionally an ox-neck soup was served, and it was considered a lucky day when dead rats weren't found floating in the mess.[1]

It was not unusual for a prisoner to go mad. The maniac would then be confined to a cell, where his screams, mixed with the curses and yells of the other prisoners and the shouting of the British troops on deck, would threaten to drive the others mad as well. Sometimes, to supply diversion for themselves, troops would rush down below deck at odd times, like one o'clock in the morning, cursing, shouting, and beating their tin utensils against bulkheads and bars. Finding it impossible to return to sleep, the prisoners devised a game of football played with tin mugs, kicking them about and keeping up the mad game until daybreak.

Mutiny by prisoners of war aboard a ship bound for the Bermudas was not unusual either. Earlier in June Boer POWs had tried to overpower guards aboard the SS *Armenian* and sail the vessel for Holland. The revolt was put down easily.

Always scheming, Fritz made his own plans for taking over the *Harlech Castle.*[2] A keen observer, he noted the layout of the ship during the few moments daily when prisoners were allowed on deck for exercise. Coupled with what he learned in brief conversations with his captors, he was sure he knew enough to take over the ship at the right moment. With his strong personality he was able to gather a group of fifteen coconspirators and told them of his scheme.

They would strike around midnight, when most of the crew and soldier guards were sleeping. Fritz and a select group of men would take the captain prisoner. The others, with the aid of all able POWs, would break down the slight partitions between them and the guards, overpower the soldiers, and take command. They would then sail for France and freedom.

But there was careless talk, and the plan was discovered by an Afrikaner detective who had infiltrated the group masquerading as a POW. At ten o'clock in the morning on the day the assault was planned, the prisoners were assembled at mess. Names of the principal leaders, including Duquesne's, were read out, and they were immediately escorted to a cell where physical conditions were even worse than what they had been experiencing. They complained later of being treated worse than animals. No food, blankets, or mattresses were given them the first night. What food they eventually got was not edible.

The *Harlech Castle* sailed up the east coast of South Africa to Durban to take on more prisoners before turning south to round the Cape of Good Hope and continue on to Bermuda. (The voyage to Bermuda usually took about thirty-three days, but the side trip to Durban for POWs extended the time to forty-four days.) It was from Durban that Fritz, apparently unperturbed by his stricter incarceration, had a letter of complaint posted to the provost marshal of Bermuda. It was never received, he was informed later.

He wrote a second letter aboard the *Harlech,* complaining about an event that had occurred prior to his latest imprisonment. It was not clear what the circumstances were that had prompted the letter, but it appeared to refer to an infraction of the rules for which Fritz had been punished. Again, as was his style, he was careful to phrase the letter most respectfully:[3]

I have been informed of your non receival of my letter from Durban. The paper I here-with enclose I wrote about. It was handed to me as I passed through the passage from one end of the ship to the other by a man who was, at one time, a friend. I understood his name was Harold Clair a musician. I did not read the paper, until I was alone, which was when the ship had left Cape Town, otherwise you should have received it that night. I hope that this will enlighten you, and let you understand why I so much object to my imprisonment.

I sent a copy of this to you from Durban. To save time I enclose the paper itself.

I hope you will investigate the case. I expected to be able to give you a description of the man so that he could be arrested for theft. But now, it is too late.

Yours respectfully,
Fritz du Quenne
Prisoner of war

Captain G. J. Traherne, commandant of Hawkins' Island in Bermuda, investigated for the provost general and attached this comment to Fritz's letter: "I have made enquiries and find that the prisoner did not pass through the passage from one end to the other—but over the bridge deck. No strangers were allowed on board and the prisoner was handcuffed. It is practically certain that he received no papers from anyone. The attached is probably written by himself."

Fritz made another attempt to escape when the *Harlech Castle* stopped at Ponta Delgada in the Azores to take on coal and water. The prisoners were brought on deck for some fresh air and exercise during the short time the ship was there.[4] Released from his shackles for exercise, Fritz saw his opportunity when a careless private on guard duty set his rifle down and stepped away to talk to a group of prisoners. While the soldier recounted his war experiences, Fritz silently took the gun, raised it by the barrel, and swung it in a wide arc, smashing it against the guard's skull and killing him. Ignoring the startled prisoners, Fritz grabbed the dead body and slipped it over the side. Then he slid down inside an open hawsehole as far as he could go. When night came and the search for the soldier had quieted down, he would climb out and swim ashore.

But an hour later a raucous voice from above yelled to the cramped Fritz, "Come up, you bloody bastard, or we'll shoot you full of holes. I see you down there." Reluctant to give up the freedom he had almost gained, Fritz didn't move. A shot was fired, which barely missed him. Then he clambered painfully up, his muscles aching from the enforced confinement, to where guards and prisoners stood surrounding the hawsehole.

"Jan told!" an indignant POW called out, Identifying the snitch. "We wouldn't have told." But it didn't matter to Fritz now. He was put in solitary in the brig, and he knew now that there was nothing but death for him.

Next morning, with the ship under way again for the Bermudas, Fritz was put on trial. But now there was no direct witness against him. Knowing that the life of a snitch was a precarious one, Jan the informer denied seeing anything. He didn't see Fritz kill the guard. His back was turned. All he saw was Fritz scuttling down the hawsehole. A guard murdered? What guard?

The frustrated prosecutor was incensed. There was the missing guard's gun and a fleck of blood on the deck. The man was missing, and Duquesne had fled. Wasn't this proof of a crime and guilt?

The judge pointed out that there was no body. Perhaps the guard had slipped ashore for an unannounced leave. So a guard was missing and a Boer had taken the opportunity to hide. Nothing could be proved beyond this. There was no case, and Fritz Duquesne was free to spend the rest of his life in the Enchanted Isles.

A few months later Fritz managed to get a letter to *Le Petit Bleu du Matin,* the official European organ of the Boer government,[5] in which he bitterly complained about his treatment aboard the *Harlech Castle* and ashore in Bermuda. He wrote that he had received "worse treatment than would have befallen the lowest criminal. After our arrival at Bermuda, my fellow prisoners and I were tortured in a way which made even the barbarian Polynesians blush. Six of us were locked up in a jail in the middle of the Atlantic Ocean (a jail which is a source of embarrassment to the savage uncivilized native girls) and surrounded by insulting British soldiers."[6] Fritz was never inconsistent regarding the treatment he received at the hands of jailers. In all his future incarcerations over the next four decades he would continue to rail about poisoned food, beatings, barbarism, and inhuman treatment, in letters, public statements, and legal appeals.

When the *Harlech Castle* sailed into Hamilton Harbor on 20 December 1901, the surprised POWs were greeted by a sizable turnout of

Bermuda's seventeen thousand citizens, many of them approaching in boats. Four previous ships with 3,020 Boers destined for island camps had preceded them, and the expected arrival of even more prisoners had caused something of a holiday air to pervade the islands. Obviously there was still some interest among the Bermudians in watching the arrival of these strange men from South Africa who were causing mighty England so much trouble. Their long beards, their ever-present pipes, the knobbed sticks that many of them carried, and their shabby clothes contrasted greatly with the style of the islanders, who, though several thousand miles from Mother England, were just as Victorian in fashion, manners, and mores as the most staid Londoner.

Rumors that Bermuda would become a penal colony for Boer POWs had been circulating since April, some time prior to the arrival of the first prison ship. The news caused mixed feelings and trepidation among the islanders. Although war news was followed with interest, the Bermudas were uncommonly peaceful. Bermudians considered themselves detached from the rest of the world, except for the five thousand tourists who visited the islands annually. The potential loss of tourism was what concerned them particularly. But there wasn't much to be done when it was announced that the imperial government had already leased Darrell's Island for a year, with an option to continue at one month's notice. The leases had been arranged without consultation with the Bermuda government headed by the governor, Lieutenant General Sir Digby Barker, K.C.B. And it was so when other islands in the sound were obtained, whether from Admiralty administrators who had governed them since 1809 or from the owners under private treaty.

Local blacksmiths were hired to make iron gates and fencing, and Prospect Garrison employed colored labor to set up the basic necessities for a large-scale occupation of the islands. Military boats ferried troops working on the islands, and at the end of May a special detachment of Royal Engineers installed and maintained condensing and distilling equipment for water on the islands.

On 28 June the SS *Armenian* dropped anchor in Grassy Bay with 963 prisoners on board under guard of a company from the Second Battalion of the Royal Warwickshire Regiment, which had been withdrawn from active service in South Africa. That same day Governor Barker issued a proclamation placing certain areas under martial law.

Every attempt was made by the British to assure that the camps were carefully prepared and would not be open to criticism. Conditions would be in direct contrast to those aboard the prison ships and in the refugee camps of South Africa. Nevertheless, life in the Bermuda camps under military rule would not be easy. Bermuda may have been an island paradise, but as far as the POWs were concerned, it might as well have been Devil's Island,

Bermuda was a Devil's Island to Fritz. Decent treatment could not deter him from making immediate plans to escape. Volunteering for work details gave him the run of the islands. Although always under the eyes of armed guards, he could see that the British had laid out the prison camps in such a way as to preclude escape. But to the dedicated escaper, such plans were never a deterrent.

The island camps were split into four sectors, Fritz learned. Each island sector was marked off with buoys as a warning to civilian boaters to keep their distance. No civilian was allowed to enter the military zones without a pass signed by the assistant general for prisoners of war. The largest of these zones contained the camp commandant's headquarters, the prison hospital, and a group of mail censors on Ports Island. Long, Nelly, and Hawkins' were the other islands in the zone.

Hawkins' Island was divided into three sections by barbed-wire fencing. The prisoner's compound was at one end, the Royal Engineer's workshop was in the center, and at the northern end lay the special enclosure for convicted rebels who had rioted or caused other difficulties. The major islands in this zone had been linked together by wooden-planked footbridges, which overcame the difficulty of transportation to some extent and enabled the prisoners to march to work in the quarries at the east end of Long Island.

To the south and forming a second zone lay Burtt's and Darrell's. On both these islands the land had been divided in two with barbed-wire fencing strung to a height of nine feet from tees and on posts, effectively placing the guards on one side and the prisoners on the other. Where the fencing met the sea, posts were sunk in concrete with the barbed wire running into the water. One iron gate connected the two compounds on each island.

To the west were Tucker's and Morgan's islands, which formed the third zone and were linked to Darrell's by telephone cable. They were also split into two sections, and extra security was afforded by a guard post on the mainland and by three Royal Navy gunboats anchored off to the south in Hamilton Harbor. Known locally as the "guardian angels," the boats played their searchlights on the surrounding waters after dark, seeking out prisoners attempting to swim to the mainland and, with luck, stow away aboard a ship bound for America and freedom. Fritz realized that he faced his most difficult challenge here. Evading the "guardian angels" would not be easy. Even more difficult would be the sharks, an enemy he could not see. But when the time came, he would have to take his chances. Anything would be better than imprisonment.

Fritz also knew that the British were especially wary of the prisoners in the second and third zones. The prisoners on Tucker's were known to be those who had signified their willingness to accept the authority of the crown. But those on Morgan's and on Darrell's in this zone were the "irreconcilables," those who had no intention of submitting—at least until the war was over.

It was not until March 1902 that the governor—now Lieutenant General Sir Henry Geary, K.C.B.—officially designated the fourth zone, which was limited to Hinson's (Godet's) Island and the water surrounding it. Close to Hamilton City, it was used as a boarding school for most of the young Boer boys who had been sent to Bermuda. Ranging in age from eight to sixteen, these youths had been taken prisoner while assisting their older relations in the front line. These Khaki Schools provided academic teaching and manual training.

Each Boer compound was provided with washing and toilet facilities. Eight hundred and fifty Bell tents, with standard wooden flooring, were erected for the use of the prisoners in the compounds. The tents were arranged in lines of about a dozen each, with seven or eight men to each tent. Each tent elected a foreman, and the foreman of the line elected a line captain, who, in return for being responsible for the affairs and conduct of his men, received the privilege of a tent, or hut, to himself. The line captains in the compound voted for one or more commandants, and these senior officers were in complete control of their fellow prisoners. The chain of command worked well, and internal discipline was maintained by the camp Landrost (magistrate's court). This form of self-government preserved discipline and morale and ensured the general well-being of the group as a whole. There was a minimum of interference from the British, although each island occupied by the prisoners had its own guard company of British troops.

Roll call was conducted by a British officer every morning at 6:30, and again at 4:30 P.M. and two hours before the sailing of any ship.[7] The irreconcilables on Darrell's Island were especially difficult. The island was a former camp headquarters and parade ground for the Bermuda Volunteer Rifle Corps. Roll call of the prisoners was taken each morning, but "dodging" had become a regular feature, and it was the practice for unarmed soldiers to check each tent for defaulters. At the other camps prisoners simply lined up in front of their tents for morning muster.

Because of the world furor over British POW camp conditions in South Africa, it was expected that the Bermuda camps would receive the same scrutiny from newspapers, the clergy, and peace organizations from abroad. And they did. Newspapers and committees sympathetic to the Boers made periodic inspections of the camps but could find no fault with their administration. There was the Lend a Hand Society of Boston, the Boer Relief Fund of New York, and the American Transvaal League of Paterson, New Jersey. Genuine philanthropy was the object of most of the societies, but the purpose of several of them was to bait the British Lion for attacking little South Africa. There was even much sympathy on the islands for the Boers. The Association for Boer Recreation, run by a Miss K. Elwes, provided the prisoners with many items to make their positions comfortable, including books, magazines, playing cards, and fishing line.

But the most active organization, and one that was anathema to British authorities, was the Boer Relief Committee under the direction of Miss Anna Maria Outerbridge, Captain W. E. Meyer—whose military title derived from commanding ships at sea—and Mrs. Selma Recht. While the other organizations were simply interested in the prisoners for humanitarian reasons, the BRC, consisting of nine members, was openly pro-Boer in its sympathies and had German connections.

Miss Outerbridge was a determined gray-haired woman in her early fifties who had no fear of the consequences regarding her position. A strict prohibitionist, she was often described as a Tartar who gave no quarter, particularly when it came to her belief in the suffragette movement. She felt that the presence of British troops in South Africa was wrong, and she would do everything she could to correct that wrong.

Many members of the Outerbridge family lived on Bermuda, descendants of an Outerbridge who had come to the island in 1609 as part of a group of shipwrecked mariners. Among the prolific Outerbridges on the islands were physicians and surgeons, auctioneers, dentists, dressmakers, bicycle agents, mill operators, ice dealers, lumbermen, painters, and even chimney sweeps. Anna's father was Charles Outerbridge, a grocer and provision merchant at Bailey's Bay who also had outlets in Hamilton and Southampton.

Anna Outerbridge regularly sent bananas to the prisoners from her father's stores. Her Boer sympathies were well known to the POWs, and when any escaped they would make their way to her home at Bailey's Bay, where she would hide them. It was a spacious home at 172 Bay View Drive, offering many places for concealment. Her actions were in direct defiance of the military regulations imposed on Bermudians when the prisoners were first brought to the islands. Obviously not liked by her fellow islanders, she was burned in effigy in place of Guy Fawkes on 5 November 1901.

The military authorities also knew of Miss Outerbridge's sympathies. Whenever a prisoner was on the loose, military search parties placed her home at the top of their list. The situation became so embarrassing to the authorities that the Colonial House of Assembly was forced to pass legislation making it an offense to assist or harbor Boer prisoners of war. The law, enacted on 18 December, pronounced a maximum punishment of five years imprisonment or a fine of £300. The only restraint it imposed on the strong-willed Miss Outerbridge was to make her act a little more prudently.

Escape from the islands was not easy, Fritz determined. But he was not deterred. It was not impossible for prisoners to swim the short distance from their island camps to the main island, if they successfully avoided sharks.[8] The next great difficulty was to leave the Bermuda Islands without detection. Once an escaped prisoner was able to evade all the military blockades and zones set up to ensure his incarceration behind barbed wire, he had to make his way to Hamilton on St. George's, the only escape route to mainland America, which was the closest country offering sanctuary. New York City was 775 miles away. Hamilton and St. George's were the only ports of entry and clearance for vessels, and there was a large amount of traffic. Fare for the fifty-hour trip to New York was $30. If a POW was even able to come up with the fare, he would then have to secure passage—which would not be easy, considering his appearance and the language barrier. Not to be forgotten were the "guardian angels" patrolling the waters of the harbor throughout the night and the sharks that patrolled night and day. A further deterrent was the penalty of solitary confinement for those who were captured attempting to escape.

Baron von Kaynach, who had walked in chains with Fritz through the streets of Cape Town on the way to the *Harlech Castle,* attempted an escape. He managed to swim from Ports Island to the Warwick shore on the mainland after two and a half hours in the water. But he was picked up quickly at the home of Mrs. Recht, the Boer sympathizer. Even he, a veteran escaper, was pessimistic about further attempts. To his British captors he said, "The whole business is really hopeless." So all in all, escape was only for the daring.

The British would soon find out how daring Fritz could be.

CHAPTER 5

Peace in South Africa, but
No Peace for Fritz

ERMUDA was impossible, hopeless, an impregnable prison of
pink beaches and sunlit waters from which no prisoner could
escape—or so believed the British.

But nothing was impossible or hopeless for Fritz Duquesne, the
man who had already escaped from a British POW camp in South
Africa, had almost dug his way out of the formidable Cape Castle, and
had almost escaped twice from a prison ship. There was no question
that Fritz possessed the daring to escape from the Peacock Isles. The
only question was when.

But first Fritz had to settle into his new life. There would be time.
He would study the islands and the impressive and discouraging
methods the British used to contain the Boer prisoners. He would find
a way off the islands, or he would make a way.

Always the enigma, Fritz was officially listed as number 24131 and
identified in a prison report as Fritz Jean du Quenne.[1] His home address was given as Brussels and his nationality as American—a masquerade he had perhaps undertaken to avoid prosecution as a rebel.
But Fritz was always playing the game, the game of the elusive spy.
English was given as the language spoken, but it was known that he
spoke fluent French and Afrikaans. The only incontrovertible fact in

54

the report was the note that his appearance was "well set up gentle-manly," a trait that would work to Fritz's advantage for the rest of his life.

And always playing the heroic soldier, Fritz gave information that he was a member of Pienaar's commando. But that is doubtful. Boer POWs usually gave the name of their units, not those of their officers. The only Transvaal senior officer of that name in 1901 was Comman-dant J. Pienaar, who served under General Lemmer in the western Transvaal. There is no reference to Duquesne in the documents of the western Transvaal commandos, or any other commando for that mat-ter. His name is also missing from the files in which POWs are listed according to their units.[2]

Because of his attempted escapes and the suspicion that he had murdered the guard on the *Harlech Castle*, Fritz was imprisoned tem-porarily on Tucker's Island in a special enclosure, or "ram camp," as the Boers called them.[3] The camp was for incorrigibles. Fritz was one of several prisoners who had their hands shackled fourteen hours a day. No chain separated the cuffs, which were clamped together; the prisoners endured the night with their hands fastened close together.

The Reverend J. van Blerk, a young Boer minister who had come voluntarily to Bermuda to administer to the needs of his countrymen, visited the incorrigibles and was particularly impressed by Fritz.[4] He mistakenly believed that the Boer prisoner was French because he was obviously educated and well spoken. He could recite poetry beautifully, van Blerk reported, and the prisoner often read or recited to him.[5] The minister described Fritz as having light blue eyes—in fact they were dark blue—and a mop of jet black hair that hung to his shoulders. Fritz had let his hair grow long again after it had been cropped prior to boarding the *Harlech Castle*. This time he apparently had not told his captors about his vow never to cut it until the Boers were free.

It was from this "ram camp" on 25 April 1902 that Fritz made his first attempt at escape from the Bermudas.[6] Among the other prison-ers were Lieutenants de Gourville and Horvung, Field Cornet Nicholas du Toit, Alfred Joubert, and Frederick H. Bosch, a fourteen-year-old boy (identified as an officer in some accounts). A British guard named William, whom they believed to be sympathetic, sug-gested an escape plan to them.

What they did not know was that guards were given a standard re-ward of £3 for each prisoner they caught escaping. The plan was for William to release them from their shackles, which they had learned to

Bell tents in the prison enclosure on Bremuda's Burtt's Island, where Fritz was imprisoned. (Bermuda Archives)

pick anyway, and allow them to escape over the barbed-wire fence. But when young Bosch made the first attempt to go over the fence, William shot and killed him. The other prisoners remained where they were. William collected his reward, and Duquesne and Joubert were transferred to Burtt's Island, where there was even tighter security. It was one of the islands to which the irreconcilables had been assigned.[7] Du Toit was sent to Darrell's Island.

The war was rapidly drawing to a close in South Africa. Lord Kitchener's scorched-earth policy of burning farms and crops was slowly eroding the Boers' ability and will to continue opposing the invader. Also to be considered was the staggering death rate of women and children in the concentration camps that had been set up by the British to care for those who had been driven from their farms. The realization of coming peace did not diminish Duquesne's hatred of the British.

Knowing he would not be allowed to return to South Africa despite an end to the war, Fritz never gave up plotting escape. He avoided solitary confinement on Burtt's because work parties were needed on the islands, hewing trees and clearing areas for new roads. As an unskilled laborer he received one penny per hour.[8]

Fritz, identified as Duquenne in back row at right, poses with three other Boer POWs. All four were involved in an unsuccessful escape attempt on 25 April 1902. The drawing was apparently smuggled out of Bermuda. (La Petit Bleu du Matin)

It was during a rest period one afternoon in Bermuda that he met the girl who would eventually become his wife.[9] Shackled together with his fellow prisoners, Fritz and the rest of his work gang were resting under the shade of a tree when a tennis ball bounced across the road and rolled to a stop at his feet. Chasing after it, a young woman came running across the road from a nearby tennis court but stopped short when she saw the prisoners.

"Don't be afraid," called Fritz. "We won't eat you." Kicking the ball to her, he stood up and tipped his hat. Despite the prison garb, he was still the handsome and dashing soldier.

They were attracted to each other instantly. She would often see Fritz and stop along the roadside to talk to him. She was rapidly falling in love with the debonair Boer. After all, he spoke flawless French and English and recited poetry beautifully.

The young woman was Alice Wortley, eighteen-year-old daughter of Samuel Sharp Wortley, American director of agriculture on Bermuda.[10] A building contractor and civil engineer from Akron, Ohio, he was also responsible for building docks in Bermuda. Earlier in his career he had worked on the Trans-Andean Railroad in South America. Fritz would later claim that the family held "vast plantations" in the British West Indies.[11]

Seven years younger than Fritz, Alice was born on 11 November 1884 in Kingston, Jamaica.[12] Always anxious to make his life appear more glamorous than it was even if it meant adding grandeur to the lives of others, Fritz always claimed that his wife was of "the noble line of Lady Mary Wortley Montague."[13] He boasted that the best blood of England flowed through her veins and made roses of her cheeks, that her family name is preserved in Burke's *Peerage* and a famous work of English literature, and that her relatives had married into some of America's most affluent and noted families. Alice had two brothers, Samuel (Jim) and Guy, and three sisters, Clare, Mae, and Daisy. Their marriage partners were not unusually distinguished by affluence, nor were they from particularly noted families.

How could a man who proclaimed such hatred of England marry a woman through whose veins flowed "the best blood of England"? It was a contradiction of everything he had dedicated his life to. The explanation was not difficult for a man who reinvented himself according to the needs of the moment. Fritz simply declared that his marriage to this titled woman was an act of revenge against England. His revenge took its form in the sexual defilement of Alice.

Alice Wortley, Fritz's wife. She divorced him when she finally realized his income wasn't all derived from writing and lecturing. (Jocelyn W. Becker)

Even though he was a lifelong womanizer who often mistreated her by neglect, Fritz was remarkably devoted to Alice, according to her sister-in-law, Mildred Una Greenidge, wife of Jim.[14] She said Fritz was very much in love with his wife. Alice, Mildred said, knew how to pose and was stunning. It's no wonder Fritz was crazy about her. Mildred always believed it was a love match from the beginning.

A favorite fiction of Fritz's was that Alice helped him escape from Bermuda.[15] The way he told the tale, he escaped from the work gang and was hidden by Alice, whom he identified this time as the daughter of the governor general of Bermuda. She brought him food and clothing, and following a torrid romance in which he ravished this flower of English nobility, she daringly helped her lover board a ship bound for New York. As we shall see, the truth was somewhat different and even more exciting.

Progress of the war in South Africa was not kept from the Boer POWs, particularly since it was obvious that the British would soon be the victors. The more pragmatic prisoners were anxious for the termination of hostilities, wanting to return to their homeland and families to resume their prewar lives.

But even on the islands there was bitter antagonism between the *hensoppers* or "uphanders," those who raised their hands in surrender, and the *bittereinders*, those who fought on to the bitter end, the irreconcilables. Spirits still ran high among the *bittereinders*, so much so that military honors, usually accorded to deceased prisoners of war, were refused. R. Albertyn, the Boer chaplain, had requested that the Union Jack should not cover dead burghers. He also ordered that the customary three volleys fired over a soldier's grave be discontinued.

The oath of allegiance to Great Britain was the greatest cause of rancor between the two groups of POWs.[16] Some had signed the oath before leaving South Africa, some during the voyage to the Bermudas, and others during their captivity in the islands. As recently as March 1902 a party of irreconcilables had attacked a group of the "uphanders" and attempted to drown them in the Great Sound. The soldiers of the Warwickshire broke up the fight, and instigators of the fracas were put in a military prison on St. George's.

Peace terms were finally signed in Pretoria on 31 May 1902, and the two republics of the Transvaal and the Orange Free State ceased to exist and became British colonies.[17] The cable company in Bermuda received the news at 7 P.M. on 1 June. Boer commandants announced it to their assembled companies in the prison camps. Generally the information was received happily, and the Boers spontaneously began singing "God Save the King." They were told that all prisoners would be returned home as soon as possible and no action would be taken against them unless they had broken the rules of war.

One stipulation prevented an immediate return of the prisoners: If any burgher wished to return to his homeland, he must take the oath of allegiance to the British Crown. The oath was signed in triplicate by the prisoner in the presence of a justice of the peace and witnesses. The prisoner retained a copy, the British government kept one, and the third copy was sent to South Africa. The oath read, "I [name and home address] adhere to the terms of the agreement signed at Pretoria on the 31st May, 1902, between my late Government and the representatives of His Majesty's Government. I acknowledge myself to be a subject of King Edward VII., and I promise to own allegiance to Him, His Heirs, and successors according to law."[18]

The vast majority of Boers willingly signed the oath, acknowledging the fact that the war was over and that the terms of surrender were generous. Home and their families and the rebuilding of South Africa were all that mattered to them now. The irreconcilables, however, thought differently. Their grudge against the British was not so easily dismissed. Although their fellow prisoners considered their zeal misplaced, many civilians and Boer aid societies hailed them as heroes and martyrs to the cause.

Fritz Duquesne in particular could not be persuaded. Until he signed the oath, he would not be released. But he knew that even if he did sign, he could never return to South Africa, because of having organized the Cape Town Plot. He had been exiled forever. That alone justified his continued hatred of the British and explained why he planned another escape that would free him not only from prison but from the pressures of swearing allegiance to Great Britain forever.

CHAPTER 6

Escape to *Who's Who*

O N 25 JUNE 1902, two months after his aborted attempt to escape from Tucker's Island, Fritz made another bid for freedom from the camp on Burtt's Island.[1] It was a night heavy with falling rain, and the guards, less alert than usual, were huddled in the warmth of their sentry boxes.

Fritz slipped out of his tent and managed to get through the wire fence enclosing the compound without being observed. It was after the 4:30 P.M. roll call, and he knew he had until the next roll call at 6:30 in the morning before he would be noticed missing.

He made his way to the shore, tied his boots and clothing around his neck, and began the mile-and-a-half swim to the main island. During the long swim he was in danger from marauding sharks and from cruising "guardian angel" patrol boats, which even on a night like this did not relax their vigilance, scanning the waters constantly with powerful beams. Several times it was necessary for Fritz to dive below the surface to escape probing lights. Fritz said afterward that the swim was "the thrill of his life" because of the constant fear of sharks.[2]

His only directional guide was the beam from King's Point lighthouse on the distant Bermuda shore, which he always kept in sight. Despite the guiding beacon, the swift current had carried Fritz several miles from his goal when he finally staggered ashore ninety minutes later.

"Willoughby," the home of Anna Maria Outerbridge in Bailey's Bay, Bermuda. She was the "notorious" Boer sympathizer and member of the Boer Relief Committee. Prisoners attempting escape from Bermuda made their way to this house first, as did Fritz when he escaped on 26 June 1902. (Photo by author)

He immediately made for Willoughby, the Bailey's Bay home of Anna Outerbridge, the "notorious" Boer sympathizer and member of the Boer Relief Committee. But once there, he was confronted by an unforeseen problem. By an odd coincidence, Duquesne's fellow prisoner and former escape conspirator on Tucker's, Nicholas du Toit, had escaped the same evening from Darrell's.

With both prisoners at her door, Miss Outerbridge was faced with a dilemma. Her sympathies were with both men, but because of the stringent law passed the previous December—punishing anyone who helped prisoners escape with a maximum prison sentence of five years or a fine of £300—she knew she would have to make a compromise: obey the law and also satisfy what she believed was a moral duty. To help both escape could jeopardize future help for prisoners not willing to sign the oath of allegiance. And after all, the war was over. Of course, for these two *bittereinders* it would never be over.

Fortunately for both Miss Outerbridge and Fritz, du Toit's physical condition resolved the dilemma. He had been weakened by the long swim, and the fight had just about gone out of him. He agreed to return with Miss Outerbridge and give himself up to the military. As for Fritz, Miss Outerbridge gave him clothes and a small amount of money, then turned him over to her fellow Boer sympathizer, Captain Meyer. He immediately took Fritz to Hamilton and the harbor Tenderloin district, where the fugitive could lose himself among sailors waiting for their ships to leave or looking for billets aboard new ships.

It was late afternoon now, and as Miss Outerbridge brought du Toit in her gig to the Hamilton office of Major Morrice, the former camp commander on Tucker's and now the assistant adjutant general for prisoners of war, she noted the increased number of troops in the streets. Their searching through buildings and questioning of civilians indicated that they were looking for the two escaped prisoners. Since her vehicle was going into the city and not away from it, she was ignored.

Because du Toit was voluntarily turning himself in, Miss Outerbridge pleaded with Major Morrice that he give him immunity against further punishment: "Major, I have a prisoner of war with me who escaped from Darrell's Island and who came to me for help. I suggested that he turn himself in, reminding him that the war was over, and he agreed. I ask you to remember this and promise me that you will not punish him and that he'll simply be sent back to camp."

Miss Outerbridge was a formidable woman, and the fact that she was turning in a prisoner gave Morrice reason to believe that perhaps it would be best to go along with her. When the news got around, he reasoned, it might prevent further escape attempts by the hardcore irreconcilables. Miss Outerbridge's conscience was clear. She had served two masters.

Morrice had to be satisfied with du Toit. But the prisoner he really wanted was the notorious Duquesne. Soldiers were placed on guard night and day at the harbor in Hamilton and at St. George's to prevent his slipping aboard a ship.

Fritz had no difficulty assimilating into the waterfront life of Hamilton.[3] Despite his vow not to cut his hair until South Africa was free, he was pragmatic enough to know that if he was to escape to America, where he hoped to continue his personal fight against England, he had better find a barber. Meanwhile, he found a prostitute named Vera and steady employment as her pimp. The sailors paid Vera 6 shillings for her product, and Vera paid Fritz 3 shillings for procuring the sailors. It wasn't bad pay, especially for a former POW who had been making only a penny a day digging holes and whitewashing fences. He also had to be constantly on guard because the whorehouses were heavily patronized by the local garrison.

Vera was a light mulatto, proud of her almost straight hair and possessing an aristocratic British style of speech that she could transform into vile bawdiness when the occasion demanded. At 6 shillings she was a bargain indeed, and the sailors never felt they had been cheated. On the contrary, they felt a little dishonest after leaving Vera.

It was an ideal situation for Fritz. With his hair cut short and a suitable wardrobe, he looked anything but the escaped prisoner. He had settled into city life and didn't move about the island where he would likely run into patrols and be questioned. And with his reputation as a "well set up gentleman" among his former warders, it was not suspected that he would be living with a prostitute. Vera's place on Front Street was also the best of listening posts. Sooner or later, or so it seemed when Fritz counted his growing fortune, sailors from all the ships making port at Hamilton or St. George's did business with Vera. Discreet questioning of customers revealed destinations and departure dates of recently arrived ships.

Fritz didn't have long to wait. On 2 July, after only a week of doing business with Vera, the American steam yacht *Margaret,* just in from a pleasure cruise to Singapore and the West Indies via the Azores and bound for Baltimore, docked at St. George's to take on forty tons of coal.⁴ The crew was given one day's liberty, and true to the instincts of most sailors in foreign ports, many of them made for the pleasure houses along Front Street. That is where Fritz met Tompkins, one of the crew and a man giddy with anticipation to meet Vera, so delightfully described by her procurer. But first a drink, then another and another. Fritz learned that the ship was leaving for Baltimore that evening. He also learned the name of the ship's owner, Isaac Edward Emerson, and her master, Captain Witer.⁵ Then it was off for a long evening with Vera.

Fritz waived his pimp's wages that night, waved goodbye to Vera, and, putting on Tompkins's uniform while the sailor was engaged with Vera, weaved his drunken way to the docks where a boat would take the liberty party back to the *Margaret*. In the dark, one drunken sailor looked much like another, and he had no trouble staggering aboard without being stopped. Thinking him hopelessly drunk, the first mate had him tossed into the brig and fed on bread and water until he "sobered up." Fritz considered it a banquet while he "sobered up" for the next twenty-four hours. He wanted to be sure the yacht was well out to sea and well on its way to Baltimore before his true identity was discovered. This would preclude the possibility of the *Margaret* turning about for Bermuda and returning him to the authorities.⁶

When he was released from the brig by the third mate the next day and his true identity learned, Fritz was charged with being a stowaway. On his way to being hauled before the captain of the yacht, he and the mate met the owner of the ship, Commodore Isaac Edward Emerson, making his way down the gangway.

Emerson was a forty-three-year-old drug manufacturer whose great wealth had been accumulated from the marketing of a headache powder he had patented as a young pharmacist in Baltimore. He called it Bromo Seltzer. With his newfound wealth he started the Emerson Drug Company and became noted as a lavish entertainer who thought nothing of taking a score or more of guests on long cruises aboard his yachts, the *Margaret* and the *Queen Anne*. Many a sumptuous party was held on their decks.

The *Margaret* was a sumptuous lady herself. A luxurious white and gold pleasure barge of 236 tons, she was 176 feet long from bowsprit to fantail and had a beam of 19 feet. By the time America entered World War I, fifteen years after the Duquesne incident, Emerson had already abandoned the *Margaret,* and she was set for the junk pile when the

Bromo Seltzer king Commodore Isaac Emerson's yacht Margaret, *on which Fritz escaped from Bermuda to the United States. (Maryland Historical Society, Baltimore)*

U.S. Navy, desperate for ships of any sort to be commissioned as submarine chasers, rescued the yacht from an ignominious end. She was commissioned S.P. (Submarine Patrol) 527, affectionately named *Maggie* by her crew, and became part of a ragtag squadron of ships called by the navy the Mosquito Fleet.[7]

Emerson formed the Maryland Naval Reserve in 1894 and during the Spanish American War provided the entire crew for the United States ship *Dixie*.[8] He was commissioned a lieutenant in the navy and after the war received his rank as captain. His daughter, Margaret, married millionaire society scion Alfred Gwynne Vanderbilt, who would lose his life in 1915 when the *Lusitania* was torpedoed.

An adventurer himself, Emerson was impressed by the personal appearance of Duquesne and by the stories he told him of his experiences in the Boer War and of his escape from Bermuda.[9] "Have you ever been to sea?" he asked Fritz.

"No, sir, but I'd make a splendid steward."

"I think everything will turn out fine for you in America," Emerson laughed. "Take this man under your special charge," he ordered the mate. "I think he'll make a splendid steward."

But Captain Witer looked at the matter of the stowaway differently, despite the fact that Emerson owned the *Margaret* and paid the bills. Witer believed it should be the captain of the ship who chose the stewards and determined what happened to stowaways. "Send that bastard in here," he thundered. "A hell of a lot Emerson knows about sea law. How do we know Tompkins wasn't killed and his clothes stolen? What kind of discipline can I have aboard if the owner keeps butting in telling me who my crew is and what they do? By god! I'll turn my ticket in at the end of this trip!"

Fritz appeared before Witer. "How did you get Tompkins's uniform, Duquesne?" the captain demanded.

Fritz told Witer the truth, hoping his story would affect the captain the same way it had Emerson. It didn't. "To hell with the Boers and your escape story," the captain exploded. "When we land in Baltimore I'll turn you over to the immigration authorities, and they'll send you back to your beloved South Africa. I should throw you in the brig. But thanks to you I'm shorthanded. You'll work your passage. Have you ever been a steward aboard a yacht before?"

"No, sir."

"Well, you won't be again. Get him out of here and into a uniform!"

Fritz was appalled. After his conversation with Emerson he was sure America would present no problems. But the irate Captain Witer appeared to be implacable in his determination to return him to South Africa. And the captain did know sea law. Fritz knew that other Boers who had escaped were well received in New York. One or another group in sympathy with their cause would take the Boers in and champion them. But to Fritz's knowledge, no previously escaping Boer had broken the law in seeking his freedom. Fritz was convinced that he must find a way to leave the yacht before it reached Baltimore. It was either that or imprisonment again in a Bermuda "ram camp."

The duties of a steward aboard a luxury yacht were light, allowing time for Fritz to study hydrographic charts in the lounge and find the best and safest place where he could jump ship. Once they entered Chesapeake Bay on the last leg to Baltimore, Fritz planned to drop over the side as soon as they were reasonably close to shore and swim for the mainland. Once ashore, he would somehow make his way to

Paterson (New Jersey) and the office of Marinus Houman, an architect and member of the American Transvaal League, closely associated with Miss Outerbridge's Boer Relief Committee.[10] Houman and his four daughters and two sons, along with a group of Hollanders in New York City, had organized an underground network to help Boers assimilate into American life.

Fritz saw his chance the next day when they passed Cape Charles and slipped into Chesapeake Bay.[11] He had already put some of Tompkins's civilian clothes on under his uniform and was ready when the yacht passed by Great Fox Island. He could see the Maryland shore. Walking quickly to the railing of the yacht, he climbed over, hung at arm's length for a moment, pushed himself out, dropped into the water, and struck out for the shore as the *Margaret* continued north to Baltimore.

When Fritz scrambled up the sandy beach on the Maryland shore, it was 4 July 1902, a significant date for the former British POW. America was celebrating its independence from Britain, and Fritz too was now totally free from that country.

The closest town was Crisfield. From there Fritz hopped freights of the Pennsylvania Railroad and walked the ties, always heading north for Paterson. He was able to buy some food with his pimp earnings, which he had exchanged for American dollars with a sailor aboard the *Margaret*. When he ran out of money he cadged the rest. He continued on through Wilmington to Philadelphia. From there he crossed the Delaware River to Camden, then on to Newark and finally Paterson, where he found Houman who took him to his home in Pompton Lakes.

And so goes the thrilling story of how Fritz Duquesne slipped over the side of the *Margaret* in Chesapeake Bay and stole ashore in America on 4 July 1902. At least that's the story as told by Fritz repeatedly over the years, orally and in print. Perhaps it did happen that way; but he told a slightly different story on form 2205 of the Department of Commerce and Labor Naturalization Service when he petitioned for naturalization as a citizen of the United States of America in 1912.

Petitioner number 21934 wrote, "Emigrated to the United States from Hamilton, Bermuda on or about the 12 day of Sept. in the year 1902 and arrived in the United States at the port of Baltimore on the 16 day of Sept. in the year 1902 on the vessel *Margaret*." A totally different date for arriving in America, and certainly a more prosaic way of entering his new life. But to say otherwise on the petition could very well have created legal problems for an escaped POW who had entered the country illegally, and by jumping ship at that. Fritz had surely thought this all out carefully before filing the form.

But what of the difference in dates? The dates of his escape from Bermuda and the sailing date of the *Margaret* from the islands are a matter of record. His petition for naturalization was dated 18 July 1912, ten years after his arrival in America. Perhaps he had just forgotten the date.

Marinus Houman was a prominent architect in Paterson who had designed factories, commercial buildings, schools, and private dwellings.[12] In classic American tradition he was a self-made man, born in Holland and coming to this country with his family in 1854 at the age of six. They settled into the long-established Dutch communities of Paterson, where as a young man Houman took up the craft of carpentry. Physically big with a fierce, mustachioed rectangular face that reflected years of hard construction work, Houman decided to become an architect in his late twenties. In 1885, after five years of night school, he established his offices at 6 Park Avenue in Paterson.

He never forgot his Dutch heritage and passionately took up the cause of the Boers. Refugees and former POWs would meet at his office and then be taken to his large home on the northeast corner of Ramapo and Passaic Avenues in Pompton Lakes. They would stay for several weeks, becoming acclimated to the new country and waiting for Houman's contacts to find them work. While waiting, some Boers would write books espousing their cause while others would prepare for lecture tours around the country, hoping to gain funds and sympathizers.

But dedicated as Houman was, not all was going well with the American Transvaal League. Finances were and always had been a continuing problem. He poured out these problems to Anna Outerbridge in a letter dated 13 August 1903 in which he detailed his difficulties during the past couple of years (a period that included the time he assisted Fritz Duquesne).[13] He told her he was not able to put into words how pained he was at "the fate in store for those poor prisoners." Like herself, he said, he had made sacrifices beyond his means, and in justice to his wife and children he must stop.

Miss Outerbridge was hoping to pass seventy-five men through New York, but she pointed out that to allow them to land under the present immigration law would require about $50 for each, or a total of $3,750, an impossible amount for him to raise.

Houman was concerned about continuing to bring Boer POWs to New York because, as he wrote, "they had never learned to work and in the rigorous winter climate they would suffer untold misery." He felt that it was kinder to leave them in Bermuda, where the English government would be responsible for them. He also felt that the irreconcilables should sign the oath of allegiance. After all, they would be doing so under duress, and by law it was not binding.

He suggested that it would behoove them to let the world know about this and that Miss Outerbridge should write all the facts to the English pro-Boer papers, the *Daily News* of London, the *Manchester Guardian,* and the weekly *New Age.* He felt it might bring good results, as it would "awaken the conscience of the better people of England." Houman particularly wanted Miss Outerbridge to write the Reverend Harold Rylett, a Unitarian minister who was editor and proprietor of the *New Age* and honorary secretary of the Stop the War Committee, the most vociferous and infamous of the antiwar organizations opposed to what they called "an unjust and unnecessary war."[14] Houman said he would write Rylett himself that night.

He also said he would contact Richard Weightman, one of the "sub editors" and a friend of his at the *Washington Post.* Richard Coxe Weightman had been the White House reporter for the *Post* during the administration of Benjamin Harrison and during both terms of Grover Cleveland. He was now an editorial writer for the paper and Boer advocate.[15]

Such was the situation when Fritz passed through Paterson and stayed at the Houman home for a few weeks.

To his surprise, Fritz was visited one day at Houman's by that "flower of England," Alice Wortley, and her mother. Mr. Wortley had left his position as director of agriculture in Bermuda and was returning to the construction business in Ohio. Miss Outerbridge had told Alice where Fritz would be in America. The reunion was a happy one, and Fritz no doubt again took his "revenge" against England. They would see each other again. It would be a stormy relationship and, for Alice, always a mysterious one regarding her masquerading lover.

Houman finally received word from the American Transvaal League in New York that Fritz was to report to them in Manhattan, where he would be given further instructions and employment. The work was not to Fritz's liking: he was a conductor on a subway train at $25 per week. When he complained, he was given a job as a subscription collector for the *New York Herald.*

Meanwhile, a dispatch issued in Bermuda by Captain C. Pyne, commandant of Darrell's Island, warned prisoner number 24131 "not to return to South Africa."[16]

Number 24131 never would.

Colonel Teddy Roosevelt Meets
Captain Fritz Duquesne

I T W A S T H E F A L L O F 1 9 0 2 when Fritz was thrust into the exciting, romantic, and adventurous world of New York journalism, a time when being a newspaperman was all of those things. It was a world into which Fritz Duquesne fit very comfortably.

To become a reporter was to join one of the most important professions a young man could aspire to at the time, with much thanks to the glamorous image created by the handsome, fashionable, and stalwart figures of Richard Harding Davis and David Graham Phillips. Davis was now a famous war correspondent, novelist, and dramatist. His was the act that every young man wanted to follow. Other reporters making strides in journalism at the time were Will Irwin, Irvin S. Cobb, Albert Payson Terhune, and former frontier lawman Bat Masterson, who had traded in his gun for a pencil on the *Morning Telegraph*.

Just two years into the new century, New York was full of the optimism generated by that knowledge and was vibrant with the exhilarating presence of such personalities as "Diamond Jim" Brady, his beauteous companion Lillian Russell, John Barrymore, who couldn't choose between drawing pictures for the *Journal* and following the family tradition of acting, and the sybaritic Stanford White, who saw beauty in every building he designed and had designs on every beauty he saw.

It was the era of the Gibson Girl, who through the artist's pen of Charles Dana Gibson became the "American woman idealized" and the "American girl glamorized." Perhaps a little more exciting and not so much an icon was the Florodora Girl, any one of six lovely ladies in the *Florodora* musical comedy, unattainable but sought after by every young—and not so young—man in New York City.

The Bowery and the Tenderloin provided sin, scandal, and pleasure. Horse-drawn hansom cabs were still the best way to get around, but electric automobiles were making headway. Broadway was an unequaled promenade for people-watching. Delmonico's and Sherry's were the most elegant restaurants in town, but you could have a lot more fun at Rector's, the "cathedral of froth." There were Churchill's, Reisenweber's, and Mouquin's, a favorite of the lords of the journals. But the newsmen also kept the beer flowing at Meehan's, Jack's, Hitchcock's, the Black Cat, Maria's, Perry's Hole in the Wall, and even a place called Duquesne's.

Theodore Roosevelt had been president for only a year following the assassination of his predecessor, William McKinley. The *Washington Post* editorial cartoonist Clifford K. Berryman was credited with sparking the Teddy Bear phenomenon when he caricatured Teddy refusing to shoot the mother of a captive bear cub. All future cartoons of Roosevelt by Berryman would include the cub somewhere in the illustration. And the president's latest book, *Outdoor Pastimes of an American Hunter,* created a national interest in outdoor activities. Pope Leo XIII, the "prisoner of the Vatican," had less than a year to reign.

Franz Joseph was emperor of Austria, and Kaiser Wilhelm II of Germany was visiting his uncle, King Edward VII, who had finally received the crown of England. A political rebel named Trotsky had escaped from Siberia and joined another named Lenin in Paris.

The kaiser had recently received as guests in Berlin the Boer generals Botha, De Wet, and De La Rey, expressing an interest in their military tactics against the British in the recent war.[1] The hated Kitchener had just taken his post as commander-in-chief of the army in India, and the London *Spectator* had criticized him for muddling through the war, suggesting that there should be a reappraisal of British tactics and urging "more adaptability in our warfare."[2]

In entertainment, Italian tenor Enrico Caruso made his first recording, James Barrie's *The Admirable Crichton* was a huge success, and

Georges Méliès's science fiction film *A Trip to the Moon* could be seen in theaters. Mrs. Leslie Carter, Ethel Barrymore, Mrs. Patrick Campbell, and John Drew were the current rage on the stage. Two of the year's most popular songs were "In the Good Old Summertime" and "Bill Bailey, Won't You Please Come Home?"

In literature, Emile Zola had died and Arthur Conan Doyle's most popular Sherlock Holmes story, *The Hound of the Baskervilles,* was being read, as was Owen Wister's *The Virginian*. Beatrix Potter's *The Tale of Peter Rabbit* hopped into public favor.

Current events showed that scientists Pierre and Marie Curie were continuing their experiments with radium and radioactivity. Captain Robert F. Scott had failed to reach the South Pole, and the North Pole proved just as elusive to Lieutenant Robert E. Peary. Mount Pelée on Martinique had erupted, killing thirty-eight thousand people, the Philippines became a U.S. territory, and Cuba was proclaimed an independent republic. The twenty-story Flatiron Building in New York City was completed, J. C. Penney opened his first store in Kemmerer (Wyoming), modern air conditioning was pioneered by Willis Carrier, Pepsi-Cola "hit the spot" for the first time, and French fashion designer Charles R. Debevoise achieved couturier immortality by inventing the brassiere. It would be one more year before the Wright brothers learned to fly.

In sports, the first postseason college football game was held at the Tournament of Roses in Pasadena, with Michigan defeating Stanford 49 to 0, and the Philadelphia Athletics took the American League pennant, with the Pittsburgh Pirates becoming the National League champions. The first World Series was still a year away. The heavyweight boxing champion of the world was James J. Jeffries.

Fritz could buy a new suit in "the very latest cut" for $7.95 from Siegel Cooper Co. or spend almost twice as much for one at Wm. Vogel & Son. He could take a forty-four-day cruise on the Hamburg-American Line to Norway, Sweden, Russia, and Denmark for $225. Or he could buy a fifteen-room house with three bathrooms for $23,500 in Brooklyn, where he would soon be living.

But on a salary of $25 a week as a newly hired collector of subscriptions for the *Herald,* Fritz could not afford much. On the other hand, he couldn't have started on a more appropriate paper. The publisher was James Gordon Bennett Jr., a slightly mad playboy, sportsman, and adventurer, and an innovative newspaperman. If a young reporter liked to travel, a position on the Bennett paper was a sure bet he'd be using a passport. It was Bennett who sent the young Henry M. Stanley off to Africa in 1870 to "Find Livingstone!"

If anything, New York had too many newspapers. There were at least fourteen major papers and many lesser beacons of journalism, most of which were centered along Park Row, also called Newspaper Row—a short street in lower Manhattan with the entrance to the Brooklyn Bridge on the north end.

The big ones were the *Herald*, the *Tribune*, the *Times*, the *World*, and the *Journal*. And then there was the *Sun*, a "newspaperman's newspaper" and the Holy Grail of almost every reporter in America. The *Sun* was housed in a disheveled five-story brick building—the former home of Tammany Hall, which was still running New York in a benignly corruptive fashion—at 170 Nassau Street on the corner of Frankfort Street next to the *Tribune* tower and close to the *Times*.

Just across the street was City Hall and its park, where almost four decades later Fritz Duquesne would be sitting with a double agent who would be responsible for putting the Black Panther of the Veld behind bars for a long time.

Fritz was not content with being a collector, and his discontent was fueled by constant contact with newspapermen who were intrigued by his stories of big-game hunting and Boer soldiering in South Africa. The years of prison and flight had not left Fritz bereft of his old charm and ability to tell a story superbly in that rich, modulated voice. He could still mesmerize his listeners.

Fritz was soon asked to write some of his experiences for publication in the *Herald*. The stories attracted the attention of the influential and respected "Gentle" George Mallon, city editor of the *Sun,* who asked Fritz to join his staff in 1904. Adding pressure to the decision to hire Fritz, no doubt, was Marius Houman's friend Weightman, who in addition to writing editorials for the *Washington Post* wrote in the same capacity for the *Sun.* Mallon was noted for training young newspapermen who later became outstanding members of their profession.

Fritz was a quick learner and was added to Mallon's string of successful young men. In two years he would be named Sunday editor of the *Sun.*[3] Later he would become a reporter for the *World* and the *Herald,* a playwright, a novelist, a bon vivant about New York, and a subject in *Who's Who in New York City and State.* The rapidity with which he adapted to life in America was remarkable. The Dutchman Houman, who had been concerned about bringing Boer POWs to

New York because "they had never learned to work" and would "suffer untold misery," need not have worried about Fritz.

Yet despite all the perks attendant to a journalist on a respected newspaper—or newspapers, since he jumped around to several between 1904 and 1909—the restive Fritz was not content. He created an impressive and chronologically contradictory background for himself in the New York *Who's Who* for those years that reflected the image he would show to the world for the next half-century.[4] He would cling tenaciously to the charade even when languishing, ill and aged, in a federal prison and later in a nursing home.

According to Fritz, he was a special correspondent for the *Herald* covering the long siege of Port Arthur and then went to Paris on a roving commission for the paper, where he joined the staff of *Le Petit Bleu du Matin*. Although the events at Port Arthur, and so presumably Fritz's stint there, lasted from February 1904 to January 1905, Fritz also claimed that in 1904 he was a war correspondent in Macedonia and Tangier reporting the difficulties the sultan of Morocco, Abd-al-Aziz IV, was having with the brigand Raisuli, who had kidnapped the naturalized American citizen Ion Perdicaris. (The abduction prompted the famed challenge from Roosevelt at the Republican National Convention that whipped the lethargic delegates into a frenzy of cheers, "We want either Perdicaris alive or Raisuli dead!")

Fritz also reported that during this time he toured the Congo Free State at the personal behest of King Leopold II, the much unloved ruler of Belgium. He allegedly served as that royal person's publicity agent, his duty being to allay charges that Leopold had approved the use of depraved and cruel practices in the slave trade so as to pillage riches from the African colony. Ever the hero, Fritz claimed to have found time in the course of his duties to the king to capture the first gorilla ever for a Belgian zoo, though the animal unfortunately died at sea en route to Antwerp. Fritz then, or so he says, returned to America, where he gave lectures of "a religious nature" on behalf of the Paulist Fathers missionaries.

Hardly pausing to catch his breath, the peripatetic Fritz was next in Australia, where he ramrodded the Eldu expedition for Sir Arthur Jones from 1904 to 1906. (There is no record of any such expedition Down Under. Note also that it is yet another version of Fritz's whereabouts in 1904.) Finally, in 1908 Fritz was building a string of theaters in the British West Indies for his future father-in-law, S. S. Wortley.

There is no evidence that Fritz, the magnificent creator of heroic hoaxes, ever participated in any of these adventures. It is doubtful that he even left New York during these years. Instead, he likely divided the time between his home at 633 Park Place in Brooklyn and the City Room on the second floor of the *Sun* building, where instead of the roar of guns he heard only the continuous thunder of the presses, which caused the old building to shake and rumble. Instead of choking on the smoke of high explosives, he gasped for air amid clouds of smoke from reporters' cigars and cigarettes. And the only battle cry he heard was "Copy boy!"

But he was not idle. While he was purportedly wandering the globe, Fritz was in fact writing—three novels and three plays.[5] The novel *Cossack Life* was printed in *Le Petit Bleu du Matin*. Two other novels, *The Spectacles of War* and *Lost in the Bush*, were published in South Africa. *Perdu* was a play produced in French in Brussels; *The Harlequin King* and *The Yankee Amazon* were plays copyrighted but not produced in the United States. It was at about this time that Fritz, considering his ascending success, began assuming the clipped, cultured accent of an Englishman. Despite his antipathy toward England, the affectation could only enhance his overall image. It also helped to eliminate his Afrikander accent.

Hatred of England and of Kitchener, now commander-in-chief of the army in India, continued to be the driving force in the life of Fritz Duquesne. The Boer War may have been over, but he never passed up a chance to generate wrath against the island empire. Fritz had a public opportunity several years after arriving in America when he gave a rousing speech in a public forum at Cooper Union in Manhattan, excoriating the treachery of England in the Boer War and its treatment of prisoners, particularly in Bermuda. Alice Wortley was in the audience, the young woman from Bermuda whom he had last seen at Marius Houman's when he first came to America in 1902. It was a short reunion. They would meet intermittently over the next couple of years, with marriage the final result.

Despite the fiction he created for future professional résumés and *Who's Who* books, Fritz continued his occupations of reporter, freelance writer, and lecturer. His articles on African big-game hunting brought him to the attention of Theodore Roosevelt.

The lame-duck president was looking toward his retirement from the White House in March 1909 and began making plans for that inevitability as early as 20 March 1908, when he wrote a number of famed African hunters, including Colonel John H. Patterson, a veteran of the Boer War and of campaigns in India, an explorer, hunter, and railroad engineer who had gained fame from his 1902 book *The Man-Eaters of Tsavo*.[6] Roosevelt considered it "the most thrilling book of true lion stories ever written." He wrote Patterson that he would be leaving the presidency a year hence and would like to make a trip to Africa.[7] He asked for some advice on hunting in Africa, particularly where he should go "to get some really good shooting."

On the same date Roosevelt also wrote Frederick Courteney Selous, an English naturalist and the premier African hunter of the day. Already a legend, Selous was presumed to be the model for H. Rider Haggard's fictional great white hunter, Allan Quatermain, in *King Solomon's Mines*. There would be an extensive exchange of letters between the two over the next year, with Selous becoming Roosevelt's chief adviser on almost every aspect of his coming expedition.

The correspondence between the president and the hunters marked the beginning of a year-long campaign of interrogatory letters and personal meetings at the White House and at Roosevelt's Sagamore Hill home on Oyster Bay. African hunters, naturalists, scientists, hunting rifle experts, and practically anyone who had ever been to Africa or gotten within smelling distance of a rhino's breath passed on their knowledge to him. These Africa sessions were squeezed between affairs of state, meetings with congressmen and senators, ambassadors, admirals, and generals, cabinet meetings, rifle practice, mornings on horseback, and discussions on fortifying Pearl Harbor.

Among these experts were Carl Ethan Akeley, American explorer, taxidermist, and naturalist of the Chicago Field Museum of Natural History; Charles D. Walcott, secretary of the Smithsonian Institution; Edgar Alexander Mearns, retired lieutenant colonel from the Army Medical Corps who would be chief naturalist and physician on the Roosevelt safari; Colonel Cecil A. Lyon, the president's former western hunting companion and Republican National Committeeman from Texas; Sir Harry Johnston, British explorer and African colony administrator; and, of course, Captain Fritz Duquesne.

It would be interesting to know what Fritz might have thought about meeting with Roosevelt if he had been aware of the president's opinions regarding the British victory in the Boer War. In an 1899 letter to his sister, Anna Roosevelt Cowles, the president had written, "The South African business makes me really sad. I have a genuine admiration for the Boers; but the downfall of the British empire I should regard as a calamity to the race, and especially to this country."[8] To British publicist and politician Frederick Scott Oliver he wrote in 1915, "Even as regards the Boer War, while I did not at all approve of some of the British actions before it occurred, I felt that when it did occur, it was essential to the welfare of Africa that the English should win."[9] But even if Fritz had known the president's position, it is not likely that his tremendous ego would have permitted him to turn down an invitation from the White House. After all, he would be able to boast about it for the rest of his life—which he did, and was not believed at a critical moment in his life.

Roosevelt was looking forward to his African safari, as he confessed in a letter to friend and western illustrator Frederic Remington, "with just as much eagerness as if I were a boy."[10] The whole world knew about the forthcoming trip, and it didn't escape the attention of Fritz. A series of syndicated newspaper articles by "Captain Fritz Duquesne" began appearing under the heading of "Hunting ahead of Roosevelt in East Africa." The features also appeared in *Hampton's Magazine* for February and March 1909. (Roosevelt, incidentally, considered *Hampton's* a "professional muckraking magazine.")[11] Pungent-prosed advance blurbs invited readers of "The Best Magazine In America" to read the articles of "the Boer ivory hunter":[12]

Would you like to go to Africa with Roosevelt? You get the thrills and excitement—without the danger.
  Like adventure? You'll get plenty of it, with thrills to spare, when you read. . . .

The "thrills to spare" were primarily Fritz's accounts of his own shooting adventures: "Like most Boers I have been hunting, on and off, and associating with hunters since I was ten years old. Danger and hairbreadth escapes have happened so frequently to me that most of my hunting experiences appear almost too commonplace to record." But he also discussed what Roosevelt could expect in the hunting of elephant, giraffe, leopard, and smaller game, as well as the eating of monkeys and the best type of weapons and cartridges to use.

"It would be impossible to hunt any length of time in Africa without having some adventure worth relating," Fritz promised, "adventures in which a steady eye, nerves of steel, and a brain quick as lightning are life-saving essentials to a big game hunter." While pointing out that "Mr. Roosevelt's reputation as a man of prowess and nerve has preceded him," Fritz subtly suggested that the president might not be physically up to the trip; the perils of Africa are so great that "he will be lucky if he comes out alive."

Roosevelt himself had hinted in his letter to Patterson that his physical condition was not up to par: "It is unnecessary to say that I shall be in no trim for the hardest kind of explorer's work. But I am fairly healthy, and willing to work in order to get into a game country where I could do some shooting."[13] To Selous in a letter dated 25 June he confided, "I should wish to travel so as to be comfortable, for when I go out there I shall be a man of fifty who for ten years has led a very engrossing sedentary life, and who is no longer fit to endure hardships."[14] The chief executive's condition was even worse than he cared to admit. He was totally blind in his left eye, had impaired vision in the other, was soft and overweight at two hundred pounds on a five-foot eight-inch frame, and suffered from a touch of "Cuban fever," an all-inclusive malady covering malaria, dysentery, and the feared yellow fever.

The Duquesne articles must have caught the attention of the man in the Oval Office. Always seeking more advice and information, the president invited Fritz to the White House where he could ply the experienced hunter with questions about hunting and the Dark Continent.[15]

Temperatures were hovering in the mid-fifties in Washington when William Loeb, the president's junior secretary, greeted Captain Fritz Duquesne outside Roosevelt's office and told him, "Go inside."[16] It was Monday, 25 January 1909. In seven years this guest of the White House would be sinking British ships off the coast of South America. In eight years he would be certified a lunatic and placed in an asylum. In nine years he would be declared paralyzed. In nineteen years he would be a press agent for Joseph P. Kennedy. In twenty-eight years he would become the hub of the largest Nazi spy ring ever to operate in the United States. And in thirty-three years he would be serving time in Leavenworth Penitentiary. But today he was a respected and acknowledged expert on big-game hunting in Africa. Theodore Roosevelt, the twenty-sixth president of the United States, was eagerly looking forward to meeting him.

It was a busy day for the president. In addition to attending a reception for the Committee of State Food and Dairy Commissioners, he met with his vice president, the secretaries of state, war, and the interior, the attorney general, and two congressmen and three senators.[17]

But Teddy was never so busy that he couldn't find time to see another African hunter. According to Fritz, as reported in a front-page story in the *Washington Post* the next day, he and the president had had a bully time.[18] This was confirmed by a full-panel illustration of the meeting, drawn by political cartoonist Clifford K. Berryman, on the front page of the *Washington Star* the same day.[19]

Roosevelt endeared himself to Fritz by beginning their meeting with the statement, "I'm a Dutchman."[20] Then followed a session of more than two hours, with the president asking questions on all facets of the safari he would embark on the following month. He wanted to know the caliber of guns to use on different animals, where to place his shots to get the best effect, where he could expect the greatest danger, and the best way to lug out hides and trophies.

"As a former president of the United States," Fritz told the chagrined Roosevelt in his acquired clipped British tones, "you will be rather prominent and may be treated differently, meaning you might be taken to game preserves where the game is plentiful and tame."

"I'll have none of that," retorted the president. "I want to take a hunter's chance. I want to shoot the game where it is most dangerous."

Saturated with a knowledge of Africa gained through talks with experts and the reading of hundreds of books, Roosevelt was the best-informed man Fritz had ever met. He seemed to have an intimate knowledge of the continent's topography and flora and fauna. "I was astonished at the thorough way he has prepared for his trip," Fritz told the *Post,* "an obvious result of having studied the country night and day through maps and books from the time he decided to go to East Africa.

"With the remarkable knowledge he is noted for," continued Fritz, "Roosevelt fired question after question at me like the shots from an automatic gun."

Despite expressing more of an interest in rhinoceros than in any other game, Roosevelt was concerned as to whether R. J. Cuninghame, a hunter/naturalist and field manager for the entire expedition—also considered Africa's first professional hunter[21]—would steer him to lions. "Will Cuninghame take me to where there are lions?" he asked. "That's what I want to get at—lions, lions! Now, they have the roan antelope, or as the Dutch call it, the bastard kind. I intend to get some of them, and the blesbok and oryx, too.

"And I want a cheetah and a leopard—they've got such bully marks. I want to run up against white rhinoceroses, because I like something that will come back at me. I don't want to have my own way," insisted the president.

"Where's the best place to get an elephant's heart? Where's the best place to use a soft ball and solid ball—on what part of the animal I mean?

"Suppose an elephant charges me, what should I do to distract its attention? I thought the natives would fire in the other direction so the elephants will run away from you."

"There are many things you could do, Mr. President," Fritz laughed in reply. "But I would suggest that one of the best is to run like the wind."

"What sort of shikaris do you suppose I will get down there?" continued Roosevelt nonstop. "I've been reading up on the names of different Arabic and Swahili words used among the shikaris on the East Coast of Africa."

Fritz was impressed by the president's equipment, saying it was excellent because he had taken the advice of Africa's greatest and most experienced hunters. Fritz said he spoke of his weapons as a parent speaks of its children. His rifles were "fine little fellows" and "dandies." Teddy expressed particular delight over the .30-caliber hand-operated bolt-action U.S. Army model rifle: "We've got a bully rifle here. I have had a sporting stock and sporting sights put on it. It's a bully boy, the best army rifle in the world."

The *Star* cartoon shows the signature Berryman bear cub clinging to Roosevelt's left leg for protection. Fritz sits at the president's feet in schoolboy fashion. At Fritz's feet is a book entitled *Rules for Killing African Game*. Berryman's conception of Fritz is all wrong. Dressed in a bush outfit, Fritz is balding and bearded, hardly resembling the clean-shaven adventurer with a thick head of hair. It is possible that Berryman, who was noted for drawing cartoons on short deadlines for use in the following day's afternoon *Star*, mistook a picture of Cuninghame for Duquesne. The cartoon figure looks remarkably like the safari leader, and even the bearded Selous. Berryman was noted for never being particularly careful about drawing correct likenesses of the president's guests if he had not met them personally or seen their photos.[22]

Cheering throngs and uniformed Rough Riders waved farewell to Roosevelt, his son Kermit, and other members of the expedition when on 23 March 1909 they sailed from Hoboken aboard the SS *Hamburg* for Naples on the first leg of their voyage to Africa. They would be

Pulitzer Prize-winning artist Clifford K. Berryman's cartoon from the Washington Star *of 26 January 1909 showing Fritz advising President Roosevelt on his forthcoming African big-game safari. Note Duquesne's name on the pugaree wrapped around the crown of the topi on the floor. (Library of Congress)*

The Travel Magazine

Registered in U. S. Patent Office

VOLUME XV—NUMBER 6   March, 1910

PRICE 15 CENTS
$1.50 A YEAR
PUBLISHED MONTHLY

Copyright by Underwood & Underwood

NEAR THIS SPOT ON THE VICTORIA NILE CAPTAIN DUQUESNE AND LIEUTENANT MARCHAND HAD A BATTLE WITH CROCODILES

WILL ROOSEVELT RETURN ALIVE?

By CAPTAIN FRITZ DUQUESNE

Shortly before President Roosevelt left the White House and started for Africa he catechised Captain Duquesne closely and somewhat anxiously regarding Uganda. The risks taken in hunting the white rhinoceros, only to be found in Uganda, are trifling as compared with the sleeping sickness peril, he was informed. Captain Duquesne, who has safaried through East Africa and speaks from experience, described Uganda to the President as 150,000 square miles of disease. If Colonel Roosevelt safely negotiates this last stage of his safari he will have surprised residents in the land of the tsetse fly.—EDITOR.

COLONEL ROOSEVELT has done what few people of the African jungle expected. He has crossed the Rubicon and entered Uganda, the land of the dreaded sleeping sickness. Practically every one of us, to whom the dangers of the jungle are a part of life, doubted whether Roosevelt would direct his safari into this enchanted land of disease that is embroidered with all the beauties of nature and cursed with all her crimes—Uganda, the solar plexus of Africa, the conservatory of plagues, the nursery of sickness, and veritable parade ground of death.

After facing every danger and experiencing every thrill of the wild jungle of British East Africa, the second stage of the Roosevelt safari has taken him into the dreaded realm of the Kabaka. None of the tales told him around the camp fires at Naivasha, of the terrible trials and dangers in the land beyond the lakes, have broken his resolution to follow the original plan he mapped out to me in the White House before he

271

Fritz speculates on the fate of Roosevelt while on African safari in The Travel Magazine *for March 1910.*

gone more than a year. It would not be incorrect to say that this marked the beginning of what has been called the era of "great white hunters," and that the Roosevelt expedition was responsible for the "industry" of safari.

In that year's time Fritz used his short acquaintance with the president to his monetary advantage by writing negative newspaper and magazine articles about the Roosevelt trip. Prior to the president's departure, Fritz's articles had gloried in the wonders of Africa and were a tribute to Roosevelt's hunting prowess. The negative approach he took now might be attributed to chagrin at not having been invited to accompany the safari. But Fritz was also a good publicist. He and his editors may have thought that a negative approach, one indicating that Roosevelt was in greater danger than expected, would sell magazines.

For instance, Fritz elaborated on the theme of the president's poor physical condition in a lead piece for *The Travel Magazine* entitled "Will Roosevelt Return Alive?" The issue was for March 1910, which means that the article was available to readers in early February and had been written at least three months prior to publication. The Roosevelt expedition was expected to end in early March.

In the article Fritz paid tribute to the fact that Colonel Roosevelt had done "what few people of the African jungle expected."[23] He had made the perilous journey of crossing East Africa and the Victoria Nyanza into Uganda, "the land of the dreaded sleeping sickness." Fritz then launched into what he considered would be the even greater perils facing the intrepid explorer:

Practically every one of us, to whom the dangers of the jungle are a part of life, doubted whether Roosevelt would direct his safari into this enchanted land of disease that is embroidered with all the beauties of nature and cursed with all her crimes—Uganda, the solar plexus of Africa, the conservatory of plagues, the nursery of sickness, and veritable parade ground of death.

None of the tales told him around the camp fires at Naivasha, of the terrible trials and dangers in the land beyond the lakes, have broken his resolution to follow the original plan he mapped out to me in the White House before he started. . . .

They have been fighting big game in a country where there is comparatively little disease, but in Uganda they face the greatest menaces in Africa. Sleeping sickness, black water fever, malaria, veld sores, spirillum fever, tsetse flies, mosquitoes, jiggers, unnamed poisonous insects and germs which so far have stood undefeated by the soldiers of science.

Another disease that adds to the sum of Ugandan terrors and is greatly feared by the whites is a particularly virulent malaria which, after a few attacks, becomes the dreaded and nearly always fatal black water fever.

Fritz ended the article with a foreboding—and actually accurate—prediction: "It will be remarkable if Colonel Roosevelt and his party pass safely through the sleeping sickness country." Roosevelt escaped sleeping sickness but did contract malaria and suffered recurring bouts of it during the next several years, which may have contributed to his early death at age sixty.

Former New York state senator Tom Platt, an old political foe, jumped in with his own thoughts on what might happen to Roosevelt in Africa. The frail senator had retired the same day Teddy had left the presidency. Platt, known as the "Easy Boss," was one of the political bosses who had helped Roosevelt get the Republican nomination for New York governor in 1898. But Governor Roosevelt fell into immediate disfavor when he refused to cooperate with Platt's machine. Consequently Platt made sure Roosevelt was President McKinley's running partner in 1900. That was one way of getting rid of the toothy troublemaker.

The tone of Platt's remarks suggests that he may have seen Duquesne's stories. When a *New York Times* reporter, visiting Platt in his New York apartment on 7 March, asked him his opinion, the Easy Boss replied, "There are a great many people who do not think Mr. Roosevelt will ever return from Africa alive. Many who have undertaken the same trip have been stricken by disease or killed by accident. He may be very strenuous and he may be physically strong, but he is taking a long chance."[24] Perhaps it was wishful thinking.

Fritz also used Teddy's safari as the subject of a successful lecture series tour, "East Africa, the Wonderland of Roosevelt's Hunt." Illustrated with motion pictures and photographs in color, it was touted in a slick four-page brochure as "A Lecture by Captain Fritz Duquesne— Soldier, Hunter, Author, Giving a Graphic Description of African Savage Life and Customs."[25] The Berryman cartoon was reproduced in the brochure, with the caption skillfully relettered to read, "Seeking Pointers from Duquesne." A stalwart Fritz in Boer War uniform was depicted on the front page with a portrait of Roosevelt in African hunting clothes. A picture inside showed Fritz with a rifle standing next to a downed rhinoceros. Mastheads from a number of newspapers along with the headlines of the "Hunting ahead of Roosevelt" stories were

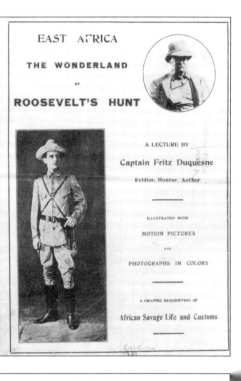

Fritz's African lecture brochure in which he expounded on the dangers facing Teddy Roosevelt on his safari. (Theodore Roosevelt Collection, Harvard College Library)

duplicated, with the information that "3000 articles were published in 300 leading newspapers." The stories were definitely syndicated to a number of papers; but with Fritz, more was more. It isn't likely that the stories appeared in all the newspapers shown. Careful examination shows that the layout was a "paste-up," cleverly arranged to link articles with the mastheads of newspapers in which they may not have appeared.

Fritz could not play it straight even when being legitimate.

CHAPTER 8

Hippos to Louisiana and
Hippo du Jour

RITZ ARRIVED in Washington on 1 March 1910 and registered
at the elegant Riggs House on the corner of Fifteenth and G
Streets.[1] The next day he landed on the front page of the *Washington Post* with an interview predicting doom and gloom for the Roosevelt expedition then drawing to a close in Khartoum.[2] With only two
weeks left until the safari was over, Fritz was still playing the harpy,
prophesying for profit, as he had been doing for months in his lectures
and articles, that members of the expedition would surely fall prey to
horrific African diseases.

He was in the capital city to testify before a congressional committee on the importation of wild animals to the United States and to give
two lectures on "Hunting ahead of Roosevelt." The publicity-con-
scious captain wasn't one to miss an opportunity. This opportunity
had been sparked by the news that Dr. Roderic Prosch, a French medical missionary who had dined with Roosevelt two days earlier, died
the following day from African fever.

"The Roosevelt expedition has been in more than a score of zones
of the sleeping sickness," said Fritz in an article headlined "HE FEARS
FOR T.R.: African Guide Thinks Him in Danger of Jungle Ills."[3] "And
it is highly probable that every member of the party now has the virus

90

of the disease in his veins. It may not develop in members of the party until they reach Europe or even America."

Fritz pointed out that it was "positively dangerous" to allow Roosevelt and his companions to return to this country without a bacteriological examination being made to assure that they were free of the germ of the sleeping sickness or the equally deadly African fever. He feared that if it broke out after an expedition member arrived in this country, it would spread everywhere through the medium of flies and mosquitoes. Fritz advised a rigid quarantine.

"I am forced to believe that the Roosevelt party must be infected with one or the other of these deadly maladies," Fritz continued ominously:

There is no escape from this conclusion, drawn as it is, from many years' observations. If the Roosevelt party escapes it will be the only example on record of an African hunting party getting off scot free, for never in the history of the country has a hunting expedition traveled where Roosevelt has been but members of it were stricken with one or the other diseases. It is simply incredible that they could have escaped. Mark my word—before the party gets to Europe, either African fever or the sleeping sickness will break out among them.

It was the same foreboding message Fritz had been preaching for the past year in his lectures and articles. As mentioned earlier, he was not far off the mark. Roosevelt escaped the African fever and the sleeping sickness, but he did contract malaria and suffered from it for the rest of his short life.

The *Post* reporter gave a capsule history of Duquesne's Boer War exploits and escape from Bermuda, with the new information that he had "fired the first rifle at the bloody battle of Magersfontein." If he did, Fritz must have had a fast pony to take him several hundred miles east across the Orange Free State so that he could participate in the battle of Colenso three days later. Fritz also offered the information that at age eighteen he had been a professional big-game hunter in German East Africa—absorbed after World War I into British East Africa and now called Kenya—and had killed fifty-five lions and innumerable other large game in the African wilds.

A surprise revelation was the information that "the President originally selected him to lead his expedition, but changed his intention when it was learned that Capt. Duquesne was *persona non grata* with the British officials of Africa. Duquesne," it was reported, "had taken a leading part in the Boer War and Mr. Roosevelt did not desire to offend English sensibilities." This was another fabrication by Fritz. But it made good copy and was another example of Fritz's aplomb. To tell such an absurdity, in the president's own bailiwick, where it would be printed in the capital's most prominent newspaper—that took nerve. Roosevelt had already selected Cuninghame in October 1908, three months before his meeting with Fritz in the White House. He was considering William Judd, another highly regarded hunter, but recommendations from Selous and Akeley settled the matter. Another story is that Judd lost his chance at heading up the safari on the toss of a coin with Cuninghame.[4]

The *Post*'s interview with Duquesne about Roosevelt's health created a furor, and Fritz was taken to task by assistant superintendent Arthur B. Baker of the National Zoological Park and newspaperman Francis Warrington Dawson, both of whom had recently spent several months in Africa. They charged that quarantine for members of the expedition was not necessary because sleeping sickness is not contagious and the white man is almost immune to the disease carried by the "tse-tse" fly.[5] The *Post* carried Fritz's retort reasserting his belief that Roosevelt had probably contracted the sleeping sickness in Uganda. "What authority had Baker and Dawson gained in a three-month visit to Africa?" asked the thirty-three-year-old Duquesne. "And what knowledge did they have to confute me who has spent his entire career in the jungles? The fellow who has spent a few months in East Africa no more knows the country than I would know America from Sandy Hook. I think it is ridiculous to argue against the superficial knowledge thus gained."[6]

It was true. Baker and Dawson had spent only a short time in Africa. The fifty-two-year-old Baker had never been to Africa except for a recent visit in 1909. He was a widely respected scientist with an international reputation for designing and constructing zoos. His trip to Africa had been undertaken for the purpose of adding African animals to the National Zoological Park.[7]

Dawson was a thirty-one-year-old newspaperman and novelist who was manager of the United Press French news service in Paris and its special European correspondent when he was assigned in 1909 to cover the Roosevelt expedition to Africa.[8] Seeking absolute privacy after twenty years of continuous public service, Roosevelt had banned all press members from covering the safari and refused all interviews. Nevertheless, the feeding frenzy of the press persisted, and he was followed by a contingent aboard the *Hamburg* as well as when he transferred to the *Admiral* at Naples for the last leg of his voyage to Africa.

Dawson won the confidence of the colonel when he assisted him in giving the press his denial of a fake interview—"an impudent fabrication"—printed in the *Paris Journal* and widely copied around the world. He became Roosevelt's trusted helper and was allowed to continue with him to Nairobi and beyond. Dawson became the colonel's part-time secretary. He helped him in answering the constant flood of mail, edited his articles on Africa for *Scribner's Magazine,* and eventually acted as his press representative, releasing official bulletins of the safari's progress.

Almost replicating his discussion with Fritz prior to his trip, Roosevelt expressed to Dawson his almost passionate desire to bag a lion along with the four other most dangerous game animals: elephant, rhinoceros, buffalo, and leopard. "If only I can get *my* lion," he told Dawson on the *Admiral,* "I shall be happy—even if he is small—but I hope he will have a mane."[9] Roosevelt appeared to be obsessed with the desire to kill a lion. On 28 December 1908 he had written Selous expressing delight that he would be meeting the hunter on safari. "It is just the last touch to make everything perfect," the president wrote. "But you must leave me one lion somewhere! I do not care whether it has a black mane or yellow mane, or male or female, so long as it is a lion; and I do not really expect to get one anyhow."[10] Roosevelt need not have worried. Selous was generous and left him a total of nine lions.[11] Some even had manes.

Dawson returned to America a short time after leaving Nairobi with the safari, because he and Roosevelt had heard that an attempt was being made to eliminate the colonel from future political activities. Rumors were being spread that Roosevelt was "directing political conditions from the jungle." Back in America, Dawson discovered that the truth, as he told it, was being deliberately "hushed." So strongly did he feel about the situation that he resigned from the United Press, thus cutting short what he called "the greatest opportunity of my life" to accompany Roosevelt down the Nile. He began lecturing on what "Roosevelt really was doing in Africa: hunting and observing local conditions," and positively not "mixing in American politics." Thus Dawson was in Washington to rebut Duquesne's charges regarding Roosevelt's health.[12]

The Associated Press representative accompanying Roosevelt was Captain W. Robert Foran of British East Africa. Foran had been aboard the *Hamburg* when Roosevelt left America. He was the only other press member allowed to join the expedition to Nairobi. In 1910 Foran would become a fellow contributor with Fritz to *Adventure* magazine as well as a founder with Duquesne of the Adventurers Club in 1912.

Fritz partially agreed with Baker, saying that in one sense sleeping sickness is not contagious. "One man cannot contract it from being in proximity to another. But the tse-tse fly may carry it from one man to another.

"Another statement of his," said Fritz, "is that the white man is almost immune from the disease. It is true that scores of blacks catch the sleeping sickness to one European, but the reason for that is obvious. They are all but naked. Only the face and hands of the white man are exposed, and the face is always covered with a netting. But the risk of contracting this deadly plague in Uganda is so great that a prudent man would not care to undertake a visit through the country, except in a rickshaw. When the Duchess of Aosta made the trip through the jungle in a rickshaw, many of the natives carrying her vehicle were stricken.

"Henry M. Stanley returned from his last trip to South Africa with the fever in his veins. He died within thirteen months. There is no cure for the 'sleeping sickness.' Science has so far been baffled in all attempts to deal with it.

"I should never have led Mr. Roosevelt into the lake country," the captain concluded. "That is the real land of the sleeping sickness. I strongly advised him against penetrating into this portion of the African continent."[13]

To further corroborate his argument that members of the Roosevelt party should be quarantined, Fritz got the support of his former enemy, Major Frederick Burnham, also in Washington to testify before the same congressional committee.[14] "The white man is subject to the disease," said Burnham, whom the *Post* described as another "soldier of fortune." Supporting Fritz's fears, he said, "Ventures into Uganda and into the head waters of the Nile are undertaken at the greatest risk."

But Colonel Cecil Lyon, the former president's close personal friend, was unconcerned: "Colonel Roosevelt is not in any great danger of death from the sleeping sickness. You might kill Colonel Roosevelt in a steamboat accident or a wreck, or drown him or something like that," he laughed. "But sleeping sickness—never! Think of that man dying with sleeping sickness! No. Never, my son!"[15]

And so the arguments went. Right or wrong, it was exhilarating reading and great publicity for Fritz's first lecture, scheduled for 4:30 Friday afternoon, 11 March, at the Columbia Theater, to be "vividly illustrated by moving pictures of hunting scenes and savage life in darkest Africa." But first Fritz hosted a party of friends at his hotel on 6 March, where the "celebrated soldier, war correspondent, traveler, and writer," as described by the *Post*, presented an illustrated lecture on the birds and mammals of eastern and southern Africa.[16] Among the guests was Associate Justice Thomas H. Anderson of the Supreme Court of the District of Columbia.

There was a lot of competition in the entertainment world that week. Fritz would be preceded at the Columbia Theater by matinee idol Douglas Fairbanks in his huge Broadway success, *A Gentleman from Mississippi,* and he would be followed that evening by musical comedy star Trixie Friganza in George M. Cohan's *The American Idea.* But his press releases were designed to overcome the disadvantage. Publicity prose described Fritz and his film in heroic phrases:[17]

No other man of his age has had a life of adventure so dramatic and marvelous in the wilds of Africa, and the story which he will bring to his audience will be the moving one of the actor, the man who knows and feels what he tells because it is what he has lived.

Or:

Perhaps no other man in the world is so well qualified to speak on the African wonderland as is Capt. Duquesne. Born in South Africa of Boer parents, and having served in many capacities in all the recent events in the kaleidoscopic history of South Africa, it is peculiarly fitting that he should bring to America the story of the land of the Roosevelt hunt.

And:

The famous Boer soldier, hunter and author, will illustrate his story with moving pictures of hunting and savage life in the Land of Roosevelt's Hunt.

The pitches worked. The Columbia Theater at 1112 F Street was filled with people willing to pay up to a dollar to hear the stout-hearted explorer.

Through moving pictures and colored stereopticon slides, Fritz took his audience on a trip through the hunting grounds of the Roosevelt party from Mombasa to Khartoum, sometimes referring to the expedition's leader familiarly as Teddy, and sometimes more formally as "your former President." He began his lecture by translating *Bwana*

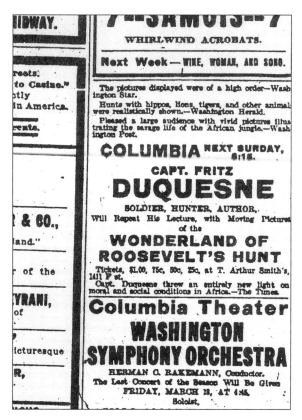

Advertisement in the Washington Herald *for 13 March 1910 describing Fritz's African lecture.*

Tumbo, the name Roosevelt had been given by African natives and which had caught on with the press in America.[18] "It means Mr. Unusually Large Stomach," explained Fritz. (He would give it a less dignified translation later, when testifying before a congressional committee.) "The savages were much impressed with the girth that Teddy had acquired, and immediately christened him with an appropriate name." The audience laughed heartily, knowing Roosevelt's style of exuding good health. But Fritz went on to explain that *Bwana Tumbo* was not opprobrious. It was actually a Swahili term of honor meaning that Roosevelt was regarded as a powerful and important person.[19]

Fritz then launched into a tribute to the bravery and hunting skills of Roosevelt but laced the compliments with his usual self-serving criticism:

Accompanied by a score of experienced hunters, Teddy never really endured any dangers during his African expedition.

Mr. Roosevelt will be hampered in the writing of his accounts of the expedition because of the inability to use the "I," as so much work was done by the native hunters in his caravan.

The presence of so many professional hunters eliminated any real danger to the former President who came to Africa not as a hunter, but as a novice willing to learn.

The big hunter from America has made himself popular in Africa because he went there posing not as a big game expert, but as a man anxious to learn and see.

The only trouble about his trip to the Dark Continent is that his expedition was too large and he had too much done for his comfort and entertainment. Under these circumstances, Mr. Roosevelt did not go through the actual dangers of big game hunting nor did he see the country like the professional hunters.

There is quite a difference in being guided to game and having it pointed out to you to shoot and in locating it yourself. He never experienced what it is to have a rhinoceros charging at full speed with four or five bullets in his hide and not a white man within four or five hundred miles to come to his rescue if the last shot fails.

Fritz was partially correct. Teddy did experience charges by wild animals, including lion, elephant, rhino, and hippo. But there was always another "great white hunter" nearby should that "last shot fail."

But the lecture wasn't all Roosevelt. Fritz also recalled some of his own former hunting experiences and commented on African life in general. He took the opportunity to expound on the theory he would be presenting to a special congressional committee in two weeks: the value of introducing wild African animals into America:

Conditions in the Southern and Southwestern states are ideal for the propagation of the wart hog, wildebeest, hartebeest, gazelle, zebra, impala and the oryx.

All of them are fine game animals, excellent shooting and several are splendid eating. As for the zebra, it's only a question of time before they are used as beasts of burden. The Germans have been most successful in breaking and training them. I have seen whole teams of zebra in German East Africa working under harness like so many donkeys.

Several times during his performance—for that's what it was; Fritz never just talked—his best pictures were marred by an operator unfamiliar with the movie projector. Unperturbed, Fritz sailed through with humor and élan, always the consummate actor.[20] He ended the lecture by comparing the Roosevelt hunting party with those of Europeans and other Americans who go to Africa under practically the same conditions. "He has done more than these other fellows," said Fritz. "He's done a lot for the first time there and he's to be congratulated on his success. It's not the work of an amateur."

Captain Fritz was also a success, if the reviews were an indication.[21] The *Washington Star* reported, "The pictures displayed were of a high order, many of them having been taken by Duquesne in his hunting trips." According to the *Washington Post*, "Captain Duquesne pleased a large audience with vivid pictures illustrating the savage life in African jungles." The *Washington Herald* reviewer was effusive:

The story which Capt. Duquesne tells is thrilling and through it all he is the principal actor.
Hunts with hippos, lions, tigers, and other animals were realistically shown. The pictures which are thrown upon the screen are most vividly illustrative of his story and serve to carry one into the very heart of the Land of Roosevelt's Hunt. His pictures are beautifully colored and are of his own accomplishing.

Fritz repeated his performance on Sunday evening, 20 March, before another large crowd. He announced at the opening of the lecture that it was not a travelogue but simply the exhibition of a collection of views made by him while at the head of an expedition sent out by Bertha Krupp, daughter of the famous German gun maker—another romantic masquerade by Captain Fritz, who never missed an opportunity to enhance his image. There is no evidence of any association between him and the future Cannon Queen of Germany, the twenty-four-year-old daughter of Fritz Krupp. (Destined to become one of Germany's most famous and revered women, she would be remembered in history, however ignominiously, as the namesake of Krupp's giant mortar in the coming Great War: Big Bertha, responsible for crushing the Belgians and giving Germany its first victory at the battle of Liège.)

More good reviews followed, with the *Herald* critic saying:[22]

An audience that seemed to be deeply interested in real Africa and its scantily clad inhabitants closely followed Capt. Fritz Duquesne at the Columbia Theater last evening and heartily applauded the lecturer at the close. . . . [The] motion pictures showed exciting hunts of alligators, hippopotami and other wild beasts together with native dances, customs, etc. Many of the colored views were very beautiful.

Reported the *Post:*[23]

The pictures (both moving and stereopticon) which are thrown upon the screen are those taken by Capt. Duquesne on some of his thrilling expeditions in the African jungle land, and are beautiful as well as instructive. His motion pictures serve to carry his audience at once to the very scene of the action, and for the time one almost feels the dangers with which the lecturer so often comes in contact.

There was competition that same week from Arthur Radclyffe Dugmore, an internationally known photographer of wild animals who had met Roosevelt in Africa at the start of his safari. Dugmore was lecturing on "Photographing Live Game on Roosevelt's Hunting Trail," a subject startlingly similar to Fritz's. Dugmore defended Roosevelt in his lecture, charging that the former president was the "subject of much unjust condemnation for the alleged slaughtering of big game in the jungles of Africa."[24] He said the report "was without foundation and that every animal killed had been either used as food or else would be added to the collection of the Smithsonian Institution which would make it the possessor of one of the finest collections of animals in the world." Fritz and Dugmore would compete again seven years later in New York, both of them lecturing on the horrors of war in Europe.

Another competitor Fritz and Dugmore had to contend with was E. M. Newman, also at the Columbia Theater. His pictures and talk were lauded by the *Herald* as the "most interesting of the African lectures" that week.[25] As this plethora of lectures on Africa suggests, there was quite an appetite in Washington for information on that relatively unknown continent. The interest was perhaps the result of the highly publicized safari of the city's most famous recent resident. Still, it's surprising that there was any space at all in the newspapers for news about Africa or that anyone even cared, considering that the raging controversy at the time was whether Frederick Cook or Robert Peary had been the first to reach the North Pole the previous year.

Meanwhile, despite Fritz's dire predictions regarding the fate of Roosevelt and the members of his expedition, the former president completed his historic safari on 14 March 1910, arriving in Khartoum to cheering thousands and "looking the picture of health, with physical fitness showing in every line."[26] Fortunately, newsboys did not deliver the *Washington Post* to his tent door flap in Africa, where he would have read about Duquesne's fears for his life. "My health has been marvelous," he said. "I have had no attack of fever for six months and this I attribute to the great care I took in regard to water and diet. I drank no alcohol on the march." He was ready to "hit the line hard."

Teddy "hit the line hard" by leaving almost immediately on a triumphal three-month tour of Europe, where he attended the funeral of King Edward VII, had a bully time with Kaiser Wilhelm II, and learned he'd rather lie down with lions than party with kings.

At 10:30 in the morning on 24 March 1910, six days after his last lecture, Captain Fritz Duquesne was facing the lions as he prepared to address members of the House of Representatives on the Committee on Agriculture.[27] The committee was meeting for the consideration of H.R. 23261, which officially, and hyperbolically, read:

Be it enacted by the Senate and the House of Representatives of the United States of America in Congress Assembled, That the Secretary of Agriculture be, and he is hereby, directed to investigate and import into the United States wild and domestic animals whose habitat is similar to government reservations and lands at present unoccupied and unused: *Provided,* That, in his judgment, said animals will thrive and propagate and prove useful either as food or as beasts of burden; and that two hundred and fifty thousand dollars, or as much thereof as may be necessary, is hereby appropriated, out of any money in the Treasury not otherwise, appropriated for this purpose.[28]

Fritz was appearing before the committee at the specific request of his old Boer War nemesis, the British army's chief of scouts, Frederick R. Burnham. The request came from a conversation Burnham had once had with his old friend Theodore Roosevelt.

Two years earlier, on 13 May 1908, Roosevelt—forever remembered as the great conservationist president—had convened for the first time in history the governors of the states and territories to consider the great common problem of the exhaustion of the country's natural resources. The purpose of the historic conference was to adopt conservation practices to stop the depletion of forest and mineral resources and to use its waterways more effectively.

Another concern at the time was uneasiness over future meat supplies for a growing American population. So a group of Burnham's well-to-do friends put up a generous sum of money to send him to

Africa and return with animals that could be bred in the United States and would thrive in similar habitats. The natural place to put these animals, Burnham and his friends supposed, would be the forest reserves and national parks newly created by Roosevelt.

As a naturalist, Roosevelt had long been interested in the domestication and hybridization of animals. As early as 1902 he believed that the eland, largest of the African antelopes, could be domesticated in the arid American West. He was even more convinced of this after his African safari. When Arctic explorer Vilhjalmur Stefannson wrote him in 1918 suggesting the domestication of the musk ox in northern America, Roosevelt expressed an interest in supporting the project.

An enthusiastic Burnham called on the president to broach his own animal domestication plan but was told that the best person to see regarding the importation of African game was Gifford Pinchot, chief of the Forest Service. According to Burnham, Roosevelt also mentioned "that he had just met a bitter enemy of the British, a Boer named Duquesne, who seemed to know much about African game, etcetera. I assured TR that Duquesne *did* know, and that I knew a good deal about Duquesne."[29]

It would be some time before Burnham and Fritz would meet, but meanwhile Burnham learned that even a letter from the president of the United States to Pinchot could not accelerate the legal process. A bill would have to be introduced in Congress that would allow the animals to be imported. Hearings and debates inevitably would follow. To get his message out and create some excitement on Capitol Hill, Burnham wrote "Transplanting African Animals" for the 10 February 1910 issue of the *Independent*.[30] Fritz saw the story, described by Burnham himself as a "dry-as-dust article," contacted Burnham, and wrote a series of syndicated articles about the plan. The two former adversaries became lifelong friends but would seldom see each other.

When Representative Robert F. Broussard Jr. (Democrat from Louisiana) saw the stories, he was immediately intrigued and invited Burnham and Duquesne to visit him on his plantation in New Iberia for further discussion of the plan.[31] The congressman wanted to import hippos to Louisiana at once so that they could gorge themselves on "the water hyacinths that were clogging the state's rivers, killing the fish and causing sickness." The result was H.R. 23261, authored by Broussard.

Meanwhile, with the zeal of a missionary, as he recounted in his autobiography, Burnham "deliberately set out to win over to genuine Americanism one of the most remarkable men I had ever met, regardless of the thousand rumors and irrefutable proofs of his black deeds—acts which could not be defended by a civilized code."[32] Burnham explained:

Duquesne was clever, educated, resourceful. He spoke several languages and wrote well. We both knew Africa. Here, I thought, was our chance—he to forget forever the old hatreds and become a valuable citizen of the United States . . . and I, to carry out a long cherished dream.

. . . I must confess that I sincerely longed to win over this man of such tireless energy and brilliant mind. So we teamed up for a while. Duquesne was a most interesting talker and had very wonderful yarns to spin about Africa and other parts of the world. A few of my friends repeated to me some of his amazing tales and believed he was just a Baron Munchausen. That clever Hoosier Senator Beveridge [Indiana Senator Albert Beveridge] asked me, "Is he really a Boer?" I told him that Duquesne was indeed a Boer. . . . I assured him that Duquesne was raised among the Kafirs and had acquired their superlative gift of oriental story-telling—a form of entertainment where the dividing line between fact and fiction is never confused by the native.

But Burnham soon learned that his fervor to convert Fritz was not shared by the Black Panther of the Veld:[33]

[On more than one occasion] Duquesne . . . revealed to me a scorching flame of bitterness and fury that sprang straight from his heart's core. It was hatred as intense and resistless as the overpowering flow of red hot lava. I was startled, but even then dared hope that his rage might be cooled by time and reason.

But at long last it was borne in upon me that he was like one of those strange characters depicted in the *Lives of the Martyrs* who in their secret hearts actually relished being tied to the stake and burned alive. Call it fanaticism, eccentricity, or what you will, this sadistic satisfaction is an obsession . . . that . . . was notably possessed by this man of extraordinary power. His source of strength was a reservoir of black and bitter hatred like the poison which the octopus spews before an attack.

Quite an indictment! And one Fritz endeavored to live up to every minute of his life. Burnham finally realized this and gave up his attempt to "save" the embittered Boer, admitting, "As a reformer I was not a success."

But the two worked well together in their attempt to bring wild African animals to America for domestication.

Fritz was charming, witty, and impressive and demonstrated his great knowledge of African flora and fauna at the committee hearings chaired by Charles F. Scott, the Republican congressman from Kansas.[34] (Scott's congressional career would end in 1911, and as publisher and editor of the *Iola Register* he would direct publicity for the 1912 Republican campaign to elect William Howard Taft to a second term. Fritz would be on the opposite side campaigning to elect Roosevelt for a third term on the Bull Moose ticket.)[35]

Broussard addressed the committee, introducing the experts he hoped would help persuade passage of his bill:

I was anxious to get a meeting as soon as possible because of the fact that three gentlemen who probably have devoted more time than almost anyone else to this matter both from the scientific and from the practical standpoint of investigating the matter, happen to be in Washington today. I refer to Mr. Irwin, of the bureau of Plant Industry of the Agricultural Department; Captain Duquesne, an Africander who has taken part in various campaigns and is a hunter of great note; and Major Burnham, who has kindly come from New York this morning to appear before the committee, and who has given a great deal of thought and study to the subject.

W. N. Irwin found it rather strange that for four hundred years only four animals had been used for supplying meat in America: cattle, sheep, swine, and goats. These four had been imported from Europe and only one native American animal, the turkey, was under domestication. He expressed concern that meat prices were going beyond the reach of ordinary people. This could be alleviated by adding a million tons of meat a year for consumption by importing the proper animals from other countries.

Irwin suggested importing the hippopotamus, "whose flesh is excellent in quality," to the bayous of Louisiana, as well as the Cape buffalo, a number of smaller antelopes, and more than one hundred other species. Other animals he recommended for domestication in America were the yak (from Tibet) in the Rockies, llamas (from Peru) in the mountain states, pigs (from Manchuria) in the northern states, and rhinoceroses in the desert states. "Our country is growing so fast that we ought to adopt every possible means of strengthening our meat supply," he urged.

Irwin quoted from an address he had given at a January 1909 meeting of the American Breeders' Association in Columbia, Missouri, in which he estimated that by 1950 there would be two hundred million people in the United States but not, at the current rate, enough meat produced for their consumption. Irwin presciently concluded:

We need every additional species that it is possible to secure before its exter-mination takes place. It is a sad commentary on our twentieth century civi-lization, that instead of preserving the wild mammals wherever found, at least until a sufficient number may be brought under domestication to en-sure their perpetuation and propagation as a heritage for our posterity, we are relentlessly hunting and shooting them down without the slightest re-gard as to whether the animals at which our guns are aimed are the last of their sex or species.

"I now desire to present to the committee Captain Fritz Duquesne," said Congressman Broussard, "formerly in the Boer army, who is lec-turing and writing on this subject in this country."

Fritz was never better than when he was the focus of attention, and he was certainly that as he sat before members of one of the most im-portant legislative bodies in the world. He cranked up the Duquesne charisma and won them over completely with his detailed analysis of need and use of animals in Africa. His enthusiasm and charm and that voice that commanded attention guaranteed him a rapt audience.

Fritz pointed out in his opening statement that he had been bred among the animals Dr. Irwin was talking about:

I am as much one of the African animals as the hippopotamus. I would be a dead animal if it were not for the hippopotamus, because most of my early life was spent eating hippopotamus.

As to the quality of this animal as food, I just want to call your attention to the vigorous race of Dutchmen that were in the Boer War. There was nothing mentally or physically defective about them; and they lived on hip-popotamus.

We have lived and our race has been built up on the wild animals, notwithstanding the fact that we have had perhaps more wars than any other race. We have been fighting the Zulus and the Kaffirs in general; and we lived on the wild game of Africa without any help from the outside. We have produced a pretty sturdy and strong and intelligent race—I think they are intelligent—just on these animals. If these animals are good to build up a white race in Africa, why are they not good to use in this country?

He urged bringing hippos to Louisiana, describing how the animal had kept streams in Africa clear of vegetation. "The hippopotamus will eat all water plants, all the aquatic plants," Fritz declared. "It lives on them. It will never leave a river where it can get food. . . . [There] are millions and millions of acres of that stuff [in Louisiana] that could be used for hippo food."

Fritz then launched into an eloquent summation of the commercial value of the African animals, explaining that the hippo is the greatest food-producing animal in the world. Its teeth are valuable as ivory, the bones good for making "a great big pot of soup," and its skin "one of the most valuable things that the Boers have in Africa"; it is "kipped" (split) into a transparent leather valuable for the covering of automobiles and automobile wheels. He went on to explain how French soap manufacturers competed with one another offering all kinds of prices to Boer farmers for hippo fat.

Not wanting the congressmen to forget how excellent hippo flesh was, Fritz eagerly expounded on the delicacy. "If those animals were castrated and treated the way you treat your domestic animals," he said, "I think their flesh would be equal to anything you have in the world. We have tried that; we have castrated them and we have used them. They have made splendid food—excellent food. They could not be better."[36]

After wowing the congressmen with that bit of animal husbandry, Fritz took America to task for its indiscriminate hunting of animals: "That has been the fault with your own country. You have exterminated even the birds that have dozens of young a year." He reiterated that African animals can be brought to the United States and would have no trouble surviving:

You have here hundreds of miles of country that is exactly like the habitat of our African game, and would breed those animals which can all be domesticated. Every desirable animal we have in Africa can be domesticated. I would not recommend bringing the lion into this country, of course; but it stands to reason that all these other animals, if introduced into this country and put into a suitable climate, could be bred here.

"It would not be advisable to introduce the elephant into this country," Fritz also pointed out, "but it would be a very fine thing in Brazil."

Fritz then discussed at length the practicality of bringing camels to Australia, which has deserts the counterpart of African deserts. He told how his father had won a contract to export camels to Australia and how he, Fritz, had brought them there. "They are excellent food," Fritz concluded, "and as Doctor Irwin says, they are fine milkers."

"Do you think animals such as you have mentioned could become acclimated here without difficulty?" asked Representative Frank Chapman, a Democrat from Delaware.

"Yes," replied Fritz. "I was over there recently in one place where Colonel Roosevelt passed through and the frost was that thick" (indicating about an inch with a thumb and forefinger). "That is where he went to get some of his best animals."

"Whom did you say?" asked Willis C. Hawley, Republican from Oregon.

"Mr. Roosevelt," answered Fritz.

"I thought he was called '*Bwana Tumbo*,'" Hawley said with a wink.

Amid much laughter from the congressmen, Fritz replied, "The white men do not like to call him 'Mr. Big Belly,' for that is what it means, you know."

Fritz was then quizzed by Congressmen W. C. Hawley (Republican from Oregon), James Cocks (Republican from Oklahoma), Robert E. Lee (a Virginia Democrat), and Pleasant C. Chapman (Republican from Illinois) regarding temperatures and the amount of snow in Africa, the flowers of the Upper Nile, the average hands high of the zebra (fourteen to sixteen), the temperament and the crossbreeding of zebras, horses, and mules (resulting in the zebrule or zebroid), and the style of the British versus the Germans of getting their percentages of profit out of Africa.

Impressively, and without a pause or stammer, Fritz answered all their questions, often adding anecdotes from his own experience. He drew laughter when Congressman Hawley asked about the zebrule, "Do they have more stamina than a mule?'

"Yes," said Fritz. "If you look at a zebra or a zebroid or a zebrule, you will find those animals have a bigger and heavier rump. They are stronger and better animals. If you were ever kicked by one, you would know all about it."

At the conclusion of his testimony Major Burnham corroborated almost everything Fritz had said. Burnham then went on to describe the success he had had in domesticating camels and zebras and importing small game animals to his ranch in California. When he had finished, his article from the *Independent* was included in the record as part of his statement.

Burnham had pointed out in the article how millions of African animals survive predators, poisonous snakes, drought, and other forces too numerous to mention. Why, then, shouldn't these animals thrive and multiply in a country exempt from these perils and in a climate corresponding to that of their native lands? Burnham answered his own question, though it showed his cattleman heritage, with a condemnation of current practices and an appeal to future generations:[37]

We ourselves are the only reason why none of this precious game can ever live in our wild plains. So intent are we on destruction that we have become the wonder of the world. We have dynamited our fish, killed all our buffalo, carried off even his bones in trainloads, then came back with herds of cattle, tramped out and ate the finest natural grass ever known. When it was eaten level with the ground, for fear it might, with its great recuperative power, renew itself, we have put that curse of God, the sheep, to tear it up by the roots and gnaw to death every little shrub left by the cattle. I have seen forest fires 40 miles wide burning in the Sierras to make early grass for herds of sheep. If it were known that a herd of eland were on the Rio Grande, a thousand guns would be after them and their hides sold to the nearest tannery; even a rare bird would surely be slaughtered. Again and again I have known of individuals trying to introduce useful birds and animals; their fate is always the same. Only a national law and a changed public opinion can make it possible to ever either save what animal life we have or introduce new and valuable additions.

Dr. Arthur M. Farrington, assistant chief of the Bureau of Animal Industry, Agricultural Department, followed Burnham, stating the department's concern about importing diseased animals into the country and insisting that there would have to be proper precautions.

"Does the present law actually prohibit the importation of the animals you name into the United States," asked Chairman Scott, "or does it merely declare that they shall only be imported when free from disease?" Farrington again answered that only diseased animals were prohibited, without specifically saying there was no law disallowing the importation of animals. Congressman Broussard repeated the question. Playing it safe, Farrington repeated his answer that the Agricultural Department would not admit diseased animals.

Fritz broke the impasse by asking Farrington, "You know that Barnum & Bailey and all the menagerie people have brought in a great number of animals from Africa. What provision is made for quarantining these animals?"

"They are quarantined under the officers of the Bureau of Animal Industry," answered Farrington.

Fritz argued that the machinery set up for inspecting worked well and prevented any disease from coming into the country and affecting domestic animals. "So far as I know," he pushed home, "there is no disease in this country now that has been imported by menagerie animals."

"You have the machinery now for that inspection?" asked Broussard. Farrington assured Broussard that the Agricultural Department did, then finally agreed that wild animals could be brought into the country under the present laws and inspection guidelines.

A discussion of possible hippopotamus diseases followed. There were none. Fritz also suggested importing warthogs to clear out forest undergrowth, adding that the warthog "is good food." He got a good laugh from the committee when he said, "Of course, I am not a very good judge of good food, because I have eaten snake and crocodile; but I have lived in Washington, too, and I can make a comparison."

The session ended around one o'clock with Fritz offering to come back and show transparencies and movie film he had taken for his lectures "of a great number of these animals that I have spoken about, taken in their various habitats in the different countries where they live."

"The zoological side of the question was hardly touched upon at the hearing," reported the *Washington Post* the next day, "although the testimony teemed with interesting and plausible suggestion . . . and the general attitude of the members seemed to be favorable."[38]

Under the heading of "A New Food Supply," a *Post* editorial predicted an immediate hearing before the Agricultural Committee of the House and expected, "in all probability, a favorable report."[39] Major Burnham was described as an "American hunter and naturalist of the foremost authority" who has "presented the subject with convincing effect, and Capt. Fritz Duquesne, an Afrikander of distinction, has been urging the same proposition before leading members of congress and in the course of his lectures. . . . Proposals which at first sight may look odd and chimerical to the mass of our readers," concluded the editorial, "will be seen to be matter-of-fact propositions when they become familiar."

So what happened to H.R. 23261 calling for the importation to the United States of wild and domestic animals? Was the *Post* correct in predicting a favorable report? The bill died in committee, with congressional opposition compounded by the fact that the Taft administration was on an economy program, and appropriating $250,000 for the plan was not practical.

The wild animal importation plan was still viable as far as Fritz was concerned. He managed to interest Ohio Columbus Barber, founder and president of the Diamond Match Company in Ohio, in the scheme.[40] He convinced the multimillionaire big-game hunter and breeder-importer of Guernsey cattle that he should import a flock of llamas for the good of the country. The idea was to have Peruvian Indians drive the animals from New York to Barberton, the factory town Barber had founded in Ohio. The publicity would be good for Diamond Matches. But Barber feared that even if the llamas survived the long sea voyage to New York, they might not survive the long cross-country trek. Dead llamas and homeless Peruvians scattered across America would not be good publicity for Diamond Matches.

Fritz was still pushing for the importation of African animals more than a year after the congressional meeting in Washington when, on 6 April 1911, he hosted the first annual—and only—South African banquet for the Beta Theta Pi Club at the fraternity clubhouse at 46 East Twenty-fifth Street, New York City. Cuts from African wildlife were the exotic meat du jour.[41]

Wily Captain Fritz had discussed the idea with fraternity members Arthur Sullivant Hoffman and Charles F. O'Brien, possibly with an eye toward launching a successful business career as an importer of African meat. (Hoffman was editor of the pulp magazine *Adventure*, which had just begun publication the previous year and to which Fritz was a frequent contributor.) The two friends had joshed Fritz so unmercifully about the idea that he ordered a shipment of meat from his brother in Mombasa, German East Africa (now Kenya). This was evidently Pedro, the brother Fritz reported to have been killed by Major Burnham during the Boer War. No matter; as mentioned earlier, Fritz could resurrect members of the Duquesne family on demand. In due time fifty pounds of dried meat and fifty pounds of refrigerated meat arrived on the *Kronprinz Wilhelm*. Fritz turned it over to Beta Theta Pi for the group's dinner.

With assurances from Fritz "that no one would be able to tell the difference between the African and domestic meats," the food was served in various ways under euphemistic names. For members curious about what they were ingesting, a menu explained the gourmet meal. Springbok (gazelle) was made into a soup, hippo meat was the basis for South African croquettes, great kori bustard (a game bird) was served up as turkey, kudu (antelope) was labeled beef, and dik dik (a small antelope) was called lamb. As further assurance that the meal was direct from Africa, a photograph was displayed showing the packing box and its Mombasa postmarks.

There was no need for the assurances, the subterfuge, or the photograph. A gamy taste was admitted by all, and some mentioned that you could tell the meat had been on an ocean voyage. Yet all admitted that it had a good flavor and enthusiastically asked for seconds.

Fritz was again the focus of attention, and he couldn't resist making the most of it. He spoke passionately about importing animals to

America, particularly hippos to Louisiana. He laughed at the suggestion that the animals would bring disease with them and then, without stopping, launched into his Boer War experiences, not forgetting his life as a POW in Bermuda and his escape to America.

He had a good audience. As usual Fritz associated with only the best of society. In addition to Hoffman and O'Brien, those present included the adventuring Presbyterian Dr. S. Hall Young, the "Mushing Pastor" of Alaska; Brigadier General Leonard P. Ayres, one of the nation's leading economists, who several years later would be one of the few finance men to predict the 1929 Crash; Dr. Samuel McCune Lindsay, retired professor of social legislation at Columbia University; Francis H. Sisson, advertising manager of the American Real Estate Company and soon to be vice president of Guaranty Trust Company; Dr. David R. Boyd, former president of the University of Oklahoma and soon to be president of the University of New Mexico; attorney David Provost; and economist Dr. Leonard P. Ayres, later to be vice president of Cleveland Trust Company.

It was a culinary idea before its time.[42]

CHAPTER 9

Last Hurrah for the Bull Moose and Gentlemen Adventurers

C OLONEL ROOSEVELT returned to America on 18 June 1910 to a staggering reception of adulation. When the *Kaiserin Augusta Victoria* steamed into New York Harbor, half a million people huzzahed from the shore, along the streets, and in boats pulling alongside the ship. A delegation of uniformed Rough Riders were on hand, and so was Fritz.

Fritz stood on the pier waving at the colonel and his son Kermit—who waved back enthusiastically, according to Fritz.[1] They must have had sharp eyes indeed to pick Fritz out of all that humanity. The next day, said Fritz, Roosevelt presented him with three of his hunting rifles as souvenirs of the trip for his aid in preparing the safari.[2] There is no record of such a gift, nor are any of the president's rifles missing from the exhibits in the Roosevelt homes or museums.[3]

Two days after Roosevelt's return, Fritz and Alice Wortley were married quietly in Manhattan. During the last several years their meetings had been sporadic, consisting of brief visits from Fritz between lectures. But their attraction for each other had not lessened. It was a sincere love. During the nine years of their marriage Alice would enjoy a life of travel and excitement. Yet she never knew "exactly what Fritz did," as her brother's wife, Mildred, related years later.[4] Mildred insisted that Fritz was devoted to Alice and that the marriage was a love match. Nevertheless, he would boast for years that she was a titled English lady and that he had married her for the sole purpose of defiling her—not for love, but as an expression of hatred for England. There was no waning of his hatred for all things British. It continued unabated.

And where was the particular object of this hatred, Kitchener of Khartoum? Fritz could not have been unaware that the man he blamed for the death of his family had been rising steadily in the ranks of the empire's pantheon of military heroes. Kitchener gave up his command as commander-in-chief in India in September 1909, when he was made a field marshal and offered the Mediterranean Command. But first he took a long holiday, touring the world and visiting the United States with stops in San Francisco, the Yosemite Valley, and Chicago. In April 1910 he was in New York and visited the Military Academy at West Point. Fritz reported that he observed the field marshal when he was in Manhattan and was only biding his time until he could destroy the conqueror of South Africa.[5]

Fritz would never be so close to Kitchener again, despite his future claims of having been responsible for his death. Kitchener cut short his tour and a visit to Civil War battlefields to return to England and press his claim for the job he desired most: viceroy of India. He was passed over, and in his bitter disappointment he turned down the Mediterranean Command. He was unemployed for the first time in forty years. But be began punching the clock again in July 1911 when the recently crowned King George V conferred on him the splendid title of British agent, consul general, and minister plenipotentiary to Egypt.

Kitchener was busy again, and so was Fritz. At least Fritz said he was. As the story is related in *The Man Who Killed Kitchener*, Fritz was traveling and studying all over the world:[6]

It is hard to keep track of his movements during this time. We hear of him in Paris, dabbling in deeper researches in explosives in a celebrated laboratory. We hear of him in India, studying in Calcutta, on the chance hint that in India England would find her most devastating foe, and he his strongest ally, in the rent triangle that lies between the undiscovered Himalaya peaks and the sultry Indian Ocean to the south, between the Arabian Sea and the farthest shores of the Bay of Bengal. What he did here is mysterious, as much that he did is mysterious. But England never gained from anything he did.

But had Fritz actually done any of this studying or any of these un-named mysterious deeds, leaving his new bride sitting patiently at home? Well, he believed he had. What is known for sure is that he and Alice went south to the West Indies in February 1912. It was the only adventure she ever shared with Fritz.[7]

Fritz was lured to Jamaica by the possibility of borrowing funds from Samuel Wortley, Alice's father, who was building theaters in Kingston. He hoped to persuade his father-in-law to finance an expedition through Central and South America. Fritz intended to make a documentary film of the trip for the Thanhouser Film Company, a short-lived production company founded in 1910 by Edwin Thanhouser.[8] Fritz had become associated with the president of the company, Charles J. Hite, and the vice president, Hans J. Spanuth. (Fritz would maintain a lifelong friendship with Spanuth's wife, Lillian—a graduate of the Juilliard School of Art and Music, tall, lovely, and always stylishly dressed.) He got the financial backing, but not as much as he sought.

A sideline of the trip was a plan to sell elephants.[9] Fritz still believed that his animal importation scheme was practical, and he planned to place orders for the large beasts with lumber camps and planters, who would use the animals as labor-saving devices just as they had been used for generations in India. Fritz and Alice would meet with prospective buyers in the West Indies and then continue their selling trip through Central America and down the west coast of South America.

Alice's brother Jim and his wife, Mildred, were also on the trip to Jamaica. As usual, Fritz contributed nothing in the way of finances. "None of us knew anything about Fritz until the government eventually got after him," Mildred said years later.[10] "We never knew how he made money. When he lived with us he never paid anything or gave my husband anything. We lived a fantastic life. We had servants and could have anything we wanted. We took care of Fritz." So in addition to all his other abilities, Fritz was also an accomplished freeloader.

Kingston was in the midst of a streetcar strike, with rioting, shootings, and general anarchy prevailing as a result of a recent increase in fares.[11] The Duquesnes and Wortleys, accompanied by a friend named Hintz and with Jim at the wheel of the car, were driving to dinner when they became embroiled in the turmoil.[12] It would seem to be an odd time for a night on the town, since Kingston was virtually under mob rule, but Fritz was always the adventurer.

Lillian Spanuth (later Linding), Fritz's lifelong lady friend. Could she have been the woman rumored to have helped him escape from the Bellevue Hospital prison ward? (Author's collection)

The car was forced to a stop by rioters armed with razors lashed to bamboo poles, who surrounded the car and began pelting it and its occupants with heavy stones. Fritz grabbed a large wrench and Jim a hammer from a toolbox, and they began flailing away at their assailants, with Alice fighting alongside. Mildred fled for safety to the porch of a nearby house. Struck on the head by a large stone, Alice was knocked insensible to the floor of the car. The gasoline tank was ripped open and the fuel set afire when it poured out. Fritz, Jim, and Hintz accounted for a few battered heads, but they were saved only by the quick arrival of troops who fired indiscriminately into the mob, endangering the Duquesnes and Wortleys as well. Seriously injured, Alice remained in the hospital for a few days. Fritz suffered a fractured jaw and a lung punctured by a rib. He wore his wounds and bandages well, later strutting about New York like a soldier returned from the wars.

Pachyderm peddling would have to wait.

Fritz visited his friend, editor Arthur Hoffman, at his *Adventure* magazine office swathed in bandages and apologizing for not having stopped by a week earlier upon returning from Jamaica.[13] "I did not know I was badly hurt in Kingston," he told Hoffman. "I caved in the day I called you up and landed in hospital. A rib was planted edgewise in my lung. My jaw was splintered so badly that my face had to be opened to put it together. While they were at it, I got them to cut a Boer War bullet out of my abdomen."

Fritz took time out on 18 July 1912, when he and Alice were living in New York at 110 West Thirty-fourth Street, to file a petition for naturalization.[14] He must have taken delight in signing the petition, which required him to renounce allegiance to any foreign country and "particularly to George V, King of Great Britain and Ireland of whom at this time I am a subject."

In August 1912 Fritz was stumping New York State for Teddy Roosevelt, who was seeking a third term as president on the Bull Moose ticket.[15] Teddy's old political foe, Senator Tom Platt, had been in error when he prophesied in his *New York Times* interview in 1909 that Roosevelt would never run for political office again.[16] In that same interview he had predicted that Roosevelt might not even return from Africa. If he did return, Platt said, he "would be likely to stay out of politics from necessity if not from choice. When a man in politics stays outside of the organization for more than a year, he is mighty apt to stay out for all time."

But Platt hadn't reckoned with Roosevelt's energy and determination or with Taft's unpopularity—particularly his unpopularity with Teddy, his former best friend.

When the enormously popular Roosevelt left the White House, he had hand-picked his former secretary of war and protégé, William Howard Taft, as his successor. It was expected that Taft would continue his predecessor's policies in tariffs, conservation programs, and foreign affairs. Such was not the case, and Taft only succeeded in disillusioning and angering members of his party, even though he won the Republican Party's nomination for president and would be running against Woodrow Wilson, the choice of the Democrats.

Equally disillusioned and angry, Roosevelt, as leader of the progressive wing of the Republican Party, announced his candidacy for the presidency in February 1912. In reply to a question regarding his health at the National Progressive Party's convention in Chicago in August, he replied, "I am as strong as a bull moose, and you can use me to the limit."[17] The press quickly picked up on the colonel's hearty response, and from then on Roosevelt was running on the Bull Moose ticket.

It was not the first time Roosevelt had referred to himself as a bull moose. On 15 August 1898, when he returned to New York aboard the transport ship *Miami* with his troop of volunteer Rough Riders following their heroics in Cuba during the Spanish American War, in response to someone's "How are you?" he bellowed, "I'm in a disgracefully healthy condition! I've had a bully time and bully fight! I feel as big and as strong as a bull moose!"[18]

Fritz's decision to campaign for Roosevelt is not surprising. Not only did he admire Teddy as a fellow hunter and adventurer, but he knew that the Rough Rider was an admirer of the kaiser. Former newspaper colleagues were also giving their support to the Bull Moose standard bearer. Richard Harding Davis and Will Irwin conceived the idea of syndicating free to newspapers pro-Roosevelt articles written by high-priced authors. Davis, Irwin, and other newspapermen who were followers of Roosevelt worked as unpaid volunteers for the candidate.

Fritz volunteered to use his undeniable ability as a speaker to tour New York State in September touting Roosevelt for president.[19] He led the First Division of the Flying Squadron, one of two big automobiles—the equivalent of a modern-day recreational vehicle—equipped for light housekeeping, complete with cots, electric lights, and a kitchenette. Each car had a movable platform, a "tail-end talker" from which "orators could orate" on the virtues of Mr. Roosevelt. Emblazoned on the side panels of each van were large oval pictures of Teddy and his running mate Hiram Johnson, separated by a Bull Moose, the symbol of their party. Underlining it all and reviving memories of Roosevelt's presidency in 1902 was the slogan, "A square deal for all the people." This "circus plan of campaigning," as it was described, required Fritz and his partners, S. C. Latta and Robert Price Bell, to distribute literature and give speeches throughout their assigned territory.

One of the pieces of campaign material was a sixteen-page brochure titled "Why Vote for Roosevelt?" and by-lined by Capt. Fritz Duquesne. Boldly printed on the front page in letters the same size as the title and three times larger than his name were the words "By A Democrat."

In his lengthy plea to the electorate on behalf of Teddy, Fritz asked if a Democrat could support his party's nominee believing that he was supporting the best man. If not, could he support the Republican nominee? Fritz seemed to think that neither was possible. He then proceeded to explain why he intended to give his vote to Roosevelt, summarily dismissing Taft as a serious contender and predicting correctly that the struggle would be between Roosevelt and Wilson. Fritz ended his appeal with an impassioned argument: "Your vote will decide whether the people shall rule or the corrupt corporations. The fight will be between Woodrow Wilson the writer of history and Theodore Roosevelt who MAKES it."

It was a noble experiment, but to no avail. Any hopes Fritz may have had of being showered with political favors for his participation in the campaign were dashed when Teddy failed to convince voters that he was their best choice. The Republican vote was split, and Wilson squeezed through the White House door with only 42 percent of the popular vote. The Bull Moose had become an endangered species by national referendum.

As for Duquesne's Flying Squadron companions, Latta wrote Roosevelt in 1916 expressing an interest in getting back into that year's election fight.[20] He had been in Washington a couple of weeks earlier circulating among Democrats at meetings where they thought he "was of them." An early "dirty trickster," he passed on what tidbits of information he had gathered. Bell, meanwhile, became a highly decorated soldier in both world wars and ended his career as a colonel and assis-

Motor van driven by Fritz during the 1912 presidential campaign. Fritz and two partners toured New York State giving speeches and distributing literature for Theodore Roosevelt, standard bearer of the Progressive Party—the Bull Moose Party. (New York World, 31 August 1912)

tant chief of staff for military intelligence in the Fifth Army Headquarters under the command of General Mark Clark in Italy.[21]

Fritz continued living the life of a gentleman, enjoying the modest reputation of a writer/lecturer and the respect usually accorded one of that profession. Success appeared to be his. The income was less than he might have wanted, but it was an easy lifestyle. When he needed extra pocket money, he could always rely on Alice to ask the Wortleys for a little help.

The dashing captain drew on his own African experiences—and, no doubt, those of others—to provide material for stories appearing in newspaper syndication and in a number of national magazines including *Adventure, Hampton's, Travel,* and *Field and Stream.* The gee-whiz yarns had such colorful titles as "The Man-Eaters of M'Wembi,"

"The Fighting Dwarfs of the Congo," "A Fire-Hunt at Kivu," "When the Rain Was Red," "Sekokoeni's Raid," "Tracking the Man-Killer," "Trapping Big Game in the Heart of Africa," and "African Big Game Hunting Made Easy."

Adventure was particularly suited to the personality, background, and writing talents of Fritz Duquesne—hunter, soldier, spy, adventurer, the man who wove together fact and fantasy with great aplomb. He was "discovered" early, with stories appearing in three of the magazine's first twelve issues.

In a 1935 article celebrating the magazine's silver anniversary, *Newsweek* called *Adventure* the *Atlantic Monthly* of the pulps (so-called because publications of its genre were printed on cheap wood-pulp paper).[22] It was considered the dean of the cheap magazines, with its first issue rolling off the presses in November 1910. If a famous writer suffered a rejection from one of the smooth-paper periodicals, he could expect an acceptance from the 15-cent thriller. Not even the slicks could boast of having a former associate editor who turned down a Pulitzer Prize: Sinclair Lewis, who said no to a Pulitzer for *Arrowsmith* in 1925 but in 1930 accepted the Nobel Prize for literature. *Adventure* was also the only pulp distinguished by being entirely illustrated at one time by Rockwell Kent.[23]

Adventure was published by the Ridgway Company—a subsidiary of the Butterick Company, still famous for its ladies' apparel patterns—one of the largest publishers of magazines in America. Novelist Theodore Dreiser was editor of the company's three magazines, *Delineator, Designer,* and *Woman's Magazine,* when it was decided to publish a "pulp" for intelligent readers. Serials, novelettes, short stories, and ballad poetry, all in a heroic vein, formed *Adventure's* contents. Writers were paid 10 cents a word, a princely sum at the time. Dreiser named Trumball White the magazine's first editor. Lanky, bushy-eyebrowed, and scholarly Arthur Sullivant Hoffman, a Phi Beta Kappa from Ohio State University who claimed he had never had an adventure,[24] took over as managing editor in 1911. The only assistant Hoffman hired in the magazine's formative years was Sinclair Lewis. Together they put out *Adventure* almost single-handedly, reading manuscripts, editing copy, correcting proof, making dummies, and doing everything else necessary to produce a magazine.[25] The only thing they didn't do was deliver the copies.

Noted writers who contributed stories of their adventures and fictional thrills were Talbot Mundy, H. Rider Haggard, Arthur D. Howden Smith, H. Bedford-Jones, Negley Farson, E. Alexander Powell, and Albert Payson Terhune, famed for his dog stories. *Adventure* discovered such renowned authors as Harold Lamb, 1932 Pulitzer Prize winner T. S. Stribling, and Octavus Roy Cohen. Also making their first literary appearances in the magazine were Arthur B. Reeve, George Jean Nathan, Gouverneur Morris, Courtney Ryley Cooper, and H. de Vere Stacpoole. John Buchan—author of *The Thirty Nine Steps* and countless other adventures, and later governor general of Canada—made his first American appearance in print in *Adventure*, as did Rafael Sabatini, Edgar Wallace, Konrad Bercovici, Warwick Deeping, and many others. Captain Fritz Duquesne was in good company. Is it any wonder Theodore Roosevelt was an ardent reader of *Adventure?*[26]

The November 1935 twenty-fifth anniversary issue of *Adventure* ran a review of the magazine's history written by Hoffman, now no longer editor.[27] A stout defense of the magazine against literary critics,Hoffman's review also set forth the editorial tradition he had established and that had remained steadfast over the past quarter-century:

We can take pride in the fact that *Adventure* has kept itself clean and decent, not only free from sex and the salacious appeal, but also avoiding false standards of ethics held up as models in its fiction. A man's magazine. Adventure and the outdoors. Action. Nothing in the decadent line. Compare it today or in the past for all around wholesomeness with most of the smooth-paper magazines of the same period.

As to its literary quality it has pretty well proved itself. During my time it had to struggle against the feeling of both the critics and the general public that no action story could be literary. That is, of course, absurd. . . . If action, however violent, evolves from character there is no higher literary expression and the ultimate crystallization of character is likely to be physical rather than psychological action.

The Butterick Building at 233 Spring Street, on the corner of Macdougal Street in New York City, was a mammoth structure of editorial enterprise, with pounding presses in the basement and offices devoted to packaging and mailing the company's various magazines. Dark wood paneling and stained-glass windows festooned the main lobby of the editorial suite, which according to *Newsweek* became "a world crossroads for explorers, big-game hunters, prospectors, and ship captains."[28]

There was a mystique about adventuring and wandering the wide world just before the Great War. The pulps brought the romance of travel to the thousands who, bound to an armchair, could experience it only vicariously. Violence, war, death, and killing—in self-defense, of course, or for a lady, for vengeance or for a righteous cause—such things were acceptable and had an aura of romance about them, especially as described in the brittle yellow pages of *Adventure*. All concerned were hail-fellows-well-met. It was all very wonderful, and editor Hoffman captured it best in the "Some Real Adventurers" section of an early issue in which he singled out one of those reckless rascals who was a regular visitor to his opulent offices on Spring Street:[29]

We never get tired of meeting them, these men who have "done things" and are still doing them, these real-in-the-flesh Adventurers from the far places of the earth. But sometimes when here in New York and in our comfortable offices, I find myself greeting these men from the Great-Out-of-Doors, shaking a hand whose fingers pulled a trigger in an African war or grasped a knife somewhere in the South Seas or strangled a throat in some forgotten corner of Asia, a certain envy and restlessness comes over me. The Spirit of Adventure, I suppose it is, that calls now and then to all of us and makes us a bit dissatisfied with our quiet, sheltered existence.

But they're fine fellows, all of them. And interesting? You should have been in here one day last spring and seen three of us standing (we forgot to sit down) for about two hours listening to Captain Fritz Duquesne's experiences in the Boer secret service and how he escaped from a British prison at eight in the morning when he was sentenced to be shot at nine. You see, his jailer came in with a basin of water and a towel—but there's no space for that now.

Fritz, ever the spellbinder, could always capture an audience with a gossamer tale. He obviously captured the imagination of Hoffman, who in a 1938 interview with the *New Orleans Times-Picayune* said, "The world's greatest adventurer is Fritz Duquesne, South African Boer, whose hatred of the British inspired him to some of his greatest exploits."[30]

All of this adventuring and roistering inevitably led to the organizing of the Adventurers Club, with Hoffman being the principal founder. Also among the founders were Fritz,[31] Sinclair Lewis, and newspaperman Will Irwin. It all started in the profusive extravagance of Hoffman's office.[32] According to the *History of the Adventurers Club of New York:*[33]

Two world wanderers happened to meet in Hoffman's office during the latter part of 1912. Both had participated in the Boer War, and discussed some of its more stirring incidents. It occurred to Mr. Hoffman that there should be in New York a meeting place for kindred spirits who had traveled the far-flung trails. He made the suggestion to a number of his associates, among them Talbot Mundy, Stephen Allen Reynolds and Sinclair Lewis. . . . The idea met with instant favor.

The two Boer War veterans were not named. Could one have been Fritz Duquesne?

Reynolds was made temporary secretary, and he sent a query to possible members, which follows in part:[34]

Your name having been suggested by one of the originators of our proposed club for adventurers, explorers, soldiers, travelers, filibusters, soldiers of fortune and other kindred spirits, I write to ask whether we can get together and give definite shape to the idea.

It has been proposed that we admit no one as a member who has not "been somewhere or done something;" that we do not welcome the professional "joiner," the bore in the dress suit, nor the mere "bohemian" or man about town, that we encourage informality but discourage anything bordering on the tough.

The response was overwhelming, and at 6:30 in the evening on Saturday, 7 December 1912, thirty-three men sat down to a $1.50-a-plate dinner around the horseshoe table in the Barn Room—a euphemistic name the adventurers had given the bar—of Mouquin's Restaurant at 454 Sixth Avenue, a favorite rendezvous for writers and theatrical people.[35] At this first informal organizational dinner, the thrill seekers exchanged lies and told their daring deeds far into the night. Naive, chauvinistic, but always sincere, they were a reflection of the times—a time that can only be described, as it always is, as bereft of complications. For these men the world was still wide, and they were seeking to narrow its boundaries. Their adventuring was motivated by a desire to see what was beyond the horizon, at the top of a mountain, or at the bottom of a sea. The naiveté and boys'-club attitude was also reflected in the three toasts offered that evening: "To the Game!" "To every lost trail, lost cause, and lost comrade, Gentlemen Adventurers, bottoms up!" And the last, drunk with the most acclaim, "To Adventure—the shadow of every red-blooded man!"

But it was Fritz, reported Hoffman in his "Camp-Fire" column in *Adventure,* who capped the evening with another of his enthralling stories:[36]

Will Irwin, for all the vast experience that has made him probably the greatest American journalist (even if he does prefer the term "newspaperman") in the United States, became so absorbed in Captain Fritz Joubert Duquesne's story of his escape from the British prison in Bermuda that, after the dinner was all over, some six or eight of us, including Talbot Mundy who served against Duquesne in the war [there is no official record of Mundy's military activities in the Boer War],[37] adjourned to a table downstairs till half-past two in the morning while the rest of that dramatic tale of the Boer's escape was being unfolded. We'd have stayed till eight in the morning if it had lasted.

The object of the club, as stated in its Certificate of Incorporation, had apparently been fulfilled to everyone's satisfaction: "For the purpose of bringing together men of all professions and livelihoods, who are adventurers, in social intercourse and fellowship, and for the purpose of the general furtherance of a healthy and wholesome spirit of adventure."[38]

The first formal dinner of the Adventurers Club was held on 15 March 1913, when the seekers after the extraordinary dined for only 90 cents a plate in Engel's Chop House at 61 West Thirty-sixth Street. The world wanderers again told tales about hairbreadth escapes from cannibals, balloon ascensions, police chases, and heroics in war. One invited guest who could not attend sent his regrets:[39]

I wish I could be present at the Adventurers Club dinner. Give my regards to Col. Church and the rest of the Executive committee. I claim to be a little of an adventurer myself, in the proper sense of a willingness to run risks and incur hardships for an adequate cause. I am sorry that all I can do is to wish you a most pleasant dinner.
Colonel Theodore Roosevelt

Branches of the Adventurers Club quickly sprang up in other cities around the country, and the club remained a viable organization for more than sixty years. Fritz attended both inaugural dinners, and through the years, whenever in New York or not in prison, he faithfully showed up at the monthly meetings to report his latest adventure. After dinner it was a common practice for Fritz, the skillful fencer, to cross foils with other members. A frequent fencing partner was his cousin, Viscount François de Rancogne.

An incident of rankling chagrin to Fritz occurred at the club shortly before his arrest for fraud in 1917.[40] Doubt was cast on some of his yarns. Charles Somerville—a fellow member, a reporter for the *New York Journal-American,* and, according to *The Man Who Killed Kitchener,* a "bide-at-home adventurer"—had become increasingly envious of Fritz's "inexhaustible fund of magnificent adventure stories and the tense attention they earned." At an Adventure Club banquet Somerville gave a talk on his own adventures, which were so exaggerated that Fritz knew he was being ridiculed. In a cold rage Fritz told Somerville that "in Europe a man would be called out for such an insult and pay for it with his life." Preferring to remain indebted, Somerville turned down the offer. Fritz refused to calm down and was forcibly ejected from the club, vowing never to return. But no one could stay angry at Fritz for long. It was not long before he was back with yet taller stories. He would be in even bigger trouble with the Adventurers in 1941 when he was called traitor. But he would be welcomed back again, for one last poignant farewell address before his death in 1956.

It was June 1913. Colonel Roosevelt was planning one more adventurous trip. At the age of fifty-five and boasting an even more expanded waistline, the colonel knew it would be his "last thing of the kind" and his "last chance to be a boy."[41] The sobering effect of the African trip had left him with the belief that "the man should have youth and strength who seeks adventure in the wide spaces of the earth."[42]

It was the last time Fritz would attempt to involve himself in a venture with the former president.[43]

Roosevelt's expedition to South America proved to be more difficult and perilous than his African trip, resulting in injuries and disease that surely shortened his life. Fritz neither wrote nor lectured on the perils facing the colonel as he had for the African trip—perhaps because his knowledge of the southern continent was limited, although that had never stopped him before from expounding on subjects of which he was ignorant.

Roosevelt had become interested in a South American journey during his last days in the White House, when he met Father John Augustin Zahm, C.S.C., "a funny little Catholic priest"[44] whose zeal and enthusiasm for the countries south of the border greatly impressed the president. The opportunity for such a trip presented itself when Roosevelt was invited by the governments of Brazil, Chile, and Argentina in the spring of 1913 to address several learned societies in those countries. His African safari had been backed by the Smithsonian Institution; for this new expedition Roosevelt sought and got the backing of the American Museum of Natural History. Cinching his decision to make the trip was that Kermit, his son and African companion, was in

Brazil at the time building bridges. Father and son would share danger and adventure again.

The original itinerary of the expedition was changed when, in October, Roosevelt was informed in Rio de Janeiro that Colonel Cândido Mariano da Silva Rondon of the Brazilian Telegraphic Commission had, on a recent expedition to the Brazilian Plateau of Mato Grosso, discovered the headwaters of a large unmapped river flowing northward toward the Amazon. Where it journeyed and where it terminated was unknown. Would Roosevelt want to explore it?

"We will go down that unknown river!" Could there have been any other reply from the man having his "last chance to be a boy"?

Thus was born the Expedição Scientifica Roosevelt-Rondon. Colonel Roosevelt joined up with Colonel Rondon in December. Five months later, after extreme hardships and encountering near-impenetrable jungle, hostile Indians, insects, reptiles, and man-eating fish, there no longer was any doubt about the River of Doubt. In tribute to his redoubtable companion, Rondon renamed the river the Rio Roosevelt. The Brazilian government later officially named it the Rio Teodoro.

Fritz was also busy. He had recovered from the injuries suffered in Jamaica and was preparing for the long-planned expedition to South America, which would be tied in with a rubber-hunting project under the auspices of the Goodyear Tire and Rubber Company headquartered in Akron, Ohio.[45] His contract with Goodyear awarded him $5,000 cash and required him to bring out of South America five tons of rubber produced from a rubber-bearing vine in the Chaco district of Argentina, an area not known for producing such a vine. Nor, for that matter, was the vine noted for bearing the milky latex necessary to make rubber. But Fritz convinced Goodyear founder and chairman Frank A. Seiberling of the possibility.

At the time, he and Alice were living with her brother Jim and his wife, Mildred, at 420 Rhodes Avenue in Akron. Fritz's in-laws were elated to hear that he would soon be off on another adventure, however scatterbrained they thought it was. Any breathing spell from the family freeloader, however brief, was always welcome.

When Fritz heard of the planned Roosevelt trip to South America, he got in touch with Horace Ashton, a thirty-year-old explorer, writer, lecturer, and professional photographer who had traveled extensively throughout the world and particularly in South America.[46] Ashton had covered the Russo-Japanese War for *Collier's Weekly* and claimed to have been an official photographer for President Roosevelt for several years, having accompanied him to Panama during early construction of the canal. At the time, Ashton's company, Argus Laboratories Moving Pictures, was at 220 West Forty-second Street in New York.

Ashton had also "discovered" Fritz Duquesne. The two met in the fall of 1908 when Fritz was writing "Hunting ahead of Roosevelt in East Africa" for *Hampton's*. "In publishing his articles he needed photographs, and he came to me," Ashton told New York police several years later following one of Fritz's arrests.[47] Fritz had apparently captivated another listener. Ashton became interested in his conversation and suggested to Fritz, "Why don't you lecture?"

"So he went down to the Pond Lyceum Bureau," Ashton told police. "He went on lecture tours for the Lyceum and later on a tour for the Keith Circuit [showing films and talking about Africa]."

Fritz made a deal with the Thanhouser Film Company and Ashton to follow Roosevelt's trek through South America for a travelogue to be presented later on the lecture platform—and particularly at the upcoming San Francisco Panama-Pacific International Exposition in 1915.[48] Thanhouser must have considered Fritz's venture a good investment. With the company's backing he purchased twenty thousand feet of film at $4 a foot. The $80,000 worth of negative was insured with the German-owned Mannheim Insurance Company on 17 December.[49] At sea, the policy protected the film from "seas, fires, pirates, rovers, assailing thieves, jettison, barratry of the master and mariners, and all other perils, losses and misfortunes that have or shall come to the hurt, detriment or damage of the said goods and merchandise or any part thereof." Another certificate insured the film against further risk: "It is agreed that this insurance covers only the risk of capture, seizure or destruction by men-of-war, by letters of marque, by taking at sea, arrests, restraints, detainments or acts of kings, princes and people, authorized by and in prosecution of hostilities between belligerent nations." Fritz's film was protected from everyone, and from every natural and unnatural disaster, except Fritz himself. The policy would prove to be his undoing several years later when he tried to collect on the loss of the film, which had been deliberately destroyed by him in his crusade against England.

Fritz's trip was to be a joint venture with his cousin, the Vicomte de Rancogne, who at that time was making final arrangements with the French government regarding the expedition as well as organizing a Paris chapter of the Adventurers Club. Their plans, according to editor

Hoffman in *Adventure* magazine, called for picking up at Kingston, Jamaica, "eight negroes as a vanguard of machete men . . . eighteen half-breeds, some of whom were with Captain Duquesne in his expedition into Colombia, Brazil and Costa Rica, and—a unique feature—a Great Dane that was trained in the Putamayo rubber country to give warning of the nearness of poisoned arrows and pits."[50] Fritz's "independent thinking" and "thorough preparation in advance" called for the wearing of "partial armor of specially prepared leather" in imitation of the old Spanish conquistadores for protection against poisoned darts and mosquitoes. Big dogs that warn of poisoned arrows and holes in the ground! Leather armor! No wonder the Adventurers Club wanted to toss Fritz out.

Additionally, it was reported that Fritz would testify again before the next congress about his scheme for introducing African wildlife into America.

Fritz and Alice (without the Vicomte) left New York for South America in December 1913, but not before Fritz made an important decision that would brand him a traitor twenty-eight years later: on 4 December he became an American citizen.[51] But for now Fritz's future was the lecture circuit. In their baggage was a trunk especially constructed to carry the movie film and still negatives destined for proposed lectures. The trunk, made of iron half an inch thick, was about 45 inches long, 30 inches high, and 26 inches deep. A hinged cover lined with packing overlapped the sides and was fastened down with two thumbscrews and a lock. Two iron bands fastened by rivets wrapped around the trunk. Overall it was painted a dark green, almost black. Solidly constructed, it required two men to lift. The trunk would figure prominently several years later when Fritz was accused of sabotage in causing a British ship to sink.

On the voyage south, Alice did not realize that her time with Fritz would be short. Nor was he aware that his life would never be the same again. He would not return to America for two and a half years, and when he did return it would be not as a writer and lecturer about his and Roosevelt's South American adventures, but as a hunted fugitive and a dedicated spy for Germany. He would continue in that profession for the next three decades.

CHAPTER 10

Kaiser Wilhelm Hires Captain Fritz Duquesne

RITZ AND ALICE did not plunge into the jungles of Brazil like the indomitable Teddy. Their journey south from New York was a rather leisurely jaunt that, despite Fritz's announced itinerary, did not retrace Roosevelt's footsteps.

Instead the Duquesnes cruised through the Caribbean; rode the Panama Railroad across the Isthmus of Panama, skirting the Canal, which would not open for shipping until 15 August 1914;[1] steamed down the west coast of Colombia; and then made the arduous journey across country by rail, train, pack mule, and stern-wheeler to the Rio Negro, where they took a boat to Manáos (Manaus), the capital of Amazonas state in western Brazil. The Negro formed a junction with the Amazon River, which flowed a thousand miles eastward to the Atlantic Ocean. The city was an important trading port accessible to ocean steamers, and an ideal location for a spy or saboteur who might want to create chaos in British shipping.

It was the summer of 1914, and world events had at last reached the long-expected cataclysmic condition. Archduke Franz Ferdinand, the crown prince and heir to the throne of the Austro-Hungarian Empire, was assassinated in Sarajevo on 28 June, triggering the series of events that led to the Great War.

England declared war on Germany on 4 August for invading tiny Belgium. President Woodrow Wilson declared America's neutrality the next day. Former president Roosevelt, long since returned to America, endorsed Wilson's policy. Fritz lost all respect for Roosevelt when he heard of his stand. "There are no good Americans except the anti-English ones," declared Fritz.[2]

War at last! It was the best of news for Fritz. The conflict returned the hated Kitchener to prominence. Created an earl on 17 June, he was appointed secretary of state for war the day after Britain declared war. The English people were elated. Kitchener of Khartoum, the country's greatest soldier, a needed father figure at this time and now the British Empire's premier warlord, would surely lead them to victory with the New Armies he would build in this their hour of greatest need. Thirty-seven-year-old Fritz swore he would get involved this time and England would lose, as would Kitchener. Shortly after contacting the German consulate in Manáos, Fritz sent Alice home. He explained that he planned to penetrate the more primitive areas of Brazil, which would be beyond her endurance—a conclusion that does not square with the durability Alice seemed to show merely in arriving at Manáos. Fritz then began a new and secret life.

He was hired, perhaps, on the basis of a directive issued on 18 November 1914, from the headquarters of the Intelligence Department of the Imperial Navy in Berlin to all naval agents throughout the world, ordering mobilization of all "agents who are overseas and all destroying agents in ports where vessels carrying war materials are loaded in England, France, Canada, the United States and Russia."[3] The directive continued:

It is indispensable by the intermediary of the third person having no relation with the official representatives of Germany to recruit progressively agents to organize explosions on ships sailing to enemy countries in order to cause delays and confusion in the loading, the departure and the unloading of these ships. With this end in view we particularly recommend to your attention the deckhands, among whom are to be found a great many anarchists and escaped criminals. The necessary sums for buying and hiring persons charged with executing the projects will be put at your disposal on your demand.

It is unlikely that Fritz worked simultaneously for both the German navy and army intelligence departments. Nevertheless, he unwaveringly boasted of having committed acts of sabotage for Captain Rudolf Nadolny, the legendary "Silent Colonel," head of the Geheime

Nachrichtendienst des Heeres (Secret News Service of the Army), known as the ND or as Abteilung (Department) IIIb.

The retainer fee of 4,000 marks (about $1,000) a year and 10 marks ($2.50) a day for living expenses did not allow Fritz to enjoy the free-spending life he would have preferred.[4] But the adventure of living on the edge must have been a fair substitute. Bonuses were paid for each individual piece of work undertaken, the amount varying with the importance of the mission. The promised bonuses may explain all the destruction claimed by sly Fritz. His claims included twenty-two British ships sunk, one hundred others set afire, and the waterfronts of two towns burned.[5] One-third of all moneys accrued were kept in trust at the rate of 5 percent interest.

Fritz Duquesne the suave, courtly gentleman with the clipped British speech was now gone. In his place was the play-actor Frederick Fredericks or George Fordham, a rumpled and doddering middle-aged Dutch botanist. To avoid suspicion, the stoop-shouldered and thick-spectacled Dutchman was constantly on the move.

Alternately using his own name and one of the two aliases, Fritz journeyed northward to Pernambuco (now Recife) on the east coast of Brazil, to Paramaribo in Dutch Guiana (now Surinam), Georgetown in British Guiana (now Guyana), Caracas in Venezuela, and Managua in Nicaragua. Like a gadfly he was back and forth, up and down the east coast, always observing British shipping. Under any one of his aliases he shipped orchid bulbs, mineral specimens, rare plants, or film aboard British ships. Mysterious explosions would follow, and the ships would sink at sea. Fritz headquartered at the port of Bahia (now Salvador), where the Dutch planter became an established figure and was free to work as a spy and saboteur.

Recalling his experience as a pimp on the Bermuda waterfront, Fritz frequented the bars and dives of whatever Brazilian port he was in. He would observe the crew of any English freighter carrying war material. Singling out the least bright sailor, he would bribe the man with 20 Dutch gulden (about $5) to carry aboard a package of orchid bulbs for a friend or relative at the ship's destination. The supposed bulbs would in fact be either high explosives or an incendiary device.

The most widely used and effective incendiary was the "fiery cigar," devised by Dr. Walter T. Scheele for the German government while employed as president of the New Jersey Agricultural Chemical Company. The "cigar" was a lead tube containing potassium chlorate or picric acid separated by a copper disc from a quantity of sulfuric acid.

Wax sealed the ends of the tube. When the sulfuric acid ate its way through the copper disc and mixed with the picric acid, the result was an intense white-hot flame that created havoc.

Another method, and a favorite story Fritz recounted many times over the years at cocktail parties and to admiring listeners, was one often challenged by experts,[6] How could the brave captain sink ships with such small amounts of explosives? Undaunted, Fritz would tell the story anyway. He believed he had done it. Besides, it was such a good story.

Fritz claimed he would approach the target ship after nightfall in a small native boat with a concealed bomb made from a five-gallon paint or oil drum filled with TNT. If discovered by the watch, Fritz would stand and hold up a bunch of bananas or a jug of local liquor and assume the guise and patois of a peddler. Then he would return to shore for another try later. There was security in the knowledge that lookouts were reluctant to open fire in a neutral port. When successful in getting close to a freighter, Fritz would dive down with the drum bomb and attach it to the ship's rudder. With each swing to the right or left of the rudder, a rod attached to the blade and drum turned a mechanism that, when wound tight, would release a hammerlike blow to a cap and explode the TNT. Detonated directly under the stern, the explosion was sufficient to sink or at least cripple the ship.

It was particularly easy for Fritz to move throughout Brazil because of the large number of German colonials who had made the South American country an outpost of the German Empire. Easing his way even more was a letter of introduction dated 6 May 1915, written in German and signed by Herr Uebersezig, German imperial vice-consul at Managua. The letter read, "It is a pleasure to me to commend to my countrymen Mr. Fritz Duquesne, captain of Engineers in the Boer Army. He has in many circumstances rendered notable services to our good German cause."[7] Sunk by a submarine off the coast of Ireland the day after this communication was the British ship *Lusitania*. The outrage in America spurred by the act eventually helped bring America into the war, an event that ended Fritz's career as a spy.

Ever the bon vivant, Fritz was a great favorite in Rio de Janeiro society, where he was known as the Boer patriot Piet Niacoud (Duquesne spelled backwards phonetically—clever Fritz would have his joke).[8] Piet was liked because he loudly denounced the Germans at every opportunity, a praiseworthy posture in Rio's Allied circles. He was doubly popular because Fritz the spy could not forget that he was also an actor. Though always alert for information that would aid the German cause, he would not deny himself the opportunity to emote in recitals before Rio society. It was a precarious position for a spy, but one he reveled in. He also enjoyed the security of acceptance by high-ranking British civilian and military figures. In the near future Fritz would be in a similar but even more daring and perilous position in New York.

Despite his caution, Fritz had not escaped the eyes of British Intelligence along the docks, where he was a more visible figure. He was being watched closely but had cleverly avoided being directly connected to any sabotage. Sir C. Mallet, the British minister at Panama, wrote to the Foreign Office in London on 16 June 1915, informing them of activities under his jurisdiction:[9]

Through a Canal Zone detective I learnt confidentially that a passenger named Captain F. Duquesne, travelling with a passport issued by the United States Consul at Manáos, Brazil, had embarked for Trinidad on the *R.M.S. Panama* on the 14th instant.

My informant stated that Captain Duquesne poses as an American officer but in reality is an intelligence officer in the service of the German government.

I have warned the governor of Trinidad by telegraph so that a watch may be kept on Captain Duquesne's movements.

Fritz may have dropped the guise of the Dutch planter for that of the American officer because he had only a U.S. passport, which enabled him to move freely through the American Canal Zone. He behaved himself and gave no reason to be arrested in Trinidad, where he was under constant surveillance.

Fritz continued his travels through Central America. In Guatemala he received another endorsement from a representative of the German government. A communiqué dated 20 December 1915 and signed by Herr Lehmann, the German consul, declared that Fritz was an acceptable guest in outposts of the German Empire.[10]

There were several narrow escapes. Fritz struggled with a purser who caught him trying to place a bomb in the hold of a vessel loading dockside.[11] He escaped, stunning the purser with a blow to the head from his revolver. Another time his lodgings in a Brazilian port were surrounded by British agents. He escaped across the rooftops. Once he was actually captured while planting a bomb aboard a vessel. Put in a boat to be taken ashore, Fritz leaped overboard and disappeared.

But the net was drawing tighter, and Fritz could not expect to operate effectively much longer. The end of his career as a saboteur began in January 1916, when he emerged from the jungle at Bahia with hired native carriers lugging the heavy green trunk. On 27 January, using the name of Francisco Figuerado—alliterative, as in Frederick Fredericks—he filed an application with Brazilian customhouse broker Raul E. de Olivera to ship one case of potter's earth samples (in dust), weighing 80 kilos (about 175 pounds) and valued at $500, to New York aboard the steamer *Verdi* sailing 28 January.[12]

Much to "Francisco Figuerado's" consternation, the explosives failed, and the *Verdi* sailed safely to New York.

Undaunted, Fritz immediately planned the destruction of the Lamport and Holt steamer *Tennyson.* On 11 February he signed an Invoice of Returned American Goods and Declaration of Foreign Exporter at the American consulate, stating that the undersigned, George Fordham, "solemnly and truly declared that the 20,000 feet of moving picture film and the 4100 negatives which he was shipping back to the United States were to the best of his knowledge and belief, of the manufacture of the United States and had been exported from the United States in 1913."[13] Sixteen boxes marked "minerals" were placed aboard the *Tennyson,* bound for Trinidad, New York, and Liverpool. The steamer's primary cargo was hides and copra. The boxes of "minerals" contained some ore, perhaps the movie film and negatives, and definitely explosives and incendiaries.

"George Fordham" was successful this time.

The *Tennyson* was halfway between Bahia and Trinidad on 21 February when she was rocked by a terrific explosion in the hold followed by a fierce fire. Three sailors were killed. The ship was foundering, but the captain managed to beach her. England was outraged. British intelligence moved swiftly. A clerk named Bauer was arrested. He confessed to working with Fritz Duquesne, who operated undercover as George Fordham and Piet Niacoud. Other conspirators, including an agent named Niewirth, were hunted, but all managed to escape.

Bauer was eventually sentenced to twelve years in prison. But his tattling led to the discovery of papers and funds of the saboteurs in a safe-deposit box registered to Piet Niacoud with an English company.[14] Niacoud gave his home address as Cape Town. The documents revealed plots that, if carried out, would have compromised the neutrality of several South American republics. American bills totaling $6,470 were in an envelope marked "On His Majesty's Service" and addressed to Niacoud. The name created shock waves in the British colony when the story was printed in the Rio newspapers. As one English-language paper reported, "Little did the English dream that they were harbouring a black-hearted spy in their midst whom they now know as one of the leading plotters whose audacity is beyond belief."

A notice was issued by His Majesty's Printing Office informing consular, military, naval, and police authorities and "all others whom it may concern, that Col. Fritz du Quesne"—note the sudden promotion—"the notorious agent of the Central Empires was wanted for trial with other German offenders for crimes against the rules of civilized warfare and neutrals." A "fugitive from justice," Fritz was wanted on charges of "murder on the high seas; the sinking and burning of British ships; the burning of military stores, warehouses, coaling stations, conspiracy, and the falsification of Admiralty documents."[15] The most serious charge was murder on the high seas, which carried an obligatory death sentence. Determined to carry it out, the British would have a long chase over the next sixteen years before driving Fritz to ground.

Fritz moved fast, south down the coast to Argentina and the gay life of Buenos Aires. Almost immediately he became involved in a plan with the Argentine Board of Education to produce a number of educational films.[16] Fritz saw it as a money-making scheme that would bring him $24,000 or more. First, though, he would have to return to America to purchase the film. But he couldn't return to America unless he was dead. Alive, he would be arrested by British intelligence. Fritz decided he must die.

The death of Fritz Duquesne got good coverage in most major newspapers. On 27 April 1916 the *New York Times* gave him a nice two-column spread:[17]

CAPTAIN DUQUESNE IS SLAIN IN BOLIVIA
Hostile Indians Descend on His Expedition and Kill Soldier of Fortune

CAREER FULL OF ROMANCE
Boer Scout at 17, He Swam to Liberty from Bermuda—
Trailed Roosevelt up the Amazon

A special cable to the *Times,* unsigned and datelined 26 April from Buenos Aires, followed: "Captain Fritz Duquesne of New York, noted adventurer and soldier of fortune, has been killed in a battle with Indians on the Bolivian frontier. His expedition was looted by the attacking band."

The story that followed told how Duquesne and his wife had gone to South America with motion picture equipment to trace Roosevelt's expedition. This was the first news about Fritz since he had left New York almost three years earlier. A lengthy obituary followed.

A follow-up story the next day reported that Alice Duquesne had received a letter two months earlier from Fritz while he was in Buenos Aires. He wrote that he was going to Bolivia and would return to New York in a few weeks and asked that no more mail be forwarded to him.

Famed photographer Arnold Genthe was a close friend who, as he explained in a *New York Times* interview from his studio at 1 West Forty-sixth Street, had received one of the captain's last letters home.[18] Genthe was famous for his pictures of the 1906 San Francisco earthquake and for portraits of Theodore Roosevelt, Jack London, and stage and silent screen personalities. His photographs of nineteen-year-old Greta Garbo in 1925 would be credited with convincing Metro-Goldwyn-Mayer mogul Louis B. Mayer to sign the Swedish actress for her first American movie.

Genthe reported that Fritz had complained in his letter of consistent "hard luck," concluding with the following (in an obvious reference to the *Tennyson*): "And now, just as I thought my expedition was coming to a close, I hear that the ship upon which I sent my picture films to America has been sunk by Germans. All the practical results of the two years I have labored here have therefore been destroyed." It was as ludicrous as John Dillinger robbing a bank and then criticizing it for not having his savings. Genthe theorized, "Having lost his films, Captain Duquesne, unwilling to return to New York with empty hands, re-entered the wilderness of South America to obtain more pictures." Fritz described his sufferings in the jungles, either real or imagined: "My body is full of sores and my mind is full of holes. I'm almost a fit subject for a hospital."

Fritz had succeeded. If the *New York Times* printed an obituary, surely it must be true. The world, and particularly the British, would believe he was dead.

But Fritz had more surprises. An Associated Press news story datelined Montevideo, Uruguay, broke on 8 May in the *New York Times* and other papers:[19]

Captain Fritz Joubert Duquesne of New York, explorer and soldier of fortune, who was in command of an expedition into the Bolivian wilds, has been found by troops at Rio Pilcomayo in a badly wounded state, after a battle in which his expedition had attacked and defeated a band of Indians on the Bolivian frontier.

Aid was sent to the wounded explorer who is expected to recover.

It was pure Fritz Duquesne: a paean to the wounded but victorious hero, found bloody but unconquered along the river border between Argentina and the Chaco region of Paraguay. He even managed to send the story out over the AP wire under the byline of his most frequently used alias, Frederick Fredericks.

Fritz Duquesne was resurrected twelve days after he had declared himself dead. Why? Speculation would suggest that he regretted the first story announcing his death even though its effect had been the desired one: to put a halt to the intensive English manhunt for him. He might have feared that if he were "dead," he would never be able to return to America, Alice, and the good life. Where else could he go? A U.S. passport was the only one he possessed.

Carefully considering his options, Fritz may have determined that in America he should be free from extradition and eventual execution because of Wilson's strict Neutrality Act. Whatever the reason, he was already on his way back to New York as the rescue story was being wired around the world. After all, he still expected to collect on the Argentine Board of Education scam. And he had another bold plan to collect insurance on the materials he had just destroyed aboard the *Tennyson*.

The plan was insolent in its daring.

CHAPTER 11

"Captain Claude Stoughton, at Your Service!"

FRITZ DUQUESNE RETURNED via a German submarine to America, where he planned to continue his fight against the English he detested so much. He landed in Baltimore aboard the German merchant submarine *Deutschland,* which, after a remarkable voyage across the Atlantic to demonstrate that the British blockade of naval vessels could be avoided, pulled into the Maryland harbor on 10 July 1916.[1]

At least that is the story Fritz would continue to tell for the next four decades. After so many years of repeating the elaborate fabrication, even he must have begun to believe what was just another of his great lies. The truth, as much as can be determined from the meager information available after some eighty years, is considerably different from what Fritz Duquesne told at the time, and from what he would have preferred history to record. But it is just as bizarre.

Fritz had been in New York since May 1916, having fled South America one step ahead of British intelligence. His only security was in the United States. Besides ensuring his personal safety, the move to America would allow him to conclude the money-making scam he had conceived in Buenos Aires involving the Argentine Board of Education. A young man about New York, after all, needed spending money.

Fritz had faced a dilemma in South America. If he stayed, British intelligence would sooner or later find him. Hence the false story in April of his death at the hands of hostile Indians. Second thoughts produced the other false story reported by the Associated Press about his being found alive along the Pilcomayo River. The British now knew he was alive, but life undercover would be better in the United States than in South America. Fritz would fight the possibility of extradition for his crime of murder on the high seas when the time came. The streets of Manhattan were safer than the jungles of Brazil. And if caught? Fritz would prefer taking his chances in the American courts. Wilson's signing of the Neutrality Act was in his favor. The Black Panther of the Veld still had a few tricks left.

Fritz arrived in New York with a man named Williamson, who is not heard from again, and reportedly purchased the movie film for the Board of Education for $24,000 cash. The reels were stored at the Fulton and Flatbush Warehouse at 437 Carlton Avenue, Brooklyn.[2] For whatever reason, they were labeled "statuary." The film was insured by "Frederick Fredericks" for $33,000—not for the $24,000 purchase price—with the Stuyvesant Insurance Company.

Later testimony in an insurance investigation revealed that Fritz had visited the warehouse frequently, once arriving after hours and trying unsuccessfully to bribe the watchman to admit him.[3] It was learned that he moved to a small hotel in Elizabeth, New Jersey, and about two weeks later the warehouse mysteriously caught fire and destroyed the "statuary."

Fritz then disappeared. But first he persuaded innocent Alice, as the dutiful wife with whom he was now reunited, to aid him in an attempt to collect not only the $33,000 insurance for this film—the "statuary"—but also the $80,000 for the film he claimed had gone down with the *Tennyson!* Fritz Duquesne, alias George Fordham, alias Frederick Fredericks, was in line for $113,000. Time dragged on as the Mannheim and Stuyvesant insurance companies investigated the claims, reluctant to pay what they believed to be fraudulent claims by Fordham and Fredericks. But they could not prove that Fordham and Fredericks were both actually Frederick Joubert Duquesne, nor could they prove that any of the three was alive or dead.

And where was Fritz while all this was going on? He had disappeared sometime in May, shortly after the warehouse fire. His exact whereabouts will probably never be known. But according to Fritz, he was executing a plan to destroy England's most illustrious soldier,

Kitchener of Khartoum. For the rest of his life Fritz claimed that he was "the man who killed Kitchener." Had he been, it would have happened at this time in his life.

The events of the Great War that formed the basis for Fritz's claim began in April 1916, when England grew concerned that the Russian people, weary of a stalemated war, might overthrow Tsar Nicholas II. Or if the expected summer offensive against the Germans should fail, the Russian government might sue for a separate peace. Hoping to negate either possibility, Prime Minister Herbert Asquith's government proposed a mission to Russia to strengthen that country's resolve and to discuss supplying weapons and munitions and methods of payment. Kitchener asked for, and was given, permission to head up the mission. With security in both countries lax, it was an open secret in government circles by mid-May that Kitchener would visit Russia. No doubt it was also known in Berlin. But no one knew exactly when or how he would make the journey.

It was decided that Kitchener would leave on 5 June aboard the HMS *Hampshire* from Scapa Flow, the chief British naval base in the Orkney Islands off the northeastern tip of Scotland. This whole area from Inverness to Durness and John O'Groats was the Zone of the Fleet—quite literally an Admiralty preserve where martial law prevailed. Kitchener would arrive in Petrograd six days later. British intelligence believed that the route selected had been swept clear of mines, unaware that on 28 May the German submarine U-72, commanded by Lieutenant Commander Kurt Beitzen, had laid a series of mines off the west coast of Orkney Island along Kitchener's precise course.

The *Hampshire*—which had returned four days earlier from the indecisive Battle of Jutland—passed out of Scapa Flow's protective basin at 4:45 P.M. on one of the stormiest days the area had seen in years. Suddenly, at a little before 7:30 P.M., the ship was rocked by a violent explosion that shook her from stem to stern. A huge hole was torn in the ship's bottom between the bows and the bridge. The *Hampshire* had struck one of Beitzen's mines. It was nearly 7:45, and the cruiser was sinking fast by the bows. Lifeboats smashed against her steel hull when attempts were made to lower them into the raging waters. Only the large oval Carley rafts remained afloat. Scores of sailors jumped overboard with little hope of surviving in the frigid sea. One of the survivors last saw Lord Kitchener walking calmly from his cabin to the quarterdeck, where he waited with equal calm for the inevitable. The

The armored cruiser HMS Hampshire *with Lord Kitchener aboard was sunk by a German submarine on 5 June 1916. Fritz claimed to have signaled the sub from aboard the ship, making him "The Man Who Killed Kitchener." (National Archives)*

Hampshire went down by the bow, a quarter-hour after striking the mine. Her stern rose high in the air before the ship turned completely over and disappeared beneath the storm-tossed sea.

Only 12 of the crew of 655 survived. Kitchener of Khartoum was not one of them.

Fritz told a different and, of course, more dramatic story.[4] Following his "death" at the hands of hostile Indians in Bolivia and before his "resurrection" twelve days later, Fritz was well on his way to a meeting with the Boer Revolutionary Committee at Breda in the Netherlands to accept a commission as colonel.[5] The committee—a complete fiction—had been organized, according to Fritz, to use the opportunity when England was occupied with a European war to take back South Africa for the Boers.

The committee informed Fritz that Count Boris Zakrevsky, a young Russian nobleman who spoke fluent English, had been assigned to accompany Kitchener from England to Petrograd. Sworn to secrecy, he had nevertheless told his fiancée of his mission. *She* could be trusted, of course. The count did not know she was a German spy. Within the hour German intelligence in Petrograd knew of Kitchener's plans. En route to England, Zakrevsky was seized by Germans on the Baltic coast and tossed into prison. German intelligence told the committee that it wanted Fritz Duquesne to replace the count. His mission was to kill England's number one soldier, either by his own hand or by signaling waiting U-boats, which would torpedo the Russia-headed ship. Would he do it?

"By my soul, by my love for all things Boer, by my hatred of Kitchener and all things English, by my love for my mother, I accept," was Fritz's unflinching reply.

Fritz Duquesne was now Count Boris Zakrevsky, or Agent A100-1-20. Fortunately his fluency in Russian was excellent. Wearing the Russian uniform and decorations of Zakrevsky, Fritz arrived in London the first week of June, when news of the Jutland battle was coming in and creating as much excitement as if the war had been over.

On 4 June he entrained at King's Cross railway station with Kitchener and his entourage. The train headed north for Edinburgh and then Inverness. They were now in the Zone of the Fleet and under martial law. There was a delay of several hours while the papers of the party were verified by telegraph from London and Scapa Flow. Then it was on to Thurso station, whence they motored to the harbor. The torpedo-boat destroyer HMS *Oak* took Kitchener and his group on the two-hour sea journey across Pentland Firth, past the islands of South Ronaldsay and Flotta, and into Scapa Flow. Here amid the massive, almost intimidating splendor of the Grand Fleet—though wounded and depleted from Jutland—secrecy was finally broken, and Fritz learned, when the party (Fritz included) transferred to the cruiser, that Kitchener would make his journey to Russia aboard the *Hampshire.*

Fritz had to warn the waiting U-boats! In his suitcase he had what looked like an ordinary book but was really a book of message sheets. The top half of each sheet was painted with a luminous substance so that it would glow in the dark. The bottom half was weighted. He would use these if his other signals could not be seen. Fritz was to write the name of the ship and the chosen course on the top half of each sheet, then drop them into the sea for a submarine to pick up. The information would be wirelessed to the rest of the squadron, and the U-boats would then converge and attack.

But the ship was under way, tossed about by violent seas that would make it difficult to pick up the message sheets. Fritz's other pre-arranged signals included a white handkerchief or piece of sheeting hung out of a porthole. It was still light, and such a signal would be intercepted. Fritz decided instead to rely on the more reliable water torch. When it struck the water, it ignited and gave out puffs of smoke at three-second intervals. For insurance he also closed the porthole on a pillowcase hanging over the side.

It was 7:44 P.M. Fritz put on a life jacket and checked the pistol he carried. If necessary he would kill the man himself. Suddenly a terrific shock threw him against the wall of his small cabin. The lights went out, and the ship began to list. Fritz stumbled out into the passageway and saw the captain's door open. Kitchener and several other officers stepped out. Fritz followed them to the quarterdeck where he stood less than twenty feet from Kitchener, who was waiting calmly. If Kitchener got into one of the boats or rafts, Fritz would shoot him. But then:

Off to starboard hardly a hundred yards away, was the conning tower of a submarine, bobbing up and down in the turbulent water, now flung back, now thrown nearer. His ears seemed to hear a wild plea across the waters: "We want Kitchener!"

At that moment Kitchener saw, and understood. Duquesne wanted to cry it all out aloud to the man: "I am Fritz Duquesne, whose people you ruined, whose land you stole, whose near and dear ones you defiled. I swore to hunt you to the death; not for one instant since have I ceased my unremitting efforts. *Now* do you see my power, my vengeance? His lips formed some of it. The wind was shrieking like hell unleashed. Could the man hear? In some sudden lull . . . Fritz thought he saw startled understanding cross the man's face.

Kitchener suddenly staggered as a wave washed over him. He lost his footing and was swept over the side. His enemy gone, Fritz jumped over the side of the *Hampshire* and desperately fought his way through the surging waters to the U-boat. He was pulled aboard. His whole body was bruised, and a rib was broken. The crew knew who he was because of the Russian uniform. They crowded around him, drinking death to all things English: "It *was* his hour, this was such a kill as no jungle beast ever dreamed of!"

In Germany Fritz was toasted and feted. He received decorations from all the Central Powers: the Iron Cross with gold leaves, worn only, but for him, by the kaiser, Hindenburg, Ludendorff, and several others. And there was the Diamond Crescent of Turkey.[6] Fritz was created baron of Brandenburg.

Ten days after the sinking, the British secretary of the Admiralty collated all the reports and discovered that one other man had been saved:

A private soldier appears to have left the ship on one of the rafts, but it is not known what became of him. Some of the reports had said the man had gone over in a small raft, some that he had been picked up by a small boat nearby—and in that sea!—and one was foggily sure that it looked like a submarine periscope. Clearly all of this was wrong, they decided. If it had been one of the Kitchener party, he would have turned up somewhere. A mere private soldier, on an unidentified raft, washed overboard somehow; so they reported the tangled stories. The man was Fritz Duquesne.

It was a wonderful story. And that's all it was—a wonderful, improbable story.[7]

Fritz finally surfaced in Washington, D.C., in July 1917, just three months after America had entered the war in Europe to "make the world safe for democracy." It would not be incorrect to speculate that he was running low on whatever funds he had, and that he saw the war as just another opportunity to provide him with what he always lacked: money. He was not concerned about being drafted, since he was now almost forty years old, beyond the age of men wanted in the military.

He immediately made contact with his old adventuring friend, Captain Horace Ashton, for whom he had conducted an unspecified expedition in South America.[8] He told Ashton he was looking for work but emphatically asked him to keep his presence in Washington as quiet as possible. Temporarily, he said, he would be using the name Frederick Fredericks.

Ashton visited Senator Robert F. Broussard, who had been elected to the Senate from his state of Louisiana in 1915. It was the same Broussard who, as a congressman in 1910, had introduced the bill for the importation of wild and domestic animals to the United States and produced Fritz as an expert witness. Ashton learned that Broussard was also in contact with Fritz.

The senator, obviously not aware that Fritz was wanted by the British for murder on the high seas, informed Ashton that he was trying to obtain a position for Fritz with General George W. Goethals, the former chief engineer on the Panama Canal and now acting quartermaster general and director of purchases, storage, and traffic for the U.S. Army.[9]

Failing that, Broussard said Fritz had an invention that might secure him work with the Navy Department. Fritz had filed plans with the Secretary of the Navy for an electromagnetic submarine mine mat. Charged with high explosives and floating just beneath the surface, it would be attracted to any steel ship passing by and blow it up.[10] For someone wanting to keep his presence quiet, Fritz was certainly getting around.

Ashton had been offered a job with George Creel, the American government's official propagandist. He introduced Creel to Fritz in Creel's office, an old brick residence at 8 Jackson Place, across the street from the White House.[11] Creel was chairman of the Committee on Public Information and was popularly known as "Uncle Sam's Press Agent." President Wilson had named the former Denver newspaperman head of the committee when the United States declared war on Germany. He was given broad powers as a censor and carte blanche to use every means possible to stimulate the spirit of Americanization everywhere in fighting the war on the home front.

Fritz never worked for Goethals, the Navy Department, or Creel. Nor was his invention ever accepted. What his position would have been with the quartermaster general was never explained. But as a writer and former newspaper editor, he would have fit easily into the Creel committee. Like Broussard, neither Creel nor Goethals was aware of Fritz's background, or he surely would have been arrested or detained rather than considered for positions with them.

What would have been Fritz's intentions if hired? Would he have worked as a spy, or would he truly have devoted his energies to the American war effort? Whether responsible for Kitchener's death or not, his quarrel with the field marshal was over, although he was still a dedicated Anglophobe. After all, Fritz had no complaint against the United States. He was now a citizen of his adopted country, and he had done quite well financially and socially in his milieu. Spying against England was only a crime in America, not a traitorous act. He would be tagged with the more onerous epithet of traitor if he were to spy against America. As matters developed, that was not in his plans. But that time would come in another war in just twenty-two years.

Fritz returned to New York when he was not able to secure a position with the government. While seeking employment he shared an apartment with Horace Ashton at 137 West Fifty-seventh Street.[12] Since the bogus insurance claims were still pending, he insisted that Ashton not reveal to mutual friends that he was in the city. It was also necessary to maintain a low profile because of the possibility of apprehension by British intelligence for his activities in South America.

Apparently he told Ashton, who later gave such a statement to the police, that he had landed a job with the J. G. White Engineering Corporation, a large contracting company responsible for building railroads, bridges, power plants, and harbor improvements throughout the world.[13] At the time, the company was gearing up for war work.

His application for employment at the White company was dated 8 September 1917 under the name of Fred du Quesne.[14] The details he supplied on the form were prime examples of the obfuscation he used to cloud his life. His present position was "none," and he indicated that he would like to work as an "inspector of military devices, purchasing agent for same, or army supplies transportation." To a man whose primary occupation was spy, any one of these positions certainly would have been acceptable and beneficial. It is not quite clear whether he ever did get work with White, but later when the police arrested Duquesne, Ashton told them that Fritz was employed by the company as an "inspector of airplanes." The statement is interesting because White did not build airplanes. But Ashton believed that Fritz was working for the company, as no doubt Fritz had convinced him he was, and in that capacity.

The nearest relative Fritz listed on the form was a sister, Jocelyn A. du Quesne, living in Los Angeles. His first impulse was to write her name as Duquesne, which he erased and then rewrote as du Quesne. But Fritz had always claimed he had only one sister, Elsbet, who was killed during the Boer War.[15] His next nearest relative was listed as Viscount François de Rancogne, prisoner of war, Germany. The third and last relative named was Edward Wortley, colonial secretary, Jamaica, B.W.I. He was referring to his father-in-law (Edward J. or Samuel Sharp), who actually had been the director of the Department of Agriculture in Jamaica, not the colonial secretary, before Fritz met the Wortley family as a POW in Bermuda.

If nothing else, the employment application provided good reading for the personnel department at the White Corporation. Some of it was true; much of it read like an adventure novel. Fritz described himself as a graduate of St. Cyr—another life-long lie—as a master of French and English, and as having lived in England, France, Africa, Australia, Central America, Brazil, Argentina, and the United States. He made no mention of Bermuda. Given as references were Thomas

O'Connell (a relative, he said, employed by White in Nicaragua), Ashton, Senator Broussard, and the Marquis (not Viscount) de Rancogne, lieutenant general of cavalry, France.

It would be difficult to determine what his previous experience would have qualified him for as an employee of the J. G. White Engineering Corporation, considering what Fritz wrote in the space provided:

1898 to 1899. Secretary to board of selection on military devices and contracts. South Africa, reporting Genl. de Villiers. [Salary] 10 pounds weekly.

1899 to 1902. South African War. Was inspector of military communication and reported secretary of war. 12 pounds, 2 shillings, 6 pence weekly.

1902 to 1903. Lived in United States to start residence. Had an experience job in the subway looking on. $25.00.

1903 to 1904. Went on tour of Congo Free State in the interests of making favorable publicity in this country for King Leopold. Gerard Harry in charge of campaign for king. Received $10,000 for the job, with expenses.

1904–5–6. Headed Eldu expedition and industrial research party in Australia. Sir Arthur Jones financed me. Received 2,000 pounds yearly.

1907–8. Toured Russia for *Petit Bleu*. Publicity. 1,000 florins weekly.

1908–9–10. Organized and built string of theaters in British West Indies. Financed and erected hydro-electric plants for S. S. Wortley & Co., Kingston, Jamaica. Made percentages.

1911–12. Lived in Nicaragua and Guatemala. Was with Mr. Thomas O'-Connell in Nicaragua for one year. Made industrial and investment investigations, especially ore, fibre, rubber. $5,000.00 and expenses yearly. Mr. Hite financed. Address New Rochelle.

1913–14–15–16. Explored and travelled in South America, Brazil, Argentine, Peru, and Bolivia, on own account. Also conducted special expedition for Horace Ashton of 220 W. 42nd St., New York.

No mention was made of his years as an editor and reporter with the New York *Sun* and *World*. His rather shadowy background would have been exposed if references had been requested from those newspapers. An inquiry would have turned up a different account of how he had spent the years 1903 to 1907, the years he supposedly spent in the Congo Free State for King Leopold and in Australia and Russia. Nor did he mention his association with Theodore Roosevelt in 1912, when he campaigned throughout New York State for the former president's unsuccessful bid for a third term. No, he wouldn't do that. Fritz was careful about anyone he listed as a family member or a reference. They were either dead or very difficult to get in touch with. There would be no trapping the Black Panther of the Veld.

So what was Fritz Duquesne doing? Always needing money to live in the style he had set for himself when he came to America in 1902, he was hardly one to remain idle. Nor was he likely to work at a regular job, which would only be tedious for him, mentally, physically, and monetarily.

Recalling his pleasant prewar days as a Manhattan bon vivant and respected Sunday editor of the *Sun* making a tidy living supplemented by a nice income from articles and lectures on big-game hunting, he called the James B. Pond Lyceum Bureau, his old agents. He was informed that there was no money in such lecturing now.[16] Because of the war, people weren't traveling, and they certainly weren't going on safari. There was bigger game in Europe. Audiences wanted war heroes, and they were willing to pay for the privilege of seeing and hearing them—anywhere from 25 cents to $18 a ticket, depending on how patriotic they felt at the box office, plus a 10 percent war tax. A top ticket price of $18 was a substantial increase over the $1 tops Fritz had been getting during his lecturing heyday six years earlier.

It wasn't long before managers and producers counting box office receipts came to the conclusion that there were not many patriotic New Yorkers. The war tax was not very popular, either with the public or with the theater people, and it was blamed for an alarming falling off of business up and down the Great White Way, which itself was facing doom: the government's fuel administrator, Dr. Garfield, was about to sign a bill blacking out the bright lights because they were considered a national extravagance.[17] It had been decreed that theater marquees were burning up coal needed elsewhere. Calmer heads prevailed, however, and a week later it was determined that signs could be made less costly by an arrangement for dimming them. The theatrical season was already suffering from a puzzling slump that, coupled with the unwanted tax, brought in a gloomy forecast of a permanent business flop.[18] Cutting actors' salaries was being considered as a way to salvage the disaster.

Despite the decline in ticket sales and the oppressive war tax, Sergeant Arthur Guy Empey—"an American soldier who *went*" as a machine gunner with the Royal Fusiliers, and author of the big-selling *Over the Top*—was drawing audiences in a return engagement at Carnegie Hall with a "Vivid, Soul-Thrilling Narrative of Life on the Front Line in France" as well as giving a lecture that included a demonstration of trench warfare. Captain Arthur Radclyffe Dugmore of the King's Own Yorkshire Light Infantry was at Carnegie Hall on another evening, talking and showing films about "Fighting It Out," with the proceeds going to the YMCA and the British-America Relief. It was the same Dugmore who had lectured in Washington in 1910 on Roosevelt's African trip at the same time as Fritz. Author-soldier Major Ian Hay, author of *The First Hundred Thousand,* was "Carrying On" with an illustrated lecture of that title on the progress of the war, also at Carnegie Hall.

Regardless of the disappointing season, the theater was offering stiff competition to the heroes with plays and stars certainly not lacking in luster. John Barrymore and brother Lionel were starring with Constance Collier in *Peter Ibbetson* at the Republic; George Arliss was *Hamilton* at the Knickerbocker; the phenomenally successful and spectacular musical tale of the East, *Chu Chin Chow,* starred Tyrone Power Sr. in its second year at the Manhattan Opera House; Peggy Wood was singing her heart out to Sigmund Romberg's music in *Maytime* at the Shubert; Blossom Seeley was belting out songs in her own special style at the Palace; Laurette Taylor was *Out There* at the Liberty; Miss Billie Burke was *The Rescuing Angel* at the Hudson; the ill-fated Evelyn Nesbit was unsuccessfully pursuing a career in *A Roseland Fantasy* at the Riverside; and Harry Lauder was beginning his farewell tour at the Lexington in *The Jolly Scot's Goodbye.*

As for the movies, Douglas Fairbanks could be seen in his latest western, *The Man from Painted Post,* Theda Bara was vamping audiences in *Cleopatra,* and William Farnum was a fugitive on the run in *Les Misérables.*

There was also competition from seventy-five thousand nationwide volunteers groomed by George Creel's Committee on Public Information to give four-minute talks on prepared topics at street corners, in movie theaters and churches, and at civic events. They were called Creel's "stentorian guard." Also flying madly about town making Liberty Bond speeches, the forerunner of stage and screen stars who would soon follow her example, was the queen of the Gay Nineties, once called "the most desirable woman in America": the legendary Lillian Russell. The Marine Corps made her an honorary sergeant after one rally at the Hippodrome that drew five thousand people, hundreds of whom stormed the stage later to buy bonds.

So considering the adulation and attention being directed toward heroes, not to mention the price of admission, Fritz Duquesne decided to become a war hero.

He immediately set about designing a uniform that would be appropriate for the British army unit he decided would best suit the heroics he had created for himself: the West Australia Lighthorse.[19] Wily Fritz had carefully selected an outfit not commonly known in New York, now at the height of war fever and patriotic fervor. The majority of war heroes and veterans of the European conflict were not Australian.

He presented a fine figure, with turned-up mustachios, slouch hat with brim on the left side turned up Australian style, and well-cut field boots. A war hero possesses badges of bravery, and intrepid Fritz was adept at creating heroes. Who was a greater hero than he? The ribbons prominently displayed on his stout-hearted chest showed that he had won the Queen's and King's Medal with seven clasps, for the Boer campaign; and for acts of bravado in the Great War in Europe he had been awarded the Distinguished Service Order, the Military Cross, the Médaille Militaire, and the Croix de Guerre. As always, Fritz did things in a big way. Dissatisfied with the standard size of these decorations, he had a tailor make each ribbon a quarter of an inch wide, bigger than stipulated by army regulations.[20] Topping off this splendid picture of military grandeur were four brazenly displayed gold wound stripes.

Swinging his swagger stick, Captain Claude Stoughton strutted down to the Pond Lyceum Bureau in suite 6056 at 1 Madison Avenue in the sprawling Metropolitan Life Insurance Building.

The bureau had been founded in 1874 by Civil War hero Major James B. Pond of the Union Army. Pond became the foremost "manager of leading American and foreign lecturers," including among his clients some of the most famous people in the world.[21] It was not unusual to see him squiring about town on their speaking tours such luminaries as P. T. Barnum, Samuel L. Clemens, Arthur Conan Doyle, Susan B. Anthony, Booker T. Washington, Rudyard Kipling, poet Paul Laurence Dunbar, African explorer Henry M. Stanley, North Pole seeker Robert E. Peary, and even African hunter Fritz Duquesne. The major had been dead since 1903, but the Lyceum continued under the management of his son, James "Bim" Pond. In later years Bim would manage the tours of Admiral Richard E. Byrd, Helen Keller, Captain Eddie Rickenbacker, John Masefield, W. B. Yeats, and many others. It was still a first-class operation.

From Fritz's point of view Bim's booking skills were ideal. He had already handled the lecture tours of visiting war heroes, among them Dugmore and Hay. But in 1917 no one at the Pond Lyceum Bureau had ever seen anyone quite like the dazzling Captain Claude Stoughton. He took them by storm. And to the delight of everyone, the brave captain possessed a theatrically resonant voice enhanced by a charming clipped English accent, matched only by his own captivating charm and gentlemanly yet military manner.

Wouldn't Bim Pond have recognized Captain Claude as Captain Fritz? Perhaps not. Bim had been between twelve and fifteen years old during the halcyon time of Fritz's African lecture days (1902 to 1905). On the other hand, there may have been collusion between Bim and his father's old friend. In a 1959 letter to Fritz's friend, Lillian Linding, Pond wrote, "When he posed as Capt. Claude Stoughton he wore the ribbon of the Victoria Cross! Nothing but the best for our Fritz!"[22] (The passage of forty-two years had either dimmed or enhanced Bim's memory. The V.C. was not part of Fritz's uniform.)

So was young Bim, only twenty-seven years old in 1917, aware of the masquerade? Whatever the answer, Bim whisked Captain Stoughton down to the photo studio of Clarence E. Hall at 1485 Broadway, just off Times Square, where the captain's grandeur was captured on film for display on the front page of the brochure to be distributed to his audiences.

The biography Fritz created for the mythical Captain Claude Stoughton was as splendid as the figure he presented to his public.[23] Showing no pretensions to British reserve, the Pond Lyceum program proclaimed that

Captain Stoughton has perhaps seen more of the war than any man at present before the public. He wears ribbons showing that he has received five medals: two of these the King's and Queen's for service in the Boer War, carrying seven clasps; one is for service in the Natal, and two for bravery in saving lives. A sixth French medal, for which he has been cited, is yet to be awarded. At the outbreak of the Boer War, Captain, then Lieutenant Stoughton, was an officer in one of Australia's crack horse regiments, the Mounted Rifles. He went with his regiment to Africa, and served in Cape Colony, Orange Free State, Transvaal, Natal and Basuto Land. He was with Kitchener at the Battle of Paardeburg when General Cronje was captured; was with Lord Roberts at the Capture of Bloemfontein; at the fall of Johannesburg and the seizure of Pretoria. Later, in pursuit of De Wet's army, he was attached to General Knox's flying column as intelligence officer and commandeering officer for the Australian Bushmen. He later entered the Cape forces and took active part in the clearing up of Basuto Land, and in the last Natal insurrection he fought with the Natal forces.

Fritz, masquerading as Captain Claude Stoughton of the West Australia Light-horse, sold Library Bonds for the Allies in New York City. (Author's collection)

The brochure went on to outline the bold heroics of this soldier who appeared to be everywhere at once overseas, who never missed a major battle, and who miraculously survived every engagement despite horrific wounds. He fought in New Guinea, Flanders, the Somme, and Arras—illustrated by motion pictures—and participated in the ill-fated invasion of Gallipoli. He was four times gassed, three times bayonetted, and once pronged by a German trench hook.

And those were only the highlights of a brilliant military career that, the public was assured, had finally brought him face to face with the most fearless lecture audience in the world: that of the United States! Stoughton, the brochure proclaimed, would be pleased to lecture on the story of the Anzacs or on underground warfare—or on "German Spy Methods," of which he had learned much in Egypt. Fritz was audacious indeed. One of the subtopics in Captain Stoughton's lecture on German spy methods was "Germany pays nothing for its spying on us. We pay it all. How long will we stand for it?" Evidently for as long as Captain Claude Stoughton would lecture American audiences about it.

So it was "Captain Claude Stoughton, at your service!" And he took America by storm. Bim Pond gave Captain Stoughton the full treatment befitting a visiting war hero who could provide inspiration on the home front to a country at war for only seven months. Fritz was set up at the McAlpin Hotel and later the Astor House, where he ran the greatest risk of exposure in his charade when he met the Right Honorable George H. Reid, formerly high commissioner of Australia, premier of the Australian Commonwealth, premier of New South Wales, high commissioner in London, and member of the British Parliament, and now a client of the Pond Lyceum Bureau.[24] Reputed to be the greatest living British orator, Reid was on a visit to New York giving addresses at Carnegie Hall in support of America's participation in the war. "What American Independence Has Done for the British Empire" was the subject of one speech. Fritz was an instant hit with him. At the Ritz-Carlton Hotel headquarters of the British Propaganda Mission and at cocktail parties, Fritz also met a number of British army officers who had no idea they were wining and dining and swapping war stories with a consummate fraud.

What was even more remarkable and audacious was that there was no such unit as the West Australia Lighthorse! Which means, of course, that brave Captain Stoughton could not have participated in the Boer battles, nor at Gallipoli, nor in the slaughter of Flanders

Fields, the Somme, or Arras. If Sir George or the British military in New York City had been more cognizant of what was happening on the Western Front, there would have been no more playacting for Fritz Duquesne.

Nevertheless, Captain Claude Stoughton had arrived on the scene just in time for the Second Liberty Loan drive during October 1917. He did his bit by whipping up the patriotic passion of citizens whose purchase of Liberty Bonds contributed to the total of $3,807,891,900 raised nationwide that month. He also made speeches raising funds for the Red Cross. It will never be known how sincere Fritz was when, like Creel's "stentorian guard," he trumpeted such slogans of the drive as "We must have dollars as well as men in the fight for freedom" or "Every bond you buy helps win the war." But as long as hero worshippers would gather to listen, and as long as the tea party invitations— and, more important, the checks from Pond—kept coming, Fritz would keep talking. He was so successful and in such demand that he continued making lecture appearances through the month of November. Pond began making plans to send him on a nationwide tour, even though Fritz was beginning to lose his voice.

A highlight of Captain Stoughton's appearances in New York was the evening of 26 November at the McAlpin Hotel, where his talk was well received by members of the popular Twilight Club, which had moved from its usual meeting place in the Colonial Dining Room at the St. Denis Hotel to the more spacious McAlpin for the occasion.[25] Ironically, the McAlpin was a favorite watering hole for the German Secret Service.[26] Von Rintelen, a noted German spy, often dined there. The attraction of the hotel for the Germans may have been the authentic rathskeller in the basement with its high vaulted ceilings.

The Twilight Club was a dining and discussion society that welcomed speakers of any political persuasion to expound on whatever topic they chose except party politics. The club considered itself an "organization for discussion of current questions of importance." Any guest could "say his say freely on any topic presented for discussion," which explained why regular speakers ranged from Russian anarchists to members of the Salvation Army to the agnostic Robert Ingersoll. Fritz was right at home. With his fine voice spieling pure hokum, Captain Claude Stoughton was a sensation.

It is difficult to explain the paradox of Fritz Duquesne at this time. Although an admitted enemy of England, he certainly wasn't in a position to hurt Britain's war effort or America's in his guise as Stoughton. On the contrary, he was helping both countries by stimulating the sale of Liberty Bonds and raising money for the Red Cross, whose help was extended to all the Allies.

Did Fritz intend to make contact with imperial Germany's espionage organization in the United States? Not very likely. The well-financed and well-organized network of spies and saboteurs had practically ceased to exist when President Wilson broke off diplomatic relations with Germany in February and Count Johann Heinrich von Bernstorff was sent packing to the kaiser. The German ambassador extraordinary and plenipotentiary to the United States of America and Mexico, von Bernstorff had been using his diplomatic immunity to hide his role as the kaiser's chief of espionage and sabotage in the Western Hemisphere.

Bernstorff's chief aides and partners in his diplomatic duplicity, military attaché Captain Franz von Papen and naval attaché Captain Karl Boy-Ed, had been recalled to Germany in December 1915 for their suspected involvement in espionage and sabotage. Even the flamboyant Franz von Rintelen, the spy who romantically tagged himself the Dark Invader, had been under wraps since August 1915, when he was arrested in England on his way back to Germany from New York. Mexico City was now the base of operations for Germany's espionage activities.

When Fritz was on trial in 1941 for espionage in the interests of Nazi Germany, U.S. prosecuting attorney Harold M. Kennedy reminded him of his lecture series and asked, "Were you at the time going around the country representing yourself as Captain Claude Stoughton of the Australian military forces?" Fritz admitted that he had done so, and that the masquerade had been for theatrical purposes, adding, "I made the speeches to pep up American defense workers and to help along American publicity."[27]

Despite that admission twenty-four years later, and even though his activities as Captain Claude Stoughton were aiding the Allies, it cannot be assumed that Fritz Duquesne had suddenly turned patriotic toward his adopted country. Nor can it be assumed that his hatred of England had ceased. But it can be assumed that his vanity was being fed by the attention and adulation he was receiving. Once again he must have been reveling in the pulse-beating excitement of living on the edge, where he had been teetering all his life. And it can definitely be assumed that he had found a solution, however temporary, to the old Fritz Duquesne dilemma: no money. The Pond Lyceum Bureau was paying him handsomely. But for Fritz, "handsomely" was never enough. His attempt to get more money through the insurance claims, capped by the indignant protestations of a patriotic New York woman, would prove to be his undoing, and he would soon totter over that edge.

CHAPTER 12

Fraud and the Bomb Squad

"I NOTICED THAT THE captain's mustaches trained upward in imitation of the well known style affected by the German emperor. I think it must have been that mustache that first aroused my suspicion."[1] So went the story Mrs. Katherine Ferguson told federal agents a few days after meeting the resplendent Captain Claude Stoughton at a social gathering on Riverside Drive. Mrs. Ferguson was a widow living on the drive near 139th Street with her son Mortimer. Because her young son was in the army's officer training program at Camp Dix awaiting orders to go overseas, she was feeling particularly patriotic and affronted by the mustaches. Stoughton expressed a special interest in her son. He wanted to know more about his activities and even said he would like to motor with Mrs. Ferguson to Camp Dix and meet the young officer.

Thus began the unmasking of Captain Claude Stoughton. Fritz could only blame his flowing mustaches, which most likely he had indeed unwittingly fashioned after the hirsute embellishment of Wilhelm II.

Mrs. Ferguson discovered that Captain Stoughton was unusually clever and amiable, and a wonderful storyteller. "He related some marvelous stories about his adventures in the Boer War and as an explorer and hunter in Africa," she reported. "But his uniform and his general manner made me somewhat ashamed of the occasional thought that he should wear different mustaches, especially since he wore wound stripes on his arm and he told me he had been gassed and wounded by bullets."

Mrs. Ferguson had occasion to talk with Claude/Fritz several more times at parties to which both she and the popular captain were invited. Young Mortimer accompanied his mother one time and had a long conversation with the captain, who greatly impressed him. "I think Captain Stoughton should come to Camp Dix and talk to the soldiers," Mortimer told his mother. "It would give them a chance to benefit from his own remarkable experiences."

But before the heroic captain could visit the military encampment, and perhaps spy on the U.S. Army, Mrs. Ferguson's suspicions were aroused at another gathering. "He was by no means thoroughly in sympathy with the cause of the Allies," she told federal authorities. "It was about the time of the great Piave drive in Italy. The Italians had been driven back and the Austrians' temporary success was the general topic at dinner that evening." (The Austro-German attack at Caporetto shattered the Italian Second Army on 24 October of that year, 1917, and drove the Third and Fourth Armies to the Piave River by early November, resulting in a disastrous defeat for Italy.) "When I mentioned to Captain Stoughton that I thought this was terrible, he looked at me oddly and said: 'The damned wops! They are not fit to clean one's boots.'"

Taken aback by this statement, Mrs. Ferguson attributed it to the fact that the normally abstemious captain had taken a glass of wine at dinner. Now suspicious, the former admirer of the captain noted that his mustaches "seemed to be standing up more pugnaciously than before." She told herself that no man could use that kind of language and wear that style of mustaches and be wholly loyal to the Allied cause. Determined to draw him out, Mrs. Ferguson led the captain off alone to another room, where the punch bowl was. Plying him with what must have been a lethal beverage, she brought up the Italians' defeat again but this time showed them less sympathy. She was rewarded with the energetic response, "We will drive them off the face of the earth."

The *we* convinced Mrs. Ferguson that she had before her a man who wanted not only the Italians but also the English and Americans driven "off the face of the earth." Not satisfied that she had already condemned and convicted the valorous Australian captain, Mrs. Ferguson forged on in her discourse to the federal agents: "My blood was up and even though I'm not a spy nor a detective, I told him that Mortimer had been to the Mexican border and that was bad enough." (Mrs. Ferguson was evidently referring to the 1916–17 U.S. Army "punitive expedition" into Mexico led by General John J. Pershing against Pancho Villa's rebel soldiers for their attack on the New Mexico border town of Columbus. Her son must have been an enlisted man with Pershing's troops.) "I was willing to go far to place this man in the toils. In order to test him I added that I thought it terrible that my son would now have to go abroad and probably be slaughtered.

"He looked at me in a new way," she recalled, and he said, "And that is all that it is, Mrs. Ferguson. It is nothing but a slaughter."

The now irate widow, who kept her true feelings under admirable control, continued pouring punch for Captain Claude, telling him she understood and that her sympathies were with him. "Sympathies are not needed by the enemies of the Allies," he sneered.

A Victrola started at that moment, breaking the tense moment, and the captain smiled complacently again, particularly when his punch pourer said, "I really believe the Germans will win the war."

"There is not a doubt of it," he answered quickly.

"That convinced me I was talking to a German sympathizer," continued Mrs. Ferguson, "so I began speaking more and more openly in favor of the Germans. His replies left no doubt as to where the loyalties of the supposed Australian captain stood."

In fact the conversation became so openly pro-German that Mrs. Ferguson became nervous, fearing that she had gone too far and that someone might overhear and believe she herself was pro-German. She asked the captain to speak in a less excited tone.

A very concerned Mrs. Ferguson notified an unresponsive police department the next day about her experience. Frustrated, she then got in touch with federal authorities and was rewarded by a visit from an agent. Her story resulted in a visit from another agent who showed her a number of photographs of wanted suspects, among whom was the man they believed to be posing as Captain Claude Stoughton.

She immediately picked out Fritz Duquesne. The agent informed her that she had run across one of the boldest and best known of alleged German spies on whose trail the government had been for some time.

Doubts began to surface elsewhere regarding the authenticity of Captain Claude Stoughton.

The Merchants Association of New York began checking the captain's military record, having learned that he had failed to register with British authorities upon his "arrival" in New York. However, doubts and unanswered questions did not lessen the popularity of the magnetic officer. Captain Claude made light of whatever did not appear to have a plausible explanation regarding his battlefield accomplishments. His unfailing supply of arguments and seeming credibility left interrogators benumbed and puzzled but apparently satisfied.

Nevertheless, the Right Honorable George H. Reid, the former high commissioner of Australia, became less sure of the genuineness of his supposed countryman, the hero he had welcomed so warmly. Swayed by the rumors he heard, he began spreading his own.

Much to the consternation of Sir George, Captain Stoughton was engaged to speak at a luncheon in his honor.[2] Sir George came to the luncheon not expecting to see the captain, since gossip about the war hero was becoming more prevalent. Sir George was surprised indeed when Stoughton appeared shortly before the luncheon was to begin. With admirable panache the captain walked directly to Sir George and reproached him for making remarks that aroused suspicion not only as to his identity but also as to his patriotic purpose. Taken aback somewhat, the legitimate Australian had nothing to say and watched silently as Captain Claude turned and walked casually to the bar and spoke to several acquaintances. His speech at the luncheon received the usual thunderous applause. Only Sir George sat silent, wondering.

Meanwhile, more than a year had passed since Alice Duquesne had filed the false claim with the insurance companies for $33,000 worth of "statuary" destroyed in the Brooklyn warehouse factory and $80,000 for the film that went down with the *Tennyson*. The Mannheim and Stuyvesant insurance companies were still doggedly pursuing the elusive phantoms George Fordham and Frederick Fredericks, whom they believed to be the equally elusive Fritz Duquesne.

Some months earlier Frederick T. Case, an attorney and counselor at law at 80 Maiden Lane in Manhattan, who may have been acting for the two insurance companies, had started looking for answers regarding the mercurial Fritz. On 9 August 1917 he wrote Theodore Roosevelt, the retired twenty-sixth president, at Sagamore Hill on Oyster Bay:[3]

I am endeavoring to make some investigation regarding a gentleman known as Captain Fritz Joubert Du Quesne. The newspapers state that he went to South America in 1913 with a moving picture outfit to follow in the footsteps of your explorations in that region, making moving pictures as he went.

The newspapers after recounting his most thrilling early adventures, state that he was a "Bull-mooser and intimate friend of Theodore Roosevelt."

I imagine much of the newspaper articles about this gentleman were for advertising purposes and that the writers did not feel themselves very closely confined but felt free to use their imagination to a considerable extent. However, if this gentleman happened to be well known to you, perhaps you will be willing to give me some information as to his operations in following your footsteps in South America, and perhaps you can advise me of people in this country who may have known the captain. Any information or assistance that you can give me in this regard will be very greatly appreciated.

Teddy's answer the next day was brief and evasive: "I don't remember even to have heard the name of the gentleman of whom you write." Twenty-four years later this negative response would be used against Fritz in his trial on charges of espionage.

Undaunted by the reply, Case wrote Roosevelt again on 17 August at his *Metropolitan Magazine* office at 432 Fourth Avenue.[4] He pointed out that since his first letter of inquiry he had learned more about "the gentleman" from other sources who could vouch for the acquaintance between him and the former president. He recounted Duquesne's escape as a POW from Bermuda aboard the *Margaret,* his newspaper career with the *Sun,* his lectures on big-game hunting in Africa, the magazine articles he wrote about Roosevelt's African trip, and his campaigning in an automobile during Roosevelt's bid for the presidency in 1912. Case concluded, "It occurs to me that these further details may recall this gentleman to your mind. If it is not too much trouble I would very much appreciate your advising me in regard to him if it should happen that you recall him with these further details before you." There was no reply.

Roosevelt may have determined that the best defense was no further denial. There was too much corroborating evidence proving that the two men had met—at least twice, and maybe three times. However briefly, Roosevelt had met Fritz in May 1908 at the governor's conference on conservation in Washington. He had met him again at the White House on 24 January 1909, when he sought advice from Fritz on his forthcoming African safari. And he must have been aware that Fritz had participated in his 1912 presidential campaign, driving one of two motor vans throughout New York State distributing literature and giving speeches for the Bull Moose standard-bearer.

But it was a critical time for Roosevelt. His three sons were in the military fighting a war he had vigorously urged America to enter, accusing President Wilson of being what modern America would call a "wimp." No, he may have thought, it wouldn't be good to have it known that the Spanish-American War hero and America's symbol of patriotism had associations, however brief and distant, with a traitor and German spy.

So the weeks went by, and Fritz still enjoyed his celebrity despite the shadow of doubt he was creating. Once again he was living on the edge, sustained by his arrogance and, of course, by the steady income of lecture fees. But the stalwart captain was nearing the end of his rope, and the noose was being drawn taut from four different sources: the federal authorities, tipped off by the patriotic Mrs. Ferguson; the pursuing Mannheim and Stuyvesant insurance companies; chief fire marshal Thomas P. Brophy, a master of his craft, intent on capturing the arsonist who had destroyed the Brooklyn warehouse in 1916; and the notorious Bomb Squad, headed by the tough, persistent, and no-nonsense Inspector Thomas J. Tunney of the New York City Police Department.

Brophy had been a reporter for the *Brooklyn Eagle,* the *New York Times,* the *World,* and the *Herald* before joining the New York Fire Department's Bureau of Fire Investigation as a deputy fire marshal, becoming its chief in 1915.[5] Because of his reportorial training and natural curiosity, the forty-year-old chief investigated most arson-suspected major fires himself. The federal government and the fire departments of other cities often requested his aid, and he was credited with investigating more fires, resulting in more arrests and convictions of arsonists and pyromaniacs, than any other city's fire chief. The year before, he had investigated the disastrous explosion caused by German saboteurs at Black Tom, the huge munitions supply terminal on the New Jersey side of New York Harbor in the shadow of the Statue of Liberty.[6]

Tunney was forty-four years old, a large man with a big brush mustache who ran the Bomb Squad his way. He had joined the NYPD in 1897 at the age of twenty-four and seventeen years later was a captain whose specialty was bomb explosions.[7] He was considered so expert that he was named by police commissioner Arthur Woods to command the Bomb Squad organized by Woods shortly before war broke out in Europe in 1914. The duties of the squad were exactly what its name would suggest. It sought out and destroyed bombs placed by members of the Black Hand Society and radical extremists, generally leftists, who created havoc with explosive devices in order to achieve their political and social goals.

When America's entry into the European war seemed imminent, the squad's name was changed to the Bomb and Neutrality Squad. In his 1919 autobiography *Throttled*, Tunney described this small group of dedicated men as "vigilant guardians of the neutrality of our country."[8] Woods transferred the entire unit to the army's Military Intelligence Division in December 1917, and until June 1919 the squad was under the orders of Secretary of War Newton D. Baker. Tunney was made a federal commissioner.[9]

Tunney was under the supervision of Lieutenant Colonel Nicholas Biddle, a former special deputy police commissioner who had been placed in charge of the MID.[10] In civilian life Biddle was a bank director and trustee of the Astor estate. After the war he was general manager of the properties of Vincent Astor and his millions of dollars. (In a neat twist of irony, in 1921 Biddle negotiated a transaction in which his close friend Astor took over the Hotel Knickerbocker and converted the hostelry into the Knickerbocker Building for offices and stores. It was in that same building that Fritz Duquesne experienced his final downfall twenty years later.)

The members of the squad performed their new duties admirably. They were not timid about trampling on the civil rights of suspected anarchists and German agents. It would not be unfair to say that an arrest was often helped along by entrapment. One of Tunney's most celebrated arrests was that of five Russian Jewish anarchists—Jacob Abrams, Mollie Steimer, Hyman Lachowsky, Samuel Lipman, and Jacob Schwartz—for violation of the 1918 Sedition Act (they had distributed two leaflets objecting to America's objection to the Russian Revolution).

The squad was also involved in the June 1917 arrest by U.S. marshals of the anarchists Emma Goldman and her former lover, Alexander Berkman. Newspapers did not mention the squad's participation, but Goldman later reported that the car in which she was riding with the arresting marshals was "followed by officers of the Bomb Squad."[11]

The quarry of these law agencies was finally targeted one night in early December when Tunney dispatched Sergeant Thomas J. Ford and Detective Thomas J. Cavanagh of the Bomb Squad to arrest Captain Claude Stoughton—who they suspected was Fritz Duquesne, Frederick Fredericks, and George Fordham—at the apartment he shared with explorer Horace Ashton on 175th Street. (Sergeant Ford became Inspector Javert to Duquesne's Jean Valjean, an implacable hunter who fifteen years later was delighted to arrest Fritz in another sensational fashion.)

The Bomb Squaders had tracked Stoughton down from information given them by Bim Pond when they visited his office seeking the whereabouts of the bold captain. It was only then, Pond always claimed, that he learned his star lecturer was none other than Captain Fritz Duquesne, the internationally famous spy and, incidentally, a former lecturer on African big-game hunting for Bim's father.[12]

But the intrepid detectives did not find Fritz. Ashton informed them that Fritz was in Pittsburgh selling Liberty Bonds and was expected back Friday evening, 7 December. Ashton couldn't understand the fuss. Fritz was "all right," he said, working for the J. G. White Engineering company. He professed no knowledge of Duquesne's masquerade as the Australian officer.

Nevertheless, and no doubt without benefit of a search warrant, Sergeant Ford and Detective Cavanagh rummaged through the apartment and found enough evidence to justify a decision to return Friday and arrest the alleged fraud. Fritz was an arrogant prisoner of his own ego and could never discard the impedimenta memorializing what he was: a monumental poseur. He collected and treasured the clippings, photographs, and documents that any other professional whose career was spying would have either disposed of or never collected. (He would make the same mistake again twenty-four years later when he eagerly and unsuspectingly showed his scrapbooks of derring-do to the FBI agent who had him under surveillance.) Ford and Cavanagh found a bewildering array of circumstantial evidence that, if nothing else, provided them with a choice of charges on which to arrest Fritz. Hardly damaging but certainly interesting was the detailed copy of his application for employment at the J. G. White Engineering company.

Impressed by the military exploits described, the Bomb Squaders asked Ashton if he knew anything about Duquesne. "Captain Fritz Duquesne," said Ashton, careful to give Fritz the military title he insisted upon, "was the leading scout for the Boers in their war against the British."[13] He also was careful, from either admiration or friendship, to make it clear that Fritz was *the* leading scout, not just *a* scout.

Of particular interest to the police officers were a number of photographs, one of which showed Fritz as a POW in Bermuda with shackles on his ankles and, as described by Tunney, a "martyred expression on his face." Other photos showed him hunting in Africa, and several depicted him in uniforms of different nations. The assumption, Tunney reported, was that "he might be another of the nervy little band of counterfeit officers which had done all its fighting in the restaurants and sympathetic check-books of New York during the war."[14]

They also found one of Fritz's prewar Pond Lyceum Bureau programs touting his African lecture tours. Ford and Cavanagh were sure they had their man when they discovered one of the West Australia Lighthorse uniforms worn, it was assumed, by the celebrated Captain Claude Stoughton. Ford and Cavanagh then uncovered a mass of newspaper clippings from the United States, England, and South America describing almost every bomb explosion aboard ships since the war began. The largest number of stories described the sinking of the steamship *Tennyson*. The two most damaging items found were a *Tennyson* shipping invoice and the letter of commendation to Fritz Duquesne from the Austrian imperial vice-consul in Managua. (The *Tennyson*, of course, was the one ship sinking that could be positively linked to Fritz and was the reason why he was back in New York.) Attached to the letter was a conventional-sized business card inscribed, "Imperial Captain Upon Service, Carl Uebersezig, Imperial Austrian Vice consul, Managua, Nic." As far as Ford and Cavanagh were concerned, the case against Captain Fritz Duquesne was now cinched. They looked forward indeed to Friday and the return of their quarry.

When Fritz returned to the apartment from Pittsburgh and another successful lecture tour that Friday, he was surprised to meet the two officers but accepted his arrest quietly, as he always had and always would in the future (except for one small show of anger in 1932, in the aforementioned roust by Ford). But for now he would accept the inconvenience. He could escape later. He always did.

For lack of a better complaint, Ford and Cavanagh arrested Fritz on the charge of "unlawfully masquerading in the uniform of one of America's allies."[15] A more formal complaint could be made later.

Fritz may have looked at the Tombs prison at 101 Centre Street with some dismay, realizing that it would not be easy to escape from that gloomy pile of stone resembling a medieval fortress with its turrets and high-pitched roof. Named for the former prison on the site, which was often described as an Egyptian tomb, the somber structure housed the Criminal Courts Building and the prison facility itself, connected by the celebrated Bridge of Sighs. It was at the booking sergeant's desk in the Tombs that Fritz met Lieutenant Colonel Norman Thwaites of the British army, who also had a colorful career.[16] Under other circumstances the two might have found much in common.

At forty-five, Thwaites was four years older than Fritz. Born in England, he was raised in Germany. He was a traveling actor in his youth and served with the British army in the South African Light Horse during the Boer War, which surely would have nettled Fritz. After the war, and for ten years, he was secretary and traveling companion to Joseph Pulitzer, publisher of the *World* at the same time Fritz was writing big-game hunting articles for the paper. After Pulitzer's death in 1911 Thwaites represented the *World* in most of Europe's capitals. He served in the British army again with the Fourth Royal Irish Dragoon Guards during the Great War and was severely wounded at Messines.[17]

While recovering from his wounds at King Edward's Hospital in London, Thwaites was asked by Sir William Wiseman to work with him in New York City. Thwaites wrote in his 1932 memoir, *Velvet and Vinegar,* that he was asked to "undertake a mission to the United States and to organize an intelligence branch in New York."[18] But Sir William, a war hero who had been gassed in Flanders, had been chief since December 1915 of the British Secret Intelligence Service (MI6) in the United States.[19] Wiseman's important role was providing the English government with precise information from the highest levels in American government. A similar role was played by Sir William Stephenson, the man called Intrepid during World War II.

Wiseman was responsible for Somerset Maugham's brief career as a spy when he sent the author to Russia in mid-1917 to report on the progress of the Russian Revolution prior to the Bolshevik October coup. After the war Wiseman stayed on in New York as a partner in the banking house of Kuhn, Loeb, and Company. Back in British service again during World War II, he briefed Intrepid on his difficult position. A personal assistant to Wiseman for a short time was a young intelligence officer named Ian Fleming.

Sir William's MI6 cover was that he was a member of the American and Transport Department of the Ministry of Munitions (more simply, it was a commission responsible for purchasing munitions).[20] But as senior of the chiefs of British intelligence services operating in America, he was the communications link between British Prime

Minister David Lloyd George and President Woodrow Wilson and his close adviser, Colonel Edward M. House. Thus he was the liaison offic er between the British and American war cabinets. Quite clearly, Sir William was no slouch. Surely Thwaites was proud of this "special mission," which was accompanied by a promotion to lieutenant colonel and the title of provost-marshal of New York City.[21]

The "special mission" of the two intelligence agents was to nudge fence-straddling America into the war. The English had also fallen prey to the wave of anti-German hysteria sweeping America. They were concerned—needlessly so, as time would show—that if the United States joined the war on the side of Britain, millions of German Americans would launch a sabotage campaign to destroy the war effort. Britain's two men in America were told to monitor the situation. The numerous Austrian, German, Irish, and Hindu groups plotting sabotage in America and sedition in the British Empire were a more serious threat. Sir William and Lieutenant Colonel Thwaites were certainly busy, which may explain why they overlooked the great game being played by Fritz.

Thwaites wrote:[22]

During my 12 months' service as Provost-Marshal, my office arrested no fewer than 199 delinquents for transgressions of various kinds. Most of these were impostors wearing uniforms or insignia, orders or decorations to which they were not entitled. By dint of hard lobbying we had succeeded in getting Congress to pass a law making this an offence: there having been no rule or regulation which enabled the police or other authorities to deal with such cases. When the law came into operation these frauds could be arrested and charged with impersonating an officer, or for wearing wrongfully the uniform of a friendly power. The penalty was six months' hard labour for such an offence, or a fine of $300, or both. For putting up unearned decorations the penalty was the same.[23]

Considering his position as provost-marshal and the fact that he was instrumental in having a U.S. law passed making it an offense to impersonate a military officer, it is puzzling that Thwaites was not aware of Duquesne's impersonation of an Australian officer at a time when other British in Manhattan were becoming suspicious. It is even more puzzling because Thwaites often worked closely with Inspector Tunney. Thwaites described the relationship between the two offices: "New York police headquarters in the Criminal Court building vied with the Provost-Marshal's Office in curbing the crooked activities of hotel beats, cheque manipulators and the nimble-witted confidence men who appeared to find the British uniform an open sesame to the generous hearts of New York citizens."[24] He also had high praise for Tunney: "This remarkable man was, in my opinion, worth at least a division of shock troops at the front in defeating the machinations of the enemy."[25] Nevertheless, it would seem that both offices were slow in their pursuit of this master impersonator among the "nimble-witted confidence men" then manipulating New Yorkers.

Thwaites recounted the story of his meeting with Fritz:[26]

One day I was asked to come round and have a look at a man calling himself Capt. Stoughton, of the Australian Horse. The police had received the tip that he was not a genuine article, and that he had been concerned in an explosion on board a British vessel which resulted in the death of several of the crew. They had decided to have a look at the fellow's papers. This inspection revealed that his real name was Fritz Joubert Ducain, that he had been born in South Africa, that he had never been in any Australian regiment, and if he had done any fighting it was not for the British but for their enemies. I must say Fritz was a fine figure of a man. . . .

Opinion among the police officers who had examined him was divided, several believing him to be all he claimed, and inclined to resent my prompt verdict that the man was a fraud. Fritz had made the mistake of trying to curry favour with the Sergeant at the desk, who was frankly anti-British, by telling him behind his hand that he had fought against the British in the South African Boer War.

"If this were so, (asks the Irish officer), how came it that the British had presented him with medals?"

Thwaites went on to tell how he asked Fritz in what brigade and division his Australian regiment had served. Fritz gave the wrong answers, particularly in mentioning a division that had not served at Gallipoli, where he claimed to have been wounded. Thwaites told the police to "lock the fellow up."

Fritz was held as a "secret prisoner" for a week before being brought before Judge Thomas C. T. Crain in General Sessions Court on 14 December 1917. Crain was one of the aristocratic "stalwarts" of Tammany Hall and in 1924 would be appointed by Governor Alfred E. Smith to the State Supreme Court.[27] In 1930 he would be elected district attorney of New York County.

The charge of masquerading as a British officer was set aside, and Fritz was specifically indicted on the charge of attempting one insurance fraud following a bomb explosion on a steamship in 1916 and another fraud following a later explosion in a Brooklyn warehouse.[28] His bail was set at $50,000—an exorbitant sum for the time—because of a suspected intimacy with the country's enemies. Fritz should have been proud. That was the total of the bail set for both Emma Goldman and Alex Berkman, considered America's foremost revolutionists and anarchists.

Fire marshal Brophy and district attorney Edward Swann testified that Duquesne had had a key and access to the room where the warehouse fire occurred, and that a man whom he had employed had since disappeared. Swann was another Tammany Hall man who was often under fire in his position as district attorney.[29] He was elected a judge of General Sessions in 1907, defeating former governor Charles S. Whitman—a future card-playing friend of Duquesne. The first anticocaine bill was drawn under his supervision, and he was instrumental in obtaining a federal antinarcotics law and a law against carrying guns in New York City. Swann became district attorney in 1916 and campaigned against vice, charity rackets, gambling, and stock swindling. He was often investigated for misconduct but always exonerated.

Fritz faced a formidable foe.

The heavy bail had been set by Judge Crain in response to the request of assistant district attorney Ryttenberg, who said at the arraignment, "The Neutrality Squad has informed the district attorney that it had information showing that the defendant was identified and connected with the enemies of this country and that if bail in a lesser sum were fixed, the defendant by reason of his connections would be able to obtain the bail and probably would not be within the jurisdiction of the court when wanted for trial."[30]

"Under $50,000 Bail as Nation's Enemy" headlined the New York Times about Fritz's latest predicament.[31]

Fritz knew he was in deep trouble—not because of the excessive bail, but because the sinking of the Tennyson had been named in the indictment, and British consul general Charles Clive Bayley had already begun legal procedures to have Duquesne extradited to England to stand trail on the charge of murder on the high seas for the sinking of the Tennyson. Fritz knew that once he was in England, it would be Cape Town all over again and death by a firing squad in the Tower of London. Only this time there would be no way out by revealing secret codes. He also knew there was no escape from the impregnable Tombs, a heap of gray granite in the heart of Manhattan. New York City was not Cape Castle or Bermuda.

But Fritz was already formulating a plan. It would lead to insanity and paralysis.

CHAPTER 13

Insanity and Paralysis

P ROCEEDINGS DRAGGED ON while Fritz languished in the Tombs. His was an interesting case containing legal peculiarities that generated lengthy discussions over the niceties of international law.

It was argued between lawyers of the British government and New York City and with Fritz's lawyer that he was a naturalized citizen of a country that had declared its neutrality in the overseas conflict, that he had planned the crime charged against him in Brazil, another neutral country, and that the crime itself had been committed in international waters on a British ship, but not with Fritz aboard. So who would get Fritz, and when?

The British hadn't quit their demands. It was April 1918, almost six months since Judge Crain had set bail at $50,000. The British were becoming more insistent. They wanted Fritz *now*. And Fritz knew that the Americans would soon weary of keeping him, and that he would be turned over to the hated English and the waiting noose or firing squad.

But he also knew that when a person's sanity was in question, he was usually immune from prosecution. The solution was simple: Fritz the actor became Fritz the lunatic.

The quiet, complacent, and even model prisoner in the Tombs suddenly became wild-eyed and uncontrollable. The neat, gentlemanly appearance was replaced by disheveled hair and clothes. The well-spoken person began babbling incoherent nonsense. Nevertheless, the British consul insisted on extradition. But the New York police and medical examiners would not be hurried.

Judge Crain set up a three-member lunacy commission that would meet for three days beginning on 2 May 1918 to determine Fritz's mental condition and to report on whether he was "in a state of idiocy, imbecility, lunacy or insanity so as to be incapable of understanding the proceeding or making a defense on the trial of said indictment now pending against him, and also as to his sanity at the time of the commission of the crime alleged."[1] The commission consisted of a doctor, a lawyer, and a layman who would call witnesses and thoroughly examine Fritz's past and present life history. He would be represented by counsel and the people by a member of the district attorney's staff. They would determine if Fritz's "hysterical insanity" was genuine. The chairman of the commission was city magistrate William A. Sweetser. The two other members were Drs. F. S. Haver and William J. Costa.

Testimony was heard from arresting officer Thomas Ford, chief fire marshal Brophy, and fire marshal Frank J. Prial. Offering their medical opinions were Dr. William Steinach, a psychiatrist and neurologist and assistant alienist at Bellevue Hospital, Psychopathic Ward; and Dr. Frank A. McGuire, visiting physician of the City Prison.

Also giving his opinion after observing Fritz was Dr. Perry Lichtenstein, resident physician of the City Prison. Lichtenstein was a psychiatrist and criminologist who had been with the prison since 1913. He held that post until 1931, when he was named medical assistant to the district attorney. Lichtenstein boasted that the door between his office and "the world's largest detention prison" stood open all the time. In a world of bars and bolts, his door didn't even have a lock. To the prisoners he was known as Doc.[2]

In attendance were assistant district attorneys Alexander Rorke and William J. A. Caffrey, on behalf of the people, and Robert P. Levis, attorney for the defendant. Levis may have formed an association with Fritz in 1912 when the two were staunch Bull Moose supporters of Theodore Roosevelt.[3]

Aware that this would have to be the best of all his playacting roles, Fritz broke loose from his guards on the first day of the three-day hearings and burst in on the commission as if charging the guns at Colenso.[4] Wild-eyed, hair and prison garb askew, he screamed over and over, "Bring up the guns! Bring up the guns! Bring up the guns!"

Then, as if in charge of a commando ready to attack, he turned and cautioned, "I want you men to watch the enemy—there—there—don't let them close on you!"

Before the guards could restrain him, Fritz threw himself at Sweetser, who almost fell off his chair in the suddenness of the attack. With the guard struggling to hold him, Fritz babbled, "I'll go right there behind the cannon." Suddenly whirling, horror etched into his face, he screamed, "The guns, damn you! Bring up the big ones!"

Then he rushed at Sweetser again. "I know you want me, need me. I'll be there when you want me—and I'll have the guns! I pledge my soul on it! We have terrible odds to fight against tonight!"

Detective Ford and his partners testified to the commission that they believed Duquesne was "so clever that he was no doubt feigning insanity." Their opinion, though correct, was probably based on professional cynicism regarding the criminal character and had no basis in science. They also testified that the evidence they had gathered from this paid German spy was "of such importance that while it would be divulged to the commissioners privately if desired, it was such that it would be unwise to place the same upon the record."[5]

This "important" evidence was not mentioned again, and its content is unlikely ever to be known. Nevertheless, this statement convinced the commission that the question of the defendant's sanity or insanity was one of utmost importance to the country at large.

Fritz appeared the first two days of the hearings.[6] But he absolutely refused to leave his cell at the Tombs afterward, forcing the commission to come to him for the last session on 4 May. His lunatic performance was consistent. At the hearings he never ceased babbling and gibbering. But once he decided to confine himself to his cell, Fritz changed his performance completely.[7] Now he refused to utter a word. He also made a show of groaning if he touched his thigh. The commission was convinced there was no feigning on his part.

Drs. Steinach and McGuire testified that in their opinion Duquesne was now insane and unable to consult with his attorney in preparation of his defense.[8] Fritz obviously had not lost any of his histrionic abilities. He was still the consummate actor.

He found a harsher theatrical critic in Dr. Lichtenstein, who was not fully convinced. His opinion was that Duquesne "developed prison psychosis some time previous to being sent to Bellevue Hospital for observation, that at the present time he has not fully recovered, but that a good portion of his conduct is put on." He concurred that at present the defendant was unable to consult rationally with his attorney.

Lichtenstein considered Fritz a malingerer and the cleverest simulator he had ever encountered among the five hundred thousand prisoners he boasted of having come in touch with during his eighteen years with City Prison.[9] He must have had high regard for Fritz. Experience had taught Lichtenstein that some malingerers are quite brilliant. With such persons it is extremely difficult to detect simulation. His opinion of Fritz was that he was a man of evident refinement and excellent education who had no other occupation than that of adventurer.

Lichtenstein could find no physical abnormalities and admitted that Fritz's manifestations did not fit any form of insanity he was familiar with. Once, while visiting his patients in the prison, Lichtenstein stood to the side of Fritz's cell on the tier while a guard was serving the prisoner his lunch.[10] Fritz suddenly bounded out of bed and demanded, "Give me an extra portion of bread." The doctor immediately swung into view. Without a word, Fritz retreated to his bed and to his silence. This convinced Lichtenstein of Fritz's sanity, and he so testified at the hearing. But to no avail.

The commission found that Fritz had been sane at the time he committed his alleged crime but was mentally incompetent at present. So on 6 May the Black Panther of the Veld was declared a lunatic and committed to Matteawan State Hospital for the Insane—now Fishkill Correctional Facility—in Beacon, eighty miles north of New York City. He must have been elated, having once again eluded the grasp of England's executioner. But it did not take long for Fritz to realize that even though his present situation offered him physical refuge, it would soon drive him mad. Bermuda and even Cape Castle must have appeared more inviting. He was in the company of imbeciles.

For five months Fritz endured the lunacies of deranged inmates. There was one who said he was not Napoleon but Napoleon's tomb. Another tapped his foot incessantly and puffed and whistled like a locomotive, claiming to be a steam engine.[11] It was more than Fritz could bear, even for a short time.

His scheming mind was never at rest. He had another plan. If it failed, better the noose than a straitjacket and rubber room. He demanded another hearing. Gone was the gibbering. Once again he was the suave, debonair, charming, and well-spoken man of the world. In an attempt to thwart England, Fritz pleaded guilty to an attempt to de-fraud the Stuyvesant Insurance Company.[12] Found guilty, he would only get a prison term, certainly a preferable alternative to execution. Unhesitatingly the commission declared him sane, and on 11 October he was returned to the Tombs.

But nothing had changed. The British still wanted Fritz. And this time it looked like they were going to get him. The United States was ready to give him up even though his sentencing on the fraud charge was set, ironically, for 11 November 1918. It would be Armistice Day. The war in Europe was over, but it didn't lessen the charge against Fritz for murder.

District attorney Swann notified Coudert Brothers, the internation-al legal firm representing the British embassy, that "in the event that the United States Commissioner . . . directs that the defendant . . . be extradited . . . this office . . . will waive all objections to the proposed extradition." Coudert Brothers replied that "the British Government would undertake, in the event either of failure to convict or of a sen-tence for less than life imprisonment, to return the defendant to the New York authorities."[13]

Fritz had gambled and lost. Still, the proceedings dragged on inter-minably. Then two women lawyers heard of his predicament while vis-iting one of their clients in the Tombs in December. They believed his story, and Fritz was suddenly overwhelmed with legal representation.[14] Through "pure feminine sympathy," Mary M. Lilly and Eve P. Radtke decided to help Fritz and offered their firm's services to Frederick A. Ware, then representing Fritz. Additionally they had the aid of another lawyer, Joseph A. Boccia, in the habeas corpus proceedings. Levis had evidently dropped the case.

"The man is apparently a bit eccentric, and the sufferings he has un-dergone in his various adventures may have affected his mind, but I cannot believe he is guilty of the crime [of which] he is accused, and we are going to try to save him," Mrs. Lilly told a *New York World* re-porter.[15] The same reporter wrote, "Duquesne is only 37. But his year's imprisonment in the Tombs, coming on top of a life of adventure, makes him look 50. He is in a pitiful physical condition and his once brilliant mentality appears to be at the lowest ebb."

Ware and his new associates firmly believed in Fritz's innocence of the charge of murder on the high seas and said they would vigorously oppose his deportation at a hearing set for 23 December before com-missioner Hitchcock.

It was about this time that Fritz last saw Alice. Having evidently had enough of Fritz's masquerades, she decided to divorce him after it became "obvious he had gone German."[16] Typically, Fritz turned the incident around and made himself the hero. In a 1939 letter to his cousin, François de Rancogne, he wrote:

Unfortunately, I have to tell you that Alice divorced me when I was a prisoner on the way to the firing squad. I didn't want to die while she was still my wife, because that way the British could have laid claim to the plantations in the West Indies that she would inherit, an enemy property. We shook hands through the prison bars and I never saw her again. She gave a very sporting appearance throughout all the trouble and did everything possible to delay my execution, which gave me the time I needed to plan an escape.[17]

According to Clement Wood, Alice married a Buffalo millionaire whom she met while selling clocks for a living at from $2,000 to $4,000 each.[18] The truth is that Alice married William Otto Carl Becker, a mechanic, on 17 November 1919 in Flint, Michigan.[19] They moved to Santa Ana, California, where they raised their son, Lyle Jocelyn. Alice died on 30 December 1965, at the age of eighty-one, in Laguna Beach, California.[20]

Mildred Wortley, Fritz's sister-in-law, and her husband also saw him for the last time while he was in prison. She said years later that he was his old charming self despite the fact that his legs were chained.[21] No wonder the lawyers believed his story. The Duquesne magic always worked.

Except in court. Fritz went before Judge Joseph F. Mulqueen in General Sessions Court charged with violating Section 1202 of the Penal Code: bilking an insurance company. The judge's reputation as a tough jurist was widely known.[22] Fritz, knowing that the British embassy's request for his deportation would take precedence over his conviction for fraud, had one last artful dodge: before Judge Mulqueen could pass sentence on the prisoner before the bar, he suddenly collapsed. Mulqueen ordered the courtroom cleared and called for a doctor, who examined Fritz and declared him paralyzed below the waist. The doctor ordered Fritz to be returned to his cell until an ambulance could take him to the prison ward of Bellevue Hospital. In the Tombs the warden and Dr. Lichtenstein warned the doctor that Fritz was not paralyzed, that he was a malingerer. But the doctor refused to listen and said emphatically, "There is no doubt that he is paralyzed."[23]

Fritz must have smiled triumphantly to himself. Maybe he couldn't escape from the impregnable Tombs. But a hospital? It might take a little time. But surely it would not be difficult for the man who had almost dug out of dreaded Cape Castle, who had escaped a Portuguese prison and then braved sharks and the Bromo Seltzer king to leave Bermuda behind. Fritz was patient. It was the first rule of the professional escaper.

He must still convince doubting doctors of his paralysis. Primitive, even medieval-torture methods were used to prove he was not disabled. Needles and pins were stuck into the muscles of his legs and inserted under his toenails. But to no avail. Not a muscle moved. There wasn't a single facial twinge. He couldn't possibly be shamming. The verdict was still paralysis. True or not, one of Fritz's claims was that he could control his body so as to avoid normal reactions.[24]

Fritz was carried on a stretcher to prison ward 26. Despite his supine position, he couldn't help but say defiantly, "I don't see why I should stay here long. There's nothing can keep me here." Jimmy Cagney couldn't have said it better—if he had been making movies then.

Fritz was assigned the last bed in the eighteen-bed ward next to a window on the west side looking out on First Avenue through three three-quarter-inch iron bars set three inches apart.[25] There would be no cruise to England, at least for a while. With no assurance that his stay would be permanent or that he would escape extradition to England, the master deceiver wasted no time in planning his next deception.

The paralytic asked that every day he be placed in a wheelchair next to the window, asserting that he wanted to study the birds lighting on the window sill.[26] When his eyeglasses were not returned, Fritz, no stranger to confinement, improvised. He pierced a piece of cardboard with two small holes, and by squinting through it he could magnify print.[27] And so the routine continued—day after day, week after week, and month after month. Fritz sat leaning on the window sill for hours, silently watching the birds, which soon began eating out of his hand. Or he squinted through his cardboard glasses, reading contentedly. During this time he never moved a muscle below the waist. He lost considerable weight. But despite the unappealing situation, the debonair Duquesne never lost what was an apparently inborn appeal. He was a favorite of all the nurses and interns and was never refused a request.

A sudden change came over Fritz when allowed to go to the bathroom, a ten-minute privilege given patient-prisoners only twice a day.

Alone and unobserved, he exercised and massaged his legs furiously to prevent muscle atrophy from lack of use.

A consistently strange behavior at night soon evoked no interest. He would pull a blanket over his head while sleeping, explaining to nurses that soldiers in the field did this as a protection against rats and insects.

Sitting by the window for great lengths of time and covering his head with a blanket at night were all part of an escape plan yet unformulated. Attendants soon became accustomed to the peculiarities of the paralysed prisoner in ward 26 and stopped asking questions.

Fritz's only—and frequent—visitor was faithful Lillian Spanuth, whom he had met in 1910 at the Thanhouser Film Company. It has been suggested that she was the one who supplied him with the means of his eventual escape: two small hacksaw blades. Years later, when asked by the author if this was true, she avoided giving a straight answer.[28] Another version was that a fellow prisoner, his time up, gave the blades to Fritz as a parting gift.[29] Everything changed for Fritz once he had the blades. To all appearances he was still the model prisoner. But now he had a purpose. Slowly, methodically, he began sawing at the iron bars of the window while hunched over the sill apparently watching and feeding the birds.

He was spurred to urgency on 19 May 1919, when he was wheeled into court to hear U.S. commissioner Hitchcock finally accede to the pleas of British Consul General Clive Bayley and approve the saboteur's extradition.[30] Fritz would be on his way to England as soon as a warrant of extradition was issued by Secretary of State Robert Lansing.

Mary Lilly, still defending Fritz, promised to carry the fight to the State Department.[31] "Captain Duquesne has been held on a chain of circumstantial evidence," Lilly told a *New York Sun* reporter. Hinting at duplicity on the part of Hitchcock, she continued: "Commissioner Hitchcock told me that his hearings were merely to determine whether there was evidence enough to justify the holding of the defendant for extradition. He permitted no defense," she said angrily. "And Captain Duquesne's American citizenship was of no value to him in a United States court." Commenting on Fritz's physical condition, the *Sun* reporter wrote, "Capt. Duquesne looked little the part of the adventurer in many lands. He has to be moved in a wheeled chair."

The old adventurer may not have looked the part, but he immediately began playing it once he was back in ward 26. Fritz resumed watching the birds and sawing at the window bars. He finally cut through two of the bars, enough to allow him to squeeze through the window on Monday, 26 May.[32] He made his escape shortly after midnight, following a final check by the police officer who passed through the ward every thirty minutes throughout the day and night. Fritz was just in time. Charles J. Murray, an orderly, had dropped off a bundle of clothes that evening and told him he would be leaving the next day: Lansing had signed the extradition papers.

When officer Charles D. Sands left after his midnight check, flashing his light down the aisle of beds, Fritz painfully and unsteadily got to his feet. The brief daily exercises hadn't been enough to restore all the strength in his legs. He pulled his clothes over the gaudy prison garb—pink striped pajamas—and arranged the bed to make it look occupied. The blanket was tucked over the pillow, of course—to keep out the rats and insects.

Fritz tiptoed to the window and noiselessly pulled loose the one bar sawn through at the top and the bottom.[33] The second bar was sawed through at the top and partly at the bottom. He forced it out at the top and pushed it aside, leaving an opening of about eight inches at the top and seven inches at the bottom. There was an opening of fourteen inches from top to bottom—an incredibly narrow space through which to squeeze. Fritz was thankful he had lost weight. Directly below his second-story window was a wooden ice shed. From the shed there stretched a thirty-foot open space bounded by a six-foot brick wall and beyond that a spiked wrought-iron fence about seven feet high. He would have to scale both obstacles to reach First Avenue and freedom. To the right of the open space was a boiler room. Unexpectedly, an engineer was sitting outside the open door of the room smoking a pipe. Fritz could only wait, hoping the man would finish his pipe and leave.

Too much time had passed. It was now 12:30 A.M. The guard returned at the far end of the ward. Fritz couldn't get back into bed, and he couldn't go through the window. He could only turn his back to the aisle of beds and hope the guard wouldn't see him pressed up against the wall in the illumination from the darting flashlight. He was in luck. The guard didn't walk the full length of the ward—confident, no doubt, because no one had ever escaped from the hospital prison. Fritz was in luck again. When he looked out the window, the engineer was gone.

Soaked with the sweat of fear, Fritz pushed up the outside sash, then heaved himself up onto the sill. He put his legs through the window first. Then, with great difficulty, he squeezed his torso through the tiny opening. Fritz had long ago made the decision not to tie several sheets together for his descent to the ground. He knew there wouldn't be time for this time-honored tradition of the escaping prisoner, even though subsequent news stories erroneously reported that this had been his means of escape.

Halfway through, the bottom sash suddenly dropped onto his shoulders, pinning him to the sill. It was Cape Castle all over again, a replay of the moment when he had been almost crushed by stones while attempting to escape. But Fritz was determined not to be caught this time. He tried hunching the sash up with his shoulders. The window wouldn't budge. Then one last agonizing effort, and the window shot up. He hung from the sill by both hands, then let go, hoping the slide down the brick facade would help break his fall to the roof of the ice shed six feet below. His weakened legs collapsed under the weight of his body. He struggled up quickly, slid down from the roof, and staggered the thirty feet to the brick wall. After repeated jumps, Fritz finally grasped the top of the barrier. He pulled himself up and over and suffered silently through the painful fall to the ground. Now for the iron fence. It wasn't easy. By clawing with his hands and gripping the vertical bars with his legs he finally managed to get to the top, ease carefully by the spikes, and drop to the ground. He was on First Avenue and free! Fritz had been right: nothing could keep him there. His getaway would not be discovered until 5:40 A.M.

Fritz stumbled and staggered on his way up East Twenty-seventh Street to Second Avenue until his rolling gait attracted the attention of a policeman who was sure he had nabbed a drunk.[34] "Prohibition's not for a month yet. Are you tryin' to drink it all up before then?" he asked Fritz. "I'll have to take you in." The officer grasped his arm and started walking him back to First Avenue, with Fritz trying to keep up on his jelly legs.

Fritz the actor began improvising. "It isn't what you think at all, officer. It's epilepsy. I have fits—epileptic fits. They don't know it at the office. I had to stay late and started walking home. And suddenly one of these fits came on. Smell my breath, officer. I haven't had a drink in months. Officer, you *can't* do this! If I'm put in jail and can't get to my job tomorrow I'll be fired. And my wife and four boys—"

"This is a case for the sarge" was the only reply. "Chronic intoxication, I'd call it."

Artist's fanciful rendering of Fritz's escape from the prison ward of Bellevue Hospital in May 1919. He did not use sheets. (Boston Sunday Herald, *31 August 1919; reprinted with permission of the Boston Herald)*

"Give me a chance. Give me a chance," pleaded Fritz. It became a monotonous litany as they headed back toward the hospital.

"Awright," the police officer finally said, moved at last by the entreaties. "I won't run you in. Maybe you ain't been drinkin.' But you certainly ain't fit to be on the streets. Whether it's chronic intoxication or fits, I know just the place for you. I'll even take you there. It's just around the corner. Bellevue Hospital. They'll treat you swell."

Incredulous, Fritz was led helplessly to the night entrance. But on the point of taking him through the doors, the officer yielded again to his pleas. "I'll give you one more chance. But don't ever let me catch you thrown' fits on my beat again."

The officer watched as Fritz teetered away. He made it to East Twenty-third Street, and for almost two miles he stumbled west, often falling, until he reached the Twenty-third Street Ferry to Hoboken. He extracted a secreted $50 bill that had been slipped to him by a friend while in the Tombs. It would provide transportation, food, and lodging until he could meet with friends.

From Hoboken Fritz took a train to Toms River on Barnegat Bay, where he stayed at a cheap boardinghouse. He spent three weeks regaining the use of his legs, soaking in the sun and saltwater. When he felt strong enough, Fritz returned to New York and then to Jamaica and Flushing, where, always on the run, he stayed with friends for only a few days at a time.

For the next thirteen years Fritz relied on other friends around the world to help him twit the New York police about his escape and evasion. Periodically cablegrams, telegrams, and postcards "signed Fritz" would be sent by these friends to the NYPD reminding them of his escape and daring them to "come and get me."[35]

His first challenge was actually a press release written in newspaper style and datelined Mexico City, 12 June 1919.[36] It was sent by messenger—thus no postage stamp—to an advertising-executive friend, Manley M. Gillam, at the Gillam Service, 110 West Thirty-fourth Street. (Gillam, a seventy-three-year-old noted advertising counsel, had witnessed Fritz's swearing in as a U.S. citizen in 1913.) The note explained that Fritz had escaped in a powerful Renault with the aid of his cousin, Major Count François de Rancogne (a recurring figure in Fritz's tales, sometimes a viscount, sometimes a marquis), and his brother (who disappears and reappears regularly, always with a different name), Captain Garnet Duquesne. The note went on to say that

Fritz had been offered a position as technical adviser to the Mexican government but that ill health prevented him from accepting.

Still a seeker of publicity, no matter the situation, narcissistic Fritz asked Gillam to type up the story and get it published. His final request: "Nota bene: As many papers as possible. Keep clippings."[37] After all, Fritz had to keep up his scrapbook.

Recalling Duquesne's announced death in Bolivia in 1916, Detectives Thomas Ford and Walter Cohane dismissed the letters as subterfuge.[38] "Duquesne is up to his old tricks," they said. "He's attempting to double-cross us in the hope that we'll give up the search for him about New York." Fritz's legal team of Lilly, Radtke, and Boccia expressed disappointed surprise at his flight. So did the friends who were paying his legal fees.

Meanwhile, on 31 May, Detective Division Circular No. 6 distributed by the Police Department of New York had announced that Frederick Joubert Duquesne—alias Captain Claude Stoughton, Frederick Fredericks, Piet Niacoud, Fritz Duquesne, and Fordham—had escaped from Bellevue Hospital's prison ward and was "WANTED FOR MURDER." The circular could have served as a work résumé for the elusive Fritz. One paragraph read, "Duquesne is of a roving disposition. He is a writer of stories, an orator and a newspaper reporter and may apply for a position as such. Is a good talker. Speaks Dutch, German, French and Spanish fluently."[39]

Fritz couldn't help but romanticize his escape. In future years he claimed that he had been aided by members of the Irish Republican Army and that he had recovered his health in a monastery.[40]

The truth is that Fritz never left the United States. Before returning to New York he spent a few years in Boston, where he thought he might start a new career in the movies with a financier named Joseph P. Kennedy.

CHAPTER 14

"A Prize Picaroon If There Ever Was One"

WHEN FRITZ DUQUESNE made his sensational escape from Bellevue Hospital, the world was between wars and looking forward to the promise of a new beginning. Woodrow Wilson was still president, to be succeeded in a few months by Warren G. Harding. Peace reigned. What was a professional spy to do?

Not much—except to make a new beginning himself. If Fritz brought any attention to himself, he would certainly be arrested and extradited to an England that had not forgiven his alleged war crime. So for the next thirteen years, a period in his life about which little is known, Fritz turned to legitimate work. He established himself in Boston and in a short time was running a modest advertising business in the Paté Frères building under the name of Frank de Trafford Craven.[1]

In 1926 Fritz became associated with a young financier whose great desire was to own a movie studio. He fulfilled that desire by purchasing the failing Film Booking Offices of America, Inc. The new movie mogul's name was Joseph P. Kennedy. Still using his pseudonym, Fritz moved to Manhattan and began working on the publicity staff of FBO, making the handsome sum of $150 a week.[2] Under Kennedy's aegis FBO soon became a viable organization again.

Not content with the success he made of FBO, particularly with the advent of sound motion pictures, Kennedy joined forces in 1928 with David Sarnoff, president of RCA, to purchase the Keith-Albee-Orpheum vaudeville circuit. The combination resulted in the creation of Radio-Keith-Orpheum. Fritz remained on RKO's publicity staff following the merger. When he was arrested by the FBI in 1941, he still possessed a number of shares of RKO stock, which he valued at $1,000 to $1,500.[3]

In 1930 Fritz went on the staff of the Quigley Publishing Company as an advertising writer and critic of vaudeville shows for the company's magazines, which included *Motion Picture Herald, Motion Picture Daily, Fame, Better Theatres,* and the *International Motion Picture Almanac.* He was then fifty-one years old.[4] Quigley was Martin Quigley, a former reporter who had covered the Bull Moose campaign and who began publishing his magazines in 1915. An originator of the Motion Picture Production Code, he was a powerful presence in the entertainment industry. His advice was often sought by established producers as well as by neophytes in the industry. Joseph Kennedy during his fledgling days as a studio owner also looked to Quigley for advice in his new venture.[5]

Fritz lived a quiet, elegant lifestyle in an apartment at 44 West Seventy-fifth Street in Manhattan, one block from Central Park. Typically, Fritz was well liked and highly regarded at the office. Polite and soft-spoken with the English accent he had never dropped, Fritz was completely accepted. Staff members noted his penchant for fine clothes and good food.[6]

As ever, Fritz could not help but attach a military title to his assumed name. He was Major Craven to the staff. He often wore a monocle and "toyed with a smart stick," according to office companions. "He wrote good copy and acted, in other respects, like the second son of an earl," said one.[7]

Quigley was captivated by Fritz's personality and background and considered him an absolutely enchanting entertainer. He often invited Fritz to his home at Greenwich Cove in Riverside, Connecticut, where Quigley Sr., his son Martin S. Quigley Jr., and Fritz cruised Long Island Sound in a thirty-five-foot Elco Cruisette power boat. The trio would have lunch aboard the Cruisette in some quiet harbor, then get home in time for dinner.[8]

Fritz would hold center stage during all this time, to his own delight and that of the Quigleys, father and son, regaling them with stories of his adventurous life. He explained in detail, and surely embellished, his methods of damaging and sinking ships during his war days as a saboteur in South America, which young Quigley wrote up for his Loyola High School semiannual paper.[9]

Fritz's run from the law lasted two days shy of thirteen years. It came to an end on 23 May 1932, shortly after noontime, when he was arrested in the Quigley offices on the fourteenth floor of the General Tire and Rubber Building at 1790 Broadway. The action, characters, and dialogue could have been a page right out of one of the pulp stories Fritz had once written for *Adventure* magazine.

Acting on what he later said was a "tip," Fritz's old nemesis, Detective Thomas Ford, posted himself in a hallway of the Quigley offices.[10] Backing him up were Detectives Charles Beakey and James Connolly and Acting Lieutenant James Pike, all of the Alien Squad—sometimes called the Radical Squad. Fritz, according to a *Sun* reporter, presently appeared, "attired like the lilies in spring." He was wearing a dark gray two-piece suit with a blue tie. His graying hair was neatly combed back in a pompadour.

Ford stepped forward, clapped his hand on the fugitive, and said dramatically, "Fritz, you're out of luck at last."

Continued the *Sun:*

The glass of fashion and mold of form—the Captain[, who] has lost none of his dapperness and jaunty effrontery in his past thirteen years as a fugitive, drew himself up haughtily and flung from his shoulder the detaining hand. Ford promptly slammed him in the jaw with a solid righthander and in the same motion pulled a gun. He was taking no chances with a man as dangerous as Fritz Duquesne.

"Now behave," said Ford, as Duquesne rubbed his jaw. "You are Captain Fritz Duquesne and a prize picaroon if there ever was one. You know me, and I know you. You know we have been after you for thirteen years on that British murder charge. You're done! Finished! Washed up!"

"I am not Duquesne," Fritz protested angrily. "There has been a complete mistake in identity."

Calvin W. Brown, vice president and general manager of the company, stormed into Quigley's office yelling, "The police are beating up Craven!"[11] The usually reserved Quigley Sr. sprang into action and stopped Ford from punching the bleeding Fritz again. A former police reporter, Quigley knew all the detectives and persuaded them to calm down.

Fritz, "attired like the lilies in spring," is arrested in New York City in 1932. (New York Sun, 24 May 1932)

Satisfied that they had their man despite Fritz's protestations of mistaken identity, the four detectives, now in a festive mood, were not taking any chances with the man who had escaped custody so often. With small .25-caliber pistols drawn,[12] they hustled the now disheveled Fritz downstairs, out to Broadway to the waiting police cars, and on to police headquarters at Grand and Centre Street.

A search of Fritz's office had turned up a copy of what must have been a surprise to the arresting officers: a book published in February by William Faro, *The Man Who Killed Kitchener,* a biography of none other than Fritz Duquesne! A copy of Detective Division Circular No. 6 circulated after his 1919 escape was pasted inside the front cover. Confronted with the book, Fritz continued to insist that he was Craven, not Duquesne, and was only an agent negotiating with motion picture companies for film rights to the book.

The author was Clement Wood, a forty-four-year-old former lawyer, teacher, historian, anthologist, biographer, and poet. The versatile author's works ranged over a wide field from religion to politics. He was a bitter foe of social and racial injustice and a romanticist, which probably explained his interest in Fritz. His most enduring work has been *Wood's Unabridged Rhyming Dictionary*.[13]

Asked by a *New York Times* reporter if the arrest was a publicity stunt for the book, Wood replied, "If it is, the publishers haven't told me anything about it. And if it is a publicity stunt, the book deserves it." A later search of Fritz's apartment turned up publicity releases touting the book as the story of the man who "attacked an empire single-handed" and who "spread death and destruction around the world." Wood said in the releases that "the book promises to cause something of a sensation" and that "Duquesne still lives and is perhaps plotting further war, ruin and disaster."[14]

(It is tempting to speculate that the whole affair was a publicity stunt conceived by Fritz and Wood. After all, Fritz was his own best press agent and had been publicizing himself for thirty years. And what better way to bring attention to the book than to have the slippery Fritz Duquesne suddenly arrested by his old enemy Ford? So who was Ford's tipster?)

Among Fritz's former friends and foes who dropped in at the police station to identify him was Thomas Tunney, now retired from his position as head of the Bomb and Neutrality Squad. In a *New York Times* interview he declared, "Certainly that's Duquesne. It's a good many years since I've seen him, but I had him in court at least 60 times. It's the same man, but he's a lot heavier. He was about 150 pounds when he escaped from Bellevue. Now he's about 180."[15] Chief fire marshal Thomas Brophy was just as positive in his identification. Reporters who had worked almost thirty years before with Duquesne at the old police headquarters in Mulberry Street also identified Craven as Fritz. Fritz calmly denied it, said the *Times*.

Continuing to insist that he was Frank de Trafford Craven, Fritz stood nonchalantly in a police lineup, said the *Times*, "with chest out and chin up with all the airs and graces of the aristocratic Englishman he claims to be."[16] Imperturbable and unblinking in the glare from powerful lights, he answered the questions of Assistant Chief Inspector John J. Sullivan, who read the old charge against him of murder on the high seas. "How old are you?" asked the inspector.

"I won't answer without the advice of counsel," Fritz replied.

Detective Thomas Ford, Fritz's old nemesis, leads the "prize pica-
roon" away in handcuffs. (National Archives)

"How old are you—52?"

"I don't know—40, I think."

"Are you wanted by the British government?"

"I will volunteer no information. I want to see my lawyer before I make a statement. I don't intend to supply the British government with any information about myself."

The police called Clement Wood, author of the Duquesne book, to the station to identify the prisoner. He denied that the man was Fritz Duquesne. Meeting him, he said, "Hello, Fred Craven."

"Craven" stared past Wood without showing any sign of recognition.

Wood said he had last seen Duquesne at Port au Prince in 1927 and in Martinique in 1931.[17] He declared that he had known Major Craven for five years, and that Duquesne and Craven were not the same person. "Craven does not resemble Duquesne, except in a superficial way," Wood said. "Craven is shorter and older. His speech is different."

Fritz was held all day at police headquarters and then booked at the Elizabeth Street station at 9 P.M. for homicide and for being an escaped prisoner. Ford and Tunney then drove him to the Federal House of Detention at 427 West Street, where he was placed in the custody of U.S. marshal Raymond J. Mulligan until it could be determined if Great Britain still wanted him on the old charge of murder on the high seas. Arthur Garfield Hays, a close friend of Wood's, was the lawyer Fritz requested to see.

Hays was a lawyer whose fame from defending civil liberty cases without pay was as important as the millions he made from representing large corporations and well-heeled individuals. Clients who paid the fifty-one-year-old lawyer money were showman Billy Rose, gambler Frank Costello, and the Dionne quintuplets. Those who paid him no fees but won him world renown included Italian anarchists Nicola Sacco and Bartolomeo Vanzetti; the eight Scottsboro blacks condemned to die in 1931 for allegedly attacking two white girls; John Scopes, accused in 1925 of teaching evolution in Tennessee; and Georgi Dmitrov, the Bulgarian Communist tried by the Nazis in 1933 for burning the Reichstag. Hays was a Bull Mooser in 1912 and in the same year became general counsel to the American Civil Liberties Union, which was then only three years old. His reputation as a defender of civil rights and free speech was considered second only to that of Clarence Darrow, with whom he worked on many of these infamous cases. Later, Hays protested the prosecution in the late 1930s of members of the German-American Bund, even though they were sympathetic to Hitler.[18]

Hays interviewed Fritz in the federal building and found him a "likeable chap," and his sympathies were aroused.[19] "The war was long over," Hays said, "and I realized that had Germany been victorious, the man would have been a hero rather than a criminal. It did not seem to me that his trial in an English court in 1932 would serve any useful social purpose." After interviewing Fritz Hays said, "This man insists he is Fred Craven. The British government will have to prove identification first." Intimating that the 1917 extradition warrant was illegal, he continued, "And they will have to prove that Frederick Duquesne was properly extraditable."

On 26 May Hays filed a writ of habeas corpus arguing that the defendant could not be extradited without evidence that he had been on English territory when the crime was committed. The writ also claimed that the prisoner was not Duquesne but Frank de Trafford Craven, and that even if he were Duquesne, his extradition would be illegal because Duquesne was in Bellevue Hospital when the order for his removal was signed.

A jovial Fritz Duquesne faced Federal Judge Frank J. Coleman on 6 June.[20] According to Hays, "We all admired the man. Even the district attorney and judge were sympathetic. It was before Hitler's time and no one then hated the Germans. After all, if there had been murder, it was homicide in a war of many years ago and homicide in war is heroic."[21]

Representing the British government again were Frederic Coudert Jr. and Frederic Coudert Bellinger of Coudert Brothers. Representing the federal government was U.S. attorney George Z. Medalie. (He would later be a New York State Court of Appeals judge and an adviser to governor Thomas E. Dewey during his administration, 1942–54.) Coudert did not contest the writ. But it was understood that the British government had made it a definite policy that wartime events are better forgotten. At the request of the Foreign Office, Scotland Yard was reluctant to rake up wartime scandals and stir up renewed bad feeling against Britain's former enemies.[22]

Judge Coleman declared Fritz Duquesne, alias Frank de Trafford Craven, a free man.

But Fritz's troubles weren't over yet. He no sooner left the courtroom than the implacable detective Ford, still playing Inspector Javert to Fritz's Jean Valjean, arrested him on the charge of being an escaped prisoner. Innocent or not, escaping custody was a violation of Section 1694 of the Penal Code and a felony. Fritz was whisked to Yorkville Court and arraigned before magistrate Alexander Brough, where he was held on $2,000 bail until his hearing on 28 June.[23] It appears that no one dared post bail for Fritz.

Defense attorney Hays and deputy assistant district attorney Howard Goldman argued the case briefly before city magistrate Benjamin E. Greenspan, a recently appointed judge noted for "lifting his courtroom out of the humdrum routine almost every time he sits on

Fritz's life story appeared in the 3 July 1932 edition of the New York Mirror Sunday Magazine following the publication of The Man Who Killed Kitchener.

the bench" and described by one newspaper as "the city's foremost producer of courtroom drama."[24] There wasn't much drama in Greenspan's opinion this day, but it was rendered swiftly: "The fact that the crime charged, 'murder on the high seas,' is not covered by the state laws; that the defendant was held for extradition by federal authorities and that he was delivered for a federal prisoner, lead me to the conclusion that no crime has been committed against the laws of the state of New York, and the defendant is discharged."[25]

Once again Fritz had beaten the system. He was a free man. But he couldn't shut up. Six months later, on 24 January 1933, he complained about his treatment by the press in a letter to William Bolger, managing editor of the *New York Sun*—the paper for which, as a young man, he had been a reporter and city editor.[26] After asking that his letter be placed in a conspicuous position in the paper, Fritz wrote, "I think it is about time that the slanderous frame-up against me by Great Britain, which your reporters played up as much as they possibly could, together with the fake accusations of the official thugs at police headquarters, ceased."

Embellishing as he did in all his communications, he complained about how much his defense had cost—in fact Hays had charged no fee—and then cast himself again as an abused hero: "Furthermore, your paper did not mention that when I was arrested, I was beaten three times into unconsciousness by the arresting six officers who covered me with revolvers, stripped me, put me in irons and then assaulted me." Fritz concluded by claiming that he was not seeking publicity and did not want any. He only wanted a square deal.

Fritz would attract some truly unwanted publicity during the next four years, when he worked intermittently for the Works Progress Administration, several right-wing fascist organizations, and eventually Nazi Germany.

CHAPTER 15

Wrath, Reds, and Right-Wingers

"I HATE THEM! I hate them! I hate them!"

Fritz was so angry, the unribboned monocle almost popped out of his eye as he reaffirmed his undying hatred of the British Empire to *New York Evening Post* columnist Archer Winsten in February 1934, almost two years after his arrest in the Quigley offices.[1] Fritz was sitting in a Radio City office answering questions for Winsten's "In the Wake of the News" column, which was devoted to "the present status of headliners of the past."

The only concession Fritz would make regarding the British was his often-quoted crack, "The English have a lot of fine points, but I don't want them stuck into me."

Fritz again showed his aversion to giving his true age when Winsten asked, "How old are you, Colonel?"

"I can't say how old I am now," he replied. "That sounds like I was a woman. But the reason is that all my people were killed by the English when I was very young. So I don't know."

"Are you willing to hazard a guess?" asked Winsten.

"Between 40 and 44," he replied, his blue eyes shining. Winsten quoted Wood's book, *The Man Who Killed Kitchener,* as saying that Fritz was fifty-four. Actually he was fifty-six.

Winsten reviewed the colonel's career up to the present, then added that Fritz was writing a military history of the South African people.

Fritz and a chest festooned with military awards, sometime in the early 1930s. He would seem to be emulating the finery of the man he hated most. (Author's collection)

They talked about adventurer Frank Buck, then enjoying great celebrity as an innovator in collecting exotic animals for zoos around the world. Buck's famous slogan "Bring 'em back alive" had become part of the language. Fritz was critical. "I was bringing 'em back alive in 1910," he said. "I invented the doping of wild animals.[2]

"I also object to being called both a soldier of fortune and a spy," continued Fritz, contradicting the obvious fact that these were his life-long careers. Dismissing the first charge with an expletive, he said, "I'm a patriot. I don't go around fighting for the fun of it." As for being a spy: "I was a revolutionary agent. I didn't report to anyone. I went out on my own to destroy the enemy, as the British say. Spies don't do those things. They are nothing but the eyes of the General Staff. I happened to be my own General Staff."

Fritz glinted balefully at Winsten through his monocle and concluded, "When the British annexed South Africa they thought they annexed me. But I'm one of the irreconcilables."

Fritz still had not reconciled himself to pursuing any form of legitimate business. Despite his age, he had no trouble attaching himself to women, not always of estimable character, who were willing to provide a livelihood for him and keep him in pocket money. But this would soon change, and he would have a steady source of income for a short while. Fritz would be hired to organize and direct the intelligence units of two pro-Nazi, anti-Semitic organizations. At the time there were an estimated eight hundred antidemocratic groups in the United States with such names as the Paul Reveres, Black Legion, Harry Jung's American Vigilantes, the American Defense Society, Yankee Freemen, and the Christian Front.[3] The Silver Shirts and the Order of '76 were interested in Fritz.

William Dudley Pelley, headquartering in Asheville, North Carolina, founded the Silver Shirts on 31 January 1932, the day after Hitler was appointed chancellor of Germany. The group was patterned after the Nazi Party, but with an American twist. Pelley was a small, dapper man sporting an unkempt Vandyke and thick glasses. Even in normal conversation he talked as if he were speaking from a podium. He claimed that one day in 1928 he died and went to heaven for seven minutes. Upon his return to Hollywood, where he had been writing scenarios for screenplays starring Tom Mix, Colleen Moore, and Lon Chaney, he renounced the fleshpots of sin, swore off tobacco, coffee, tea, and liquor, and decided to dedicate his remaining days to saving

America from the Jews and Communists. He also wrote for the *Saturday Evening Post, Adventure,* and other pulp magazines.[4] Pelley said he would not die again until 1962. (He outlived his prediction by three years.)

Pelley liked to strut about in a self-designed uniform of silver shirt, black military jacket with an embroidered silver shield, black breeches, shiny tall boots, and a tightly drawn Sam Browne belt.[5] All this splendor was often enveloped in an aviator's flying coat.

Royal Scott Gulden, head of the Order of '76, was tall, gaunt, graying, neatly dressed, and somewhere in his early forties. He was a superpatriot dedicated to saving America for Americans and protecting it from the Jews, who were going to take it over any minute for the Bolshevists. A sometime realtor, he claimed a long-distance relationship with the Gulden mustard family.[6] Gulden believed that Pelley would one day rule America.

When a merger was planned between the '76ers and the Silver Shirts, Gulden was appointed secretary to direct espionage and propaganda activities. Gulden admitted that he knew nothing about spying and looked around for someone to do the job. Fritz was recommended to him by Colonel Edwin Emerson, another one of those odd figures like Fritz who hovered and strutted around the fringes of history.

The sixty-five-year-old Emerson started his career as a reporter for the *New York Evening Sun*—Fritz's old paper—but didn't last long.[7] He managed to join Roosevelt's Rough Riders as an interpreter and dispatch rider, but Teddy was unhappy with him for writing "a description of the personnel of his regiment" he didn't like. Emerson claimed that the article, written for *Collier's Weekly,* was intended to be humorous. But Teddy was not humored. The Emerson article implied that the Rough Riders were rustlers and thieves.[8] For the next several years Emerson covered battles around the globe as a war correspondent. During World War I he was captured and interned by the Germans. In 1934 he was president of the Society of American Friends of Germany, another pro-Nazi propaganda organization, with offices in the German consulate at 17 Battery Place. With this background, it was not surprising that Emerson and Fritz were acquainted.

Fritz and Gulden met in the late spring of 1934 at 41 West Forty-sixth Street.[9] After a discussion of more than two hours, Fritz accepted the job of intelligence officer. Colonel Duquesne found the offer irresistible. He would be paid for doing what he had devoted his life to: spying. Life could not be sweeter for Fritz. He had money, and he was playing spy.

Every effort was made to keep Fritz's name and purpose secret, even from members of the organizations. But the secret was ferreted out by John L. Spivak, a thirty-seven-year-old renowned reporter. A professed Communist and "left-wing rabble-rouser," he was noted for defending the rights of the underdog.[10] At the time, Spivak was writing for *New Masses*, a weekly magazine with a small circulation. It was regarded as a pro-Communist publication and a voice of intellectual rebellion.[11] Through his sources Spivak learned about the hiring of Duquesne and sought an interview with the reluctant Gulden. They met in the Order of '76 offices at 1 East Fifty-third Street. A black 76 encircled by a gold band was on the door.[12]

"Isn't it rather strange that this 100 per cent 'patriotic' organization is working so closely with a German spy in this country?" Spivak asked Gulden. "We will cooperate with anyone who will help drive out the Jewish pest!" Gulden replied.[13]

When Spivak's "Plotting America's Pogroms" series broke in the *New Masses* edition of 2 October, the circulation of the magazine tripled overnight. The demand was so great that the 10-cent magazine was bootlegged at 25 cents a copy. Gulden mustard sales dropped, even though Spivak was careful to say Gulden had nothing to do with the business and was only a distant relation.[14]

The day after the issue identifying Duquesne appeared on the newsstands, Spivak received a phone call from a woman in a New York State government office (Spivak did not identify her in his account of these events).[15] She sounded dismayed, disillusioned, and bitter. "I am Jewish," she said, "and if you can prove to me that Fritz Duquesne is distributing anti-Semitic propaganda or is working with Nazis and anti-Semites I think I can be of help to you. I have a key to his apartment." When asked how she came to have a key, she replied harshly, "Because I am his mistress. And if he is working with the Nazis, I'll get you anything he's got."

Spivak met with his caller, a woman in her mid-thirties, at a Greenwich Village restaurant. To show how close she was to Fritz, she told him that Fritz had met with Arthur Garfield Hays that day asking him to sue Spivak for libel. "Hays won't sue you," she revealed. "He told Fritz that if you said he was a Nazi agent he was sure you could prove it. He not only advised against suing you but bawled the hell out of him for spreading anti-Semitism after all the help that Hays, a Jew, gave him over the years without compensation.

"I want no part of Duquesne anymore," she concluded.

"If you are Jewish and if you really want to help, this is exactly when you should not break with him," Spivak told her.

"I can't go to bed with that son of-a-bitch now," she said with revulsion,

"If you want to help you'll bury your loathing. Act as if nothing has happened and you do not believe what I wrote. Say it's just communist propaganda. This is the time when you must cultivate him. I want to get the names and addresses of all his friends; where and how and from whom he gets money to operate with; his meetings with Emerson—everything he does. I want letters, documents, anything that will show his connections with the Nazis."

Finally convinced, she said, "All right. I'll get you everything I can."

Spivak said that Duquesne's mistress, despite her revulsion, kept him informed for several years of his activities. Journalistically, Spivak had no further use for Fritz. He turned over what he had learned to the Anti-Defamation League. Spivak speculated that either his informant's loathing became increasingly difficult to conceal or Fritz found another woman. In any case, Fritz moved out of his apartment in April 1940 and into that of an attractive sculptress—Spivak did not identify her, but he is referring to Evelyn Clayton Lewis—whom Fritz was said to have seduced into becoming a traitor.

Was Fritz Duquesne an anti-Semite?

If working for an anti-Semitic organization made him one, then he was. There is no other indication in his career that he was. But the Order of '76 and the Silver Shirts were also pro-German and pro-Nazi, which made them anti-British. This was attraction enough, as was the added inducement of a steady income for doing what he did best: spying. Despite its ramifications, it was quite simply just a job to the amoral and opportunistic Fritz Duquesne.

How long Fritz continued his affiliation with the right-wing organizations is not known. Spivak said Fritz's mistress kept him informed for several years. But Fritz became an employee of the Works Progress Administration on 29 January 1935, under the name of John du Quesne, less than a year after his agreement with Gulden.[16] He was employed as a supervising material inspector—whatever that might have been—until 4 February 1937, when he was terminated for insubordination. Fritz claimed that he was a research worker on a theater project making $15 a week and was fired because he wouldn't lie. That was, no doubt, a lie.

On 22 November 1937 Frederick Joubert Duquesne filed with the county clerk of New York a certificate indicating that he was the sole owner of, and doing business as, the Air Terminals Company at 2 West Forty-fifth Street.[17] He claimed to be servicing securities. Fritz was also registered with the Securities and Exchange Commission as a broker and dealer for the purpose of dealing in RKO stock.

No real money. But don't cry for Fritz. In just nine months he would reach the pinnacle of his espionage career. He would be handpicked by Admiral Wilhelm Canaris, the head of the German Abwehr, to be Nazi Germany's major intelligence link in America.

CHAPTER 16

Colonel Ritter Hires
Colonel Duquesne

F RITZ DUQUESNE's long record of spying for Germany and his hatred for the British had not been overlooked during the early 1930s in Hitler's Germany, then girding for another war.

Hitler's intelligence organization, the Abwehr, was delving deep into the military secrets of its enemies and even those countries it did not expect to war against—in particular the United States. Admiral Wilhelm Canaris, chief of the Abwehr, wanted information about America's potential war machine.

One key to that information was Fritz Duquesne. His previous service to the Fatherland during the Great War had not been forgotten, and considering his long years of living in America, Canaris was sure Duquesne would be able to uncover information of benefit to Germany.

Canaris, born in 1887, enlisted at the Imperial Naval Academy at Kiel in 1905.[1] He had risen to become head of the Abwehr in 1935 by dedicating himself to slow but sure advancement through the naval ranks, using all political means within his power through the successive military regimes of the kaiser's imperial Germany, the Weimar Republic, and the Third Reich. Following World War I Canaris rose steadily in rank with commensurate gains in influence and power. When Hitler came to power in 1933, Canaris believed that the new chancellor would return Germany to its former glory and position as a world power. Although he came to despise the Nazis, there is no evidence that he was a double agent and worked with British intelligence to depose Hitler, despite popular romantic legend.

Small-boned, with wrinkled, sallow skin, Canaris appeared to be older than his forty-eight years when he took command of the Abwehr. Those who worked with Canaris called him *der Alte*—the Old Man. Behind his back friends called him the White Admiral.[2]

The Abwehr was the Intelligence Department of the German Armed Forces High Command, which had been created to continue the work of Colonel Walthar Nicolai's World War I Stabsgruppe IIIb. *Abwehr* was a cosmetic term meaning *defense,* considered a less threatening word than *espionage* to Germany's friends and possible enemies.

Immediately upon his appointment to command the organization, Canaris restructured the Abwehr into three groups.[3] Group I was responsible for gathering intelligence and conducting espionage; Group II conducted sabotage operations and fomented insurrection and sedition; and Group III was responsible for counterespionage and penetrating enemy secret services.

Enter Nikolaus Adolf Fritz Ritter—an extraordinary espionage agent who put together the largest spy organization ever assembled in the United States, with Fritz Duquesne as its key member.[4] Ritter was especially valuable because of a fluency in French and "American" English. According to his 1972 autobiography, *Deckname Dr. Rantzau* (*My Covername Is Dr. Rantzau*), his code name was Dr. Johnson or Alfred Landing in America, Dr. Reinhardt or Dr. Weber in Holland, and Dr. Jansen in Hungary—countries in which he concentrated his espionage activities throughout most of the war. He was known as Dr. Renken in Germany.[5]

The spy ring Ritter organized in America—known as the Ritter Ring—became the most successful of all his operations, albeit the most notorious and the most famous following its eventual breakup in a brilliant stroke of counterespionage by the FBI in 1940 and 1941. It was Ritter's agents who stole the Norden bombsight and Sperry gyroscope, two of America's most closely guarded secrets, gaining possession of these instruments years before the United States even knew Germany had them.[6]

Ritter was born in Essen in 1899. Although his father had hoped he would study theology, he was attracted to military life. Following ser-

Colonel Nikolaus Adolf Fritz Ritter, the Abwehr
officer who hired Fritz to spy for Germany in 1937.
(Irmgard Ritter)

vice with the German army during World War I, he attended the
Prussian Technical School for Textiles in Sorau in der Niederlausitz, a
manufacturing city noted for its textiles and porcelains. (Originally located in the province of Brandenburg, Sorau was assigned to Poland at
the Potsdam Conference in 1945.) Ritter's first professional position
was as director of a textile factory in Silesia.

When Ritter was twenty-four years old he decided to further his career in textiles in America, and on 19 December 1923 he sailed from
Bremen for New York aboard the North German Lloyd liner *Bremen*
(launched in 1900 as the *Prinzess Irene* and renamed that year as the
Bremen). On a clear, crisply cold New Year's morning in 1924, Ritter
first saw the country he would live in for a good many years and about

which he said in his autobiography, "I would learn to love [it] as a second home."[7]

The war had been over for five years, but Ritter discovered that there was still a great deal of resentment toward Germans. "Germans Not Wanted" and "Germans Need Not Apply" were signs often posted in personnel offices. The same advice appeared in newspaper help-wanted ads. After three attempts and as many turn-downs from the Title Guarantee and Trust Company, he was finally told he was not wanted because he was a German.

"I did not know I was the man responsible for the war," Ritter replied. The sympathetic personnel director suggested that he apply for work at one of the company's affiliates in Jamaica on Long Island. Ritter was not turned away this time, and it was the beginning of his textile career in America. He began as a weaver with the Mallenson Silk Mills in Astoria and succeeded through a number of positions to become technical director of a department with sixty weaving desks.

Ritter was eventually dismissed following a dispute over wages and managed to make a living in a variety of jobs—as a typesetter, an iron-worker, a painter, and a layer of parquet floors. Then he and a group of friends traveled through the United States in an old Dodge. Among the many other odd jobs he worked at on their journey, he was a bus-boy on the Menominee, or Wild Rice, Indian Reservation in Oshkosh, Wisconsin.

His travels and the variety of work he undertook gave Ritter an invaluable understanding and grasp of the English language and American idiom as well as an insight into American culture that would be an enormous aid to him and Germany in another decade, when he began espionage operations in the United States.

Ritter obtained work again with a weaving factory in Washington, D.C., married an American schoolteacher, fathered two children, had visitor's cards to the Senate and Congress, and lived a pleasant and comfortable life in the country he would one day conspire against. But with Hitler's rise to power and what appeared to be the creation of a new and proud Germany, Ritter began feeling the old patriotic fervor for his Fatherland, and he had an overpowering desire to seek a new future in the country of his birth. He made a quick decision to return when the German consulate office asked him if he wanted to soldier again. Then General von Boetticher, military attaché in Washington, told Ritter that the *Oberkommando* of the Wehrmacht was interested in him.

On 1 September 1936, at the age of thirty-seven, Ritter began a new military life in Bremen. In January 1937 he was placed in the *Oberkommando* of the Wehrmacht foreign office—Abwehr I—under Admiral Canaris. *Hauptmann* (captain) Ritter's official office was on the second floor of a large military building in Hamburg on the General Knochenhauerstrasse (Sophienstrasse before the war and again after), with rooms for officers and employees on each side. The address was Generalkommando X. Armeekorps (Wehrkreiskommando X), Abwehrstelle.[8]

Ritter's duty was to build a nest of agents as fast as possible in Europe and America. As head of the air intelligence section, his primary function was to obtain information on England's Royal Air Force and the aircraft industry in America. He admitted that he had no background in aviation. His entire aerial experience consisted of his service as a ground observer in a Bücker-Jungmann biplane during a tour of duty with the German army in 1935 and 1936. Ritter also admitted that his only knowledge of espionage was gathered from books and that he had no formal training. But he did possess what few men in Germany at the time did: an incredible facility with the English language as spoken by Americans, and a great knowledge of America that gave him the ability to move with ease and freedom around the country.

Ritter's American wife was not happy with his new work. She divorced him in the fall of 1937 and took their children to America. He was embittered over the loss of his children, but not enough to abandon his new career. It was not until after the war that Ritter saw his children again.

As his espionage operations against Great Britain and the United States grew, Ritter, now a major, moved to new offices in Hamburg's Gerhofstrasse and Ballindamm. They were cover addresses at which the *Herr Doktor* was named on his office doors as managing director of an export-import firm, camouflage for his meetings with agents. Each office consisted of only one small, barely furnished room. Ritter would meet agents at the hotel where he stayed with his new wife, Irmgard, then walk to one or the other office, often having his secretary come along. To assist communication between his offices in Hamburg and his network of agents in America and England, Ritter employed seamen and stewards of the Hamburg-Amerika and North German Lloyd luxury liners sailing between New York and German North Sea ports.

Ritter and his acting chief, Captain Kurt Burghardt of the navy, realized that to get the information they needed and to assure its constant flow to the Abwehr, a stronghold must be established in the United States. The only way to procure that stronghold was for Ritter to travel to America and set it up himself. Canaris objected to Ritter undertaking the mission, fearing that if one of his top agents was arrested it would tip Germany's hand and expose the web of intrigue already set up. But Ritter overcame his resistance by pointing out that he was the best person for the job. With his knowledge of the country and people in America, he could accomplish in two months what would take another agent two years.

For Ritter's planned tour of America, his cover story would be that he was obtaining new business for his textile company. He would travel to America and arrive in New York using his own name. He was confident with his own name and did not want to complicate matters by changing it. Once in America it would be necessary for him to take on a new identity. This would help him disappear into the general population and make him untraceable once he started spinning his network of agents.

The one person he planned to meet whom he had known previously while living in America was Fritz Duquesne. Fritz would surely be eager to work again for Germany because spying was what he knew best, and Ritter also knew he would be in need of money. Fritz always needed money.

Ritter had also determined that none of the new agents he recruited, mostly German-born naturalized Americans, should know one another. Each would work independently and give his reports directly to the person Ritter would eventually engage to oversee the whole American operation. The theory was that if one spy was apprehended he would not be able to betray the others if all were ignorant of each other. As it turned out, several did know each other.

Ritter never feared that his role as a businessman would create a problem for him. The United States and Germany were not at war—though he believed the two countries would be eventually—and the American people had not yet been stricken with the psychosis of war. Additionally he believed that an overwhelming number of Americans were neutral regarding Nazism, though there were a great many outspoken opponents. And there were still others who were friendly toward Germany despite Hitler's threat to world peace.

Ritter felt secure in his deception for another reason. He believed that Americans had a peculiarity, far more prevalent in them than in other people, that would make his job much easier. That peculiarity was gullibility. Americans had unbounded faith in the goodness of other people.

Canaris ordered Ritter to refrain absolutely from making contact with his friend, General von Boetticher, the German military attaché in Washington. Canaris said the general had no real understanding of intelligence gathering and could only complicate Ritter's mission. Additionally his orders were to contact no German officials. Canaris was taking no chances. He had no wish to have a top Abwehr official arrested in the United States.

On 1 October 1937 Ritter boarded the North German Lloyd ship *Bremen*—not the same *Bremen* on which he had sailed to America in 1924—in Bremen for the Atlantic crossing to New York. The sleek luxury liner served the Abwehr well, until war was declared in 1939, as a carrier between the two countries of couriers and espionage agents and their precious cargoes of intelligence information. Ritter made a practice of traveling tourist class in a comfortable cabin amidships. Under no circumstances would he go first class, reasoning that all first-class passengers are listed in the New York papers, and he had no desire to draw attention to himself. When Ritter awoke ill one morning with the shivers, he refused to ask for medical help because his name would then appear on the sick list aboard ship. On the third day out he even refused to dine with Adolph Ahrens, the *Bremen*'s captain, for fear of being noticed. There were 1,921 passengers aboard, and among the first-class travelers Ritter missed mingling with were publisher Nelson Doubleday, party-thrower Elsa Maxwell, and concert pianists Sergei Rachmaninoff and Walter Gieseking.[9]

In the best James Bond tradition—or Bulldog Drummond tradition, Drummond being the popular fictional English secret service hero of the time—Ritter wore on his right hand a simple gold ring with a flat blue stone that he could use as a mirror to observe what was going on behind him by simply lowering his elbow. He also carried an unusual umbrella encased in a thin wooden sheath that made it look like a cane.

Ritter was aware that his personal appearance was not the kind to attract attention. He was rather innocuous-looking and appeared to be the average middle-class businessman. His habit of carrying an umbrella was the only thing to distinguish him from an American businessman. Capping the deception was that he walked with quick, officious steps, not an uncommon gait for a New Yorker.

Best of all, Ritter did not look like a spy. Physically he did not fit the image of what people thought a spy should look like, but mentally he was perfectly suited for the position. He was intelligent and shrewd, and he thoroughly enjoyed what he was doing. Ritter never considered himself a spy. He was an officer of the Abwehr doing his duty.

Arriving in New York City on 7 October,[10] Ritter passed easily through customs, although an inspector expressed curiosity about his umbrella, which was not of a kind to be found in America. The inspector removed the cover and said, "This is a good hiding place."

"Sorry to have disappointed you," Ritter laughed in reply.

When approaching the exit, the colonel was suddenly surprised to hear "Ritter!" called in a loud voice.[11] Startled, he thought to himself that he had been discovered before he had even begun his mission and that he would be quickly deported. Gathering himself, he turned around and was greeted with another exclamation. "Man, Ritter! How come you are here?"

Ritter was annoyed but also relieved to see that it was a reporter he knew very well from the *New Yorker Staats-Zeitung und Herold,* the largest German-language newspaper published in the United States. He pretended to be happy to see him and shook hands. "I thought you were still a captain in the Luftwaffe," said the reporter, still speaking loudly.

Ritter took pains not to look around and see if anyone nearby was listening, then answered in the same loud voice to throw off suspicion, "No, I'm just with the reserves. Otherwise I would hardly be here." Trying to get rid of the reporter, Ritter said he must be there for a special reason. Yes, said the other, the prince of Wales—he meant the recently married duke of Windsor—was aboard, and he was to interview him at a press conference.[12] The colonel wished him well and then quickly left.

Ritter registered under his own name at the Taft Hotel on Seventh Avenue at Fiftieth Street.[13] The Taft was an "Abwehr hotel," a favorite place for members of the agency to stay, just as the McAlpin had been the preferred watering hole for German spies prior to America's entering the Great War in Europe in 1917.[14]

To establish a business identity, Ritter conducted himself in a manner contrary to his nature. He gave addresses to taxi drivers and the doorman in a loud voice and in an equally resounding voice would make business appointments on the telephone, always within earshot of the staff. He would also make a point of having the desk clerk accept his messages from different textile companies. He had his laundry done at the hotel to assure getting the Taft's laundry mark on the garments. He nearly made one slip in security when he suddenly had to grab back a shirt he had just given the Chinese boy. The Luftwaffe tag was still on the shirt. When the boy left, Ritter removed the tag and burned it.

Ritter tried not to stay more than two or three days at any one hotel. Constant movement was his security. After several days at the Taft he slowly began establishing a new identity as Alfred Landing, under which name he would make contact with those Germans in America who were sympathetic to Hitler's cause and willing to spy for Germany. Thus would he begin building the largest spy ring ever to operate in the United States.

He called the Wellington Hotel from a drug store and made reservations for Mr. Landing. Ritter then returned to the Taft and wrote a postcard to Landing, informing him that he would be unable to see him over the next several days. This was followed with a letter to Landing written on Taft Hotel letterhead and addressed to the Grand Central Station post office on Lexington Avenue and Forty-fifth Street.[15]

Ritter checked out of the Taft the next morning, making a big fuss at the desk to assure that the staff knew he was leaving. He took a taxi to the Wellington, just a few blocks north at 871 Seventh Avenue, registered as Alfred Landing, and asked if he had any mail. He was handed the postcard, which he took to the post office at Grand Central Station where he asked for any mail in Mr. Landing's name. Asked for identification, he showed the postcard. "That was all I needed to identify myself," wrote Ritter. He recalled that he then went uptown to the next National City Bank on Ninetieth Street and, on the strength of his credit as Nikolaus Ritter, withdrew a large amount of money, enough to carry him over for the next several months during his journeys in the United States acquiring agents.[16] He placed his passport and all papers identifying himself as Colonel Nikolaus Ritter in a safe-deposit box. He then had lunch with an old war comrade, Brandts-Sobieski— at that time a painter and sculptor living on 179th Street—and gave his friend the key to the box, telling him it contained things he didn't want to take with him on a trip through the Midwest.

As Ritter wrote, "The textile engineer Nikolaus Ritter now ceased to exist in America. I was Alfred Landing on the search for new agents."[17]

Ritter's first *Treff* (meeting) was on Saturday, 9 October, with "Pop," a code name for squat, middle-aged Fritz Sohn,[18] a longtime German

agent who lived at 262 Monitor Street in Brooklyn. Sohn was not necessarily a spy. He was a "mailman" who forwarded to Germany material gathered by the real spies. But his role as a go-between was one in
which he took special pride. Ritter's real interest in visiting Sohn,
though, was to find a man known only as Paul.

Through Sohn, Paul had sent on to Germany a portion of the plans
of what appeared to be the Norden bombsight, an incredibly accurate
instrument that allowed precision bombing from high altitudes. The
first crude model of Carl Norden's famed bombsight was put together
in 1921, and from that moment on it was one of the world's most
sought after technical secrets. It wasn't until 1931 that the bombsight
was completed and patents granted. It became America's most closely
guarded secret—or so it was thought.[19] When Abwehr officials saw
what Paul had sent them, they were astounded by the coup. But the
plans were not complete, and more details were needed.[20]

"Paul" was Hermann Lang, a thirty-six-year-old German born 11
August 1901 at Schwarzenbach am Wald.[21] He was particularly proud
of the fact that he was an *alte Kaempfer* (an old follower) of *der Führer*.
This distinguished him as one of the four thousand Nazis who had
participated in Hitler's ill-fated Munich beer hall putsch, his attempt
in 1923 to overthrow the Weimar Republic and establish the German
National Government.

Lang was a naturalized American citizen who had been living in
America since 1927 and working since 1929 for Carl L. Norden, Inc., at
80 Lafayette Street in New York. His position as an assembly inspector
for the makers of the famous bombsight allowed him access to blueprints of the instrument. To maintain the secrecy of that desired device, different elements were made in a number of other plants until
final assembly. But Lang had all the plans and each night would take
some home with him. An expert draftsman, he would lay them out on
his kitchen table and painstakingly copy them, making full-scale du-
plicates.

Sohn arranged a meeting between Ritter and Lang at the Monitor
Street apartment for Sunday afternoon. Ritter observed that Lang was
stocky and dark-haired, with bushy eyebrows, sparkling brown eyes,
and a snub nose. His demeanor was self-assured, though he was perpetually sad-faced. Nevertheless, Ritter had an instant liking for the
man. He was surprised to discover that Lang was a rather simple man
who had no real aspirations except to provide for his wife and daughter. He did not consider himself a spy. Even after thirteen years in his

adopted country he remained a German in spirit—a patriot—which was his reason for stealing the bombsight for the land of his birth.

Authorized to pay $1,500, Ritter offered Lang payment for the plans and was instantly ashamed when the sparkling brown eyes looked at him with indignation. Lang refused to accept any money for his efforts. Ritter was astonished. "It was the first time," he wrote, "that I had encountered a spy who was stealing secrets purely for ideological reasons and not for monetary gain."[22] He also admired Lang's courage: "What nerves this man must have had to take drawings in and out from such a strictly watched organization."[23]

Lang turned over the remainder of the bombsight plans to Ritter, who immediately made arrangements to get them to Germany. Ritter would send them via courier-steward aboard the HAPAG-Lloyd liner *Reliance* on her next return voyage.[24] The steward was Herbert Jaenichen, the Abwehr's chief courier on the transatlantic route. His registry number was F.2341, code name Oskar. The *F* indicated that he was a scout and a courier.

Ritter met Oskar at 4 P.M. on Monday, 29 November 1937. The liner had arrived in New York that day at 1 P.M. Ritter handed Oskar his umbrella with the Norden bombsight plans wrapped inside. Oskar refused to take it, explaining that he had left the ship without an umbrella and could hardly return with one without having it examined by customs authorities. Ritter and he would meet again the next day, but this time Oskar would leave the *Bremen* carrying an umbrella.

Ritter was having an ice cream soda at the fountain of the Whelan Drug Store in the Hotel Astor at Forty-fourth and Broadway when Oskar arrived for their second meeting on Tuesday. This time he had an umbrella, but he was also limping. Oskar explained that he had pretended to sprain his ankle and was using the umbrella for support. How else could he explain carrying an umbrella on such a sunny day? (Oskar need not have worried. It would not have been unusual for a New Yorker to be carrying an umbrella that day. The temperature was in the fifties, and though the skies were clear, light rain had been expected for the last couple of days.) They exchanged umbrellas, and Oskar limped back to the *Reliance*. The final complete plans of America's most heavily guarded military secret sailed for Bremen shortly after midnight on 30 November 1937. Except for the breaking of the German and Japanese military codes by American intelligence, it was probably the single greatest espionage coup during that tenuous time before the war.[25]

In essence, that is how the *Norden-Bombenzielgerätes* and Oskar left America for Germany according to Colonel Nikolaus Ritter, Ladislas Farago, and other chroniclers of this espionage case. However, there is disagreement on which vessel sailed with Oskar and the bombsight plans and on which date. Farago says in *Foxes* that they left aboard the *Bremen* on 31 October.[26]

Ritter and Farago should have checked the arrival and departure times of the ships in the "Shipping and Mail Schedules" of the *New York Times*. Neither the *Bremen* nor the *Reliance* was in New York on either date. The schedules show that the *Bremen* sailed from New York on only two days in October—the 8th (the day after Ritter had arrived) and the 26th.

The *Reliance* had actually been long gone from Atlantic service. Her last regular voyage to New York from Hamburg was in August 1935. The ship would not steam into New York Harbor again until Wednesday, 5 January 1938, following a West Indies cruise. She would leave pier 86 at noon on Sunday, 9 January 1938, on the first leg of a 136-day world cruise.[27]

So Oskar and the Norden bombsight plans most likely left for Germany on that date. Ritter and Oskar would have first met on Friday, 7 January, and again on the next day to exchange umbrellas. Saturday was a clear, cold, and sunny day, which would have explained Oskar's concern about carrying an umbrella. It is also a more realistic date, considering all that Ritter had to accomplish on his mission. Farago's dates gave Ritter less than a month to acquire the plans, contact his brother and Fritz Duquesne, and spin a web of agents in New York, Philadelphia, St. Louis, and Detroit.

Confusing the issue even more is that Farago says Ritter gave the plans to Oskar not at the Whelan Drug Store but in Ritter's room at the Irving Arms. Ritter was registered at the Wellington Hotel.

Ritter now took the opportunity to visit his brother, Hans, who had been in America for several years as a representative of the Chase National Bank in Manhattan. Hans had been living for five years in a brownstone house at 120 Riverside Drive in a common-law arrangement with Else Weustenfeld, a plump thirty-eight-year-old divorcée born in Essen, the hometown of the two brothers. A few years older than Hans, Else was working as a stenographer and notary public in the law offices of Topken and Farley (Harald R. and William J. Topken and Philip F. Farley) located in the Whitehall Building at 17 Battery

Place, which coincidentally also housed the offices of the German consulate. Ritter discussed with Hans his future espionage plans in America and in particular singled out Fritz Duquesne as a prize secret agent. Hans would serve as a contact for Fritz and future Ritter spies.

Both Hans and Else were personable people who never discussed politics and were well liked by acquaintances.[28] Hans had a disturbing habit of constantly taking in gasps of air as if, some friends surmised, he were under a great deal of pressure. It would be some years before they would learn the truth about Hans and Else. Hans returned to Germany by way of Mexico in 1939 and was not heard from again. Else did not fare as well. Although she would testify at her trial in 1941 that she had wanted nothing to do with his "monkey business" and that Hans had urged his brother to "keep Else out of it," Ritter hired Else as a paymaster. He was pleased that she was a naturalized American citizen because of the freedom of mobility it would give her, especially since she spoke English without the trace of an accent. Else would be the conduit through which Fritz would receive future payments and microphotographs of instructions.

Ritter looked forward to seeing his old and good friend, Colonel Fritz Duquesne.[29] (Fritz was never questioned by anyone about which country's army had honored him with the colonelcy. Indeed, it was a rank conferred on Fritz Duquesne by Fritz Duquesne. But the title was accepted by Ritter and used by the press whenever writing about him.) The spymaster called Fritz at his private number, Trafalgar 4-9867, and arranged a meeting in Fritz's apartment at 144 West Fifty-seventh Street, where he had lived since 1935.[30] Fritz suggested lunch and a glass of whiskey in his fashionable rooms just four doors east of Carnegie Hall.

Ritter first met Fritz in 1931 through a mutual friend, Colonel Uldric Thompson. Thompson must have been aware of Fritz's military, espionage, and inventing background, which was perhaps the common link that galvanized their friendship. Thompson himself was an inventor and industrial engineer who during the war had invented a device for safely loading artillery shells with TNT.[31] The invention was credited with saving thousands of lives in munition factories.

Thompson was a member of the University Club and of the Alpha Delta Phi Club in New York, and he, Fritz, and Ritter often had a glass of forbidden booze during Prohibition in the seclusive confines of the clubs.[32] The University Club at 1 West Fifty-fourth Street was a particular favorite of the friends, with its interior embellishments designed by the tragic Stanford White. The liquor for social drinks was provided from the private stock of members and was stashed behind oak paneling in the mezzanine taproom.

Two other prominent club members who occasionally joined them were former New York governor (1914–18) and police corruption fighter Charles S. Whitman and Royal E. T. Riggs, a prominent corporation lawyer and lieutenant colonel in the U.S. Army Reserve.[33]

The connection between Fritz and Riggs went back many years to Duquesne's stint as a reporter and editor for the *New York Sun*. Riggs was the son of Edward G. Riggs, acclaimed political reporter for thirty years at the *Sun* until 1913.[34] The senior Riggs must have known Fritz when the two were on the paper, and no doubt they discussed the politics of the Boer War. One of the editor's closest friends was Theodore Roosevelt, a fact that may have influenced Fritz's decision to support the former president during his 1912 campaign on the Bull Moose ticket.

Ritter remembered Fritz then as being in his early forties, with a small intelligent face and aristocratic nose, gray eyes (his eyes were in fact steel blue), and graying hair.[35] He was distinguished-looking and had the appearance of an adventurer. Fritz never had much money, but Ritter always admired him for the way he managed to move in the best circles despite his lack of funds. His chief means of support, aside from his excellent social contacts, was the writing of articles for newspapers and magazines and the giving of lectures on his hunting and travel adventures before ladies' clubs. Fritz was particularly successful at this because he was innately charming. Ritter admitted that even he was beguiled. (Undercover FBI agents were also entranced by Fritz's spirited yarns while investigating him in 1941.) Ritter knew that Fritz sometimes worked as a spy, that he was a daredevil with steel nerves, and that whatever came his way was okay, as long as it involved money.

Ritter apparently believed Fritz's Münchausen memories. He recalled in his autobiography that Fritz had shown him, with much satisfaction, a photo of himself taken in 1916 on board British Admiral Sir John R. Jellicoe's flagship, the dreadnought HMS *Iron Duke*. Perhaps the satisfaction was due to pride in a nicely doctored photograph. Fritz was not in England in 1916, a year he had actually spent mostly hiding out in Brazil following his damaging of the British steamer *Tennyson*. England would have done its duty to a saboteur at that time, and as noted earlier, Fritz went to great lengths in New York to avoid being extradited to England for execution.

When the two old friends met again on 3 December 1937, Ritter noted with a smile that Fritz was still the suave ladies' man. He was sixty years old now but was living with an attractive thirty-four-year-old woman named Evelyn Clayton Lewis.

Lewis was born on 23 February 1903 in Batesville, Arkansas, and raised in Fayetteville (Arkansas) and Dallas (Texas). In 1924 she attended the fall semester only at Southern Methodist University, where she was an average to below-average student.[36] A naturally talented sculptress and artist, she was also a writer of unproduced plays. Fritz liked to say that she sculpted the figures in front of the Riverside Church in New York City. The claim was just another of his many fabrications.

Lewis was leading a moderately successful life as a designer of toys and as a sculptress when she met the spy. A woman named Helen, a former girlfriend of Fritz's and a good friend of Evelyn's, introduced the two at a cocktail party. Fritz knew a good thing when he saw it, particularly since Evelyn had a few more bucks than Helen. She also had respectable friends from Long Island, associations made through her art contacts. Fritz was never one to pass up an association with respectability. Despite the difference in their ages, Lewis was captivated by this handsome gentleman who spoke with a clipped English accent and who seemed to move in an aura of international intrigue. She soon became his mistress, which put an abrupt end to her blossoming career. According to an FBI report, she was "completely subjugated to his will."[37]

An attractive woman, Evelyn was a prize catch for Fritz with her wavy brown hair, large brown eyes, and full figure always smartly dressed in the latest fashions.[38] Later, when Fritz became more deeply involved in his work with the Ritter Ring, she would function chiefly as a lookout, spending long hours at their apartment window watching for "suspicious persons" who might be the law.[39]

Because Ritter had already determined that none of the spies he recruited should be in touch with one another, he told Fritz it would be necessary for him to work alone. For the present his contact man would be Oskar.[40] A second contact would be Ritter's brother, Hans, the representative of the Chase National Bank in Manhattan.[41] Fritz's code number was A.3518. The A indicated that he was a producing agent.[42]

Before leaving Fritz, Ritter gave him a check for $100. Nothing had changed, he noted: Fritz still needed money. But Fritz's lifestyle was about to change. With added income arriving on a regular basis from the Abwehr, he and Evelyn would soon move to better quarters at 47 West Fifty-fourth Street, next-door to the Warwick Hotel. The two would move again to an even more upscale place that would become the focus of an intense FBI hunt in 1940.

Ritter continued on his trip across America, building his network of spies in Philadelphia, St. Louis, and Chicago. In Detroit he visited another old friend, identified in Ritter's autobiography only as Mr. X and described as a very wealthy man, one of America's leading industrialists and a staunch anti-Communist. In later years, Ritter said, the man, by then quite elderly, was a supporter of Ronald Reagan, campaigning for governor of California in 1962.

His work finished in America, Ritter returned to New York and sailed for Hamburg in early 1938.

As for Fritz Duquesne, the old spy was once again out of the cold, doing what he loved best and fulfilling his destiny as he saw it. As a naturalized American citizen he would be spying against his adopted country, but ultimately he would be working toward the destruction of his hated enemy, England.

Fritz would gather and send information on to the Abwehr and operate undetected for a little more than two years, until Ritter sent over William Sebold, the chief contact for the nest of spies he had created in America. But Sebold was not what he appeared to be to his Abwehr mentor and would be responsible for unraveling Ritter's web of spies in one of the FBI's most unusual and letter-perfect operations.

Ritter would unwittingly destroy all of his own meticulous work.

CHAPTER 17

William Sebold Goes to Germany

W ILLIAM GEORGE SEBOLD was a German-born naturalized American citizen whose nostalgic visit to his homeland in 1939 was the catalyst that eventually led to the destruction of Nikolaus Ritter's carefully constructed spy ring in America
and the final adventure of Fritz Duquesne.[1]

Sebold was born in 1899 in Mülheim an der Ruhr in Germany's industrial Ruhr Valley. At forty years old he was six feet tall, weighed two
hundred pounds, and walked with a slight limp, or rather trudged, it
was said, with a heavy, flat-footed gait that compared favorably with
that of a bear. Sebold was described as having a stolid face. He combed
his light-brown hair carefully.

According to the FBI, Sebold served as a private in the engineering
corps of the Imperial German Army during World War I.[2] His real
name was Wilhelm George Debowski (or Debrovsky).[3] He changed his
name to William G. Sebold in 1922 when, after tramping around the
world, he jumped ship in Galveston to take up residence in America.
Following employment in various industrial and airplane plants
throughout the United States and South America, he eventually drift-
ed to California, where after a series of odd jobs he secured steady
work in 1938 as a mechanic in the San Diego plant of the Consolidated
Aircraft Company. He became an American citizen in New York on 10
February 1936.

Nostalgic for his fatherland and anxious to see his elderly mother,

Sebold decided he would return to Germany in 1939 for a short while and visit his mother, two brothers, and a sister who still lived in Mülheim.[4] It would also give him an opportunity to recover from a recent ulcer operation at Bellevue Hospital.

When the Hamburg-Amerika (familiarly known as HAPAG-Lloyd) Line's *Deutschland* pulled slowly away from Pier 84 at midnight on 1 February, William Sebold was aboard. He was certainly thinking about the impending joyous reunion with his family. But just as certainly he and his fellow passengers were concerned about the fears of a world drifting closer every day to another war.

The night before, Adolf Hitler, celebrating his sixth anniversary as chancellor of Germany, had given a speech in the Reichstag challenging the claim of England's prime minister, Neville Chamberlain, that he, Chamberlain, wanted peace, not Hitler. "Peace proceeds," Hitler said, "not from a gentleman with an umbrella but from the man with the sharpest sword in the world." Cool and guarded, Chamberlain called Hitler's response "not the speech of a man who was preparing to throw Europe into another crisis." Certainly that was wishful thinking on the part of the "gentleman with the umbrella," as was his clinging to "appeasement," a failed policy that he nevertheless emphatically told the House of Lords was "steadily succeeding."[5]

The reaction on the Stock Exchange was one of great relief, and prices shot up so fast that the day's trading was described as a "Hitler boom." Describing the world situation as "alarming," President Franklin Roosevelt said the United States would back Europe's democracies against dictatorships in every way short of war.

The world was in turmoil, but the *Deutschland* continued peacefully to Cherbourg and Southampton before docking in Hamburg on 10 February. Despite the imminence of war, there was still talk of peace. The bells of St. Peter's in Rome tolled the mournful news that same morning that Pius XI, the Pope of Peace, had died after a lengthy illness. The Spanish Civil War was winding to a close, and Eduard Beneš, former president of Czechoslovakia, had just met with New York mayor Fiorello La Guardia. While recognizing the continued danger of war, Beneš believed that war "was not inevitable." Asked if he thought a strong stand by the democracies could avert war, he replied with emphasis, "Of course."[6]

It was when Sebold stepped off the liner at Cuxhaven, Hamburg's port at the mouth of the Elbe River, that the facts become muddled in what is one of the most written about espionage gambits of World War II.

The motion picture *The House on 92nd Street,* loosely based on the Ritter spy ring case, added to the confusion with an infusion of melodrama and juggling of the facts. Even the street name was changed—perhaps for aesthetic reasons. A very successful semidocumentary film released in September 1945 by 20th Century–Fox, the film starred William Eythe as Bill Dietrich in the William Sebold role and Leo G. Carroll as Colonel Hammersohn in the Fritz Duquesne role. Fritz would have much to say about this later. He can even be seen briefly in newsreel footage at the end of the picture as he sits sullenly in a Brooklyn courtroom during arraignment. Charles G. Booth won an Academy Award for writing the best original motion picture story for 1945.

According to some reports, Sebold was met by Gestapo agents either aboard the *Deutschland* while at sea or when the liner arrived in Hamburg.[7] He was either met by two men in dark green suits or by one man in a dark overcoat—all of whom were members of the Gestapo and who questioned him at length about his work as a mechanic in America—and given vague warnings that he would be contacted again.

There is some truth in all of this. But here is probably what really happened, since it is not likely that the Gestapo was previously aware of his being aboard the ship: It would not have been unusual for the authorities to scrutinize Sebold's passport and visa carefully upon his arrival in a country that was now a police state, particularly since he was German-born and his occupation was that of an airplane mechanic in America. This was a potentially sensitive job, of interest to a Germany intending to go to war under Hitler. He could not have escaped questioning.

Following his interrogation, Sebold was left alone, free to pursue his journey of nostalgia, visiting his family and the places of his youth. He was in no hurry to return to America. It had been almost twenty years since he had been home. Mülheim, though surrounded by coal pits and iron works, was still a quaint and lovely town in its setting by the Ruhr River. His stay was made financially possible when, fully recovered from his operation, he obtained employment with the Mülheim Works of the Siemens-Schuckertwerke, then making steam turbines for the Westinghouse Electric Company in the United States. He would not enjoy this pleasant idyll for very long.

A few months after having settled down with his family and new job, Sebold received the first of three letters from Dr. Otto Gassner of the Gestapo, telling him he would like to meet with him in Düsseldorf regarding a matter of importance. Sebold ignored the letter. He would soon learn that it was a follow-up to the attention given him upon his arrival in Germany. It was the first in a series of events that would change his life forever in a way he could never have conceived.

Gassner wrote Sebold again, suggesting dire consequences unless he cooperated. Sebold wrote back, telling Gassner he was not interested.

A third and "particularly lurid" message, as Sebold described it later, followed in several weeks.[8] He was threatened with *Unterstützung*—that is, the "pressure of the State" would be brought down upon him unless he complied. He was told that he would be "taken care of," and he was given a description of the "funeral clothes" that "we give you when you're laid out here."

Meanwhile, Gassner was investigating Sebold's background, having noted with surprise that his real name was Debowski (or Debrovsky). The fact that the name of Sebold on his passport did not agree with the name of Debowski at the family home in Mülheim was not only obvious but curious to the esteemed *Herr Doktor* from the Gestapo. Equipped with the intriguing information that his prospective spy possessed another surname, Gassner now uncovered the unpleasant information in the Mülheim police files that under his real name Sebold had a criminal record dating back to early 1920 and had been jailed for smuggling and unspecified felonies. Sebold obviously had not volunteered this information when applying for American citizenship. Had he done so, he would have been denied his papers and most certainly would have been deported to Germany for having a criminal record.

Angry at the lack of response from Sebold, Gassner finally forced a meeting by going to his home in Mülheim. He suggested to Sebold that because of his work as a mechanic in an American aircraft factory, he could be helpful to his native country by supplying it with whatever information he might gather. In short, Gassner wanted Sebold to spy for his fatherland. (Actually, Canaris and the Abwehr were on tenuous ground. In an attempt to keep the United States neutral in the war, Hitler had ordered Canaris to avoid giving America a pretext for joining with Great Britain. Hitler was supported by Foreign Minister Joachim von Ribbentrop, who strongly opposed any espionage or sabotage activities in the United States.[9] Canaris assured Ribbentrop in April 1940 that he had no agents spying in America, despite the fact that Sebold was in full swing with Fritz Duquesne and other agents of the Ritter Ring. Ribbentrop was not a happy man when he learned the truth more than a year later. As will be seen, the admiral would do some fancy dancing to justify misrepresenting the truth to the foreign minister.)

Sebold balked at being a spy, pleading that he was now an American citizen and did not wish to betray his adopted country. Expecting this, Gassner confronted Sebold with the unhappy facts of his past, which he was sure would guarantee cooperation. Gassner gave Sebold a choice: either cooperate and return to America as an agent for Germany, or his fraudulent past would be revealed to authorities and he would never be permitted to return to his adopted country. Sebold would remain in his homeland permanently and in a concentration camp. Additionally, and ominously, it was pointed out to the reluctant spy that his maternal grandfather was a Jew. There could be reprisals against his family in Germany.

"I accepted 100 per cent after that," Sebold related later.[10]

It was then necessary to have Sebold approved by Dr. Renken, the German pseudonym, it will be remembered, of Fritz Duquesne's old friend Nikolaus Ritter, now head of the Abwehr's air intelligence division. A *Treff* was arranged for the two at AST VI, the Abwehr office in Münster. Renken was looking for men who could operate the clandestine radios the Abwehr would soon be setting up in America.

Shortwave communication would certainly be swifter and more efficient than the current courier system aboard "fast" transatlantic liners—now restricted to neutral American ships—which sacrificed their potential crossing speed of five days or less to lollygagging in Cherbourg and Southampton, often taking at least eleven days to reach New York from Europe. In addition to the clandestine radios, plans were being made to transfer courier activities to Pan American Clippers flying from Lisbon to New York, thus avoiding the British naval blockade, which conceivably could stop American liners for boarding and inspection.

Renken/Ritter hired Sebold, realizing that he had a "find." Sebold had spent enough years in the United States to have become thoroughly Americanized in speech and habits. Ritter saw in Sebold what he recognized and valued in himself: a German spy operating openly and above suspicion in a neutral country that surely would one day be an enemy.

Although Sebold agreed to cooperate with the Germans, he had no intention of carrying out their orders to the detriment of the country to which he had sworn loyalty. He planned to notify American authorities in Germany and follow their advice on how best to defeat the Abwehr's espionage plans for him.

There are various versions as to how Sebold communicated all this to the Americans. One account says he simply called on the American consul and told him his story; another says he called on the consul furtively. Some reports say that the Gestapo had stolen his passport or that he had lost it, and that it was necessary for him to obtain a new one from the American consul. An official FBI summary of the case tosses off this delicate and dangerous ploy of Sebold's by erroneously stating, "Sawyer"—a code name assigned Sebold, as will be seen— "succeeded in obtaining a new United States passport through the American consulate in Cologne."[11] All of these accounts are inexplicable, since a new passport was needless. Sebold would be returning to America not as William G. Sebold but with a new identity and with a "legitimate" passport given him by the Abwehr.

The most probable explanation is that Sebold—with the blessings of Ritter, who never suspected him of betrayal—went to the American consulate in Cologne and met with the vice-consul, presumably, as he told Ritter, to arrange for the support of his wife in New York.[12] This was necessary, he said, because his cover by the Abwehr required him to remain in Germany for an extended period of time for his training as a spy. Ostensibly, though, he was still working at Siemens-Schuckert. Actually Sebold was taking a calculated risk. He had no wife. The Abwehr, or the Gestapo, had stumbled badly in screening his background in the United States.

A man identified as "vice-consul" Dale W. Maher was, according to one source, "unquestionably the unsung hero of this major coup" for advising Sebold to continue the charade with the Abwehr until he came to America, at which time he could cooperate with the FBI in apprehending his spy contacts.[13] But Maher was not the vice-consul at the time Sebold visited the Cologne consulate, nor was he ever vice-consul.[14] Maher was appointed consul, not vice-consul, on 16 January 1940—only eleven days before Sebold and Ritter left Hamburg by train for Genoa to board the SS *Washington* for America. In his testimony before the court during the spy trial Sebold said, "The war had begun that day," which would be 1 September.[15] The American consul in Cologne at that time was Franklin B. Atwood. The vice-consul was Edward S. Parker.[16] Was one of these two men the "unsung hero"?

Sebold could not have picked a worse time. It was 1 September 1939. Germany had just invaded Poland. World War II was on, and the consulate was in turmoil, with Americans seeking to leave and refugees hoping for visas. Sebold found a harried consul and explained his situation. "You're in a tough spot," was the reply. "You'd better beat It."

Rebuffed but not defeated, Sebold returned a second time, this time with the threatening letters. Expressing more interest than previously, the consul declared, "You're in a bad spot. There's nothing I can do for you. But I have to copy these letters for the State Department."[17]

When Sebold returned for the letters, the consul told him he had been in touch with his superiors in Washington and had been advised to tell Sebold to go along with the Abwehr's spy school plans for him. He would be met by the proper officials, he was told, when he returned to New York. But he must notify consular officials in Cologne when he was leaving for America. (During the trial of the captured spies in New York in 1941, George W. Herz, lawyer for Hermann Lang, charged that Sebold had joined the German spy ring because of pique at the rebuffs from consular officials.[18] Sebold denied this, stating, "Their attitude was explainable, though. The war had begun that day and everybody was bothering them to get out of the country. Inside," he confessed, "I was a little hurt.")

Sebold was trained at the Klopstock Pension, the Abwehr's espionage school housed in a nondescript four-story building located in a middle-class neighborhood in the Klopstockstrasse, about a ten-minute walk from the ornate Hamburg city hall. The head of the school was Heinrich Sorau, whose real name was Captain Hermann Sandel, a deputy of Ritter's and a pilot during World War I.[19] To William Sebold, Sorau's code name was Hugo Sebold, or Uncle Hugo. In addition to the names of Sandel, Sorau, and Sebold, he also used the name of Kurz. Sorau was noted for being principally a recruiter of women, perhaps because of his appearance, which was considered typical of a German army officer: blond pompadour, highly polished boots, ruddy complexion, be-medaled chest.

Sorau used a variety of ruses to recruit a spy and secure the victim's devotion. He might get the prospect drunk, or compromise the person with a loan or bribe. He prided himself on being a gourmet and connoisseur of wines. He was equally at ease in high and low society, often having to eat knackwurst and sauerkraut washed down with the poorest of beers in the sleaziest of restaurants to obtain either information or a new recruit. Curiously, having toured the United States as a hotel dishwasher prior to the war, Sorau spoke his native German with an American accent.

During the intense four-month course under Sorau, beginning in September, William Sebold learned how to microphotograph documents, how to use secret ink, coding and decoding, and International Morse Code, and how to build and operate shortwave transmitters. As a respite from the grind of school, Ritter often entertained his special agents at the Cafe Alster-Pavillon on the Alter Jungfernsteig along the banks of the Binnen-Alster Lake, or put them up at the five-star Hotel Vier Jahreszeiten at Neuer Jungfernsteig 11. It is most likely that Sebold enjoyed both these privileges. Set in the heart of Hamburg, the school was only a short distance from Ritter's office on the Gerhofstrasse.

Sebold was taught the complicated square code system the Abwehr had found successful in two wars. The code assigned to him used as a basis the English edition of Rachel Field's popular novel, *All This, and Heaven Too.*[20] The day and date on which a radio message was sent provided the key to unraveling the code; thus the cipher was different every day. Twenty added to the sum of the month and day the message was sent gave the page of the book containing the message. To decode the message, the agent started with the first line of the given page and then worked up and down the page in a complicated series of squares until the message was deciphered.[21]

Using novels as a key to deciphering codes was a popular device with German intelligence. It was always a current novel, the theory being that if the book was seen on a spy's bookshelves, it would not arouse suspicion. During World War II a German spy in England used *Oil for the Lamps of China* by Alice Tisdale Hobart. A spy ring in Rio de Janeiro based its transposition cipher on an edition not available in the United States or the British Empire of Axel Munthe's *The Story of San Michele*. In the United States the Jahnke-Wheeler-Hill spy ring, contemporaries of the Ritter Ring, used David Hume's *Half-Way to Horror*. Daphne du Maurier's *Rebecca* was part of the Abwehr's plot to win Egypt over to the side of Germany.[22] Ritter would be deeply involved in that scheme with two young Egyptian officers seeking independence for their country: Gamal Abdel Nasser and Anwar el-Sadat.[23] If nothing else, German spies were well read in English and American literature.

When Sebold's training was completed in January 1940, he was given a new identity. He was now Harry Sawyer. His code name was

Tramp, and his number as an Abwehr agent was A.3549. He also had a new passport, compliments of the Third Reich.[24]

Prior to leaving for America Sebold was given the names and addresses for four "collectors" to memorize.[25] They would gather information for him to transmit over the secret radio to Hamburg. The first was Ritter's old friend Frederick Joubert Duquesne, Air Terminals Company, 120 Wall Street in Manhattan. The second was Lilly Stein, 127 East Fifty-fourth Street in Manhattan. Third and fourth were Everett Minster Roeder, 210 Smith Street in Merrick, Long Island, and faithful Hermann Lang, who had stolen the Norden bombsight for his *Vaterland*, at 59-36 Seventieth Avenue, Ridgewood, Queens.[26] Other names given Sebold to memorize were C. S. Wang Travel Service, Szechuan Road, Shanghai, China; L. E. Moeller, São Paulo, Brazil; and Dr. Alberto Beau, a college professor in Coimbra, Portugal. They would also be used to transmit reports to Hamburg.

Sebold was also given an advance of $1,000 and was told that another $5,000 would be deposited in the name of Sawyer in the Chase National Bank in Manhattan—not coincidentally, where Nikolaus Ritter's brother Hans was a representative. This sum would be used to pay agents. Other sums would be made available when needed.

Half of the $1,000 was to be paid to Roeder; the other half was to be used to purchase radio and photographic equipment. Roeder was a very respectable engineer and designer with the Sperry Gyroscope Company who was continually demanding more money from his German masters. He was well worth the investment.

Concealed in the back of Sebold's pocket watch in small cellophane envelopes were five microphotographs, each one no larger than a postage stamp, that could be read easily with a magnifying glass of moderate power. Two of the microphotographs were to be retained by Sebold. One contained instructions on how he was to prepare a code for communicating with Hamburg. The other gave detailed instructions on passwords and how to contact courier Irwin Siegler. The three remaining microphotographs were to be turned over to Duquesne, Stein, and Roeder.

Ritter and Sebold left Hamburg on 27 January by train for Genoa. Ritter was glad to use the extra time on the way to the Italian city to continue briefing his protégé. From Genoa the new spy would embark for the United States.

In an effort to make an impression on the spy chief he called the "brain guy," Sebold suggested that perhaps he could obtain the Norden bombsight and give it to Ritter as a present. Ritter replied, "Don't worry. It's already in our possession."[27] He then took leave of Sebold and continued on the way to his Egyptian adventure.

William Sebold—alias S. T. Jenkins to the State Department and the FBI,[28] and alias A.3549, alias Tramp, alias Harry Sawyer to the Abwehr—boarded the SS *Washington* on 29 January 1940, bound for America. The Abwehr evidently liked its agents to travel first cabin on their missions. The *Washington* was the largest American luxury liner at the time and was completing the second leg of a maiden voyage to Genoa from New York. To emphasize America's neutrality in the war, now almost five months old, and to lessen the chances of being torpedoed by a German submarine, the ship's name and the words "United States Lines" were prominently displayed between two huge American flags painted on both sides of the ship.

It was a stormy crossing for Tramp on the eleven-day voyage to New York, perhaps signifying a prelude to Fritz Duquesne's last hurrah and the foiled spy operation that would be such a shattering experience to the Abwehr, Admiral Wilhelm Canaris, and Colonel Nikolaus Ritter.

Harry Sawyer Arrives in America

I<small>T WAS THURSDAY</small>, 8 February 1940, a clear, crisp day, when the
SS *Washington* slipped into Pier 50 at the end of West Eighteenth
Street in New York Harbor.[1]

Oddly, there was less news of world conflict now when Europe had
been at war for five months than when William Sebold sailed to Germany almost exactly one year earlier. The opposing armies of the Allies and Axis were in what Neville Chamberlain called the "twilight
war." France called it *la drôle de guerre*, or the odd war. To the Germans
it was the *Sitzkrieg*. Americans called it the "phoney war." And Winston Churchill termed it a "sinister trance" as the armies waited for the
signal to pounce upon one another. They had been crouching since 7
September.

The biggest war news was that fierce little Finland was throwing
back successive waves of Russian infantry and tanks rolling against the
Mannerheim line in the battle-scarred Summo region. But it would all
be over in a month when Finland capitulated to the massive military
machine of the Bear from the North. The Japanese government was
preparing for "anticipated difficulties" in its economic relations with
the United States; a Russian commercial plane arrived in Berlin, mark-
ing the opening of regular air service between the two countries; and
the new 4,300-ton British motor ship *Munster*, making a run from
Belfast to Liverpool, sank after a mysterious explosion. The British

government suspected it was retaliation by the outlawed Irish Republican Army for the hanging that morning of two IRA terrorists. Fear was expressed that Nazi and Irish-American sympathizers would contribute financial aid to their cause.

William Dudley Pelley, Duquesne's old friend and founder of the fascist Silver Shirt Legion for which Fritz had once spied, was making news again. Pelley was under investigation by the Dies Committee on Un-American Activities for his pro-Nazi and anti-Semitic rantings and was appearing in Washington before the congressmen.

Reserved seats could be purchased at a top price of $2.20 to see *Gone with the Wind* at the Astor in Manhattan two months after its original release. Nonreserved seats were going for a top of $1.65 at the Capitol. The *New York Times* was hailing Walt Disney's new full-length cartoon *Pinocchio* as the "happiest event since the war." And Babe Ruth had just celebrated his forty-sixth birthday. If Fritz Duquesne read the sports pages, he would have noticed that Duquesne University's basketball team had brought to an end the eight-game winning streak of Long Island University with a 36–32 victory at Madison Square Garden. Basketball scores in 1940 were notoriously low. Fritz was often heard to remark that the Catholic university was named after another ancestor of his, the Marquis Ange Duquesne de Manneville, the governor general of France from 1752 to 1755.

It isn't likely that William Sebold was aware of any of the day's news, considering that he was now entering the most dangerous phase of his duplicitous operation. He was actually in less danger during his training as a spy under the aegis of the Gestapo and the Abwehr than he would be now when dealing with spies in America who were wary of any danger to themselves.

Several FBI special agents waited patiently in the pier area while the 424 passengers debarked from the *Washington*.[2] The agents were alert for anyone who might show an interest in that very special passenger aboard the ship. They had arrived earlier that morning to survey the vicinity, assuring themselves that no German agents were waiting for the passenger. Incredibly, the Abwehr was so confident of Sebold's loyalty that no agents were assigned to watch him upon his arrival in America. Apparently there was no fear that he might communicate with American authorities. Two other automobiles with two FBI agents in each were parked nearby.

Heading up the FBI group was Special Agent William G. Friedemann. Because of his fluency in German he had been pulled off a white-slavery case in the Cincinnati office.³ He had grown up in Oklahoma, but his parents were German-born, and he himself had traveled in their homeland. A lawyer who had also received a degree in farm management, Friedemann aspired to be a prison farm manager.

Assistant director P. J. Foxworth, in charge of the FBI's New York City Division, had gone to the bureau in Washington and personally reviewed the records of agents, carefully selecting those he believed were best qualified to investigate what would later be called the Ritter Ring, and in some instances, though erroneously, the Duquesne Ring. "Sam" Foxworth had been born in Purvis, Mississippi, thirty-four years earlier.⁴ The *P* was for Percy, but he always insisted, "That P in my name stands for Sam." Quiet and mild-mannered, he was filled with energy and noted for his cordial relations with reporters. He became a special agent in 1932 and was J. Edgar Hoover's administrative assistant from 1935 to 1939. He collected books on American history and wanted to write a book on Aaron Burr. Foxworth and Special Agent Harold D. Haberfield were on a special mission to North Africa in January 1943 when they were killed in the crash of an Army Air Corps plane near Paramaribo in Surinam (Dutch Guiana).⁵

Foxworth put between sixty and seventy agents on the case. Since neither Washington nor New York had enough men for the job, agents were borrowed from bureaus around the country. One special agent was assigned to each suspect, with the task of becoming thoroughly familiar with the individual under his constant surveillance. A central telephone system was set up in the New York office to allow agents to call in daily reports regarding the activities and whereabouts of their charges. During the lengthy investigation of seventeen months, some agents were transferred to other cases while others asked to be relieved of the tedium and reassigned. As new agents were brought in, it was necessary for them to spend some time reviewing the mass of information accumulating on the case.

The bureau had only recently become a clearinghouse for all matters concerning espionage, sabotage, and subversivism when on 6 September 1939, only five days after England declared war on Germany, President Franklin D. Roosevelt issued a special directive intended to combat the threat of German and Japanese espionage in America. His purpose was to end the conflict and jealousies between the different law agencies involved in apprehending spies and saboteurs. The presidential directive read, "To this end I request all police officers, sheriffs, and all other law enforcement officers in the United States promptly to turn over to the nearest representative of the Federal Bureau of Investigation any information obtained by them relating to espionage, counterespionage, sabotage, subversive activities and violations of the neutrality law."[6] It was probably the most important task ever given the bureau: protecting the internal security of the United States from enemy agents. A prophetic note, one that should have been heeded by Colonel Ritter, was added by Attorney General Frank Murphy in a follow-up statement to the press: "Foreign agents and those engaged in espionage will no longer find this country a happy hunting ground for their activities."[7]

The Federal Bureau of Investigation was exploring new territory, moving into entirely new areas in investigative technique. There had not been many opportunities before the Ritter Ring to use these novel methods. In addition to the routine detective work of daily surveillance of the suspected spies, sophisticated recording equipment and movie and still cameras would be used extensively, recording their every move and word. Hundreds of recordings would be made, thousands of candid photographs taken, and thousands of feet of movie film shot. It would be a learning process for all concerned, however primitive by modern standards of electronic gadgetry.

Tall, lumbering, and slightly nervous, Harry G. Sawyer, now no longer William Sebold, limped down the ramp of the SS *Washington.* Friedemann and another agent named McMahon recognized him immediately from passport photos given them by the consul in Cologne.[8] After passing through customs, Friedemann and McMahon took Sawyer—as we shall now call him—in their car, followed at a discreet distance by the other FBI vehicles, to bureau headquarters in the Federal Office Building at Foley Square. They were met by assistant director Earl J. Connelley, who would be in charge of the whole operation. After assigning agents to the case and placing Connelley in charge, Foxworth had bowed out and divorced the New York office from the operation. Hoover and Foxworth knew it would be a long and important investigation, and they determined that it would be best to have Connelley and his men go solo, leaving the New York office to investigate other cases.

Connelley was something of a legend in the bureau.[9] He became a special agent in 1920 and an inspector in 1936, and then served as a field assistant director from 1940 until his retirement in 1954. Known in the bureau as a quiet, calm operator, he participated in the investigation of many of the most prominent criminal cases in the nation's history. These included the kidnapping of Charles Lindbergh Jr. in 1932, at which time Connelley was chief of the New York bureau of the FBI. He investigated the Kansas City Massacre and was in at the capture of "The Terrible" Roger Tuohy. Connelley commanded the special squad in Chicago responsible for rounding up members of the Dillinger gang in 1934. And he bossed the squad that cornered Ma and Freddie Barker in their final hideout at Lake Weir, Florida, in 1935. Additionally, he played a leading role in the Alger Hiss case in 1948.

If Hoover was devoted to the FBI, agents said, Connelley lived it twenty-four hours a day.

Sawyer turned over his watch with the microphotographs to Connelley. Copies were made of the instructions for his contacts, and the watch and its contents were returned to him. He was told to cable Hamburg the message that would let the Abwehr know he had arrived safely in America and would soon begin his assignment: "Arrived safe. Had pleasant trip." The Abwehr had given him an alternate message if he felt he was being watched: "Am under doctor's care." If he fell under suspicion and could not cable, Sawyer was to write a letter, greeting his superiors with "Dear Old Bean" or "Dear Old Friend."

Actually, the FBI had not fully accepted Sebold/Sawyer as a double agent.[10] The bureau was skeptical of his story, fearful he might be an Abwehr plant, and planned to deal with him at arm's length until convinced he was genuine. Connelley had come to three conclusions: Sebold was crazy; or he had concocted this story, hoping for financial remuneration; or he had put his foot in something he could not quite handle. If this last were the case, the bureau was ready to jump in and take full advantage of the situation.

Friedemann registered Sawyer at the New Yorker Hotel at Thirty-second Street and Broadway. But before allowing him to begin the bureau's counterespionage coup against the Abwehr, Connelley decided to place Sawyer under surveillance for four weeks to determine his legitimacy. When that time had elapsed, Connelley, still cautious, had him observed for another two weeks. Special Agent James C. Ellsworth was actually assigned to live with him. During those eight weeks Sawyer was not approached by anyone. Again the FBI was amazed by the incredible naiveté, if not arrogance, of the Abwehr. Sawyer was a classic example of a loose cannon.

Special Agent Raymond F. Newkirk came down with pneumonia

and spent ten days in the hospital as a result of standing in the snow outside the New Yorker waiting to follow Sawyer whenever he left—which was seldom.[11] Newkirk's attitude echoed that of Connelley and other agents. "We didn't believe him," he said. "You don't believe it when something like that falls into your lap. The head spy comes over and says, 'I'm a spy and want to give myself up and work with the FBI.' We all finally came to the conclusion he was telling the truth. Of course, the microphotographs were pretty conclusive."

Newkirk was slightly built, just under six feet, and weighed 135 pounds. He had entered the bureau in 1936 and resigned in 1942 to join the service, having a reserve commission from Georgetown University. He was a security officer with the Defense Department when Secretary of Defense James V. Forrestal was organizing the fledgling agency. He then went with the Army Air Corps Office of Special Investigation before going into the infantry as an officer. Intrigued by "Wild Bill" Donovan's Office of Strategic Services, Newkirk applied for service in that forerunner of the Central Intelligence Agency and served in England, France, and Germany. He retired from the FBI in 1966.

All the agents who worked with Sawyer found him to be pleasant and easygoing, with no temperament. All his years in America had left him with only a slight German accent. An odd peculiarity was that he was not clean about his person or his clothes. Agent Richard L. Johnson, whom Sawyer called "that old boy from Texas," found Sawyer to be phlegmatic if not aromatic.[12] Johnson's opinion of Sawyer was that he fell into the category of so many naturalized Americans: "More loyal and patriotic than those of us born here."

Johnson had been a practicing lawyer before joining the bureau in 1940. He spent the rest of the war working on cases in New York City. His work in rounding up Duquesne and the rest of the Ritter Ring brought him a good reputation that generally got him assigned to special cases.

It was the middle of March when Connelley was finally satisfied that Sawyer was telling the truth. He gave orders to the reluctant spy to proceed with his mission for the Abwehr. The bureau would cooperate with him, making his assignment that much easier. According to orders from the Abwehr, Sawyer rented post office box 67 at the Hudson Terminal Station, 30 Church Street, where he would receive replies to letters written to spy contacts. And then, as ordered by the Abwehr, he rented a room at the YMCA at 5 West Sixty-third Street, where he would stay for the duration of his assignment. "Most of the crooks in

America stay there," Uncle Hugo had told him.[13] He was either speaking in jest or had a rather low opinion of the YMCA.

Now that he was officially accepted by the FBI, Sawyer was placed on the U.S. government payroll at $50 per week—a princely sum, considering that the American factory worker's average weekly pay in 1940 was $24.96.

During his training in Hamburg Sawyer had learned that there were five divisions in the Nazi spy system.[14] *Collectors* obtained the desired information. *Transmitters* forwarded it to Germany by shortwave radio or by mail. *Couriers,* working aboard passenger liners or transatlantic clippers, physically carried messages and other information to Germany. *Drops* were innocuous addresses of businesses or private citizens in South American or neutral European cities to which reports were sent for forwarding to Hamburg. *Specialists* were expert saboteurs.

Sawyer, a transmitter, would be dealing with only three of these categories: collectors, couriers, and drops. The Abwehr, though circumventing the orders of Hitler and Ribbentrop regarding no espionage activities in the United States, had no intention of resorting to sabotage in neutral America.

There was still a sixth category: *paymasters.* Sawyer's duties included paying the spies for their information with funds regularly deposited at the Chase National Bank. The FBI would make use of these funds in a manner not expected by the Abwehr.

Special Agents Friedemann and Johnson set up Sawyer's cover office, which according to the Abwehr plan he would use as a central meeting place for contacting other agents.[15] Room 629 was a three-room office suite on the sixth floor in the Newsweek Building, formerly the Knickerbocker Building and before that the Knickerbocker Hotel at 152 West Forty-second Street on Times Square. It was chosen because the landlord could be trusted. He was Vincent Astor, millionaire real estate owner and head of the American branch of the dynastic family. He also was a commander in the U.S. Naval Reserve, having served in the first world war. He would soon see navy service in the second. (It will be remembered that Nicholas Biddle, who had been supervisor of the New York Bomb and Neutrality Squad which had arrested Fritz in 1917, was a financial adviser to Astor and negotiated Astor's purchase of the Knickerbocker Hotel in 1921 for its conversion into an office building. Fritz could escape prisons but could not escape the irony of history.)[16]

Astor was twenty years old in 1912 when his father, Colonel John Jacob Astor, had the distinction of being the richest man to go down with the *Titanic*. The sinking made Vincent the richest young man in the world. It was his grandmother, Caroline Schermerhorn Astor, who was *the* Mrs. Astor and who, as the leader of 1890s New York society, established the famous Four Hundred.

The FBI may not have known that Vincent Astor was an amateur intelligence agent who reported directly to President Franklin D. Roosevelt.[17] After all, he was a close friend, a cousin by marriage, and a contributor of funds to the president's political campaigns. Along with Kermit Roosevelt and Theodore Roosevelt Jr., Astor formed a private intelligence society in 1927 called The ROOM—code-named The CLUB —into which they recruited about twenty wealthy and well-connected men. They met monthly in an apartment at 34 East Sixty-second Street to discuss financial and international topics. Eventually, through their contacts, The ROOM became an important source of information to Roosevelt, particularly since the group worked in collaboration with the British Secret Intelligence Service (MI6). Astor also maintained close ties with the Office of Naval Intelligence, which had been informed by FDR in 1941 that he wanted the millionaire "spy" to coordinate intelligence activities in the New York area. Astor obeyed the president's request until William "Wild Bill" Donovan organized the OSS in June 1942. There is speculation that Donovan may have been a member of The ROOM.

One interesting member of The ROOM was Sir William Wiseman, who, it will be remembered, was chief of the British Secret Intelligence Service in New York during World War I.[18] Another member was publisher Nelson Doubleday. It is intriguing to speculate that Doubleday, a passenger aboard the *Bremen* when Nikolaus Ritter came to America in 1937 on his spy-recruitment mission, may have been shadowing the Abwehr officer, but it was a missed opportunity. Another member was banker Winthrop W. Aldrich, chairman of the board of Chase National Bank. Under his direction the Chase was investigated as a conduit for espionage and sabotage money. Remaining undetected was Hans Ritter, a representative of Winthrop's own bank through whom such money was filtered—another opportunity missed by the amateur spies!

So considering his background, it is no surprise that Astor, who purchased the struggling *Newsweek* magazine in 1937, was delighted to offer offices in his building to the FBI agents and do anything necessary to assist them. He maintained his own offices in the building until his death in 1959. Astor even offered to transfer the building manager and replace him with an FBI agent, but it wasn't considered necessary.[19]

Multimillionaire Astor still collected his rent, of course. But then Hitler was paying for it. Agent Johnson paid the rent from the money funneled to Sawyer by the Abwehr each month. There was always enough to pay the Nazi agents and the office rent too. Any amount left over was used by the FBI for expenses during the operation. The bureau felt that this was one time it was operating at a profit. The total amount of money placed at Sawyer's disposal by the Abwehr during his nineteen months working undercover was $18,325.[20]

Friedemann and Johnson had the door between the two smaller offices in room 629 closed up, leaving Sawyer the bigger office.[21] Cameras and recording equipment were installed in the office immediately adjacent to Sawyer's, and the common wall was soundproofed with Rock Wool. Johnson set himself up in the next office with personnel files and other office equipment to give it a look of authenticity. It served as an office for communicating with bureau headquarters and as a rest area for agents keeping Sawyer and his visitors under constant surveillance. "Albert F. Rich—Diesel Research Company," Sawyer's cover name and occupation as a German agent in America, was painted on the door to room 629. It was a name Johnson "just pulled out of the air." The name of Rich was certainly appropriate, with Johnson handling so much of the *Führer*'s money.

Incredibly, without thinking and in his naiveté—there can be no other explanation—Sawyer listed his real name with the New York City Telephone Company instead of requesting an unlisted number. Uncle Hugo and Colonel Ritter would have been understandably upset if they had looked on page 932 of the June 1941 *Manhattan Telephone Directory*. They would have found "Sebold Wm G engs 152W42 BRyant 9-1609." The *Manhattan Address Telephone Directory* for March 1941 carried the same listing on page 549. Theoretically there was no harm in it, of course, since presumably only the Abwehr knew who Sawyer really was. The German agents in New York knew him only as Sawyer and would never have connected him with Sebold. Even the FBI—which of course did know Sawyer's identity—was unaware of this breach in security. (As will be seen, Sawyer/Sebold would later make one more potentially dangerous slip.)

As for "Albert F. Rich," he was in the *Address Directory*, but his phone number was not listed.

Shop By Telephone—The Classified ·   , To Buy It"   - name denotes business ⋏.

William G. Sebold evidently forgot he was working undercover for the FBI and the Abwehr as Harry Sawyer when when he obligingly blew his cover and listed his real name on page 932 of the June 1941 Manhattan Telephone Directory. It went unnoticed by his two employers.

Because there was no precedent for an investigation on this scale, weekly meetings were held with the special agents working the case.[22] Connelley and Tom Donegan, special agent in charge of special cases, presided over the meetings. They were not reluctant to ask for suggestions from the other agents. Again, because of the lack of precedents, there were no guidelines They made new guidelines. The questions Connelley and Donegan asked most frequently were "What do you fellows suggest? What should we do here?"

Out of one such meeting came the idea for a clock and a calendar. They would be placed in juxtaposition to each other, facing a hidden camera, so that the time and date of Sawyer's meetings with each foreign agent would be permanently and unquestionably recorded on film. So Friedemann and Johnson went shopping for a big clock and a big calendar, the "bigger the better." The two agents spent more time than they expected in their search. They were surprised to discover how few clocks and calendars had large numbers that could be read at a reasonable distance. They obtained an appropriate calendar from Harriet Ziegler, an insurance broker, whose Ziegler Insurance Company was located at 100 East Forty-second Street, a few blocks east of the Newsweek Building. The calendar had single-date tear-off pages displaying numerals about five inches high. The agents found a clock with a face about six inches in diameter. The calendar was hung on the wall above and behind the desk, on which was placed the clock, in front of Sawyer and to the right of whoever was sitting in the chair in front of him.

Two dynamic microphones—possibly the Western Electric 632 model, about three inches in diameter and one and a half inches deep—effective for the time, but necessarily large, were strategically placed to pick up the voices of Sawyer and his visitors.[23] Friedemann carved a crude stand for the clock to hide the first microphone.[24] The second mike was placed under a draftsman's board behind the visitor to pick up conversations should any of the spies decide to wander around the room.

Two Presto Disc Recorders, each costing $1,100, recorded Sawyer's meetings on lacquer-covered aluminum-based discs. Hundreds of recordings would be made during the next sixteen months, the voices picking up well in the small, acoustically clean room. As it developed, almost all the meetings were in German, which required Friedemann, because of his fluency, to handle the recordings. But he was often spelled by agents Jim Kirkland and Tom Spencer or by Joseph T. Fellner, another German-speaking agent.

Agent Newkirk installed a standard medicine cabinet with a mirror over the washbasin in room 629. It was a decoy designed to divert attention from another mirror across the room over Sawyer's right shoulder. It measured twelve by eighteen inches and was securely fastened to the wall, covering a similar-sized aperture that enabled an agent, usually Johnson, to focus a Kodak or Bell & Howell 16 mm movie camera through the glass, recording all meetings between Sawyer and his contacts. A 35 mm Leica camera was used to make still photos of the meetings. Pinned to the wall next to this mirror was a large map of Manhattan.

Because of the slow speed of the film available in 1940, fast lenses and a brightly illuminated office were needed to produce decent pictures. Wiring was changed in the ceiling so that low-watt light bulbs could be replaced with 150-watt bulbs. A lamp with another bright bulb was placed on Sawyer's desk so that its light would fall on the person seated across from him. An additional aid was that the walls and ceiling were painted a bright white.

Agents held many conferences with Sawyer, briefing him on what to do and what not to do during his forthcoming meetings with the German spies. Sawyer was particularly requested to hold up and position all photos and printed materials brought to him so that they could be photographed by Johnson.

The filming of spies on New York streets was handled by Agent Downey Rice, who was usually hidden with his movie and still cameras in a truck or a van.[25]

Now that Sawyer, according to his instructions from the Abwehr, had established an office where he could hold *Treffs* with German agents, the next step was to set up a shortwave radio transmitting station for communicating with his bosses in their underground bunkers at Wohldorf, just outside Hamburg. Secret traffic from all over the world passed through this listening post. Max Lowenthal, in his highly critical study of the FBI, claimed that "the FBI converted a German radio station on Long Island into a decoy operation, and established communication with a German station abroad, but had to get the name and location of the foreign station from the Federal Communications Commission"[26]—an obviously untrue statement, and another example of the muddling of the facts in this unusual case.

William Friedemann was assigned the task of finding a suitable location for the shortwave radio. The Abwehr had suggested to Sawyer

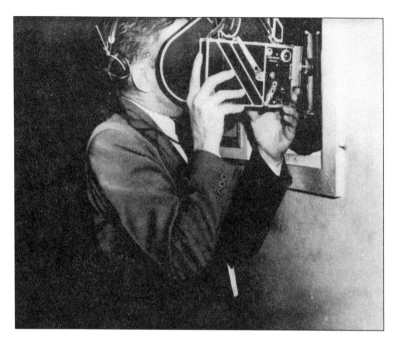

FBI special agent Richard L. Johnson behind the camera and behind a two-way mirror in Harry Sawyer's office. He filmed most of the spy meetings with the double agent. (FBI)

that he find a remote area where he could rent a farm with no high buildings around that would interfere with radio transmissions. A place where he could come and go like a weekend farmer and not attract undue attention would be best.

Friedemann found the ideal place on Long Island in Centerport, a small village of about three thousand population and forty miles or an hour's drive from Manhattan, depending on traffic. Centerport was located on a wishbone-shaped inlet at the extreme southeast end of Huntington Bay on Highway 25A. The site for the shortwave station was a nondescript wood-frame cottage at 28 Hillside Avenue—since renamed Bankside Drive North—on a high hill just off 25A overlooking Centerport Harbor on Long Island Sound.[27] It was not on a plot of land suitable for farming but had the advantage of being screened from the road by thick foliage and trees. The cottage was approached by a path from the rear leading to a garage built into the hillside. Stairs on the right turned left, then went above the garage and up the hill to

The "spy cottage" at 28 Hillside Avenue (now Bankside Drive North) in Centerport on Long Island where the FBI built a clandestine shortwave radio for transmitting military secrets to Hamburg in the name of Harry Sawyer. (Photo by Kerriann Flanagan-Brosky)

the cottage. The "cottage" was actually a split-level house with three bedrooms and two full baths. The house was in a sparsely populated area, which meant that the activities of the agents who would actually operate the radio would not come under the eyes of the curious. All locks in the house were changed as a precaution against previous owners letting themselves in.

It was never necessary for Sawyer to visit the station in Centerport, but to protect his cover later, he let his German agents believe he was there every afternoon sending to Hamburg the information gathered by the spies. Special Agent Maurice H. Price was in charge of the operation, since he was licensed by the Federal Communications Commission as a holder of a Class A radio amateur operator's license and had experience operating his own station. Agents James Ellsworth and Jack Brennan assisted him. Price planned to simulate Sawyer's touch on the key, which would further convince the Abwehr that all was right with their man in New York. Counterespionage sources had informed the FBI that agents trained in the Hamburg school had their "fist" recorded to make radiotelegraphy forgery by the Allies that much more difficult.[28]

All incoming messages were recorded by the FBI on wax discs to assure that no part of a message was lost and to preserve the transmissions for use as evidence. The messages were based on the code derived from the novel *All This, and Heaven Too*. (Sawyer could never remember the correct title, often calling it *All This Is Heavenly* or *All This in Heaven*.)[29] Later in the war agent Newkirk was with the OSS in Europe working with MI5, the British Secret Service. He was informed that MI5 had picked up the transmissions from Centerport and that their code breakers had a "helluva time trying to decipher it." When they did break the code and told American intelligence that German spies were operating in their own front yard, the polite reply was "Thank you, but we know all about it." MI5 was not told that the FBI was running the station, to avoid jeopardizing relations between the two countries.

Eventually almost daily communication was maintained between Centerport and Hamburg, with FBI agents sending information collected by Sawyer's agents after it had been carefully screened by military intelligence and the bureau. If, as occasionally happened, vital information had been gathered, it would be either deleted or altered to confuse the Abwehr. Thus there was always enough information to seem authentic and enough false data to be misleading. It would not be unusual for the FBI also to send false information to cause confusion if it could be done without arousing suspicion. During the station's sixteen months of operation, only one amateur operator reported the transmissions from Long Island as being suspicious.[30]

For transporting microphotographs and bulky items to Germany, Sawyer took advantage of the established courier-and-drop-system. But generally, according to an FBI report, the shortwave radio would be used for transmitting particular kinds of information obtained by enemy agents:[31]

[Information] relating to improved methods of manufacture and industrial development in the United States, particularly those phases of industry connected with production of war materials, improvements, and developments in armaments, with particular stress on military aircraft and the training of Air Corps personnel; the identities of ships and the nature of their cargoes leaving the United States for British and other Allied ports carrying materials and supplies necessary to the prosecution of the war; weather and various sundry other items which they believed to be of interest and assistance to the Fatherland.

The courier system imposed an unwanted but unavoidable delay in the delivery to the Abwehr of films and items such as the plans for the Norden bombsight. But for the type of information described in the FBI report, the importance of immediate delivery was obvious. With proper weather reports and a knowledge of the arrivals, departures, and courses of ship convoys, the U-Boat Command and the Luftwaffe could plan their attacks accordingly.

Sawyer/Sebold/Tramp/A.3549, with the assistance of the Federal Bureau of Investigation, had now completed all the tasks assigned him by the Abwehr except for contacting the four agents whose names and addresses he had memorized before leaving Germany. Sawyer and the FBI knew they must now move quickly. Much time had gone by since Sawyer's arrival in New York, and Captain Hermann Sandel, head of the espionage school in Hamburg, would be getting impatient, if not suspicious, at not having heard from the Abwehr's American plant.

Sawyer would have to get to Sandel, by courier, the information that the radio station was almost ready to begin transmitting. The instructions on one of the two microphotographs brought from Germany told him how to prepare a code, as mentioned earlier, and instructions on the other told him how to get in touch with the courier, Irwin Wilhelm Siegler, and what passwords to use in contacting Duquesne, Roeder, Lang, and Stein. Sawyer and the FBI had already made use of the details regarding the shortwave station as to location, wattage, frequency, and call letters.

When contacted, Siegler showed up at room 629 in the Newsweek Building and explained that he would handle all communications for Sawyer until the radio station was completed. Siegler was a butcher on the United States Lines ship SS *Manhattan* and former chief butcher on the same line's SS *America*. Sawyer's timing could not have been better. Siegler had already had an impatient message from the Abwehr: "Have you put up the radio station yet?"

Sawyer knew that since the outbreak of war, Germany's luxury liners had been converted to military use and no longer sailed the Atlantic routes. The Abwehr's couriers were forced to ply their spy trade aboard American ships, which did not dock in Germany. Because of his spy school training, Sawyer knew that the courier system was efficient and well developed, and that Siegler would be prepared with contingent plans. But he took this opportunity to ask Siegler how he would deliver his messages, pumping him for information in an exchange that was being recorded by bureau agents in the next office.[32]

"Through letter boxes in our ports-of-call," replied Siegler. "We've Duarte in Lisbon, Carlos Pitzuck in Genoa, and so on." Duarte was a code name for Dr. Herbert Dobler, who boasted that he had agents planted in the British embassy in Lisbon. One was an Englishman working as a courier between Lisbon and London. Duarte would see the contents of diplomatic pouches first, photograph them, and have the information in the hands of the Abwehr in Germany by the time they arrived in England. The spy also claimed he had access to all telegrams from London before they reached the diplomatic office.

Siegler had served a prison term in Germany for trying to smuggle money but had been released upon agreeing to act as a courier. Another courier was Erich Strunck, who had also been a partner in the money scheme and made the same deal with the Abwehr. Strunck, now a waiter on the Export Lines ship *Siboney*, was like most of the couriers recruited by Ritter: a naturalized American citizen with an unsavory past who had kept his prison record a secret. The thirty-year-old waiter had been serving time in a German jail for the same harsh law that had imprisoned Siegler. The law required any native German, under penalty of death, to register his holdings of foreign currency with the government. When given the opportunity to trade his remaining prison time for service as an espionage agent, Strunck and his fellow spies accepted it as the classic offer that could not be refused.

There was so much traffic in messages crisscrossing the Atlantic between New York, South America, and Europe that it seemed as if all the passengers and crew aboard the American luxury liners enjoying their last cruises before the war were couriers and spies for the Abwehr. Sawyer may have encountered them all at one time or another, and particularly through Siegler, who also functioned as a contact man introducing spies to each other.

Among others, Sawyer met Franz Joseph Stigler, former chief baker on the *America* and now working on the *Manhattan*. He had become a naturalized American citizen the year before. Because of the similarity of their names, Sawyer often confused Siegler with Stigler. To solve the dilemma, he called them by their spy aliases. Siegler was known as Metzger, German for butcher—a most appropriate name, since he was a butcher. Stigler was Aufzug, the word for elevator or lift. The significance is elusive.

Sawyer also met Paul Fehse, a cook aboard the *Manhattan* who claimed to be head of the Marine Division of the German espionage system in the United States. He too had been trained at the Klopstock Pension. Fehse was a leader among Sawyer's agents, arranging meetings between them, directing their activities, making sure they were paid, correlating their information, and planning its transmission via Sawyer's radio or by courier.

There was Adolf Walischewski, a steward aboard the SS *Uruguay* of the Moore-McCormack Line, who primarily transmitted information to German agents in South America.

Also working South American ports was Conradin Dold, a naturalized American who alternately worked as chief steward aboard the American Export Lines ships *Excalibur, Excambion,* and *Siboney.*

Aboard American Republic Lines' SS *Argentina* sailing between New York and Buenos Aires was seaman Heinrich Clausing.

Oscar R. Stabler was another naturalized American and a barber aboard the *Excambion.*

There was Heinrich Karl E. Stade, a stocky thirty-nine-year-old musician who played the bull fiddle. Stade was naturalized.

And there was Richard Hardwig Kleiss, forty-four-year-old chief cook aboard the *Manhattan* and formerly a seaman aboard the *President Harding* and *America.* Kleiss, who sent his messages under the name of Jimmy Hard, was called an "important courier" by FBI director Hoover.[33] He became an American citizen in 1931 but five years later moved his wife and sixteen-year-old daughter to a permanent residency in Germany. It was an indication of his true sympathies. A short time later he was arrested for trying to smuggle money out of Germany.[34]

Chief of the transatlantic couriers of the Ritter Ring was Heinrich Carl Eilers, forty-one years old and a naturalized American. He was the library steward aboard the spy-infested *Manhattan.*

Not all the couriers served at sea. Swifter delivery of information, instructions, and payroll was assured via scheduled airlines flying the Atlantic. Rene Emanuel Mezenen was a steward on the Pan American Airways *Dixie Clipper,* a four-engine Boeing B-314 flying boat, which flew between New York and Lisbon. (The plane had inaugurated transatlantic passenger service between New York and Marseilles in June 1939. Fearing the pending war, Pan Am made the usual neutrality gesture in August, displaying large American flags on the bow of the clipper.) Born in France, Mezenen came to America in 1910 and later became a citizen by virtue of the fact that his French father had served in the American army during the world war.

Richard Eichenlaub was a thirty-six-year-old naturalized citizen and proprietor of a bierstube, the Little Casino restaurant at 162 East Eighty-fifth Street. Sawyer often rendezvoused with his agents here. "This restaurant was a principal rendezvous of most of the agents arrested," said Hoover when the spies were eventually rounded up.[35] Eichenlaub was well known in police circles. He had been investigated in connection with the bombing of the British Pavilion at the New York World's Fair in 1939.

Among the other spies was Paul Bante, a fifty-one-year-old ironworker and tool- and die maker. A naturalized citizen, he liked to bluster in pro-German circles that he was a Gestapo agent. He told Sawyer, "I've got a lot of dynamite hidden away, and if we lose the war I'm going to blow up some nice bunches of people." His job was to obtain ship schedules.[36]

Sawyer, who had foolishly and unthinkingly listed himself under his real name of Sebold in the Manhattan phone directory at his office in the Newsweek Building, almost blew his cover again when Bante introduced him to Rudolph Ebeling, a forty-three-year-old shipping clerk and foreman, also a naturalized citizen. Bante told Ebeling, "I will introduce you to Harry Sawyer, a big shot with plenty of money in his pocket." At the introduction, Sawyer handed Ebeling his card and said, "I am a diesel engineer. Why don't you come to see me in my office?" Later Ebeling told Bante he had doubts about Sawyer "because the business card says William Sebold."[37] Why didn't Bante or Ebeling report it? Perhaps the answer lies in the opinion of Dr. Hans Thomsen, chargé d'affaires for the German embassy in Washington, who described the spies as "useless braggarts" and "people . . . completely unadapted for such activity."[38]

Max Blank, a thirty-nine-year-old German citizen, worked with Stabler (the *Excambion*'s barber). Employed by the German Library of Information in the German consulate, Blank told Sawyer he could obtain the secret process for making rubberized self-sealing airplane gasoline tanks and a new aircraft braking device.

Employed on the waterfront, thirty-nine-year-old Alfred E. Brokhoff was a naturalized citizen who reported on the comings and go-ings of Allied ships.

Edmund Carl Heine was a naturalized citizen living in Pleasant Ridge, Michigan, who sent all his information through Lilly Stein. Fifty years old, glib, suave, and cosmopolitan, he was a former sales representative for the Ford Motor Company and the Chrysler Corpo-ration in Germany and Spain whose annual salary often reached $30,000. He was one spy who didn't need money. He had been recruit-ed to spy for Germany by auto designer Dr. Ferdinand Porsche and Dr. Wertz, manager of the Aviation Department of the Volkswagen Werke and an Abwehr executive. They recruited him when he applied for work to promote a cheap automobile that Hitler promised everybody would be able to afford—a "people's car," the Volkswagen. It would cost $400.[39]

Gustav Wilhelm Kaercher was a Staten Island Bund leader and utili-ty company draftsman.

George Gottlob Schuh, a fifty-five-year-old carpenter, was another naturalized American.

And there was Leo Waalen, a thirty-four-year-old carpenter consid-ered by Hoover to be a "particularly active member of the ring."[40]

It was a great cast of characters.

For each of the couriers Sawyer met and reported to the FBI, the bu-reau had to place more men on the case to keep the spies under con-stant surveillance while they were laying over in New York between cruises.

Sawyer replied to the Abwehr's impatient message asking about the status of the radio station. His message, carried by Siegler—or Met-zger, as Sawyer now called him—told Uncle Hugo that he was ready to begin his espionage tasks as outlined by the Abwehr and that the shortwave radio should begin operating by 15 May. Metzger returned with a reply on the next crossing of the Atlantic by the *Manhattan*. He called Sawyer and told him he had a message from Lisbon relayed from Hamburg. "Meet me in an hour at the Black Eagle Cafe on 11th Avenue near 21st Street," he told Sawyer.[41] (Whether intended or not, it was an appropriate meeting place, steeped in German tradition. The Order of the Black Eagle was a decoration created in 1770 on the day of his coronation by King Frederick I, the first sovereign of Prussia.)

At the Black Eagle Metzger gave Sawyer a brown envelope contain-ing a single microphotograph. Enlarged, the tiny film contained last-minute instructions for contacting Hamburg by shortwave radio. Sawyer's code signature "Seeb" and his German counterpart's signature "TH" remained the same. But the message called for a change of Hamburg's previously determined call letters:[42]

Dear Friend—I gathered from your explanation that you probably will be ready for operations on May 15. Beginning on the appointed day, call for 14 days at 6 o'clock Eastern Standard Time, every 10 minutes calling CQDXvW-2. We will recognize you in that you will give the small letter "v." We will look for you between 14,300 and 14,400. For our call letter use AOR instead of DOR and keep it up until 7 o'clock at 10-minute intervals.

A great deal will depend on atmospheric conditions. Don't become impatient if it shouldn't work for days.

Because the Abwehr had chosen the call letters AOR, the station would be considered an "outlaw." Use of the letters *A* and *B* had been banned by the Cairo International Convention of 1938, which promulgated shortwave radio regulations. The convention had determined that every country would be assigned certain letters of the alphabet from which call letter groupings are derived. The letters *A* and *B* were not assigned to any nation at the time of the Cairo convention. The Germans may have chosen the combination for the Centerport station believing that it was least apt to attract the attention of the American monitoring system and the thousands of licensed operators in the 14 MHz ham band.

An amateur wishing to communicate over a long distance usually makes the general call *CQ*, followed by *DX* meaning "long distance contact desired." The small *v* meant "from." *W-2* was the prefix for amateurs in the second call area, which included Long Island. The Germans did not add the two or three letters that normally follow the prefix.

Obeying Sawyer's instructions from Hamburg to the letter lest he arouse any suspicion, Special Agent Maurice Price began transmitting CQDXvW-2 into the ether over and over every ten minutes beginning at 6 P.M. on Wednesday, 15 May 1940. Would Uncle Hugo buy his "fist"? He rested for ten minutes, then began again. He continued for one hour without receiving a reply from AOR. He would have to try again the following evening.

It was not until one week later on 22 May that AOR crackled through across the Atlantic. Using a copy of *All This, and Heaven Too*, the message was decoded to read "*Sehr gut! Sehr gut!* Very good! Very good! Grand work, old bean. Keep it up." There were no more messages that evening. Agents Ellsworth and Brennan congratulated Price. Uncle Hugo had bought his "fist."[43]

Transatlantic radio reception was so bad for the next few days that it wasn't until 27 May that another message came through. Price wrote down the dots and dashes even though they were being recorded on wax discs: "Send only two times per week. We are prepared to receive and send daily. Furnish days you expect to send. For your security also send at other times. We are prepared to receive at 7 a.m. and 5 p.m. Call signal only three letters. No CQ. Furnish frequency outside amateur band." Price answered immediately, giving the details requested.[44]

The following night's message contained more revisions: "Your signal is very weak. Can you improve it? I will send Tuesdays and Thursdays at 1 and 5 p.m. EST. After that will listen daily except Saturday night and Sunday. Saturday, 12 noon, OK. Will furnish you new frequency later." More power was added immediately by the agents to assure continued contact with AOR. Now that they had progressed this far, they did not dare chance losing further contact.[45]

During the operation of Tramp's station, which continued until shortly before the trial of the arrested spies in September 1941, more than 300 messages were transmitted to AOR, and 501 were received by CQDXvW-2.[46] To assure that the FBI would have no future legal difficulties in proving that AOR operated from Germany or German-occupied territory, exhaustive tests were conducted by government monitoring stations throughout the country from September 1939 to August 1940. Albert Leroy McIntosh of the National Defense Operations of the FCC definitely located the station's transmitter in the vicinity of Hamburg. Its exact location in the city was changed frequently to avoid destruction in British air raids.[47]

Now all Sawyer had to do was contact the four agents whose names and addresses he had memorized before leaving Germany: Frederick Joubert Duquesne, Lilly Barbara Carola Stein, Everett Minster Roeder, and Hermann Lang. They in turn would contact other agents who would meet with Sawyer in room 629 in the Newsweek Building.

The result thirteen months later would be exposure of the largest and best-organized German espionage ring in America. It would be the most sensational spy case of the war, creating headlines around the world.

The Abwehr would be in shock and disarray.[48]

CHAPTER 19

"Get Duquesne to Forty-second Street"

B UT WHERE DID Frederick Joubert Duquesne live? Not even the Abwehr knew. The only address given Sawyer was 120 Wall Street in the Exchange Building, where Fritz maintained an office on the thirty-first floor for his bogus business, Air Terminals Company, which he had registered in 1937 as a business servicing securities. If Fritz was to be placed under constant surveillance, it was imperative to know where he lived as well as worked. He didn't work much in his office, the FBI learned quickly, because he didn't show up for the first several days after a watch was put on the place.

Agents never did learn what constituted the business of Air Terminals Company or what Fritz did in the office when he was there. All they really learned was that his mail was delivered there and his rent for the one-room office was cheap. The Wall Street address was considered only a front where Fritz posed as a stockbroker engaged in selling RKO stock. Whether he was actually selling the stock is not known. Perhaps he was using the famed initials either for the sentiment or in irony, reaching back into his past when he was a publicist for the film company. The truth is that he was correctly registered as a broker and dealer transacting business on over-the-counter markets as of 23 March 1939.[1]

While checking out Fritz's office, agents thought they had discovered something of importance when, after jimmying the lock on a desk drawer, they still couldn't get it open.[2] Crawling under the desk, they found that Fritz had bored a hole through the bottom of the drawer and through the drawer port, then stuck a nail up through the hole. They pulled out the nail and opened the drawer. It was empty—much to their disappointment. It was determined that the office was just a place for Fritz to kill time.

Fritz finally showed up at 120 Wall Street, but it took four nights and some exhaustive gumshoeing to find where he lived, even though the bureau maintained that New York was the easiest place in the world to tail someone because of the crowds.

The old fox, whom agents had now named the Duke,[3] had learned something about evasion and ducking a tail during his more than half-century of stalking big game and playing at being a spy. There were some leg-weary agents who learned that Fritz was a very good walker.

Special Agent Raymond F. Newkirk, who was personally assigned to Fritz for about sixteen months, said he was the only man he had ever encountered to whom spying was a way of life. "I had never come across anyone like him before, and because of his paranoia about being followed, he was the most adept individual at avoiding surveillance I had ever known," Newkirk said:

He lived like someone was following him all the time, which he really believed was happening. It is true we were doing just that at the time; but it made no difference, he lived that way anyway.

We thought it would be easy to follow him in the subway; but it was routine for him when traveling by underground train to take an express, change to a local, change back again to an express, and so on. It was a matter of habit for him on going through a revolving door to keep right on going around and out again. He would take an elevator to one floor, then walk down the stairs and out another door. He liked to walk around a corner, stop abruptly, and wait to see if anyone came hurrying around the corner after him.

That's why we had trouble finding his home, because we had never followed anyone like him. He was so good it took us four nights to follow him from his so-called office to his apartment, because he was able to lose us the first three nights.

Tom Donegan followed the Duke the first two nights and lost him. "Get Duquesne to Forty-second Street and I'll take him from there," he said. That night, four or five of us followed him and lost him. He must have been in a hurry because he fooled us and took a train straight home. We never got him to Forty-second Street. Five men shadowed him again the fourth night and this time followed him all the way to 24 West Seventy-sixth Street. [This

The house at 24 West Seventy-sixth Street in New York City where Fritz lived on the first floor with Evelyn Clayton Lewis and where the two were arrested by the FBI in June 1941. (Photo by author)

was *The House on 92nd Street.*] He and his mistress, Evelyn Clayton Lewis, lived in a one-bedroom studio apartment on the second floor of the four-story apartment building, where they paid a monthly rent of $45. Surveillance could be maintained from panel trucks and from the apartment across the street. Every visitor was filmed by movie and still cameras.

The Duke's landlady was Mrs. Stanley Jareski, a Polish woman who had lost two brothers in the war, which made her very pro-American and all the more eager to cooperate with the FBI when she was informed of Fritz's identity and the bureau's plans. She set Newkirk up in an apartment directly above Fritz's and arranged for an apartment for the surveillance team directly across the street. The irony must be noted that one of Fritz's neighbors across Seventy-sixth Street at number 25 was Mary Jobe Akeley, former wife of Carl Akeley, the naturalist/explorer who had been one of the many African experts, including Fritz, called to the White House in 1908 and 1909 by Teddy Roosevelt for advice on his forthcoming safari.

Agents lived in close proximity to all the spies being watched, and microphones were placed in their apartments. Six or seven agents spelled off Newkirk during the constant twenty-four-hour-a-day, seven-day-a-week operation. Agents would check in at 8 A.M. and leave the same time the next morning. According to Newkirk, most agents tired of this kind of work, which was stressful in its boredom. But he was temperamentally suited for it because he enjoyed reading and spent most of his time in the apartment reading "more damn' books."

The much-used dynamic microphone was installed behind the doorbell above the door in Duquesne's large, high-ceilinged apartment. The bell was actuated by a button pushed at the entrance downstairs. Agents keeping monotonous vigil in Newkirk's apartment above sat out the long hours with earphones to their heads, listening to every word said in the Duke's room. If their eavesdropping revealed plans for the day, the agent on duty would pass on the information to the surveillance team across the street. It made following the Duke much easier when his destination was known beforehand. Now that they were familiar with the ways of the wily old Boer, they never lost him again. "Every time the bell rang it about knocked my ears off," recalled Newkirk, who was often deep in concentration reading a book when a visitor stopped by to see Fritz.

Newkirk was quick to respond once when the clanging in his ears wouldn't stop. Obviously the bell was stuck. He ran downstairs and asked Duquesne what all the racket was about. "The damn' doorbell's out of order," Fritz replied.

Fearful that the Duke might call a repairman who would discover the microphone, Newkirk volunteered to fix it. The doorbells to the four apartments were operated by batteries set in the back of a box next to the door downstairs. Not wanting to make a mistake regarding the Duke's bell, Newkirk pulled the wire leads to all the tenants' bells, putting them all out of commission.

Newkirk then told Mrs. Jareski and Fritz he would have someone up the next day to fix the bells. He called the FBI office, and Harold G. "Robby" Robinson came out to do the repair work. Robby attached all the leads again. He then went to the Duke's room to confirm that the bell was in working order and made sure the microphone was connected. The unsuspecting Fritz held the stepladder while Robby adjusted the dynamic mike.

It was the policy then of the bureau for agents to arrange their own cover. Newkirk's cover was that he worked in a Manhattan pharmacy. He chose the name of Ray McManus, that of a friend he recalled from law school who had worked in a drug store. If Fritz asked Newkirk anything about his background, he would give that of the real Ray McManus.

Ray Newkirk discovered that Fritz was an outgoing person who delighted in making friends. The two became acquainted by "chance" in a meeting arranged by Newkirk, who timed his departures by listening to Fritz's goodbyes to Evelyn. Hello and how-are-you greetings were exchanged on subsequent meetings. They were soon on a first-name basis. Fritz never suspected him of being an FBI agent, Newkirk believed, because, with his slight build, he didn't project the public's image of an agent. Except for an occasional hello, Newkirk never got to know Evelyn well, since she spent most of her time in the apartment serving as a lookout and writing letters seeking military information for Fritz. Newkirk considered her not glamorous, but a nice-looking, clean-cut woman. Knowing that the Duke always had plenty of money in his pocket—for the first time in his life, Fritz was flush with funds, thanks to the Nazis—Newkirk was amused to observe that he was always crying poor mouth and borrowing a dollar or two from Evelyn for expenses.

Newkirk actually developed a fondness for the Duke: "I couldn't help liking him. He was so entertaining. His English was excellent with no accent. When he wanted to impress someone among his friends, particularly a lady, or someone newly met, he would affect an English accent." Considering that he was a dedicated Anglophobe, it was an interesting and odd quirk in his character that he would resort to a British speech pattern to make an impression. But then he never shrank from doing what was best for Fritz, however repugnant.

Newkirk never got so close to Fritz that he was invited to the spy's private parties. But he observed that the Duke always had to be the center of attention. If someone appeared to be more informed about a subject than he, Fritz would work the conversation around to a subject he was sure his audience was ignorant about. Then he would take over. He would inquire as to whether any of them had ever been to certain places, such as South America, Africa, or even Bermuda. When he found a place none of them knew anything about, he would dwell on that country and entertain them with fascinating stories about his exploits there, knowing full well that he could not be contradicted.

Like Nikolaus Ritter before him, who had also been beguiled by Fritz's stories, Newkirk found the old spy to be a fascinating talker. Best of all, he was never boring. Newkirk confirmed that Fritz's pleasant, well-modulated baritone speaking voice was the key to his ability to spellbind listeners. Fritz freely discussed his past and was not a bit reticent about telling every detail of his imprisonments and escapes. He would talk to anyone who would listen and took narcissistic pleasure in showing to anyone who would take the time to browse through it a meticulously kept scrapbook containing clips and stories about his life. He said he planned to write a history of his exploits. (It will be remembered that a scrapbook was found among his possessions when he was arrested in New York in 1917. Ever the self-aggrandizer, Fritz was quite proud of his publicity, good or bad.) The Duke and Newkirk would often sit on the front steps of their apartment house and chat for hours, Fritz going on endlessly about his past. Whenever he discussed the Boer War, Newkirk noted, his anti-British feelings were evident. But the agent admitted to learning more about the war from Fritz than he ever did from books.

Surveillance of Fritz and other members of the spy ring never ceased. He never left his apartment without being followed. He was the one spy among the thirty-three being watched with whom the bureau had to be particularly careful.

Once, Fritz caught an agent following him, a newly sworn man just placed on the case. He was too close to the Duke, and coming up the stairs out of a subway, Fritz suddenly turned and accosted him. "I say,

Perhaps wondering where the FBI camera might be, a puzzled Fritz scratches his head on a New York street on 29 May 1940. (FBI)

Fritz (left) and an unidentifiable William Sebold/Harry Sawyer cross a New York street on 29 May 1940. Not even Sebold knows that an FBI camera is watching. (FBI)

young man," he said calmly, "can you tell me why you are following me?"

A tyro but quick-witted, the agent grabbed Duquesne by his coat lapels, shook him and banged him around a bit, and said, "I've heard about you sons-of-bitches approaching people on the subways, but this is the first time I've ever met one. I've a damn' good mind to turn you over to the cops!"

Still being roughly pushed around, but now convinced that he had made a mistake and not wanting to create a bigger scene or have the police called, the Duke apologized profusely. "I thought you were somebody else," he said meekly. And the two parted.

Another time Newkirk overheard Fritz on the sound system boasting to Evelyn that he had spotted an FBI man following him, but that he managed to elude the agent and then followed his follower without being seen. Fritz toured New York for a couple of hours, he claimed, shadowing the man's every move through Central Park, art museums, and other tourist attractions. Newkirk called the agents across the street and relayed the information. They laughed and told him that Fritz had been under surveillance all day and that the agent, although led on a merry chase, had been undetected. The Duke had been dogging an innocent tourist.

Agents believed that the Duke was color-blind. When he drove a car—which, fortunately for others, was not often—he would consistently run red lights. He was simply, in the words of the agents who followed him, "a lousy driver." On one occasion he drove to Washington, D.C., to check at the Patent Office on either the electromagnetic mine device he had submitted to the U.S. Navy Department in 1919 or a floating-dock invention he had also devised, which would allow seaplanes to be serviced without having to be removed from the water. His companion was Helen, the blonde who had introduced him to Evelyn. She must have been an understanding mistress indeed. Helen, incidentally, was a frequent visitor to their apartment.

According to Newkirk:

He left New York City at about 7 A.M. with two cars following him. Both lost him a short time later in midcity. At that time, only U.S. 1 was used to travel between the two cities. So we drove directly to the highway, waited for him to go by, and then fell in behind. The drive to Washington should have taken only six hours; but sixteen hours later at 11 P.M. he had gotten only as far as the University of Maryland in Baltimore. They checked in at a hotel and the next morning we followed them the rest of the way.

I don't think he knew he was being followed, although he might have thought he was. He drove us nuts. He went around in circles, took wrong turns, got lost, and finally arrived in the early evening in Washington. We waited until the two settled into a hotel room, then turned them over to the Washington office and returned to New York. The Washington office reported to us later that the Duke completed his business at the Patent Office and returned to New York.

It is not known whether Fritz found the papers relating to his invention for a floating dock or for the device to destroy mines in harbors. What would he have done if he had found them? Sell the inventions to the Germans? Have the mine developed for the purpose of destroying ships in American harbors when, and if, he made the transition from spy to saboteur? Then there was the alternative: sell the plans to the United States. Why not? Bizarre, certainly. But not beyond the schemes of a man who, after all, had sold Liberty Bonds in New York shortly after destroying British ships in South America during World War I. The answer will never be known.

During the time he was under surveillance Fritz took one other trip out of New York. Newkirk overheard him tell Evelyn that if things ever got too hot for him, he could hide out in a friend's cottage in Vermont where the FBI would never find him. He told her in great detail the route he would follow and pointed it out on a map. Newkirk traced the route himself on a map while listening to the two discuss the forthcoming trip.

On the day he planned to visit his Vermont friend, Fritz told Evelyn, "I'll go downtown today. If any of the FBI guys are following me I'll lose them, then meet you at 125th Street. If I walk by the car and tip my hat, that means they're still with me. Then you meet me in the car at the next subway stop." (Again, he only assumed he was being followed. He did not know it to be a fact.)

The Duke went through all these elaborate arrangements to shake a tail that never was, nor did he have to tip his hat to Evelyn, since the agents never followed him to Vermont. They didn't have to. They knew exactly where their quarry was going. Newkirk took a train to Albany and met another agent who knew the territory. Knowing approximately what time Duquesne would pass by, they drove to the highway and waited. Their timing was good. They didn't have to wait long, and they followed the Duke to pinpoint his possible future hideout. Then they returned to New York.

The most suspenseful moment during Newkirk's surveillance of

Fritz occurred one day when the Duke and Evelyn left the apartment together. This was unusual, because one or the other always stayed behind, either for messages or, in Evelyn's case, as a lookout. This gave Newkirk a long-awaited opportunity to enter their apartment and obtain typewriter print specimens. He slipped into the downstairs apartment when agents following Fritz called to let him know that the two were now far enough away that it would take at least an hour for them to return. No one else was in the building except the landlady, because all the other tenants worked.

But Newkirk had carelessly left the door open, and Fritz's cat got out while he was taking samples. He immediately went after the animal and spent almost half an hour chasing it around the interior of the building, during which time agents signaled him by phone that Fritz was on his way back. Newkirk caught the cat, returned to the apartment, shut the door carefully, and obtained the rest of the samples just five minutes before Fritz and Evelyn returned. It would have been the end of the operation if he had been caught, because Fritz would have had to be arrested. If this had occurred, Newkirk's greatest fear— "catching hell from Hoover"—would have become a reality. The specimens proved in court later that the reports Fritz gave to Sawyer had been typed on this typewriter.[4]

Fritz was soon to meet Sebold/Sawyer. When he did, he believed he had finally reached the pinnacle of his career as a professional spy.

But the Black Panther of the Veld would have only a short time to bask in his own glory—and much time to look at his scrapbooks.

CHAPTER 20

The Rest of the Players

NTER LILLY BARBARA CAROLA STEIN, the femme fatale of the Ritter Ring.

Once a brunette, now a blonde, hazel-eyed Lilly was an attractive, albeit plump, twenty-five-year-old former artist's model who would become known as the glamour girl among the Nazi spies. Born into an affluent Austrian family, Lilly had all that money could buy as she matured, but strict family discipline estranged her from her parents.[1] By the time she was fourteen she was better known in social circles than at home. An interest in figure skating, fueled by the ancillary privileges of partygoing, made her well-known in international skating circles and at winter carnivals, which also brought her to the attention of another ice-skating enthusiast: Heinrich Sorau, head of the espionage school in Hamburg, whose real name was Captain Hermann Sandel. Code name, Uncle Hugo.

According to Lilly when arrested by the FBI in 1941, she and Sorau had been frequent traveling companions since their meeting when she was quite young.[2] She knew him only as Heinrich Sorau, she said, not as Hugo Sebold. He identified himself as an international businessman with widespread interests and considerable government influence.

Financial difficulties crashed down on Lilly following the 1938 Anschluss in Austria. Her parents died, her income stopped because of the estate being tied up in litigation, and she lost many of her former friends because of her Jewish ancestry.

Good old Uncle Hugo to the rescue!

An attractive woman in distress was his specialty. He could use such a woman to his and Germany's advantage. Sorau was convinced that Lilly would be of more value to the Abwehr for her physical attractiveness than for her mental abilities, which were, to put it kindly, suspect. (J. Edgar Hoover called Lilly "a Viennese prostitute.")[3]

Lilly and the Abwehr were in similar positions but had dissimilar priorities. If Lilly were to succumb to Uncle Hugo's carrot, she would betray her Jewish heritage. Money again, and a return to the social whirl, was a prospect too tempting to turn down. Escaping execution was a nice prospect also. It didn't take Lilly long to make a decision.

Uncle Hugo—and the Abwehr—would have to compromise Germany's "final solution" by hiring Lilly. But it had been done before. Look at William Sebold. Considering Lilly's previous lifestyle, she probably gave little thought to her choices and took the easy way. It was also easy for Uncle Hugo and the Abwehr.

Uncle Hugo trained darling Lilly personally at the Klopstock Pension in Hamburg.[4] Following graduation it was planned to dispatch her to the United States, where her task would be to establish herself socially in Manhattan, visiting the best hotels and nightclubs and patronizing the opera, seeking out what significant information she could from the prominent people she consorted with.[5]

Lilly would also be a link between German military intelligence and its agents planted in America. She would request funds as needed, which would be forwarded to her through Amsterdam and South American banks and which she would then pass on to paymaster Else Weustenfeld for payment to agents.[6]

Meanwhile, though, Lilly was very busy elsewhere, even while being trained for her future spy work. In fact she was establishing social contacts even before leaving for her mission in America. Lilly had made the acquaintance of Ogden H. Hammond Jr., vice-consul in Vienna and son of Ogden H. Hammond Sr., U.S. ambassador to Spain from 1925 to 1929.[7]

It seems that Ogden Jr. rather enjoyed life, so much so that in October 1940 the State Department's Bureau of Foreign Service Personnel, which included on its staff future secretary of state Dean Acheson, attempted to force the young Hammond to resign for publicly mimicking President Roosevelt at a Newport social gathering and for "disloyal dealings" with an unnamed female agent of a foreign power.[8] It was only after Lilly's arrest in June 1941 that her name was linked with Hammond's name in print. Hammond admitted at the time that he had known Lilly slightly in Vienna, but he referred to her as a "pathetic little creature" and denied any wrongdoing. In March 1940 he filed a petition in federal court for an injunction against the State Department to bar his Foreign Service status from being altered.[9] He eventually lost the suit in a court of appeals and was denied a Supreme Court review in March 1943 to get back his old job. In later life Hammond was involved in mining prospects in Australia and oil exploration in Texas. He died in 1976.

It was during Lilly's training that Hitler's blitzkrieg thundered through Poland. She graduated from Klopstock, but German ships could not get through the British blockade to America; so Lilly was sent on a roundabout route through Sweden, leaving Göteborg on 13 October 1939 aboard Swedish American Lines' *Drottingholm,* which arrived in New York on 24 October.

Lilly registered at the fashionable Windsor Hotel—now the Helmsley-Windsor—at 100 West Fifty-eighth Street.[10] For what the Abwehr expected from its Lilly, anything less would not have been proper. Once settled in at the Windsor, Lilly sent a letter to Else Weustenfeld, enclosing a note signed by Sorau: "I am sending this woman to you. Will you please help her?"

Else arrived at the hotel on 20 October and was greeted by Lilly with the password: "I bring regards from your friends from Verden an der Aller." (Verden an der Aller was a small manufacturing city on the Aller River fifty-seven miles southwest of Hamburg. The choice of password normally had some significance: the agent being contacted might have a family connection with the city named or be well known to the person named.)[11]

"What else did you bring?" asked Else.

Lilly was also a messenger. Before leaving Germany she had been given a microphotograph of instructions for Fritz Duquesne, whom the Germans still considered their most valued agent in America. The small piece of film was dutifully placed in the bottom of a box of face powder, a not too subtle trick Lilly had learned in spy school. She also carried something Fritz would appreciate more: $500. It seems Fritz had been complaining bitterly to Else about a lack of funds. "How can I work if I don't get any money?" he asked Else. She replied that she couldn't pay him anything until she was authorized to do so by Hamburg. She passed the demand on to the Abwehr and added that Fritz was getting impatient.

"The money is for Jimmy Dunn," said Lilly, handing the cash to Else.

Lilly did not know, nor did it matter, that Jimmy Dunn was just one of Fritz Duquesne's many aliases. She was also unaware that Fritz, having seen some photos of her in the nude, was anxious to meet her.[12]

A few days later, when "Jimmy Dunn" visited Else's apartment at 312 West Eighty-first Street, she gave him the money and micro. "So Jimmy is becoming useful to them again, is he?" said the elated Fritz.

On her own initiative and with two friends, Lilly wasted no time in opening an exclusive women's clothing store in the smart retail district along Madison Avenue, specializing in exotic and high-priced beachwear for the Upper East Side Florida-bound trade.[13] The enterprise provided her with extra income as well as a cover to the inquisitive. But primarily she anticipated using the shop as a tool to gather the secrets she had come to America for. She acquired a list of wealthy clients, all wives of industrialists and financiers. Tea or cocktails served in a friendly atmosphere, mingled with shop talk, could be expected to elicit useful information regarding the business of her customers' husbands. But, as will be seen, it did not quite work out that way for poor Lilly. She had fallen on hard times.

Glamorous Lilly was no longer living at the Windsor in May 1940 when Sawyer got in touch with her. She was living in a ground-floor apartment at 127 East Fifty-fourth Street.[14] "I bring you greetings from Bachenal and Grinseng" was the password this time.

"Yes. I was notified to expect you," said Lilly.

The meeting was short, necessitated only by the need to make contact and for Sawyer to give Lilly her microphotograph with new instructions and to let her know they would have regular meetings so that she could pass on to him whatever information she had collected.

Sawyer discovered that Hermann Lang, who at his arrest in 1941 was described by Hoover as "one of the very active members of the ring," was no longer living in Ridgewood, Queens, at 59-36 Seventieth Avenue, the address given him by the Abwehr.[15] He managed to find a janitor who gave him Lang's new address in Glendale, Queens, at 74-36 Sixty-fourth Place. Glendale, like Ridgewood, was noted as an ethnic mecca for German Americans.

On Saturday, 23 March, at twelve noon, Sawyer introduced himself to a wary Lang with Ritter's personal password: "I bring you greetings from Rantzau, Berlin and Hamburg."[16] There were no microphotographs containing instructions for Lang. Admiral Canaris and Ritter were clearly worried about their treasured spy's safety and did not want to place him in jeopardy if Sawyer were caught with a micro.

Lang let Sawyer into his apartment but, suspicious of his visitor, refused to open up to him. He could be an FBI agent. Lang responded indifferently, becoming animated only when Sawyer said, "Ritter wants you and your wife to return to Germany by way of Japan and the trans-Siberian railroad. All expenses will be paid and there will be a job for you."

At this point in his spying career Lang actually did want to return to Germany. He was becoming more apprehensive about being discovered and daily feared exposure. "Sad-faced," as he often was called, accurately described him. Nevertheless, he was still not sure of Sawyer's Abwehr credentials. "I have no desire to go to Germany," he replied. "I am an American citizen."

"So am I," said Sawyer. "But I'm also with German espionage and I'm here to deliver the message I just gave you and to transmit whatever information you can give me."

"I want nothing to do with you. I don't trust you" was Lang's only reply.

Realizing he was not making progress, Sawyer cut off the visit, indicating he would see Lang again. He decided that patience and a little time would soften Lang's attitude, allowing him to get through to the spy and perhaps obtain incriminating evidence against him. The FBI still had nothing but suspicions.

Sawyer visited Lang again several weeks later.[17] This time the reluctant spy expressed a wish to go back if an easier route could be found, since his wife's health was not good.

Sawyer asked Lang how much he had received for delivering the Norden bombsight to Germany. Lang replied that he had not received money but that he relied on being "taken care of" when he returned to Germany. "Aren't you afraid of being cheated of your honors?" asked Sawyer.

"If any cheating is done," said Lang, "I can write Göring in person."

"You must be a big shot," said Sawyer admiringly. "You know Hitler and Göring."

"Sure," answered Lang boastfully, "I know Hitler and Göring. I know all of them. I've known them for years. I fought with Hitler from 1923 to 1927."

Lang reiterated that he hadn't "received a cent" for stealing the bombsight. He then demanded some compensation. (A request for money from Lang was contrary to Ritter's high regard for him. Ritter wrote in his autobiography that he was astonished to encounter a spy "who was stealing secrets purely for ideological reasons and not for monetary gain.")[18]

Sawyer said he would look into it.

A week later Lang had another reason for declining to return to Germany. For security reasons all Norden employees were being fingerprinted, and those with vital jobs were informed that they would not be allowed to leave the country.[19] Lang also refused to cooperate any more in providing vital information unless he was paid for his work on the bombsight. This was certainly a different Lang. "I was offered $10,000," he complained, "and it's about time I got paid."

Sawyer again said he would see what he could do. The FBI radioed AOR with the information that Lang was impatient for payment. AOR sent a coded reply: "Tell Lang that 10,000 marks are here waiting for him."

Lang was not happy. "I was to be paid 10,000 *dollars,* not *marks,*" he said. "At the present rate of exchange that is only about 4,000 dollars." The "ideological spy" could compute faster than an abacus.

Sawyer said he had no control over how much or how Lang was paid. "All right, I'll accept," said Lang. "But explain to them that the air is thick here. I am not allowed to go to Germany."

"Then you want the money sent to you here?"

"No," Lang replied. "One of these days, Germany will fight America and win. American money will be worthless. I want that money to be given into the care of my sister."

The next message to AOR read, "Lang requests that the money be deposited, in marks, in the Dresdener Bank, in the name of his sister, Johanna Lang, who should be notified. He cannot come himself. The air is too thick."

AOR replied, confirming that Lang's requests had been complied with. When Sawyer gave the message to Lang, the spy had valuable information to give in return: the monthly production figures of the Norden company. AOR did not receive the correct figures.

After his first meeting with Lang in March, Sawyer visited Everett Minster Roeder at 210 Smith Street in Merrick, Long Island. Roeder was the engineer and designer with the Sperry Gyroscope Company whom Sawyer had been instructed to give $500 to before leaving Germany. A forty-six-year-old pudgy little man who wore thick-lensed spectacles, Roeder was the only native-born American, aside from Evelyn Clayton Lewis, among the twenty-eight spies Sawyer would contact.

Admiral Canaris claimed that among the precious American military secrets Roeder obtained for Germany since he began working for the Abwehr in 1937 were the blueprints of the complete radio instrumentation of the new Glenn Martin bomber and, among the Sperry developments, classified drawings of range finders, blind-flying instruments, a bank-and-turn indicator, a navigator compass, a wiring diagram of the Lockheed Hudson bomber, and diagrams of the Hudson gun mountings. Roeder's future plans included delivering the latest developments in Sperry's new bombsight.[20] Additionally, Roeder delivered a speech scrambler and a remote-control machine-gun sight.[21]

Roeder was a respected citizen in the Merrick community and a well-regarded draftsman and designer in his field. It is not likely that he would ever have been suspected as a German spy had the Abwehr not given Sawyer his name. In addition to his salary from Sperry, Roeder realized a good income from inventions related to firearms, a subject in which he was an expert. Roeder was a member of the National Rifle Association and several other gun clubs. He had a private arsenal of nine rifles, six pistols, several shotguns, and a cartridge-filling machine.[22] State and town permits for the weapons made everything legal.

Roeder went on the Nazi payroll during a visit to Germany in May 1936 when, as in the case of Sebold, the proper authorities noted his affiliation with a defense company and approached him with the suggestion of working for the country of his ancestors. The proper authorities were the omnipresent Heinrich Sorau—Uncle Hugo—and an associate, Hans Dreier. Pride in his German background no doubt was used as a gentle persuader, but Roeder was not the type who needed much persuasion. Greed was his motivation, not ideals. It was strictly a business proposition with him. He liked money. He was the kind of spy Ritter was used to: the agent whose only allegiance was to money.

Sawyer gave Roeder his micro of information and the $500, which he accepted more eagerly than he did the orders. The two would have subsequent meetings later, usually in railroad stations and other public places. Roeder seldom went to Sawyer's office, and he would never turn over any information unless he was assured that there would be money forthcoming. "Chicken feed!" Roeder retorted when Sawyer some time later gave him a payment of $240. The odd figure may have raised his ire.

Sawyer continued carrying out the instructions in his own micro orders and wrote a letter to Colonel Frederick Joubert Duquesne at his Wall Street address:[23]

My dear Colonel:
I have arrived from Hamburg where Nikolaus and George informed me that you are a patent attorney interested in matters similar to mine. I would like to know where and when it would be possible to meet you.
Believe me to be most sincerely—
Harry Sawyer

Fritz telephoned Sawyer at his office and asked him to come see him in the office at the Exchange Building.

Sawyer and the FBI had already read the uncoded German on the micro intended for Fritz and knew that the Abwehr had laid out eighteen important assignments for their most valued espionage agent in America.[24] Fritz would be busy for a long time.

Fritz was to learn whether it was true that the American Telephone and Telegraph Company had invented a secret bombing ray that would guide bombers to their target; a second ray would release the bombs. If such a ray existed, Fritz was to steal it. His other instructions were:

Find out all you can about Professor Bullard of Hobart College, the chemical warfare expert, and the Army uniform that will stop mustard gas which he is supposed to have perfected.[25]

Is there being manufactured in the United States an anti-aircraft shell with an electric eye? What is the shell's caliber? How does the complicated, delicate mechanism in the shell stand up to firing shock? How does this shell compare in accuracy with the ordinary shell?

Provide all new developments in bacteriological warfare—the spreading of disease germs—from airplanes.

What are the new developments in American Army gas masks?

How about the new trench-crusher? We hear that the United States has developed such a mysterious machine which will ride over trenches and destroy them.

Furnish the names of the manufacturers, the size of deliveries, and for whom they are being made.

What are the new developments in the gun turret design for Sunderland flying boats which Captain Lungstedt is working on?

Find out if there are going to Europe any single warplanes, or squadrons, with personnel of the U.S. Army and Navy camouflaged as volunteer troops. Report immediately when there are any signs of war mobilization in America like calling up volunteers, establishing draft offices and calling in reserve officers and reservists on a large scale.

We have read in a magazine about a metal-cleaning fluid developed by the Curaz Company, Malden, Mass. Get some of it for us.

Additionally, Germany wanted to know about a new antifog device and about a Sperry range finder. Fritz was to report on leading manufacturers of airplanes and airplane engines, obtaining names of the types of planes and their performance figures, as well as determine the production capacity, floor space, shifts, and other details of each company. The Abwehr conveniently provided Fritz with a list of twenty-three aircraft and engine makers in twenty-two cities throughout the United States, which included Douglas, Grumman, Curtiss, North American, Martin, Boeing, Consolidated, Lougheed (Lockheed), Pratt & Whitney, Ryan, Bellanca, and Stinson.

Fritz was warm and friendly at the meeting with Sawyer, as was his way. (The date would be late March or early April, according to the chronology of the FBI agents. A date for the Sawyer/Duquesne meeting was given in the spy ring's 1941 court trial as 26 February 1940. Puzzling is the date in his prison records, which states that Fritz became a German agent as of 1 April 1936.)[26] But the wary professional never let his guard down, even in his small, bare office. Ever vigilant for unwanted eavesdroppers, he slipped a note to Sawyer after the two had exchanged a few pleasantries: "We will go out. Cannot talk here."[27]

They walked to a nearby automat, where Sawyer wordlessly slipped Fritz his micro, which he dropped casually into a pocket. Their small talk continued, with Sawyer telling Fritz about his work as a diesel engineer with the Mülheim Works of Siemens-Schuckert. "They are interested in my invention of a floating dock," replied Fritz. (If true, this interest might explain Fritz's hurried automobile trip with Helen to the Patent Office in Washington with the FBI in pursuit.)

Despite the pleasant tone of their conversation, in which they only discussed inventions, Sawyer could still sense an underlying skepticism, evidenced by the spy's taciturnity. But Sawyer had been warned by the FBI to be particularly careful in his dealings with the Duke. After all, the man had spent a lifetime playing the game—perhaps not very successfully, but he was perceptive and not a fool. And it was suspected that Fritz would contact Hamburg regarding Sawyer's authenticity.

"You don't speak English badly," Fritz said suspiciously. "How'd you learn it?"

"I was here once before," Sawyer said guardedly. "But I didn't make out very good—sold silk stockings door to door, and like that."

They parted amicably, with Sawyer telling Fritz he would contact him again in about a week.

The second meeting was again in the automat. Then they walked to City Hall Park, where they sat on a bench. "We call this La Guardia's Ranch," Fritz said with a sarcastic laugh, making reference to the then mayor of New York. But again, after an hour's conversation about inventions, Sawyer had to leave with no information forthcoming from Fritz.

But Fritz was more forthcoming on their third meeting, which was prompted by a microphotograph for him delivered to Sawyer in his office by the Pan American clipper steward Rene Emanuel Mezenen. "It's from Dr. Dobler in Lisbon," said Mezenen.

"I don't recognize the name, but I know of a Duarte there," said Sawyer.

"It's the same man." (This is first time Sawyer had heard Duarte's real name.) "You are to deliver the micro to Jimmy Dunn, but what it says for him to do applies in general to all the other agents."

Sawyer took the micro immediately to the FBI before setting up an appointment with Fritz, alias Jimmy Dunn. The micro showed that Germany was becoming concerned about American military strength:[28]

In the future, technical questions do not interest us as much as military ones. Get us:

A—Exact strength of the U.S.A. Air Force, listing separately the number of men in flying and ground crews.

B—Details concerning location of flying schools for fliers, length of training, number of students.

C—Especially interested in all kinds of instruction books and manuals, particularly those not available on open market.

D—Of paramount importance, if pilots are being trained for England, where are they trained, how many, when and where expected to leave, by ship or air, what route expected to take, the days of their departure. These questions pertain to Canada as well as U.S.A. It may be necessary to find friends in air force itself. I am sending $500 for this purpose.

Fritz was more relaxed and outgoing when he met with the bureau's double agent this time—no doubt, Sawyer reasoned, because Fritz had received word from Hamburg that the diesel engineer was okay. Fritz might not have been so relaxed if he had known that several FBI agents were always nearby when he met with Sawyer. He was the one spy treated with respect.[29]

"I'll enlarge it tonight," said Fritz upon accepting the micro. "Meanwhile, I've been doing some pretty hard work on those other assignments and I've sent considerable stuff across. But how much do they expect a man can do with only $300 a month? They'd better raise the ante—and you can tell them so for me." Fritz was not concerned about upsetting Uncle Hugo, who wrote the checks that then came to his American spies by way of a Pedro Gonzales in Mexico. (Pedro Gonzales? Surely a cover name.)[30] He knew he was the Abwehr's best contact in America and that he deserved more money. Nothing had changed for Fritz.

Fritz was enthusiastic at his next meeting with Sawyer a few days later: "The micro says $500 is coming for me to use in bribing American Army aviators. That shows that maybe Hamburg is loosening up a little with the purse strings. Let me know right away when the dough comes. Will you, Harry?" (When Fritz started receiving payments, he dutifully gave Sawyer a receipt each time, written in this fashion: "Received 300 pamphlets from H.S.")[31]

Sawyer was chagrined that Fritz was still using an Abwehr letter box in China to send materials to Germany. He also had sent a new army gas mask through Italy. If this continued, Sawyer would have no evidence against Fritz. But he needn't have worried. Fritz, as well as his fellow conspirators, would soon be sending a constant stream of information to AOR. Often the information would be alarmingly accurate, so much so that the FBI would become increasingly concerned about the threat to America's national security.

The old pro Fritz was riding high, doing what he loved best and getting more money for it than ever before. The pimp who had procured Vera's tricks along the waterfront in Bermuda had come a long way since 1902—or so may have thought Fritz Duquesne, now Abwehr agent A.3518.

CHAPTER 21

"You're under Arrest, Fritz"

S O S U C C E S S F U L W A S S A W Y E R in transmitting reports from his collectors in New York that he was considered the wonder of the Abwehr, respected for his brilliance and looked on with delight for evading FBI surveillance for so long.[1] Managers of other rings in the United States asked Ritter to let their spies use Tramp for sending their information. They also wanted to use him for contacting their own agents. It was an unexpected gift to the FBI.

Meanwhile, the Ritter Ring continued to operate unabated. And despite her reduced circumstances, partygoing Lilly Stein was in great need of money. Lilly told Sawyer she was prepared to turn over more material from Edmund Heine but complained that she was flat broke and absolutely needed more compensation for her work.[2] This message went to AOR: "Stein destitute. Got new contact, but must have money at once." Weary with her whining for money, AOR replied, almost ignoring Lilly, "Need urgently from all friends monthly production of airplane factories; exports to all countries, especially England and France; number, type, date of delivery by steamer or air; armature and armament; payment, cash and carry, or credit. Rose [an unidentified secret operative in Germany] has $200 for you, not for Stein. Greetings."

Another time Lilly said she would like to visit California with Hamburg's permission:[3] "Stein wants to go to California for two months with her cousin. She asks if she can make contacts or work for you there. She got letter from Heinrich [Heine's alias], Detroit, regarding plane motors. How shall I send it and other things I have?" The answer was for Lilly to stay in New York and for Sawyer to send his information by air. Wary of Lilly, the Abwehr was keeping a tight rein on her despite the good reports she was delivering from Heine.

Sawyer finally had good news for Lilly, Fritz, and Roeder—the three spies most demanding money—on 29 June 1940. Payday was arriving, along with instructions on delivering material too lengthy to transmit by radio. There was also another admonition regarding Lilly:[4]

Deliver all material through Metzger to H. Duarte at Lisbon, Duos Nacoes. Password on meeting, "Sesan Greek Franz." Duarte will hand over $500 for Roeder, $300 for you, $300 for Lilly and $250 for Dunn [Fritz].

Distribution of money by you. Don't borrow any money for Lilly. All should report military and technical information on deliveries to England. Hearty greetings.

And so it continued. Sawyer kept gathering material from the collectors, and the FBI, after the usual doctoring of important material, passed it on to Hamburg via shortwave or courier. It was an ideal, albeit one-sided, partnership. The Abwehr was ecstatic, and the FBI was delighted as its list of enemy spies in America continued to grow.

Agents enjoyed keeping an eye on Lilly.[5] Because of her affluent family's prewar contacts and because of her ice-skating interests, Lilly was good friends with French actress Simone Simon and Olympic skater and movie star Sonja Henie. Agents would vie with each other to follow Lilly on days she was meeting with these friends, who had no suspicion of Lilly's double life. The lucky agent shadowing her would give particular attention to his dress that day, because he knew he would be having lunch or dinner in a first-class restaurant. Lilly was profligate, spending money as fast as she got it. When paid, she would usually entertain friends at the Twenty-one Club for an evening of fun.

When Hamburg specifically requested photos of the Sperry gunsight, the FBI took pictures deliberately out of focus. Sawyer defensively blamed the problem on poor light and a camera that would not focus close up. To correct the problem, courier Erich Strunck returned from Germany with a new Leica and instructions on how to operate it.[6] The Nazis frequently complained about poor-quality microfilms, blurred blueprints, and pied type in communications. But they remained unsuspecting of the FBI operation.

Still fearful that he might be under surveillance by the FBI or local police, the ever-cautious Fritz continued to meet Sawyer at different locations or at "La Guardia's Ranch," where they could be in the open. During these meetings Fritz passed on information about national defense, technical data, and sailing dates for ships to British ports. However, some of this information was readily available to the average American through newspapers, publicity releases, and technical magazines.[7] Hamburg was aware of this fact, and of Duquesne's constant need for money and his trick of producing voluminous reports, often signifying nothing, to justify his pay. Hence this cautionary word: "Tell Duquesne that we are not interested in information that has been published several weeks ago in the *New York Times* and the *Herald-Tribune* and also carried from Washington by the Associated Press and other news gathering services."

The Abwehr must have been happy with the scoop sent by Fritz on 24 June 1940, which was coded SSD—*sehr sehr dringend,* very very urgent: Roosevelt was releasing the Norden bombsight to Great Britain.[8] England had been asking for the instrument since the beginning of the war, but the War and Navy Departments opposed the move, unaware at this time that the bombsight was no longer a secret. But Great Britain and its allies were now in a precarious position and conceivably could lose the war. How Fritz obtained the news is not known. But the FBI allowed it to be sent.

Tramp sent the message at 6 P.M.:

From A.3518 in New York via A.3549 via Afu 24.6.40—1800 *SS Pasteur* ten sets drawings Norden and Sperry bombsights to Vickers Co. London for manufacture sight released for use of allies. Vickers Detroit will also manufacture sights. Sperry will make 1200 and Norden 1200. Both firms must spend at least three months in tooling before production in any quantity begins.

On the same date, Fritz passed on the hard information to Sawyer that the United States had sent ten destroyers and four battleships to the Caribbean "to scout for the British." Fritz also had the information that the Todd shipyards had been given a contract to install laminated antibomb decks on twenty World War I–era destroyers and twenty newer destroyers. On 25 July Fritz informed Sawyer that President Roosevelt and William Bullit, former ambassador to France, had conferred with members of the British diplomatic corps at Hyde Park on the effects of Hitler's most recent speech.

The FBI was learning new tricks in the spy game, but Fritz still played with the old toys. He was fond of gimmicks. Invisible ink was a

FEDERAL BUREAU OF INVESTIGATION
UNITED STATES DEPARTMENT OF JUSTICE
★ ★ ★ John Edgar Hoover, Director ★ ★ ★

Rubber Stamp Comparison

One of the many Laboratory identifications which helped greatly in convicting members of a notorious spy ring, headed by Frederick Joubert Duquesne, was that of the rubber stamp of a cat, used by many of the members as a seal on their letters. Directly below appears an enlargement of a questioned specimen which was identified with the known specimen appearing on the right. In the lower right is a photograph of one of the numerous letters exchanged between members of the ring showing the questioned "cat".

New experimental fighting bomber made at United A.Co. Has besides the ordinary armament three midway turrets that cover a complete circle with their machine guns. The turrets revolve inside streamlined blisters. Still in building stage.

The green "cat's paw" rubber stamp used by Fritz to identify all his communications to Harry Sawyer. (FBI)

great favorite. He used wax paper instead of carbon paper to type out secret messages. Dusting what appeared to be blank wax paper with graphite brought out the message. Documents were concealed by wrapping them around electric wire and then covering them with friction tape. To authenticate all information submitted by him, Fritz identified the documents with a rubber stamp that left the imprint of a cat in green ink, its back bowed and fur raised.[9]

All in all the Abwehr was delighted with the information sent by Fritz, and surprised that the old spy who had served them so well in the first war was coming through again for the *Vaterland*. Generally he was gathering more and better information than his younger compatriots.

The FBI often employed a red herring to occupy the Abwehr in useless projects. One tip—ostensibly from Fritz and intended to help the Abwehr intercept messages from "American spies" in Germany—read, "Duqn says USA Intelligence sends messages out of Germany by engraving them on silverware, camera parts, and so forth. Then they spray it with a metal which is removed when parts arrive here."[10] The FBI no doubt envisioned German agents scraping silver tea sets and silverware looking for secret messages.

The old audacious Fritz Duquesne surfaced when he brazenly wrote the Chemical Warfare Division of the War Department seeking information:[11]

Gentlemen:
We are interested in the possible financing of a chemical war device which may or may not be original. This we do not know. However, we would like to study the subject in order to get a little understanding on the subject before we commit ourselves.

We understand that the Government published a pamphlet on this subject to those interested in the subject. If this be true and if you have the authority will you please inform us how we might be able to procure a copy of the same.

If it has any bearing on the matter, we are citizens and would not allow anything of a confidential nature to get out of our hands.

Very truly yours,
F. J. Duquesne

Fritz received a polite reply from the War Department written by the FBI. He was told that though his request could not be granted, the department had no fear that such a good citizen would misuse the information.

Still, the FBI was concerned when Irwin Siegler, the butcher aboard the *Manhattan*, gave Sawyer important news on 27 January 1941, which was sent on to Hamburg after the usual clearance: "Churchill here in battleship *King George V*—visited on shipboard by Roosevelt and Knox."[12] It wasn't completely true, but the facts were close enough to amaze the Abwehr and worry the FBI. The British battleship on her maiden voyage visited Annapolis on 24 January, but not with Churchill aboard. Its distinguished visitor was Lord Halifax, the new British ambassador to the United States. And Roosevelt and Secretary of the Navy Frank Knox did greet Halifax. The FBI was worried about the near accuracy of the report. They feared that the Ritter Ring might have established new lines of information they were not aware of.

Meanwhile, relations between the United States and Germany were changing and moving rapidly to a diplomatic break. On 16 June 1941 the United States ordered the closing of all twenty-four German consulates in America, as well as the German Library of Information, the German Railroads Information Office, and the Transocean News Service. The reason for the action, said Undersecretary of State Sumner Welles, was that the consulates had engaged in activities "of an improper and unwarranted character" and had acted in a manner "inimical to the welfare of this country."[13] It was a devastating blow against the German espionage machine. On 19 June Germany and Italy retaliated by closing their American consulates.

The FBI investigators were becoming concerned that perhaps they had let the Ritter Ring dangle too long. They knew who all the members were and were able to control the information they had gathered. They were also aware that new rings were being formed with new radio setups they might not be able to control. Also, with the new Leica sent Sawyer, they could hardly continue to fool Hamburg with out-of-focus photos. These concerns, coupled with the fact that one destroyer had been sunk leaving the United States, prompted the decision to round up the spies.

Special Agent Richard Johnson sat in on several conferences to determine what to do regarding the ring.[14] One concern was that Paul Fehse, the cook aboard the *Manhattan,* had become suspicious of Sawyer. The FBI agent assigned to Fehse also learned that on the *Manhattan*'s next trip to Lisbon he planned to jump ship and return to Berlin to check on Sawyer. To silence Fehse the FBI arrested him on a charge of violating the Federal Registration Act. He was happy to plead guilty on the lesser charge, believing that the FBI did not know he was a spy. (Ironically, he had told Sawyer in March that he had received his draft notice.[15] "It will make me sick inside to serve in the American Army," he told Sawyer. He would serve a different time, one year and a day in Atlanta Federal Prison.) As planned, the arrest received little attention. Publicity would have panicked the other spies and alerted the Abwehr that the spy ring had been uncovered.

Bertram W. Zenzinger was another spy picked up early on 16 April and charged with violating the Registration Act.[16] Although he lived on Skyline Drive in Topanga Canyon, California, he had a direct link with Sawyer.

But before moving on the other spies, the bureau wanted Duquesne on record and on film. Although they had had about twenty meetings, Fritz had never been to Sawyer's office. All the other spies had passed information at one time or another in the office. The game was to save the Duke for last. The FBI considered him a cunning, intelligent, and resourceful old professional who could very easily discover the setup. Extra agents were assigned to the room next-door should there be trouble.

Sawyer arranged a meeting with Fritz on Wednesday, 25 June, at 6:15 P.M. in room 629, the Diesel Research Company office in the Newsweek Building. Fritz promised to have important information.

Fritz played the role well of the wily old spy when he entered the office at 6:16 by the clock on the desk. William Friedemann and Richard Johnson were two of the agents on duty. This would be one session in the office not conducted in German, because Fritz did not speak the language.

"Gee, it's very bright in here," said Fritz, standing in the doorway.[17]

"You know, when you get older, you have some problems in seeing. Especially when you do hand printing," replied Sawyer, covering rapidly to explain the bright lights necessary for photography.

"It's probably best we do meet where it's well lit," said the ever wary Fritz. "If the room were dark it might make people suspicious about why we're meeting."

Noting "Albert F. Rich—Diesel Research Company" printed on the door, Fritz asked Sawyer—although it would seem self-evident—what business he was feigning. "I'm in the research business," replied Sawyer, "since that's the kind of business which will cover up almost any kind of sin."

Blinking his eyes in the glare, Fritz walked all around the office in-

A dapper Leo G. Carroll is Colonel Hammersohn, a thinly disguised portrayal of the equally dapper Colonel Fritz Duquesne in the 1945 film The House on 92nd Street. *(© 1945 Twentieth Century Fox Film Corporation, all rights re-served)*

In a scene from The House on 92nd Street, *Leo G. Carroll as Colonel Hammersohn (Fritz) reenacts Fritz primping before the two-way mirror in Sawyer's office while FBI agents filmed and recorded his conversation. (© 1945 Twentieth Century Fox Film Corporation, all rights reserved)*

specting everything. Friedemann and Johnson, watching from behind the two-way mirror, got the impression that Fritz wanted to impress Sawyer by playing the overly suspicious superspy. The movie camera ground away, recording Fritz's every move. Always meticulous about his person, Fritz went to the washbasin, washed his hands, and combed his hair—to "make himself real charming," supposed Friedemann. Still roaming the small room, he went to the second mirror— the two-way mirror—and examined his face carefully. Johnson took a photo of him through the mirror, filling the entire 35 mm frame. The two agents relaxed after that, assured that Fritz suspected nothing.

Sawyer was nervous. He got up and walked with Fritz around the small office, maneuvering him to the chair by the desk. "Sit down!" Sawyer finally demanded, almost shouting.

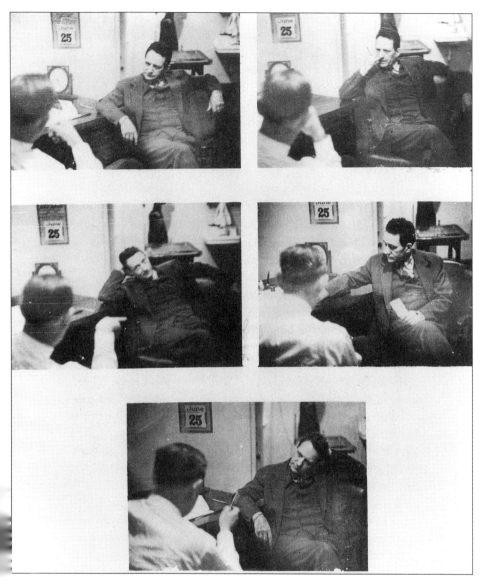

"The Duke" passing military information to double agent Harry Sawyer is recorded by hidden FBI cameras. (FBI)

"Well, it looks like everything is all right," Fritz conceded. He sat down opposite the mirror, and Sawyer, who sat in his shirt-sleeves and chain-smoked nervously, listened transfixed for the next two hours.

Fritz had lost none of his power as a speaker. He suddenly launched into a narrative—complete with dramatic gestures—of his life, from fighting Zulus as a teenager through the Boer War, his career as a lecturer, and his hatred of the British. He told Sawyer of his intense patriotism. And he capped it all by extolling his romantic prowess with women. Because of it, he claimed, no woman wanted to leave him. He bragged that he taught his girlfriends all of the refinements in sexual arousal and climax. He had made a trip to Italy to study the erotic works of art found on the walls of Pompeii and put into practice what was depicted along with what he had seen in Oriental and Greek works. "Our boss" (the *Führer*) has a mistress, Fritz pointed out, and we should emulate him: "Marriage has obligations which prevent us from being dedicated to the cause."

Despite Fritz's reputation for sartorial splendor and personal fastidiousness, during this meeting with Sawyer he displayed an annoying habit of spitting on the floor. When agents went through his apartment later, they marveled at how neat and clean he kept his clothes and quarters. Everything was perfect.[18]

Fritz asked Sawyer if he could still send material overseas. When assured that he could, Fritz got down to business. Putting on a pair of horn-rimmed glasses—which he removed and replaced repeatedly while he talked—he took off his left shoe and pulled from his sock a long white envelope. Taking out the contents, he began handing reports and drawings to Sawyer. "You've got to be careful carrying dangerous stuff," Fritz explained. "I covered the army maneuvers in Tennessee and got some pretty good stuff." Occasionally punctuating a statement with spit, Fritz gave Sawyer information about a new anti-aircraft range finder, new tanks, photographs and diagrams of a Garand rifle and mosquito boat, a new gas mask diaphragm, a one-man pillbox antitank device, and a baby tank that could be carried in a plane not yet designed. It must have been a very big sock. As Sawyer took each item, he held it up at such an angle that the FBI cameras behind him got a clear shot of the material through the two-way mirror.

"These 28-ton tanks have just been turned out by the Chrysler Motor Company," explained Fritz earnestly. "They are powerful-looking things. I think their value has not been proved, however. They have had only limited field tests. There is one at West Point, and I saw one at the Tennessee maneuvers. They have 3-inch armor and flexible guns of great power. It has one 75 cannon, one 37 cannon, eight machine guns and a two-way radio.

"The one-man pillbox," he went on, talking constantly and rapidly, "can be assembled and installed at the point of usage by American soldiers. It can withstand the weight of a tank and permit the man inside the box to destroy the tank as it passes over. All it does is to squeeze it into the ground a little. The government regards it as a deep-dyed secret, but I have the plans." Fritz gestured animatedly as he described the explosive powers of various bombs. He pantomimed firing the new Garand rifle.

While they talked, Sebold was eating a chocolate candy bar made in sections (probably a Three Musketeers). Anxious to show his expertise, Fritz told Sebold how the candy could be made into an incendiary bomb. "If those bars were broken in two," he explained, "some combustible phosphorous could be placed inside it making it a very effective though small incendiary bomb. Among its advantages is its inability to explode in temperatures under 72 degrees. A better bomb can be made of Chiclets which I've used in the past. Chew the gum thoroughly, then fold it around a phosphorous compound. You can plant them on docks by carrying them in a pocket with a hole in it and letting them fall down the inside of your trouser leg onto the pier while talking to your boss. Then, in a few hours or a day or two a fire starts and nobody knows who did it.

"I plan to do it soon," he said without further explanation.

"But I prefer the lead-pipe bomb," said Fritz. "Can you get some dynamite caps and slow-burning fuses?" Sawyer replied that he could.

"I want to blow up the machinery in the General Electric plant at Schenectady. I looked it over a year ago and I can do the job with a slow-burning fuse."

The meeting ended at 8:30 with Fritz suggesting that he could plant a bomb at Hyde Park when Roosevelt was visiting his family home.

The FBI decided it was time to round up the spies, not only for the reasons already stated but because it was clear that Duquesne was planning to make the transition from espionage to sabotage.

Four days later in the early evening on Sunday, 29 June, FBI assistant director Earl Connelley briefed a roomful of agents on the sixth floor of the Federal Building at Foley Square. The bureau would scoop up

The thirty-three members of the Ritter Ring—not the Duquesne Ring—arrested by the FBI in "the greatest spy roundup in U.S. history." (FBI)

A hidden camera captures Fritz leaving the house on Seventy-sixth Street on 1 July 1940. (FBI)

the spies that night.[19] Special Agent Hugh Small was in charge of the arrests. Twenty-three spies were to be arrested, nineteen in New York and four in New Jersey. Normal procedure called for the assignment of two agents to a spy. But no chances were being taken. Four agents were assigned to each spy, for a total of ninety-three. But there were many more working that night. Agents had to be borrowed from Newark, Boston, Philadelphia, and other cities around the country. Logistics of cars and warrants had already been worked out by the efficient Connelley.

It was a hot and humid evening in New York City when the simultaneous arrests of the spies in their homes began. A legal search would follow their arrests.

Raymond Newkirk, who had been assigned to Fritz since the beginning of the case, went with Special Agents Lawrence J. Quinn, David M. Harris, and Paul W. Walz to the apartment on Seventy-sixth Street at about 7:40 P.M.[20] Fritz, a copy of the *New York Times* in hand, answered Newkirk's knock.

"I have some friends with me, Fritz."[21]

"Bring them in, Ray," he welcomed.

Although armed, the agents did not draw their guns, even though they knew Fritz had a small inconsequential gun in the apartment. Evelyn Lewis was in a dressing gown sculpting the Christ child.

Inside, Newkirk flashed his badge and said, "You're under arrest, Fritz."

Fritz never said a word, and they never spoke to each other again. He and Lewis were handcuffed. Several hundred dollars were found in Fritz's pocket, which Newkirk believed may have shocked and disappointed Lewis, since Fritz was always borrowing from her.[22]

The agents asked Lewis if they could look through the apartment, since they didn't have a warrant and she was the renter. Cooperative, she agreed. The agents turned up maps, pictures, diagrams, notes, and letters addressed to "Jimmy," Fritz's code name of James Dunn. They also found instructions for Fritz to get information on airplane production in the United States, convoys to Greenland and Iceland, and plane shipments to England.[23]

Fritz and Lewis were on their way to Foley Square by 8:15 P.M. By 9 P.M. Walter Winchell, perhaps the most listened to newsman and gossip reporter in America and a close friend of J. Edgar Hoover, had begun his regular Sunday night nationwide radio broadcast over WJZ with the scoop that the spies had been arrested in what Hoover called "the greatest spy roundup in U.S. history."[24] Most of the spies were probably still on their way to bureau headquarters when the fifteen-minute broadcast was over.

"The importance of the arrests," said Hoover in statements to the press,

was indicated by the fact that since the enactment of the Espionage Act in 1917 there have been only 19 convictions for its violation. I would consider this to be the largest espionage case developed since the enactment of the act. The arrests were made as a result of counter-espionage activity by our agents in which we used the "flytrap" method, which made it possible for us to apprehend such a large number at one time.[25]

The top G-man did not name Germany as the foreign power the suspects were spying for but said the ring members were in communication with "representatives of a foreign country."

Hoover singled out Fritz as the "most important" of the prisoners, and he described the ring as "one of the most active, extensive and vicious groups we have ever had to deal with."[26] Hoover also said that regardless of their background or their motives for entering the field of espionage, these spies were without exception a sorry lot, "the most miserable lot of chiselers and racketeers" he had seen since becoming director of the FBI in 1924.[27]

At a press conference in New York, acting attorney general Francis Biddle, who had authorized the roundup of the spies, said, "The apprehension of these men represents the culmination of two years of thorough and painstaking work by the Federal Bureau of Investigation. It required months of careful preparation followed by additional months of investigation of the most difficult character. Perfect coordination was necessary to assure simultaneous arrest of all the men involved."[28]

Immediately upon arriving back at FBI headquarters, the spies were interrogated, some for up to about three hours. All were behind bars by 10 P.M.

William Friedemann was assigned to arrest Lilly Stein in her new apartment at 232 East Seventy-ninth Street. But there was a delay because she was entertaining a person of "considerable importance."[29] (Was it the disgraced Ogden Hammond Jr.?) "I've been expecting this for a long time" was her only comment.

Friedemann accompanied Lilly to Foley Square. Contrary to the Abwehr's opinion of Lilly, Friedemann considered her sharp and clever, willing to play both sides to her advantage.[30] The only incident worthy of note that night, he believed, was when Lilly propositioned Special Agent Wayne Klemp, a six-foot three-inch former Kansas State typing champion. He turned her down.

Newkirk was assigned to interrogate Lilly and later spent many hours with her.[31] "Lilly thought it was all a big joke," he reported:

She knew she was going to jail but was satisfied that she had made enough money to make it worthwhile. She figured she had taken the Germans for a ride because she was always hollering for money for information she knew wasn't worth a damn.

She was a caution to talk to. She often called for me in her jail cell just to talk.

"How long do you think I'll get?" she'd ask.

"I haven't the faintest idea," I would tell her.

"Where will they send me?"

"Probably Alderson in West Virginia. That's where most of the women go."

"You mean just women?"

"Yeah, just women."

"No men?"

"I don't know, I've never been there. They probably have men guards. Why?"

"Don't you worry. Lil's gonna do a little business between the bars."

Among the twenty-three spies arrested that evening were five not directly linked to the Ritter Ring. They had been in contact with Hamburg through a radio set in the Bronx. They were Felix Jahnke, Josef Klein, Carl A. Reuper, Paul Scholz, and Axel Wheeler-Hill.

Heine, the car salesman, was arrested in Detroit, and Strunck was picked up in Milwaukee the same evening. On 1 July Clausing was tossed into the brig aboard his ship the *Argentina* in Santos, Brazil; Dold was arrested when his ship the *Excalibur* docked in New York, as was Walischewski when the *Uruguay* docked. The FBI net gathered in a total of thirty-three spies, cinching Hoover's statement that it was the largest espionage case ever developed in the United States.

There was no joy in Hamburg when reports of the "greatest spy roundup in U.S. history" moved on the wires of the Associated Press, United Press International, Reuters, and other news agencies. It was a shocking debacle for the Abwehr. The agency was in a quandary when the list of spies was released. Not listed was William Sebold/Harry Sawyer, the wonder of the Abwehr, the Nazis' most respected contact in America. So there was still hope. But where was Tramp?

On 7 July AOR warned Tramp, "Suspend contact with Hamburg until further notice in the interest of your security."[32] But Tramp was silent. Nothing would be heard from him until September. Then it would be news the Abwehr doesn't want to hear: Tramp would be revealed as a double agent for the FBI.

Admiral Canaris began tap-dancing on a tightrope. Having long boasted of the success of his agents in the United States, he made feeble attempts at proving that he had been suspicious of Sebold/ Sawyer's loyalties from the beginning.[33] Considering the length of time Sebold was involved with the ring, it would be a difficult contention to prove.

Colonel Nikolaus Ritter was furious Tramp had betrayed everyone.[34] He cursed Tramp, calling him a *Schwein* and a *Verräter* (traitor). Colonel Hans Piekenbrock, head of Gruppe I and Canaris's right-hand man, calmly reminded Ritter that Tramp was not a traitor at all. He was working for his new *Vaterland*.

Dr. Hans Thomsen, chargé d'affaires at the German embassy in Washington, had complained as early as May 1940 that the Ritter Ring operation was sabotaging his own mission, which was to keep the United States out of the war.[35] "Useless braggarts" was his description for most of the spies. Thomsen was incensed at the news of their arrest and, surely with an I-told-you-so smugness, excoriated the ring with even greater vehemence. "Most, and apparently all, of the people involved in this affair were . . . completely unadapted for such activity," he cabled his foreign office on 7 July. "It is to be assumed that the American authorities knew of the entire network, which certainly was no work of art in view of the naive and, to a certain extent, down right stupid manner in the way these people carried on."

Canaris angrily replied on 23 July that Dr. Thomsen didn't know what he was talking about. He cited Duquesne, Roeder, and Lang for special commendation.[36] Duquesne, according to his report, had "delivered valuable reports and important technical material in the original, including U.S. gas masks, radio control apparatus, leakproof fuel tanks, television instruments, small bombs for airplanes, various airplanes, air separators, and propeller-driving mechanisms." Information from Fritz was given high marks of "valuable," "very good" and "good."

The incident was a major blow to the relationship between Canaris and Foreign Minister Joachim von Ribbentrop. It will be remembered that in April 1940 Canaris had assured Ribbentrop—who was opposed to spy activities in the United States—that he had no agents operating there. Ribbentrop was so outraged by the exposure that he told Canaris, "If the United States were to declare war, it will be your fault."[37] Nevertheless, the storm passed and Canaris survived as head of the Abwehr.

Publicity-loving Fritz couldn't have complained about one of the headlines in the *New York Times* the day after his arrest: "Veteran Spy of Boer War Called Leader of Ring." Not exactly true, since he wasn't the ringleader. But if allowed to see a paper, he would probably have been delighted at seeing his name in print again. Additionally, the paper ran on page 3 a lengthy biography of Fritz, the only spy to be so singled out.[38]

Fritz would have lots of material for his scrapbook. And lots of time to fill it.

CHAPTER 22

Bombshells in the Courtroom and Fireworks from Fritz

THEY WERE ALL WELL DRESSED, though a little mussed from a night in jail. And despite an effort to appear calm, the twenty-four alleged spies—twenty-four because Heine had joined them—looked worried when arraigned on Monday morning, 30 June, before U.S. commissioner Martin C. Epstein in Brooklyn's U.S. District Court. Even Fritz, who had been in this position many times before, was grim and uncomfortable.[1]

It had been a chaotic scene a few minutes earlier when they arrived, shortly after noon, in sedans and the traditional Black Marias guarded by FBI special agents and the U.S. Army. About three hundred people lined up on the Johnson Street side of the building to watch them unload, eager to see what the people looked like who had been plotting against the defenses of their country for Nazi Germany. Mounted police officers kept order.

Hustled out of the vehicles, the spies hid their faces with their raised arms or hats when confronted by the battery of reporters, press photographers, and newsreel cameramen. The ladies used their purses and hats, even the woman from the FBI who was escorting Lilly, Else, and Evelyn. Agents not wanting to be photographed inclined their heads or subtly covered their faces with their hats.

Handcuffed by their right wrists to an agent and flanked by another, the spies were led into a third-floor hearing room. More agents stood guard in the outside corridor. Only court attendants, newspaper reporters, and federal officers—more than fifty G-men—were allowed into the sweltering room. Powerful lights for the newsreel cameras added to the temperature. Most kept their coats on during the proceedings.

As each suspect was led before him, commissioner Epstein explained that they had a right to counsel, and he read the charges against them. The indictment contained two counts. The first charge was violating Section 233, Title 22 of the United States Code: failure to register as agents of a foreign government. It carried a maximum penalty of two years in prison. The second, more serious, charge was conspiring to violate the provision of Section 32 of Title 50 of the United States Code, which makes it a crime to transmit unlawfully information affecting national defense and to utilize that information to the injury of the United States or to the advantage of a foreign power. The maximum penalty was twenty years. Later, on 15 July, a federal grand jury formally indicted the spies and named the German government as a co-conspirator as well as many of its agents, including Nikolaus Ritter.

The suspects were then asked to plead. Those who pleaded guilty were told to step to one side of the room, and those who pleaded not guilty went to the other. In a surprise move, seven of the suspects pleaded guilty. Among them were Lilly Stein and Evelyn Clayton Lewis. Wicked Lilly couldn't help but flash a smile at the photographers as she joined the "guilty" group. Among the remaining seventeen willing to gamble their fates before a jury by pleading innocent were Else Weustenfeld and the Big Three: Fritz, Lang, and Roeder. Three of the seventeen would change their pleas to guilty during the trial, leaving only fourteen defendants.

When all pleas had been recorded, bail was set at $25,000 each. Only wealthy Edmund Heine, the auto company representative, could come up with the money. Ironically, he paid it in bonds of the country he had been working to destroy.

U.S. attorney Harold M. Kennedy of the Eastern District of New York was assigned by acting attorney general Biddle to "prosecute the defendants vigorously and without reservation as the case involved one of the greatest counter-espionage efforts ever made by an enforcement agency." A trial date was set for 3 September 1941. It would mark

Fritz is arraigned in Federal Court on 30 June 1941. Prosecutor Harold M. Kennedy stands with folded arms at right. (Wide World Photos)

the beginning of what would be the longest trial ever recorded in the Eastern District. At about the same time that day at Hyde Park, New York, President Franklin D. Roosevelt was dedicating his presidential library with "a declaration of faith in the future of free America." The $350,000 building was the first such library.

The prisoners were then transported under guard to FBI headquarters in the courthouse at Foley Square. Later the men were placed in the Federal House of Detention at Greenwich and Sixth Avenues.

The accused spies displayed a jauntiness and confidence that belied their less than tenable positions as they walked through the corridor of the old rococo courthouse on Washington Street in downtown Brooklyn on the first day of trial.

Fritz and several of his co-conspirators flashed a "V for victory" sign with their fingers.[2] Fritz, always a little flashier, held up two hands. Unwittingly, he was mimicking Winston Churchill, wartime leader of the country he professed such a hatred for. Winnie had popularized the signal. And from Fritz, of course, there was the continual spitting—except in the courtroom.

The presiding judge was Mortimer W. Byers, who had a reputation for being tough and strait-laced. The sixty-three-year-old jurist had an aristocratic face, steel-blue eyes framed by white hair, and a predilection for high Buster Brown collars.[3] (He would preside over another prominent spy trial in 1960, sentencing Russian spy Rudolf Abel to thirty years in prison. Abel would be exchanged in 1962 for American U-2 pilot Gary Powers.)[4] During the trial Hermann Lang had difficulty pronouncing Byers's name and called him Bias. When Fritz, who was not without humor in the courtroom and often made loud wisecracks, heard this, he said aloud, "Absolutely!" From then on the defendants and their lawyers referred to the jurist as Judge Bias.[5]

Another time, Judge Byers was charging the jury on the law, giving a definition of *conspiracy*. "If you and I agree to run down these courthouse steps," he said, "it's not an unlawful conspiracy, it's just an idle agreement up to that point. But if you or I go out and buy a box of matches and ignite the courthouse, we now have an unlawful conspiracy."[6]

Fritz cracked to Lang's lawyer, George Herz, who sat next to him throughout the trial, "What a dope I've been. Why didn't I think of that? We should have burned down the courthouse a long time ago."

Harold Kennedy, the forty-six-year-old U.S. attorney, would be specially commended by Secretary of the Navy Frank Knox for his handling of the espionage case. President Roosevelt appointed him a federal judge of the Eastern District in 1944. Kennedy would begin a new career as an admiralty lawyer in 1952, his most notable case being the collision in 1956 between the luxury liners *Andrea Doria* and *Stockholm* in which he represented the Italian Line.

Kennedy's prosecution team consisted of assistant U.S. special assistant attorney general James M. McInerney, chief of the National Defense Section of the Attorney General's Office; McInerny's assistant, Paul J. Cotter; and assistant U.S. attorneys T. Vincent Quinn, James D. Saver, and Frank J. Parker.

Representing Fritz, Stade, Wheeler-Hill, and Waalen was Frank J. Walsh, a small, thin, wiry, and feisty Irish lawyer. Quick to jump to his feet and object, he did so vigorously—and often. A novice in federal court, he became more sure of himself and more bellicose as the trial proceeded.[7] Walsh became so volatile at one point following a heated verbal exchange with Saver that a fistfight seemed inevitable. Walsh objected angrily to a snicker by Saver following a complicated question to Fritz. At lunch Walsh told Saver he was "willing to go any place you want to go and we'll settle this matter." Saver, a six-foot tall two-hundred-pound former Fordham football star, suggested his office. The slight, stoop-shouldered Walsh, weighing in at 150 pounds, agreed. But Quinn, Saver's superior, stopped the fracas.[8]

George Washington Herz and Herbert P. Georgio were the lawyers for Lang, the sad-faced spy accused of stealing the Norden bombsight, now looking every day as if he were going to burst into tears. Herz, a former newspaperman and U.S. attorney, believed implicitly in Lang's innocence and "broke his neck" to defend him.[9] Herz later handled the case of bank robber Willie "the Actor" Sutton, who robbed banks "because that's where the money is." In 1952 he defended Mickey Jelke, the twenty-two-year-old heir to an oleomargarine fortune charged with providing call girls for "café society." Jelke was convicted.

Edmund Heine, the well-heeled spy, could afford the best. He hired well-known criminal attorney George Gordon Battle and his assistant, Edgar A. Buttle. While the rest of the accused were locked up each day at the end of the trial, Heine would walk out of the courtroom arm in arm with his attorneys and return home.

Other lawyers represented one or several of the remaining spies. The majority of the lawyers were of German descent.[10] Charles A. Oberwager, a former magistrate representing five defendants, spoke fluent German and attended the same church as FBI man William Friedemann, who years later remembered the lawyer as being "typically German, about five feet three inches tall, and very overweight." Oberwager would often walk into the courtroom humming and speaking a few words of *Horst Wessel,* the official song of the Nazi Party and its second official anthem.[11]

A jury of nine men and three women and two alternates was selected in three hours and twenty-five minutes. The short selection time was a surprise to everyone. Expected to be a week-long task, it ended so suddenly that Kennedy asked for an adjournment until the following Monday.

The trial resumed during one of the summer's last humid heat waves at 10:30 A.M. on 8 September 1941 in the shabby and high-ceilinged federal courtroom in Brooklyn, packed with spectators for the historic legal battle that would see bombshells from the prosecution and fireworks from Fritz. The only display lacking during the turbulent trial would be bombs bursting in air.[12]

Fritz and his co-conspirators entered the courtroom joking and smiling. Among the spectators was the faithful Lillian Spanuth, now Linding, having remarried. She would be present at the trial every day, which was a surprise and delight to Fritz.[13]

Kennedy's solemn forty-five-minute opening statement charged that America's most closely guarded military secret, the Norden bombsight, had been in German hands since 1938. He flatly accused Lang of being responsible. The courtroom alternately giggled and became appropriately somber during his address.

Kennedy singled out Fritz, describing him as a longtime spy who had been "so bold" as to write letters to the army's Chemical Warfare Section seeking information. "We'll prove," said Kennedy, "that at the time he wrote this letter he was in the pay of the German government."[14]

In closing he said, "Whether the motive was money, whether the motive was hatred of one's country or love of another country, the fact is, they transmitted information which affected our national defense."

Pretrial full disclosure of evidence and witnesses was not required at the time.[15] This meant that the defense was neither aware of nor prepared for William Sebold and his role as Harry Sawyer. It was a dramatic bombshell when Kennedy revealed that the government's star witness was an FBI "counter-espionage agent."[16]

The demeanor of the defendants visibly changed when Sawyer, now Sebold, entered the courtroom under the protection of three FBI agents. To preserve his identity and to protect him against future reprisal, photographers were forbidden to take his picture. The Abwehr finally learned what had happened to Tramp.

On the stand, the slow-spoken Sebold told in his guttural accent the story of how he had been recruited to become a spy by the Abwehr; how he came to America, made contact with the other spies, and held meetings with Lang; how the Norden bombsight was brought to Germany through Ritter; how a shortwave transmitter was to have been set up for contact with Hamburg; and how he had been schooled in secret codes using a best-selling novel as the key.

"What was the name of your novel?" Kennedy asked.

"*All This in Heaven,*" the glum Sebold replied as the court roared in laughter. Kennedy hastily added that the correct title was *All This, and Heaven Too* by Rachel Field.[17]

Frank Walsh, George Herz, and Charles Oberwager, counsels for seven of the defendants, could not shake Sebold's story after four and a half hours of direct examination. So intense was their questioning that Judge Byers rebuked them on numerous occasions for their methods.

Walsh declared that his clients, Fritz and five other defendants, had done nothing to affect the United States and therefore violated no law. "There is no law forbidding the giving of information to Germany using methods to circumvent the British blockade if it does not harm America," he pointed out. "We were not at war with Germany in 1936 when this conspiracy allegedly began. We are not at war now. Nothing has been shown to indicate anything transmitted by these defendants affected the United States. They may have affected Britain and others, but not this country."

Walsh charged that the "plot" had been engineered by the FBI and that a government "informer," whom he described as an "out-and-out double crosser," had persuaded the defendants to become unwilling victims of the conspiracy.[18]

"I wasn't scared to become a spy," declared Sebold in response to a question by Herz. "I was an American citizen and I wouldn't give in to force."

"But you agreed to become a spy," persisted Herz.

"They had me in a corner."

"What do you mean, did they punch you or use violence?"

"They don't do those things—they do it in a nice way, you know," Sebold replied amid courtroom laughter.

Sebold told again about the threats of reprisals against him and his family unless he agreed to join the spy ring. "So then you agreed to become a spy?" Herz asked.

"Yes, wouldn't you?" Sebold retorted.

"No, I wouldn't," replied the attorney emphatically.[19]

Attorney Walsh was sternly reproved by Byers when he tried to draw an incorrect inference from Sebold's confinement in the psychiatric ward at Bellevue Hospital following his ulcer operation. Walsh had asked Sebold what happened upon his release "after it was shown you were not feeble-minded."

Judge Byers leaned forward and looked sternly at the lawyer. "There is nothing in the record to show that this man was examined for feeble-mindedness and you know it," he snapped. "Now change your line of questioning at once."[20]

Sebold lacked confidence in himself as a witness.[21] To lighten his load, the prosecution frequently called to the stand many of the FBI agents who had worked the case for almost two years to corroborate Sebold's testimony. Richard Johnson was required to be in court every day because he was one of the few agents who had witnessed all the spy meetings with Sebold/Sawyer.

William Friedemann once testified for seven days straight. Highly intelligent and excellent under cross-examination, he was a substitute for the hundreds of recordings, which were never introduced as exhibits, partly because the sound in many instances was poor. He was a qualified translator, and his copious notes quoted the spies verbatim in their conversations with Sebold.[22]

David Harris, one of the agents who had arrested Fritz and Lewis, took the stand. Walsh asked him if the FBI men had obtained warrants for the arrest and for the search of the apartment. Byers asked why he was interested. Walsh answered that he wanted to show that "these men entered and searched that apartment like a bunch of vandals." Byers admonished him for making "speeches" and again later for "roaring at the court" while arguing the admissibility of a question Walsh had posed on the law governing search and seizure.[23]

The appearance of Sebold as a witness was less of a bombshell than the showing on 18 September of the films made of Sebold's meetings with the spies.[24] The jury was asked to move to the other side of the room, and a five-foot screen was placed behind the jury box. Even Sebold returned to the courtroom to watch the films. Every time the courtroom was darkened, Fritz was immediately surrounded by eight U.S. marshals. Well aware of his past record of escapes from custody, the law was treating him with respect.

The films were silent. Even without sound they were damning, with Friedemann or Johnson describing the action and dialogue. The film was on the jerky side, Johnson explained, because of the office's inferior lighting. It had been necessary for him to crank the camera at eight frames per second rather than the usual sixteen.

Fritz watched himself arrive at 6:16 P.M. by the clock on the desk. He watched himself remove the documents from his sock and then gesture and spit while describing the contents. He listened as the audience and his co-defendants snickered when he pantomimed the shooting and noise of a rifle. The film even captured debonair Fritz in unguarded moments picking his nose and scratching himself. Surprised, Fritz commented to attorney Herz sitting next to him, in a voice loud enough for half the courtroom to hear, "Here I've wanted to get into movies all my life and I finally do and there I am picking my nose and scratching my ass."[25] More snickers filled the courtroom when Sebold held up for the camera amateurish drawings of an airplane, a mosquito boat, and a rifle.

When the twelve-minute film—consisting of two hundred of the nine hundred feet taken—concluded, Fritz leaned across to his co-conspirators grinning and whispering, perhaps pleased with his performance. But despite his humorous remarks and his occasional show of camaraderie with the other defendants, Fritz maintained an aloof and superior attitude. The other spies, whom he considered bums, were beneath him. According to Agent Raymond Newkirk, who had arrested Fritz, "It was a horrible blow when he was arrested. He believed he was so damn smart he would never get caught."[26]

The government rested its case shortly after noon on Friday, 17 October, as the spy trial rounded out its sixth week. Monday would be taken up with motions by defense counsel.

Fritz, described by Kennedy as a "veteran espionage agent of more than forty years and an inveterate Anglophile," took the stand in his own defense on 21 October. He was the first of the spies to do so. Using all his skills as an actor learned in a lifetime of deception, Fritz spent several hours telling such a spellbinding tale of his life of adventure that the New York Sun described it as "bizarre" and "a story of adventure that bordered on the fantastic."[27] The Sun speculated that Fritz's defense might rest on insanity, or at least irrationality. Why not? It had worked once before.

In his clipped English accent and well-modulated voice, Fritz spun out the half-truths and half-lies he had been telling all his life, probably no more sure of what was reality than was his audience. Chronologically, he was as accurate as a four-bit watch. But what did it matter? Fritz was always entertaining. His blue eyes would dart continually around the courtroom as if looking for a friend, or they would ogle the women jurors. Calmly and eloquently he continued, showing emotion only when expressing his hatred for the British and telling of beatings at their hands in all parts of the world. He was frequently interrupted by Kennedy's objections to his irrelevant and at times fiery speeches. Fritz used such picturesque phrases that Kennedy objected to it as the "technique of an erstwhile drama critic."[28]

Fritz may have been irrelevant and often on the verge of losing control, but the courtroom was enthralled, impressed by this alleged spy who was remarkably vigorous for his sixty-three years. "The dark, beetle-browed native of South Africa" (as he was described by the *New York Times*) began his testimony by reviewing his early years and "outlining in dramatic detail a career of adventure, intrigue, and mystery" involving friendships with kings and presidents, bizarre wartime captures and escapes, and admitted lunacy.[29] "I was born in 1877 or 1878 in the South African Republic. It is now a British colony," he added bitterly. "It was a republic, the same as America, under Paul Kruger."

"Do you have brothers?" asked his attorney.

"I have one brother. I did have brothers and sisters. But they were killed in the Boer War." The reference to the Boer War was stricken from the record on Kennedy's objection.

Fritz told of his skirmishes with Zulus as a teenager and his early education in South Africa, at Oxford, and at St. Cyr. Following his capture in the Boer War, he testified, he continued his education in Bermuda. "What was the nature of that education?" asked Walsh.

"Carrying a ball and chain." Kennedy protested this answer but was overruled.

"Perhaps he regarded it as education," Judge Byers observed.

"I escaped from Bermuda aboard the Vanderbilt yacht when I came to America," continued Fritz, forgetting or intentionally upgrading the vessel's ownership from Isaac Emerson, the Bromo Seltzer king. "As an observer for South African forces in the Russo-Japanese War I was wounded and hospitalized for ten months in Brussels, a shell shock victim."

"When you returned to consciousness, approximately how old were you?" asked Walsh.

"It was 1905," returned Fritz. But the answer was nearly lost in the laughter that rang out from the court. Byers banged his gavel, and the marshals demanded silence.

Fritz told of lecturing "in behalf of the Paulist Fathers," being a reporter for New York newspapers, suggesting African wildlife as a possible new food supply in the United States, and advising Theodore Roosevelt. "When he was president," Fritz said, "I could visit him any time at the White House, and I did. I gave him instructions on hunting big game in Africa. I also invented a humane method of killing animals with drugged bullets."

He recounted his rambles around South America in 1914 and 1915, coming to America and masquerading as an Australian officer. "I invented a magnetic mine and turned the secret patent over to the United States Navy," he said.

Walsh asked Fritz to describe some of his inventions.

"There were thirteen, nine of which have been patented, including a device for warming up airplane engines and a floating dock. I also developed a blackout lamp that was the idea of Evelyn Clayton Lewis.[30]

"A few weeks later I was arrested as a German agent. On leaving court, British agents accosted me and beat me up. I woke up in Bellevue. I escaped and went to Boston, where I ran an advertising business for four years. I did publicity for Joseph P. Kennedy, the former ambassador to Great Britain, who was a motion picture executive then.

"While working for Martin Quigley's magazines in New York, British agents walked into the office one day and beat me up." (Fritz later amended this statement, declaring that his assailants on this occasion had been New York policemen.) "They falsely accused me of murder on the high seas. It related to an incident during the world war for which Germany still owes me $10,000 for my services as a spy. The American Civil Liberties Union got me off on this charge."

"Since when have they been British agents?" asked Judge Byers.

Fritz continued, "I was then an inmate in an asylum for the criminally insane at Matteawan, and spent a period of time in a New Jersey monastery."[31]

Under direct examination by his own attorney, Fritz alternated between being suave and composed and then openly clashing with Walsh and shouting, "Don't put words in my mouth!"

Fritz denied, under direct questioning, that he had ever consorted with any of his fourteen co-defendants. "I never saw one of them before in my life until we were arrested," he swore.

"Sebold came to my office in February 1940," said Fritz in describing his first meeting with the double agent, "and first talked to me in German. When I told him I was unfamiliar with that language, he apologized for his broken English.

"He introduced himself as Harry Sawyer, a trusted employee of the Siemens-Schuckert Werke and something of an inventor and therefore interested in my floating-dock device for rescuing disabled seaplanes. I offered it to Germany after American and British naval authorities turned it down.

"Some Germans eventually became interested in the dock and sold some in Europe, including Holland. I received 10 percent of the selling price, which accounted for the $500 cabled to me from Holland. The money was not for espionage work.

"I also submitted rewrites of articles from American magazines to Sawyer because he had described himself as a sort of literary agent for European newspapers."

Fritz concluded his account of his first meeting with Sebold thus: "For want of anything better to say, I asked him, 'How is the war going?' He replied, 'All right—for Germany.'"[32]

"The FBI agents who arrested me are guilty of outrageous atrocities, and Sebold is the real villain," Fritz declared theatrically the second day on the stand in his defense. He admitted giving Sebold information but said he hadn't thought it would go to the Nazis in Germany. He denied again and again that he had helped send American defense secrets abroad, and that until the British had arrested him in 1916 he had supported this country in the world war by making patriotic speeches.

"Sebold wanted me to spy for him, but I said no because I was too old and high blood pressure made me practically an invalid."

"I once gave Sebold a picture of a boat from a children's book, but I only did it to humor him."

"Did he pay you for it?" asked Walsh.

"He gave me $100 for it."[33]

On cross-examination Walsh intimated that Sebold had offered Fritz $3,000 to donate to the America First Committee for the rally in New York the previous May addressed by Senator Burton K. Wheeler of Montana and aviator Charles A. Lindbergh.

"Sebold asked me what I thought about the America First Committee," said Fritz. "I told him I had no connection with the committee but that I approved of its principles. He said I could do a good thing for myself by contributing some money to the committee at a rally in Madison Square Garden. I said I had no money and he said he would supply it. There would be $1,000 for Lindbergh, $1,000 for Senator Wheeler, and $1,000 for somebody on the World-Telegram. I told him I didn't see the object and I refused. He said I was a damned fool, that money was money, and that it was being supplied by friends in Germany.

"I remained a damn fool," Fritz added.

"It was Sebold's idea that I blow up the General Electric plant at Schenectady, but I said no. He told me I'd be a hero if I did something like that. Sebold also told me that he knew a mechanic who would give me some dynamite I could put in President Roosevelt's Hyde Park church and that it would be a big stroke for Germany. He promised that he would see to it that within a week of the bombing I would be safe in Dakar.[34]

"I told him he was insane, and he replied, 'I'm not—not now.'"

"When he approached me with this proposition a second time I warned him I would inform the police. So I called the FBI about the actions of this dangerous lunatic."

"Did they send a man to see you?" asked Walsh.

"Did they?" Fritz almost shouted. "Six or seven came to see me. They burst in the door with guns drawn and handcuffs dangling. With me when the ruffians broke in was Evelyn. She was making Christmas ornaments and was wearing nothing but a studio coat. When she asked permission to change her clothes, one of them"—he pointed to Raymond Newkirk—"whipped off her smock. A steel corset she wore to support a broken back was torn from her bare body and there she stood, naked before eight men."[35] Fritz added, "Then Ray took her into the other room and they were there a long time." (The accused Newkirk was ribbed about this later by his fellow agents.)[36]

Fritz testified that one of the agents pulled out a revolver and pointed it at his own head in a "significant gesture" of shooting. "If you had any guts you'd do that and go down in a blaze of glory as the great Colonel Fritz Duquesne!" Fritz quoted the agent as saying.

This was too much for the prosecuting attorney. "I object to this man employing the art which he learned as a dramatic critic," protested Kennedy.

But there was no stopping Fritz. He was wound up and determined to play the martyr. He said the apartment was ransacked and property was scattered, smashed, torn, and thrown on the floor. "The hundreds of pictures, diagrams, and blueprints found there concerned only my various inventions," said Fritz. "Some of these papers were planted and some of my files were stolen.

"The G-men stripped me and paraded me naked through corridors, called me vile names and accused me of living off women," Fritz went on. "They forced me to sleep on a cot covered with excrement. I finally signed a statement at the point of a gun. I didn't want to be blackjacked into an insane asylum. It had happened to me three times before and I don't want to die mad." Fritz declared that a doctor hurt him and made dire threats when he declined to take a pill that was offered him.

"Since the trial began, I have been in isolation. I've never been out in the sunlight. Even my guards have been unkind. When I asked one his name, he said, 'Just call me God.'"

Kennedy protested again, calling Fritz's long, rambling story inflammatory. "The jury realizes," warned Judge Byers, "this is a highly inflamed recital by a man who in the past, as he has indicated, has been engaged in making speeches for publicity purposes."

Undaunted, Fritz referred again to his experience with the FBI. "There was a noise like falling beams. One of the agents shouted, 'War is declared! The people are waiting downstairs to tear you to pieces. You haven't a friend in America.' They certainly bulldozed me," Fritz ended ruefully.

"This is an act!" Kennedy interrupted angrily.

"You ought to know," barked Fritz. "You're an actor yourself. I'm up here talking for my liberty." He related several more of the hardships he had suffered at the hands of the bureau, then: "It's hard for me to go on with this."

"It ought to be," Kennedy said sarcastically.[37]

Under Harold Kennedy's searching, rapid-fire questions on the government's first day of cross-examination, Fritz lost the cool eloquence he had exhibited during his first two days of direct testimony. His total recall of truths and studied lies was replaced by sudden lapses of memory when confronted with a landslide of exhibits representing his radioed correspondence to Germany and the testimony of eavesdropping G-men. When convenient—which was often—he complained, "I'm suffering from high blood pressure and often get confused."[38]

It quickly became evident that Fritz and Kennedy were not going to get along. The prosecutor had scarcely opened his mouth with his first question when Fritz shouted, "I understand bullyragging. I've had enough of it from the FBI!"[39]

The accused Nazi spy became involved in one tiff after another with Kennedy as the prosecutor tripped him up. At one point Kennedy vigorously objected to Fritz's habit, when answering Walsh's questions, of embellishing his answers with invectives against England or the FBI. At another point, while swinging his arms in anger—Fritz tended to gesture and shout when unable to verify previous statements—he broke his glasses. They were sent out to be repaired. Then Fritz complained that he couldn't read exhibits of his alleged reports to Hamburg. Judge Byers sternly rebuked Fritz for his conduct, warning him that his actions came close to contempt of court.

Finally, losing patience when Fritz was asking as many questions as the prosecution was putting to him, Byers told Walsh, "I see no way short of ordering him off the witness stand to eliminate this exhibitionism."

Calm restored, Walsh asked Fritz flatly, "Are you or are you not a spy?"

"I am not," replied Fritz with studied emphasis.

Responding angrily to another Kennedy objection, Fritz ignored the court's recent ruling on asking questions and, shaking a finger at Kennedy, snapped, "Are you cross-examining me or is Mr. Walsh?"

In response to a plea from Kennedy, Byers ordered Walsh to direct his client to answer questions and not talk when the prosecution was making objections. Walsh did so, but ineffectually. When Fritz talked over Kennedy's next objection, Byers told Fritz directly, "I've been as patient with you as I can. You'll either follow the instructions of the court or take the consequences. You'll answer the questions and nothing more."[40]

Fritz settled down some but caused considerable courtroom laughter when later asked to point out an FBI man he said had followed him and Sebold on one of their meetings. He was unable to find the agent in the courtroom. "How did you know he was an FBI agent?" asked Kennedy.

"Well—he had on a brown coat, gabardine suit, and fedora hat—the regular uniform of the FBI."[41]

With great braggadocio Fritz described how he caused Lord Kitchener's death, leading to his arrest by British agents in New York in 1917: "It interrupted a series of lectures I was making to pep up American defense workers," he said.

"Were you at the time going around the country representing yourself as Captain Claude Stoughton of the Australian military forces?" asked Kennedy.

"Yes, that was for theatrical purposes. It was to help along the American publicity."

Kennedy showed Fritz a photograph of himself with a number of medals dangling from his uniformed chest and asked him to identify the picture. "Yes, that was me twenty-five years ago," confirmed Fritz, smiling and straightening his shoulders.

When Judge Byers asked him some questions about his native South Africa, Fritz replied, "I am a rebel. I'm a member of the South Africa Republican Party."

"What would happen to you if you went back to South Africa?"

"I'd be shot."

On re-cross-examination Walsh asked Fritz more about his stated friendship with Roosevelt. "When did you first meet President Theodore Roosevelt?"

"In 1907, the time he founded the Adventurer's Club and I was a charter officer of that club. Once he asked me to visit him at the White House during one month in 1907, or 1908, or 1909. I visited the White House three or four times within one week.

"Mr. Loeb would meet me," Fritz continued. We would talk and he would say, 'Go inside.' And I would, and there would be President Roosevelt. Our conversation always was about hunting lions and elephants. Once President Roosevelt told me he was a Dutchman."

Judge Byers addressed Fritz: "I suppose you realize there is no possibility of calling witnesses to present the other side of this. Mr. Loeb died not long ago, and President Roosevelt died quite a while ago."

Walsh changed the line of questioning to aliases Fritz admitted to using.

"I did so in 1919 because I was a fugitive from a bughouse."

"A what?" asked Walsh.

"A bughouse. I was rescued from Bellevue Hospital by members of the Irish Republican Army and I changed my name to hide my identity as an ex-lunatic."

The morning session ended with Fritz saying he wanted "to die on the Prairies of Paradise"—evidently an allusion to South Africa.

There was drama in the afternoon session when Kennedy introduced a surprise witness from among the court spectators—an elderly black man. "Do you know this man?" Kennedy asked Fritz.

"No," replied Fritz after studying him at length.

"Don't you know that this man between 1901 and 1909 was Theodore Roosevelt's valet?"

"No," insisted Fritz.

The man was John Amos, a special agent for the FBI who as a young man had been a valet to Theodore Roosevelt. He took the stand and repudiated Fritz's claim to knowing the president. It was grandstanding by Kennedy, but it worked. Fritz looked foolish and was apparently exposed as a liar. Poor Fritz. The one time he was telling the truth—or half-truths, at any rate—he wasn't believed. Amos may have been Roosevelt's valet, but it would have been impossible for him to have seen, or remembered, every person who met the president.

Why didn't a reporter check the newspapers of 1909 to corroborate Fritz's story? Why didn't Fritz, who kept meticulous scrapbooks—which must have been in the possession of the FBI—have them brought forward? These are questions that will never be answered.

Referring to the letter written by attorney Frederick Case to Roosevelt inquiring if he knew Fritz, Kennedy asked, "Didn't Theodore Roosevelt write a denial on August 10, 1917, that he had ever known you?"

It was a spurious question, because Fritz couldn't possibly have been aware of the letter. But he answered with a smile, "That was during the world war."

"What?" demanded Kennedy.

"I was in an asylum then," finished Fritz. The "asylum" ploy was one he often used to avoid giving direct answers.[42]

In further cross-examination Kennedy asked Fritz if he told lies. "Plenty," confessed Fritz heartily. "I lied to prevent being blackjacked and I made hundreds of falsehoods in order to get things." He admitted he had lied about his birthplace in a WPA application, and he had lied in claiming that he had a dependent (a girl named Corbett), that he had been a lieutenant, a captain, and a major in the world war, and that he was a graduate of Oxford. But he insisted these were "wartime lies."

Fritz ran off a dozen or so names when Kennedy asked him what aliases he had operated under. He said that he used the alias Kain in 1932, and that he gave his birthplace as Melbourne, Australia, in order to obtain a British passport so that he might thwart his exile from all territory flying the British flag and return to South Africa. "I wanted to go home to the graves of my people and die," Fritz explained.

"That was a lie, wasn't it?" asked Kennedy, referring to the alias.

"Of course it was a lie. It was a war lie."

"Was there a war in South Africa in 1932?" asked Kennedy in feigned surprise.[43]

Fritz leaned forward, pointed a finger at Kennedy, and said menacingly, "There's always a war in South Africa because Englishmen are there. Britain is always a belligerent there and I'm one of the revolutionists. I am an exile from there."

"Tell us something about the Boer War," suggested Kennedy.

"Let's get down to cases," Fritz said petulantly. "You are not trying the Boer War or any other war. Why don't you ask about the war between Germany and England? You're trying to shove things down the throats of the jurors."

Asked again about his meetings with Sebold, Fritz said, "I suspected he was a foreign agent when he was willing to pay good money for junk. But I never suspected he was a German agent. I thought he was a Russian agent or English. As a matter of fact I suspected he was insane. To be frank, I thought he was nuts." Nevertheless, Fritz continued taking money from Sebold for what he termed harmless material cut out of magazines and bought from toyshops. "Sawyer asked me to get him a code to use in case this country went to war. So I told him I would invent one for him."

"And did you?" asked Walsh.

"I sold him a code used by Benedict Arnold in the war between England and the United States in 1776." (Arnold had appropriated a centuries old-method involving a book, often the dictionary. A series of numbers would guide the user to a certain page and a certain word needed to decode the message. It was the system the Abwehr taught Sebold.) "It's also used by sweethearts in France," Fritz added.

"Where did it come from?"

"I got it out of the public library. Sebold seemed very pleased and accepted it."[44]

Then, pointing a finger and gesturing angrily at Kennedy, Fritz shouted, "I'm not going to be killed on a dirty guillotine on mere words. The FBI has all my drawings, notwithstanding what they say, and they refuse to produce them."[45]

With unexpected suddenness, Walsh stepped back from the rail and announced that he had completed his examination of his client.

Following the testimony of the other spies, Hermann Lang, third of the triumvirate and forever to be known as the man who stole the Norden bombsight, began his defense on 2 November.

Lang denied all charges against him. He had an explanation for everything, even for his on-camera statements to Sawyer: "I was afraid of Sawyer, and I did not want to give him any information about the bombsight. So just to get rid of him, I told him that I already had given the full details of the bombsight to the Abwehr on a visit to Berlin. Naturally this was not true. I am not a spy."

In an unusual move, but one intended to prove the innocence of his client, George Herz had earlier planned to subpoena Secretary of War Henry L. Stimson. The move was prompted by a statement Stimson had made at a press conference on 23 October that there was "no reason to believe" that the secret of the Norden bombsight was in the possession of the Germans. It was certainly not a complete denial and a guarded statement at most.

A subpoena was served on the secretary on 29 October. At a press conference the next day Stimson said, "I do not have any personal information of a type that could be used as evidence in a court of law. I cannot talk of hearsay on a witness stand. I think it would be an idle trip for me."[46]

Herz withdrew the subpoena—thinking it would be an "unpatriotic act" on his part in view of Stimson's preoccupation with the defense program—on the condition that if called, Stimson would testify to that statement without appearing in court.

Leo Waalen was the last of the fifteen spies to take the stand in his own defense. The government and the defense rested their cases at 4:02 P.M. on Tuesday, 3 December 1941.

Summations for the defense were expected to take at least a week beginning 8 December. But on the day before, an event occurred that almost precluded any fair judgment on the part of the jury: the Japanese attacked Pearl Harbor. There was another stir over the weekend when it was reported that Fritz Duquesne had slashed his throat with a razor in a suicide attempt. Walsh quashed the rumor when he told reporters that Fritz had suffered a slight stroke—a harbinger of what was to come—which would not prevent his appearance in court.

The Pearl Harbor attack prompted attorneys Edmund Donald Wilson (for Eilers) and David S. Kumble (for Ebelling) to preface their arguments with pleas to the jury not to let the outbreak of hostilities between the United States and Japan "prejudice" them against the defendants. Herz felt he was bucking a stone wall during the six hours he summed up the case for Lang. "I could see the hatred in the jury's eyes. They were literally manifesting their hatred for me because I had the nerve to get up there and speak on behalf of Lang."[47]

Harold Kennedy began summing up the case for the government on 10 December. He asserted that "the evidence produced during the fourteen weeks of the trial clearly demonstrated that the alleged conspiracy to transmit information about the U.S. defense effort had emanated from the German Reich."

Calling it "specious oratory," Kennedy vigorously denied accusations by some of the defense counsel that the FBI and its counterespionage agent, William Sebold, had cooperated in an effort to "entrap" a number of the defendants, or that the information transmitted by the defendants to Germany was of general public knowledge. He called the FBI the "finest law enforcement agency I ever saw in my life" and assured the jury that "elaborate steps were taken not to lead the defendants into crime." Kennedy asserted that an acquittal would be tantamount to a "collapse of good government." Commenting on Sebold's reporting to the FBI, immediately upon his return to this country, the Nazi plans for an espionage ring here, Kennedy asked, "Isn't that the conduct of an honest American who has been invited to stick a knife in the back of his adopted country?"

Kennedy ended his summation on the next day, declaring that the acquittal of any or all of the fourteen defendants accused of espionage and failure to register as agents of a foreign government would be a "disaster" to the United States. Without referring to the state of war then existing between this country and the Axis powers—Germany and Italy had declared war on the United States that very day, and the United States had responded in kind—Kennedy warned the jury of the effect an acquittal would have on German nationals at this time: "Think of the joy in Yorkville [New York's "Little Berlin"] over what they can get away with on American juries"—an unwelcome slur against loyal German Americans.[48]

Judge Byers revoked the $25,000 bail of Edmund Heine and then, referring to the declarations of war, began his two-and-a-half-hour charge to the jury at 10:30 A.M.:

About twenty-four hours ago, the incident which has been forecast, eventuated. It would be sheer affectation if we tried to ignore it. It is unfortunate that this development should have taken place. In my opinion, the duration of the trial has been very considerably prolonged, and unnecessarily so, by the strategy on the part of some counsel for the defense. I hope you will be able to disregard it entirely.

Without mentioning his name the judge accused Frank Walsh, Fritz's attorney, of seeking—either "willfully" or through ignorance—to mislead the jury. He declared that George Herz, counsel for Hermann Lang, had been guilty of "calculated impudence" toward the court.

The jury was told to disregard the arguments of defense counsel that the defendants' actions were motivated solely by a desire to hurt Great Britain and not the United States defense effort: "It is my duty to tell you that from and after March 11, 1941, the safety of Great Britain became a matter of the national defense of the United States," Judge Byers declared. He then read an excerpt from a letter of that date, when the lendlease law became effective, from President Roosevelt to Secretary of the Navy Frank Knox. The letter stated that the "safety of the United Kingdom is vital to the defense of the United States."

"Consider the evidence carefully," Judge Byers said to the jury. "If you are not familiar with it after these three months, there is nothing I can add to help you."[49]

It was 1 P.M. when Byers finished his instructions. The jury began deliberation after lunch, at 2:20. They recessed for dinner from 6:40 to 9:20 P.M. A verdict was reached a few minutes before midnight, after eight hours of deliberation. Edward A. Logan, foreman of the jury, announced that all fourteen defendants accused of espionage and failure to register as agents of a foreign government, namely Germany, had been found guilty on both counts.

In dismissing the jury Judge Byers said, "It will readily appear that you have rendered a very substantial contribution to the welfare of the country which you and I hold very dear."

T. Vincent Quinn, assistant U.S. attorney, told the jury that it had "done a hard job very well."[50]

"Possibly the most fantastic spy trial in the history of our country came to its inevitable conclusion the week following the Pearl Harbor attack," said J. Edgar Hoover. "It broke the very spine of German intelligence in the United States."[51]

Judge Byers set the date of Friday, 2 January 1942, for sentencing.

Typically, Fritz remained unrepentant, steadfastly maintaining his innocence as he always had in previous arrests over the last four decades, and as he would until he died. On 29 December, while awaiting sentencing, he wrote a letter to Herman, Lillian's husband (he could not write to Lillian because prison rules did not permit correspondence with married women):

The time is drawing near for the pronouncement of my doom. I assure you Herman that this whole thing is a miscarriage of justice as far as I am concerned. I know what a patriot you are and how you hate the nazis and I want you to believe me. I never have done a thing at anytime anywhere against this, our country. I am sure that if I had been *courtmartialed* I would have been freed. The jury was overcome by the declaration of war. Furthermore they did not understand the military significance of the things they listened to or saw. The papers of course tried the case in headlines. On account of the war I expect the judge to be harsh. I am innocent and that is what is driving me mad. I cannot believe it all and yet I *am* here. The poor sailors and stewards that were tied into an alleged conspiracy with me were just suckers for a German wharf rat [Sebold] who made $15,000 in a year out of them.

The letter was postmarked 8 January 1942, six days after Fritz was sentenced.[52]

Relatives and friends of the defendants crowded the courtroom on the second day of the New Year. All thirty-three spies were to be sentenced, including Fehse and Zenzinger, who had been arrested earlier, and Clausing and Walischewski, arrested off their ships.

Hermann Lang was called to the bar at about 10:45 A.M. Attorney Herz pleaded clemency for his client, saying that Lang had a "weakness" but had never deliberately given the German government any information.

"He of all men," replied Judge Byers slowly and gravely, "knew the value of the Norden bombsight. "He of all men knew to what use it might be put by the 'chivalrous' powers of the Axis in waging their war against civilization. I sentence you, Lang, to serve eighteen years in prison on the second count and two years on the first count."

Having always given the impression that he was about to break into tears, Lang finally did so. He showed no other emotion as two deputy marshals hustled him off to the prisoner's pen across the hall.

George Gordon Battle also asked leniency for his client, Edmund Carl Heine. But the man who was going to promote the Volkswagen received the same sentence plus a $2,000 fine.

Fritz stepped forward next. Described by the government during the trial as "a naturalized American, writer, lecturer, and professional spy," he was now described by prosecutor Kennedy as "a bold and unscrupulous liar."

Judge Byers said, "I find no mitigating circumstances in this man's case. I shall not indulge in expressing my own opinion. My views might be less temperate."[53]

The usually glib Fritz for once had nothing to say. It is possible that he was finally reacting to what Heine, who had been gentlemanly throughout the trial, had told him: "You get farther by being a gentleman than being an obnoxious little boy."[54] But it was too late for Fritz.

He was sentenced to two years on the first count and eighteen years on the second and fined $2,000. His sentences, like those of the others, would run concurrently.

The lightest sentence was given Fritz's lady friend, Evelyn Clayton Lewis. She was given one year and one day to serve in prison. "My family has been in this country for more than two hundred years," she pleaded. "I was not aware I had done anything wrong."

"I cannot understand," Byers responded, "how an American citizen could engage in the promotion of anything seriously inimical to the United States."[55]

"Glamour girl" Lilly Barbara Carola Stein was sentenced to two years on the first count and ten years on the second.

Roeder, of the triumvirate, was given sixteen years.

The remaining twenty-seven spies—those who had been on trial and those who had pleaded guilty—received sentences ranging from fifteen months to sixteen years. Nine were fined. The figures were between $1,000 and $2,000.

It took two and a half hours to sentence all the spies. As they walked through the corridors of the old courthouse for the last time, the jauntiness and confidence they had showed at the beginning of the trial was gone. No "V for victory" signs were flashed.

"Look up, please!" a press photographer shouted.

"I'm through doing favors for you fellows," growled Axel Wheeler-Hill.

"You're through doing anything," shot back a bystander.[56]

In what may have been one of the first government witness-protection programs, Sebold was given still another new identity and set up with a chicken farm in California.[57] He then faded into obscurity. His fate was melodramatically described in Alan Hynd's *Passport to Treason*, published in 1943 at the height of the war: "In the shadows there walks today a man who is a fugitive from Nazi vengeance—William Sebold. 'No comment' is what Washington is giving out as to the fate of William Sebold's kin. Sebold himself will not emerge from the shadows until the bells of victory toll."[58]

As for Fritz, he knew his forty-year career as a spy was over. There would be no more escapes. There would be no more adventures. There would be only one last loud, defiant shout as he walked through the courthouse corridor: "Long live America!"[59]

CHAPTER 23

No Escape for 5051-H

Memo to Mr. N. F. Stucker, Captain
From George H. McCullough, Jr. (Geo.)
October 6, 1942
Duquesne is classified maximum custody.

At present he is confined in a locked room in "E" ward hospital. Room has metal door with a standard type Yale lock. Door has ventilating vents near bottom that are large enough to permit contraband passed through them. Room also has ventilating window opening on hospital corridor. Window when open creates aperture about 8" × 10" thereby enabling this man to make contact with other inmates, receive contraband and send information and oral messages to other inmates. Believe it has been practice of some officers not familiar with this man's record, to leave his cell open during mealtime. I believe this man to be one of the most dangerous criminals in the United States.[1]

"One of the most dangerous criminals in the United States" was sixty-five years old, suffering from high blood pressure and cerebral arteriosclerosis, showing signs of mental deterioration, and in no way deserving of the criminal esteem in which he was held by George H. McCullough Jr.

Nevertheless, 59008-L would have been delighted to know that he reflected such an aura. It surely would have been some consolation for the dreary existence he was now living in solitary confinement. Since 9

February 1942 Fritz had been behind bars at Leavenworth Federal Penitentiary in Kansas.

His rebellious nature had not adapted well to imprisonment, and only in his last few years of incarceration would he find some peace. As a young prisoner, in jails not noted for security and in times less perilous, Fritz had always had some hope of escape, at which he had been a master. Not to be forgotten was his British jailer's assessment of him during his imprisonment in Cape Castle forty-one years earlier: "He is reported as troublesome and dangerous."[2] But now a prison psychiatric report noted, "It is possible that this man who has been an active adventurer for many years, now having been arrested and sentenced a long time, has about given up hope of being free again, and thus having no hope, physical and mental deterioration are to be expected."

Fritz was now ten months into his eighteen-year sentence, with a maximum release date of 1 January 1960. He would be eligible for parole in 1948. His conditional release date was 1 February 1954. It was not a happy outlook. Life in prison was a continuous series of psychiatric examinations, physical calamities, lost appeals, and violations of prison rules by Fritz that only succeeded in causing him to lose good time, thus extending his bad time.

When interviewed upon his arrival at Leavenworth, Fritz was "extremely talkative." His colorful account of past adventures and escapades suggested to his interviewer that he had delusions of grandeur and imagined much of what he believed to be fact. Noting that he had once been declared insane, the interviewer thought he might still be suffering from a mental disorder.

Another interview on 6 March took note of Fritz's idiosyncrasies: "This man has an undying hatred of England which he not only admits but boasts of. He claims that he never would aid or do anything that would injure the U.S. He repeatedly corrects statements, indicating [that] he was either falsifying his statement or had difficulty recalling his past life. He claims his sister was raped before his eyes, yet in other interviews he says it was his mother." Fritz boasted of his past "prowess with women as well as with countries." He particularly and often expressed bitterness over the conviction of Evelyn Clayton Lewis.

The summation on his arrival was that Fritz was in poor physical condition with evidence of mental deterioration and cerebral arteriosclerosis. He was of below-average intelligence and below-average manipulative dexterity. Yet the psychiatrist's report made at the same time said, "He has undoubtedly been a man of exceptionally brilliant intelligence." It was recommended that he be placed on general labor or moderate duty only.

Fritz was judged self-assured and extremely glib—perhaps more glib than the psychiatrists realized. A year later a psychiatrist penciled on his report that Fritz possessed "superior" intelligence. It was thought that he might be "trying to make a poorer score than the maximum of his abilities." As late as 1947 he was considered devious by the warden of the Medical Center in Missouri, where he was then imprisoned. Fritz made quite a nuisance of himself while there, causing the prison undue work and embarrassment by having his rejected letters referred to famed civil liberties lawyer Zachariah Chafee Jr. It was presumed that this gave Fritz great satisfaction. And in 1953 the warden considered him "a versatile egotist whose unswerving self-confidence gave him a flying headstart in every exploit he attempted." In short, no one was ever sure with Fritz. The 6 March report, a month after his first examination, stated, "Psychiatric picture at present time must be given tentatively. This man, is, of course, a skilled espionage agent and is trained in dissimulation. He will be seen further and attempts will be made to catch him off guard."

Fritz's twelve years, seven months, and sixteen days in prison are told best through his regular psychiatric and medical summaries. While these reports document a slow physical and mental breakdown punctuated by bouts of clarity and a return to his old conniving ways, they also show a repetitive pattern consistent with his personality and the actions of his life prior to prison. Although Fritz was failing mentally and physically, the federal prison system remained skittish for years about "one of the most dangerous criminals in the United States." Continuing the 6 March report: "He is, of course, an utterly untrustworthy individual who has been brilliant in his many activities. . . . He is, at the present time, a pitiful individual."

15 October 1942: Fritz does not eat his peanut butter for supper and is warned for the last time. He says he hadn't asked for it and is told he should have told the steward to take it back. His expression and tone of voice are insolent: "I thank you for informing me the way the 'company' runs things."

3 April 1943: Fritz is moved from D-4, his regular cell, and placed in close minimum segregation in cell 6 for making constant attempts to smuggle out about fifteen letters, some written on toilet paper, through other inmates. The letters are addressed to newspapers, asking them to work toward clearing him of the false charges against him. Fritz is reported for refusing to take his clothes off when going to bed.

9 April: At a meeting before the Good Time Board to hear his case for attempting to smuggle out the letters, Fritz acknowledges his guilt: "I feel that the doctors hate my guts. Everybody does, and I sent out those letters as the last thing I could do because I wanted people to know that I was framed up by a dirty German punk that got $20,000 for the job. I wanted those people that I worked with on the newspaper to know that I wasn't guilty."

13 April: The penalty for the letter-smuggling attempt is forfeiture of six hundred days statutory good time.

3 June: At about 4 P.M. Fritz is found reading a contraband newspaper concealed in his locker. Both he and L. Kuehn, the man it belongs to, say they do not know who gave it to him. Kuehn says he picked it out of the trash can in the bathroom. Fritz says he didn't know it was against the rules.

5 June: Effective immediately, Fritz is confined in segregation. He is not permitted to have writing paper, pencils, books, magazines, or papers. Only toilet articles are permitted. Outside of the cell he is supervised by an officer at all times. No correspondence.

28 June: A lead pencil, about two inches long and shaved flat on both sides, is found in a small recess over the upper left-hand side of the door.

1 July: Fritz suffers from extreme headaches causing vertigo. "This man appears to be at the end of his rope. He has been an adventurous, rather glamorous espionage individual who has associated with the high and the mighty . . . and it is believed he is breaking down and cannot stand it. He is very emotional, and at times tears come to his eyes when talking about his troubles." He accuses guards of trying to poison him. It is recommended that he be transferred to the Medical Center in Springfield, Missouri, as psychotic.

2 July: Before a Psychiatric Examining Board Fritz gives evidence of what is probably an episodal hallucinating state. "He complains bitterly of people calling him 'Fritz' and 'Dutchman.' He claims he sees men at night peering into his window and taunting him. There is always the possibility he feigns these symptoms; but he is very intense about them. He has great hatred for the FBI. These are not delusions but the natural hatred of a frustrated individual who was finally caught."

21 July: James V. Bennett, director of the Federal Bureau of Prisons from 1937 to 1964 and the leader of a revolution in prison reform, replies to the Leavenworth warden's request to have Fritz transferred to the Medical Center in Springfield. The prison system still fears what Fritz, given the opportunity, will do despite his obvious illnesses and incapacities:

This is a most extraordinary case. The past history and institutional progress of Duquesne have been of such an unusual and menacing nature as to cast much doubt on the advisability of transfer at the present time. . . . [Mention is made of his deceptions and escapes from Bermuda and Bellevue.] It is also a matter of record he has boasted of his ability to deceive physicians and other officials.

[Recent] testimony of certain inmates clearly indicates he still harbors ideas of escape.

Although it is obvious that important medical problems are involved in the welfare of this prisoner, it is equally clear that the elements of control and security are so great [as] to overshadow all other matters. For this reason, it is advisable for him to remain in your institution . . . until it is so obvious he is so incapacitated as to be unable to carry out any of his nefarious plans.

Bennett adds a handwritten note: "And besides we're crowded at Springfield now & they have lots of problems with the C.O.'s [conscientious objectors]. Hold him for a while & we'll reconsider it later."

30 December: Fritz is locked in a single room in the psychiatric section of the hospital without any activity whatever and no diversions except for his own thoughts and the little conversation he has with the doctor and officer on the floor. He is deprived of writing and other privileges and is still considered a menace to the institution. Maximum restriction is ordered in the "disciplinary hole." Fritz is sixty-six years old.

5 January 1944: He is allowed library privileges—one book at a time in his quarters, which is picked up in the evening and checked for contraband.

July: Fritz is transferred from the hospital to the segregation unit to live with several of the spies he was arrested with. They are Lang, Fehse, Stigler, and Kaercher. He makes a fairly good adjustment but constantly bickers with them. Yet they take excellent care of him.

1 January 1945: Fritz continues to deteriorate, showing considerable evidence of nervous and mental disease. Though declared psychotic on 1 July of last year, he has not been transferred to the Medical Center because of "the dangerous character of this individual. An interna-

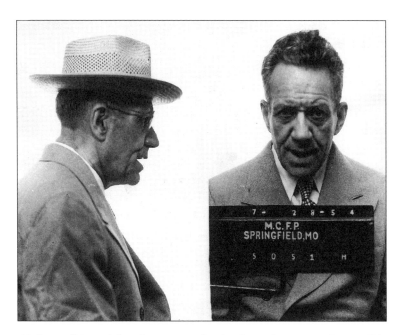

No longer "Europe's handsomest man," Fritz shows the ravages of prison life. Mug shot taken several days before his transfer to Springfield Medical Center. (National Archives)

tional rogue, he has led a glamorous and adventurous life . . . and is now at the end of his rope." Fritz has many dizzy spells and has fallen many times. He does no work and is idle in segregation.

6 March: Bennett finally accepts the fact that Fritz is "unable to carry out any of his nefarious plans," and he is transferred to the chronic ward at the Medical Center for Federal Prisoners in Springfield, Missouri. Fritz is now number 5051-H. Bennett may have been convinced by the most recent news on Fritz's condition, which reported that he sleeps lightly and has terrifying dreams that frequently waken him. A definite "paranoid tendency" causes him to believe that people are peeking at him. He claims to abhor being called Fritz. Assistance is needed in dressing and keeping clean.

16 March: Fritz is considered quite senile and a rather irrational individual. He has aged considerably, walks with a stoop, is extremely unsteady, moves about only in a stumbling fashion, and needs aid in sitting or standing. He has difficulty hearing and often cries in a most despondent fashion. He has difficulty concentrating and answering the simplest question. He expresses a sense of persecution and a fear of bodily harm and poisoning. Fritz says that he has been swindled of all his money and that "they took my car away from me and then said that I gave it to them. I did no such thing." He is depressed all the more because he appears to have some insight into his condition. Asked why he is in prison, he says, "They said that I was insane. I guess they were right if they said so." Asked how he feels, Fritz chooses his words carefully and slowly replies, "I have always been a man of vigorous nature and in this debilitated condition I am very unhappy. I hate it. I hate it." Fritz has a search made for his commitment papers to Matteawan. If he can prove he had once been certified a lunatic, an insanity plea might release him from this hell. The papers are never found.

26 March: The first of many requests to "detail the glamorous career of Fritz Duquesne" comes through prison director Bennett. William P. Kennedy, a friend of Bennett's and a "Washington correspondent for several newspapers," wants to write about Fritz. He sends along a copy of Frederick Burnham's autobiography, *Taking Chances,* which has a chapter about Fritz. Warden M. J. Pescor replies that "Duquesne has deteriorated to the extent that any information he may furnish is unreliable." But he expresses no objection to a visit from Kennedy. Kennedy does not pursue his request.

19 May: Fritz is termed completely enfeebled and inarticulate, although it is believed that he simulates the feebleness somewhat. If he is interested in a subject he becomes quite voluble. The spy whose neatness was once marveled at by FBI agents is now sloppy in person and quarters. Fritz pays little heed to rules and regulations and has a poor attitude toward personnel. He spends most of his time in bed reading nonfiction and gets other inmates to write letters for him. During the war he was permitted to write to only one correspondent. The restriction was lifted with the end of the war.

June: Fritz persists in being concerned about the fate of Evelyn Clayton Lewis, so much so that C. R. Hagen, supervisor of classification at the Medical Center, writes to her in Houston, where she has begun a new life. She wants nothing to do with Fritz and refuses to correspond with him. "The tragedy and suffering which his activities and connections in this war have brought upon me and my family have been almost beyond repair," she writes, "and any thought of any future connection is quite impossible."

6 August: Fritz is a conniver on the ward, using other inmates to his advantage. He seems incapable of doing any work. His medical report states that he denies the use of alcohol, tobacco, and narcotics. Noted are numerous war wounds, including a shrapnel wound on the back and on the right temple. This would lend some credence to Fritz's war stories.

1 December: Apparently, according to a report signed by R. Duncan, a medical consultant, Fritz was seriously injured at Leavenworth in the summer of 1943. He was forcibly thrown down a flight of stairs and forced to eat his food from the floor. He was kicked at the base of the spine (coccyx), causing him to collapse in pain. It was impossible for him to sit without great pain, with the condition becoming progressively worse, impairing his actions, causing headaches, insomnia, and extreme nervousness. His right shoulder was thrown out of alignment—an injury later shown to be a fracture—was not treated, and was "united with misalignment." No operation or medical treatment to correct the condition was considered possible. "The prognosis is a gloomy one."

25 December: Clement Wood, author of *The Man Who Killed Kitchener,* requests permission to correspond with Fritz. Fritz is sixty-eight years old.

21 January 1946: A single-edge razor is found in his locker.

25 January: Keeps other inmates awake with loud hollering.

During the next several months Fritz's condition does not improve, although it is suspected that he is augmenting his ailments. He generally appears confused but is bright and clear when a subject is to his liking. He complains of hearing voices and says the radio sounds like drums beating. He sits with a hot water bottle, filled with cold water, on his head for long periods of time. But the old Fritz, the garrulous person everyone—even his law enforcement enemies—liked, often shines through. An attendant reports on 10 March, "He seems like a nice guy."

Despite his presumed mental deterioration he carries on an incredible correspondence of special-purpose letters to lawyers, companies, politicians, and friends, always protesting his innocence and seeking help. Senators Burton K. Wheeler and Joseph McCarthy are on his list. So are Billy Rose and the chief of police of Poughkeepsie.

He asks George Gordon Battle, lawyer for fellow spy Edmund Heine, to take his case. Battle obtained Heine's release on bond by court order on 4 February, but he declines to help Fritz because of his own age—seventy-eight. He lends his Heine briefs to Fritz and suggests that he obtain a young lawyer for advice regarding clemency. Instead Fritz becomes a jailhouse lawyer, concentrating on conspiracy law. Prison psychiatrists make no note of it, not thinking it odd that a prisoner suffering from increasing mental deterioration and advanced senility possesses the capabilities to file intelligent briefs and continues to do so over the next several years.

15 October 1947: Fritz files a brief to have his conviction set aside. The arguments are the usual paranoid lies and claims of bodily harm. "Your appellant states that during the time the aforesaid government agents spent in his residence he witnessed a display of barbarism and indecency unprintable." Or regarding FBI headquarters: "He should forever after remember more vividly as a chamber of torture and relentless and merciless inquisition rivalling its counterpart in the middle ages." Fritz's training as a pulp magazine writer serves him well. The tone and complaints are almost identical to those found in his 1902 letter to *Le Petit Bleu du Matin* regarding his treatment as a POW in Bermuda. The appeal is, not surprisingly, denied by Fritz's old foe, Judge Mortimer W. Byers.

17 November: Three razor blades are found in Fritz's locker, along with a kitchen cup and a package that appears to contain fish food. It is also reported that he has an enormous number of books and enough personal effects to fill two lockers. Fritz claims that all the books and writing materials are needed for his defense. The razor blades are for personal hygiene.

December: Fritz manages to win the support of Dr. Zachariah Chafee Jr., Harvard University professor emeritus, a champion of civil liberties, and a defender of personal liberty. Chafee prepares a memorandum seeking amnesty for Fritz and points out the similarity between his case and Heine's. He sends the memorandum to prison director Bennett, who then forwards it to G. Lynn Barry, acting pardon attorney in the Department of Justice. Amnesty is denied. Fritz is seventy years old.

3 May 1948: Fritz is reprimanded for his last major violation when he is found wearing a web belt as a truss for a rupture.

20 January 1949: Paul Hollister, co-author with Inspector Thomas Tunney of *Throttled* (published 1919), requests information about Fritz. Perhaps wanting to write about Fritz, he nevertheless does not pursue his request further.

26 January 1950: Fritz appears to be alert, intelligent, and very cooperative. Apparently there has been a great improvement physically and mentally.

12 February: During his twelve years in prison Fritz and faithful Lillian Linding have corresponded regularly. He often sends her poems he has written, and his letters become increasingly endearing. They go from "Sincerely" to "As ever," then "Darling," "Love and hugs," "Caresses to you," "A thousand kisses to you," and "Wishing you love forever." He asks her if she has seen the movie *The House on 92nd Street.* "I would like you to save all the clippings on me that you can find," he tells her. Despite his mental and physical problems, Fritz cannot forget his press clippings.

24 February: Fritz associates only with the better class of inmates.

23 March 1951: Fritz writes Lillian, "Please do me a favor. The *Baltimore Sun* is, or was, running a comic sheet like *Hop-a-long Cassidy* and [I] would like you to buy a few copies to keep in my archives. Just a bunch of the usual rot dished out for kids. However, I am interested as I am the VILLAIN, a sort of APE from Africa." So Fritz is now in the funny papers. In pain (imaginary or not), physically debilitated, not sure he will ever again experience freedom—Fritz cannot forget his scrapbook.

July: Martin Quigley Sr. responds to a poem Fritz sends him. Quigley likes the verse and says he will send it to *Sign,* a "lively" Catholic magazine that will pay a nominal fee. Fritz replies that he does not want the verse published. Quigley admonishes him regarding his bitterness: "It seems to me at this late time in your life it would be best for you to direct your thoughts to the time ahead, rather than agitating yourself with recollections of the dead past."

19 March 1952: The Department of Justice asks Fritz to register as an agent of a foreign principal, since he had "executed an assignment in the espionage service for the former German government." Fritz, still declaring his innocence, denies the allegation and refuses to sign.

April: However ill he is, Fritz persists with his legal battles. He sues the 20th Century–Fox Film Co., charging that the news about him and his alleged co-conspirators was responsible for the success of the motion picture *The House on 92nd Street,* in which he is the villain. The film had made $4 million, and it is this financial influence that is keeping him locked up. Fritz loses.

9 May: The psychiatrist who ten years ago said that Fritz "has about given up hope" would be surprised: Fritz continues to adjust to imprisonment and improve. He maintains his person and quarters in passable condition and obeys ward rules. He has a better attitude toward officers. Still believing that he was railroaded by "special interests," Fritz continues to write numerous letters. The defects of arteriosclerosis, hypertension, and a hernia remain. Fritz is seventy-five years old.

15 July: Occasionally Fritz "gets started" and regales personnel and inmates with his Boer War experiences and other tales of adventure.

7 August: For good behavior, two hundred forfeited good-time days are restored.

2 September: Following another request from a writer for his life story, Fritz becomes "exceeding vehement" and says, "He can find all he needs to know in the New York Library."

September (undated): Surprisingly, prison director Bennett sends a memo to Dr. Ivan Steele, warden of the prison: "I would certainly like to know more of the details of this man's life. If you can encourage him to write his exploits and adventures, I wish you would do so."

11 September: Dr. Steele replies, "I had a long talk with Duquesne yesterday and he is unwilling at this time to write about his exploits and adventures. From his attitude I doubt that we will ever be able to get him to do this as long as he is incarcerated."

27 April 1953: Two hundred more good-time days are restored.

24 November: Fritz's remaining two hundred forfeited days are restored.

It must have been a matter of frustration and great distress to Fritz to be aware during his years of imprisonment that his co-conspirators had been released years before. He was the only one to serve such a long term. It was perhaps the penalty he had to pay for being "one of the most dangerous criminals in the United States" and an "irreconcilable."

Evelyn Clayton Lewis—his paramour, as described by the government—was released in 1942. Six spies were paroled in 1943, seven in 1945, five in 1947, four in 1948, three in 1949, two in 1950, and one in 1951.[3]

Hermann Lang, one of the Big Three and the man who stole the Norden bombsight, was deported on 25 September 1950. While he was in prison his American citizenship was revoked. His lawyer, George Herz, who still believed in his innocence, said that Lang "was caught in a swindle he couldn't get out of." Herz told him he could fight the action. But Lang responded, "I loved this country and sincerely appreciated the opportunity it gave me. I thought I would get a fair trial. I don't want my American citizenship. Let them have it. I don't want it."[4] Like Fritz, Lang never wavered in protesting his innocence. It would have been news to Colonel Nikolaus Ritter.

And what of Ritter himself? Following the Tramp calamity, Ritter could not continue undercover work because of his notoriety. He was made a commander in a Luftwaffe Panzer division named for Hermann Göring, and he took part in the battle of Sicily. Near the end of the war he was a *Brigadeführer* with two flak regiments containing Panzer and Luftwaffe groups. They were surrounded and taken prisoner by American troops in the Harz mountains on 20 April 1945. Ritter worked as a translator for the U.S. Army until arrested by British troops and placed in a POW camp. He was released on 22 May 1947. Ritter resumed a business career in postwar Hamburg and died on 25 March 1974.

In January 1954, with only nine months left to serve in his sentence, audacious Fritz filed one last brief against "the United States of America, Francis Biddle, ex–Attorney General; J. Edgar Hoover, Director of the Federal Bureau of Investigation; a said small, FBI Special Agent" (Ray Newkirk, perhaps, who was tall and thin). In February 1942 Fritz had successfully sued the FBI for the return of $400 taken from him when arrested. (Ironically, it was money paid to him by Harry Sawyer/William Sebold.) It had worked before, so why not try again?

This time Fritz was asking for a judgment of $3,254,655 and punitive damages of $250,000. He claimed the loss of valuable properties and monies taken from him when arrested in 1941. The property included three bags of uncut diamonds worth $3 million, two albums of stamps worth $150,000, an original history of the Boer War valued at $10,000, maps of the Kruger gold location in South Africa worth $40,000, and various rings, watches, and cameras.

The appeal was dismissed.

What Fritz got was an extra thirty days because of his inability to pay the remaining $351.20 of his $2,000 fine, and he was released on 19 September 1954 instead of in August. This inability marked him as an indigent convict, and he was required to sign a pauper's oath. He also got $65 in cash, a check in the amount of $150 to be mailed later, and a handshake from the warden, Dr. Ivan W. Steele.

But the Black Panther of the Veld was free. Fritz was seventy-seven years old.

Last Adventure for the Black
Panther of the Veld

RITZ WAS FOND of saying, "There's nothing a sleepy man hates
so much as being shot at at 1:30 in the morning."[1]
He may have felt that way when he was released from prison
at exactly that time on Sunday, 19 September 1954. He was placed on
board the Frisco train at 3:05 A.M. and arrived in St. Louis at 8:10. His
final destination would be New York City. At 10:15 A.M. he boarded
Pennsylvania Railroad Pullman car number 25. His one-way fare was
$55.93, plus $18 for roomette number 13. It was his last free ride at government expense.[2] Twenty-five pounds of legal papers, clippings, and
personal correspondence would be shipped to him later via Railway
Express—collect.

Fritz arrived at New York's Pennsylvania Station the next day at 7:25
A.M. He was met by Lillian Linding and longtime attorney friend John
J. Coyle, who had taken care of his business affairs for many years.
Upon seeing him for the first time since he was imprisoned, Lillian's
reaction to herself was "What a sight!"[3]

It was not the same New York City, nor was it the same Fritz who
had arrived there fifty-two years earlier. He was an escaped convict
then. He was a paroled convict now. In 1902 he managed through self-
confidence and youthful swagger to cut a niche for himself in the city's

tough newspaper world and society's higher echelons. In 1954 it would be a struggle just to survive.

A stroke had caused partial paralysis, and the handsome features of Fritz Duquesne had become slack and distorted. The once precise and well-modulated British-accented voice was slurred, and he spoke barely above a whisper. He was ambulatory, walking with the aid of a cane, but occasionally he used a wheelchair. Despite all these infirmities, Fritz's hair remained wavy and jet black.

Prison authorities were concerned that Fritz had no assets and no potential resources, but they anticipated "the possibility of future income in the event writers who have desires to exploit his life are still interested." Dismissed as having no factual basis was the "persistent rumor among Afrikaanders that Duquesne retains knowledge of the whereabouts of a mysterious hoard of gold concealed by him during the Boer War."[4]

Coyle took Fritz to the YMCA and then registered him at the Nash Hotel at 120 West Forty-seventh Street. Fritz had an appointment with his parole officer on 21 September. He was not scheduled to be free from supervision until 3 July 1959. His probation officer, Evelyn Panella, had the Department of Welfare place him in the London Arms Nursing Home at 443 West Twenty-second Street on 1 November.[5]

Fritz found conditions at the home unendurable. He wanted to get out before he died there. He almost strangled from a throat hemorrhage and feared he might die before he could get out of the home. He planned to write his memoirs.[6]

Life in the nursing home became increasingly difficult. He was disappointed because Coyle had made no effort toward fulfilling his promise to move him to a boarding home. He did not understand why he had lost a $3-a-day welfare stipend. On 10 July 1955 Fritz wrote Lillian, "I'll go mad here. I sleep between rotting patients whose bowels are festering all the time. The stench is awful. I eat it, I breathe it, and smell it continuously. To go out to the Berkshires with you would be lovely. An hour or two spent with you would aid me greatly. I want to see you and talk to you. I have not held you to my heart yet."[7]

Fritz was not willing to waste his last years. The two redeeming features possessed by this not particularly desirable character were hope and an iron will. He still maintained his innocence and continued to seek out lawyers who would handle his case. He was never successful.

Fritz was encouraged when he received a letter from movie director Marshall Neilan, who apparently expressed a renewed interest in making a movie based on Fritz's life. Fritz remembered that Martin Quigley had introduced them in the 1930s, and Neilan had wanted to make the movie then.[8] (Neilan had gained fame during the silent movie era as an actor and director, particularly of Mary Pickford's *Rebecca of Sunnybrook Farm* and *Daddy Long Legs*. He directed his last movie, *Sing It, Professor,* in 1937, by which time he had frittered away his talent. He too may have been chasing a dream, just like Fritz.)

Gambling on not being caught breaking his parole, Fritz went downtown to meet with Quigley in his office on 13 July, expecting also to see Neilan. He had not asked permission of his parole officer, Evelyn Panella. He was terribly disappointed: Neilan had not arrived from Hollywood. Quigley treated Fritz royally and said, "You are an iron man." He called Panella and praised Fritz extravagantly. "I never heard a man get so much praise," Fritz later wrote Lillian. Quigley turned Fritz down for a job, but the two had lunch.

It had been a trying day for Fritz, one filled with disappointments and aggravated by temperatures of 85 degrees and humidity of 50 percent. He wrote Lillian:[9]

I am so tired I can hardly write. My legs are paining with fatigue. When I came out of Quigley's office and started home I was in a hell of a mess. It was a terrible ride and walk I took. It was a great struggle. The trip nearly broke me down but I fought it out. I started home to this place and on account of there being two Dyre Avenues, one going to Brooklyn and the other to [the] Bronx, I had to get on the wrong one. I had the damnedest ride of my life. I did a terrible lot of walking about N.Y.C. It was eleven o'clock before I got back. I rode New York to Brooklyn and then to White Plains and back to this place. I'm too tired to go on, forgive me. I proved that I am not decrepit. I cannot go on, dear love. I am lying abed. I cannot be proven to be an invalid. I broke the spell. And I felt a brief hour of freedom. But I won out my dearest dear. The Duquesne blood is still holding up. I didn't limp very much. You'd never notice it.

Fritz finally got his wish and on 12 October was moved to another place, the Pelham Manor Nursing Home at 1011 Pelham Parkway North in the Bronx. But he was no happier and wrote Lillian, "It is a stink pot and is more insufferable than ever. I cannot stand it much longer."[10] He still hoped to move to a private apartment.

Around this time Bim Pond, son of Major Pond, the impresario who had arranged Fritz's African lectures and his Liberty Bond–selling appearances, renewed the friendship with Fritz begun when Bim was a teenager. He wanted to write Fritz's biography and had a publisher interested. He had once discussed collaborating on such a book with Stuart Cloete, the best-selling South African novelist. But Cloete finally said no. Pond believed he did not want to share any "cash return" or credit.[11]

Fritz was welcomed back to the Adventurers Club through the efforts of Pond. Some of the members were unforgiving and called him a traitor. Others recognized Fritz as one of the last of the old adventurers, a disappearing breed—and certainly one of the few charter members still alive. Pond arranged a program at the club that would feature Fritz, Stuart Cloete, modern adventurer Harold Manser, and private detective Raymond Schindler. Fritz would deliver a talk on "My Life—In and Out of Prison."[12]

The expectation of being the focus of attention again and reliving past glories made life at the home almost bearable for Fritz. He was fearful that he might miss the event when he suffered a slight stroke and was injured in a fall, striking a bedpost. Pond might have to give his speech for him. But the adventurer rallied. It would be his farewell address.

On the evening of 21 December 1955, Fritz's birthday, the adventurers gathered for cocktails at six and dinner at seven in the Patio of the Hotel Delmonico at Park Avenue and Fifty-ninth Street. Cloete spoke on "African Transition," followed by Pond who introduced Fritz. Pond took them back to the days of World War I when a "most beautifully and immaculately attired individual" entered the office of the Pond Lecture Bureau. Audiences were as impressed as we were, recalled Pond, and Captain Claude Stoughton was an immediate success. He sold thousands of dollars worth of Liberty Bonds.[13] Pond continued with a brief history of Fritz's adventures and imprisonment.

Fritz apologized for not being able to talk as he would have liked, but age and the ordeal of many years in prison—five of them in solitary confinement—left him unable to speak above a hoarse and halting whisper or to stand for any length of time. The voice that for so many years had been a spellbinder was gone. But the stories were still there. And the adventurers listened in rapt attention as Fritz rolled the years back to the turn of the century. He was adventuring again. He told them about the Boer War, Bermuda, his escapes, his activities in Panama during the building of the canal, more details of his role as Stoughton, and his long stay in federal prisons.

Cloete was impressed enough to call Fritz "a great talker." The evening provided Fritz with the opportunity to ask Cloete's help in obtaining some medals due him from South Africa. But he never followed up with particulars.[14]

It was a last hurrah for Fritz. No longer able to stand the indignities of the nursing home, Fritz felt strong enough to take an apartment of his own, an old-fashioned walk-up at 526 East Eighty-third Street. He was on relief.

But Fritz was not as strong as he believed. He had a bad fall in the apartment, fractured a hip, and was taken to City Hospital on Welfare Island. Pale and drawn, he weighed only 140 pounds. He recovered nicely and had been assigned to the hospital's rehabilitation service when a stroke proved fatal at 3:50 P.M. on 24 May 1956. Fritz was seventy-eight years old.

Dr. Herman E. Bauer, medical superintendent of the hospital, announced, "He was doing pretty well. But a stroke—he had suffered a previous one some years ago—was fatal."[15]

Lillian Linding identified the body when it was brought to the morgue at Bellevue Hospital, the scene of his triumphal escape exactly thirty-seven years earlier. But Frederick L'Huguenot Joubert Duquesne would no longer hear the drums. The Black Panther of the Veld, as the Adventurers Club would have said, had embarked on his last great adventure.

The body lay in state at the Andrett Funeral Home on Second Avenue, where a few friends said their last goodbyes. Fritz was then cremated at the United States Crematory in Niaspetto on Long Island. Lillian asked a friend, U.S. Air Force Colonel Mitchell J. Mulholland, to retain the ashes for her.[16] The plan was to return them one day to South Africa, where she and Fritz had once hoped to spend their last days together.[17] Mulholland, who never knew Fritz, held on to the ashes until 1984 when, on a ferryboat ride between Portland (Maine) and Yarmouth (Nova Scotia), he scattered them to the wind in the Bay of Fundy.[18] The disposition was appropriate. Never settled in life, the wanderer would continue to do so.

At the time of her own death, on 7 May 1974 at the age of eighty-six, Lillian was a well-known portrait painter and designer of wallpaper.[19] Fritz's medals passed to Mulholland, who still possesses them.

On 21 October 1956 Lillian had written the Marquis François de Rancogne to inform him of the death of Fritz, his cousin. "Fritz's life was too sad to even think about," she said. "With his mind and personality he could have been a great leader."[20]

Fritz Duquesne's one-man crusade to destroy the British Empire was an eminent failure. So what did it all mean, his lifetime of hate and deception? Not much. As the FBI observed, he "never pursued a legitimate business for any length of time." But to put it another way, Fritz was able to beat the system for more than fifty years. Playing by his rules, he had a lot of fun doing it and probably had few regrets. Perhaps his only legacy was that he was a colorful if somewhat unsavory but not entirely disagreeable character. He was a footnote to the history he wanted to influence. But he neither created nor changed history. He was only there to boost it along.

His was a fascinating story.

Fritz should have told it.

But no one would have believed a word of it.

"The Ballad of Fritz Duquesne"

Clement Wood, author of the Duquesne biography *The Man Who Killed Kitchener* (1932), wrote the following paean of praise to Fritz in 1946. Prison officials would not allow Fritz to see it until 1950. Perhaps it was considered inflammatory. Fritz said it showed "his prowess in battle." Never published, the poem resides in the FBI's Notorious Offenders File.

"Where are you riding, Fritz Duquesne?"

"Over the charred South African plain;
over a land that once was green,
now ashen, dead, defiled, obscene;
seeking the home where a Boer boy grew,
that nestled all that his young heart knew,—
a sister's love, and a mother's love,
green veld, and the high white sun above."

"Why do you seek them, Fritz Duquesne?"

"The English have ferried the bitter main,
and they swarm like locusts over the land;
till veld and kopje and burnished rand
are eaten bare by their fouling greed,
and the green heaven is a hell indeed.

We woke, we fought them; they staggered. But still
unending hordes swarmed out to kill.
I was shot. I was plucked by a bayonet.
But I am free, and riding yet

for a sister's arms and a mother's arms,
man's shield from red harms."

"And did you find them, Fritz Duquesne?"

"I found death on the seared plain,—
a sister speared by English lust,
flyblown, rotting into the dust;
a mother fouled and gross with child,
where red rapine had defiled
her body with red rotting ill. . . .
But I am free, and riding still—
for a sister slain, and a mother's stain. . . .

"Empire greed and tradesman wit
stole my veld, the all of it;
fouled the nest where I learned to fly. . . .
In every land and sea and sky
I will pay the bitter score,
till the name of England breathes no more.
I have been shot—lashed—jailed.
I am homeless, hunted, harried, trailed. . . .
But for every drop of her poisoned blood
I shall deal death like a spring flood.
Men will go screaming to their death,
and women shriek with their ravaged breath;
towns shall burst into towers of fire,
and tall ships crumble, to pay this score;
and her tallest captains shall gasp and die,
as Fritz Duquesne goes riding by."

"Ride on forever, Fritz Duquesne,
for a sister slain, and a mother's stain.
For the slayer dies, and the spoiler dies,
though hate is a sickness, and love is wise.
Evils are mortal, Fritz Duquesne.
Your name is a star; and England's, a stain.

"Death gives no life to the ravished dead;
but for this your soul has been appointed,
and, till honor rots and right is vain,
they will net not you, Fritz Duquesne.
No jail can hold you. No bars can bind.
You will travel the lands like a searing wind,
cleansing the shambles their sin has made,
Death's blade of vengeance for the dead.

"Ride on to glory that can not die,
till the velds are free, and their men stand high,—
and into the eternal heavenly plain.
And our hearts ride with you, Fritz Duquesne."

Aliases of Fritz Duquesne

Following is a list of the many aliases used by Fritz Duquesne during his four decades of spying, fraudulent activities, lunacy, and masquerading. Not all of the names appear in this biography. The list was compiled by the FBI and is available in the Notorious Offenders File. FBI parole report, file no. 66-1819, 5 Jan. 1942, 1.

Arnstein
D. F. Barron
Frederick Barron
Col. Bezin
Fred Duquesne
F. Crabbe
Frank Crabbe
F. Craven
Major Frederick Craven
Frederick De T. Craven
F. Detrafford Craven
John DuCain
Dunn
Fritz Duquesne
Captain Fritz Duquesne
Colonel F. J. Duquesne
Fritz J. Duquesne
Fritz Joubert Duquesne
Colonel Marquis Duquesne
Paul Duquesne

J. Q. Farn
Fordham
George Fordham
Frederick Fredericks
Fritters
J. Hernandez
Fred Howe
"Jim"
Nio Panaar
William Smith
Captain Claude Staughton
Fred Stoughton
Berthold Szabo
Vam Dam
Von Goutard
Worthy
Julian Zeller
Jimmy
Piet Niacoud

Fritz's Medals

Were Fritz Duquesne's medals as counterfeit as many of his claimed heroics?

Fritz was proud of the medals he wore and boasted that they had been won in battle, awarded by the countries he fought for. Even at the age of twenty he displayed a chestful of shiny decorations bright as sunbursts. In middle age the ribbons, sashes, and stars of courage covered a proud chest and dangled from a neck unbowed by the weight. What feats of bravery and derring-do did they represent? What wars had Fritz fought in to deserve these battle baubles?

Not many, according to Dr. Harold A. Lubick of Burbank, California, a member of the Orders and Medals Society of America and an expert in the field. The photos in chapters 1 and 15, showing Fritz with his medals, reveal a common thread, says Dr. Lubick. Several could not be identified and could have even been forged. Colonel Mitchell Mulholland, present owner of the medals, believes they may have been purchased at a beaux-arts ball (Mulholland phone interview, 11 Nov. 1972). Most were obscure decorations from duchies and principalities with Graustarkian and Zendian names, deliberately picked, perhaps, to fool admirers. More familiar decorations would have been recognized, revealing Fritz as a possible fraud. Most appeared to be house orders awarded not for bravado but for civil service and private services rendered by low-level bureaucrats. Even the Austrian uniform, designed for either a soldier or a diplomat, was adorned with apparently inconsistent orders.

These are the medals worn by Fritz (because of a lack of clarity in the photos, Dr. Lubick cannot guarantee the identification of decorations twelve through seventeen):

1. *Order of Osmania:* Second highest order of the Turkish Empire. Created to award outstanding Turkish civil servants. Awarded to foreigners for rendering valuable service to the sultan.

2. *Star of the Order of Osmania*

3. *Order of Franz Joseph:* Honoring special civil or military merit, particularly in the field of diplomacy. Almost all imperial Austrian ambassadors were recipients.

4. *Order of National Merit Military of Bulgaria:* For outstanding service to the throne.

5. *War Merit Cross:* For special merit in war (Sachsen-Meiningen, Germany).

6. *Star of the Order of Saint Alexander of Bulgaria:* For outstanding courage and services to the throne.

7. *Sash to Order of Saint Alexander of Bulgaria*

8. *Order of the Iron Cross (First Class):* For significant military merit (Germany).

9. *Order of Berthold:* A higher degree to the *Order of the Zahringen Lion* for civil or military merit (Baden, Germany).

10. *Order of the Crown of Württemberg:* Cross of the Honored Knight with Swords or Knight First Class. Originally a hunting order, but changed to recognize especially meritorious service in peace and war (Germany).

11. *Order of the Griffin:* An order of civil or military merit (Mecklenburg-Schwerin, Germany).

12. *Knight's Cross of the Crown of Württemberg*

13. *Star of the Order of Scanderberg of Albania:* For civil merit.

14. *Royal Military Order of Bulgaria:* For outstanding courage in war.

15. *Order of Henry the Lion of Brunswick* (Germany)

16. *Order of St. John of Jerusalem*

17. *Class of the Order of the White Falcon*

"The House on 92nd Street"

Thomas and Solomon, in *Films of 20th Century–Fox,* 161–62, give this account of the film *The House on 92nd Street:*

Louis de Rochemont, the skilled documentarist who had excelled with his *March of Time* series, brought the documentary style to Hollywood with *The House on 92nd Street,* an espionage story based on fact and filmed with the cooperation of the FBI. It dealt with the pursuit and capture of a German spy ring in Washington [actually, New York], a ring attempting to gain U.S. atomic program secrets. William Eythe plays a federal undercover man posing as a member of the ring led by Signe Hasso, and Lloyd Nolan is the chief of the FBI unit involved. Director Hathaway skillfully matches his live action with actual footage and gives an exciting account of this particular operation. The film proved to be a pioneer in bringing documentary techniques to films dealing with crime and espionage.

20th Century–Fox production head Darryl F. Zanuck feared that the picture was "singularly lacking in personal drama" and that it would "fall into the category of documentary features," for which there was no market. But by "blending at least partially true case histories, on-location filming, and a mixture of professional actors and 'real people,'" the picture "became the initial 'semidocumentary' feature film" (Behlmer, *Memo from Darryl F. Zanuck,* 87–88).

Signe Hasso plays a dual role, partially based on Lilly Stein's New York lifestyle. As Elsa Gebhardt she is the proprietress of a successful dress shop. As Mr. Christopher, and disguised as a man, she is the head of the spy ring. In dramatic *March of Time* tones, narrator Reed Hadley describes her dress shop: "Just off Madison Avenue in uptown New York, there was a five-story dwelling. This was soon to become known among all FBI men as the house on 92nd Street."

The final script for the picture differed considerably from the original screen treatment by Charles Booth, which dealt more specifically with the real characters. Ritter, the Abwehr officer who hired Duquesne in 1937, is mentioned briefly by FBI inspector Briggs (Lloyd Nolan) in one scene: "Major Nickolaus [sic] Adolph Fritz Ritter, smart boy of the German Secret Service. I knew him when he was over here—posing as a textile engineer—he had an office on Fifth Avenue."

The narrator describes Colonel Hammersohn (the Fritz Duquesne character): "At a Lexington Avenue intersection, a tall, wiry, intense elderly man, who probably takes himself with great seriousness, is waiting impatiently. None of the contacts that Bill [Dietrich] had already begun to establish was cagier than the veteran spy, Colonel Martin Luther Hammersohn, who regarded himself as the king-pin of German espionage in the United States, although his importance was somewhat less than his own estimate of it." The script describes him as being in his late fifties and says that he "has considerable presence and an excellent opinion of his own intelligence." It is also pointed out that he carries a gold-headed cane. Carrying a cane, not necessarily gold-headed, was often an affectation with Fritz.

Fritz's antipathy toward the British is expressed by Hammersohn's character when he meets Bill Dietrich, the William Sebold/Harry Sawyer character. Hammersohn says, "I'm an old hand at this business. I fought the English in the Boer War—I cannot begin to express my contempt for them. I was very active in the last war. I had the sinking of seventy cargo ships to my credit. Captain Boy-Ed and Franz von Papen were my friends. I knew Count von Bernstorff very well indeed."

The goal of the spy ring is to obtain the formula for Process 97, the "secret ingredient of the atomic bomb." Gene Lockhart portrays Charles Ogden Roper, a government laboratory worker sympathetic to the German cause. He has access to the formula, and his photographic memory allows him to exit the facility undetected with the figures of the formula.

The Roper character is obviously patterned after Hermann Lang, the man who stole the Norden bombsight. But by 1945 the bombsight was no longer news. The atomic bomb, however, was—which perhaps explained the script change.

Intriguingly, the tag line in the original script dated 16 April 1945, four months before atomic bombs were dropped on Hiroshima and Nagasaki, reads, "From the body of the espionage agent Elsa Gebhardt—alias Mr. Christopher, the FBI recovered the final data of Process 97, a secret—the ———— (name withheld until release from proper authority can be obtained)."

When Mr. Christopher is killed in the film's finale and the spies are rounded up, the narrator intones, "Process 97, the atomic bomb. America's top secret, remains a secret."

Hollywood legend says that script pages mentioning the atomic bomb were withheld from cast and crew and not filmed until after the bombs were dropped in August 1945. If this is so, 20th Century–Fox must have moved rapidly with last-minute filming and editing to release the picture only one month after the bombs destroyed the Japanese cities.

The written introduction to the film that appears on the screen states, "This story is adapted from cases in the espionage files of the Federal Bureau of Investigation. Produced with the FBI's complete cooperation, it could not be made public until the first atomic bomb was dropped on Japan."

Reed Hadley then picks up the narration in his well-measured tones to the stirring music of composer David Buttolph. It is a paean of praise to the FBI, but it succinctly implies, without providing the details, the story of the Ritter Ring and the new frontiers of investigation forged by the FBI:

Vigilant, tireless, implacable, the most silent service of the United States in peace or war is the Federal Bureau of Investigation. The Bureau went to war with Germany long before hostilities began. No word or picture could then make public the crucial war service of the FBI. But now, it can be told. [*Now It Can Be Told* was the working title of the picture.] In 1939, with thousands of known and suspected enemy agents invading the Americas, the FBI started building up its force of Special Agents and employees from 2,000 to a war peak of 15,000. Before being sent into the field, each new agent had to learn all the modern techniques of crime detection.

The popular film was broadcast several times on radio. The first broadcast was on the official FBI program *This Is Your FBI*, which "dramatized cases taken from the files of the Federal Bureau of Investigation." The original film cast was heard in the program, which aired on 12 October 1945 on the ABC network. *Screen Guild Theatre* broadcast the drama over CBS on 10 June 1946 with Lloyd Nolan as Briggs and William Lundigan as Dietrich. Using the same SGT script, Humphrey Bogart portrayed Briggs in the *Stars in the Air* version, which aired on 4 May 1952 on CBS. Keefe Braselle was Dietrich.

All three programs were half-hour shows, which did not allow time for all the characters introduced in the movie. If Fritz heard any of the shows from his prison cell, his ego may have been bruised when the character of Hammersohn was deleted.

Notes

Chapter 1: Huguenots and Boers

1. Unless otherwise noted, all details of Fritz's early life as described in this chapter are from Clement Wood's 1932 biography, *The Man Who Killed Kitchener* (hereafter *TMWKK*).

2. Duquesne, "Autobiographical Letter"; naturalization petition no. 21934, certificate no. 400139, 18 July 1912.

3. Papen, *Memoirs*, 49.

4. Duquesne, "Sekokoeni's Raid," 289–92.

5. Burnham, *Taking Chances*, 17.

6. FBI photo, *Justitia*, Jan. 1963, 111; Tully, *FBI's Most Famous Cases*, 149.

7. Sampson, *Capture of De Wet*, 273.

8. Kruger, *Good-bye Dolly Gray*, 20–21.

9. Arthur Pound, a friend, biographer, and former managing editor of the *Akron Beacon Journal*, wrote years later about Fritz's speech: "He speaks beautiful English, the English of the universities and authentic society. He can talk in as many minutes the lingoes of Glasgow, Aberdeen, Yorkshire, Wiltshire and Cockney London with enough fluency to deceive natives of those parts." Pound, "Is Fritz Duquesne Alive?" 5. Mildred Wortley, sister-in-law of Alice, Fritz's wife, said, "He spoke the most beautiful English you ever heard." Wortley interview, 1 Sept. 1973.

10. Benbow, *Boer Prisoners of War in Bermuda*, 85; Dath, letter to author, 2 June 1972.

11. Duquesne, "Autobiographical Letter," 2.

12. Duquesne, 1913 letter to Stephen Allen Reynolds of the *New York Morning Telegram*.

13. Duquesne, manuscript pages (Col. Mitchell Mulholland collection).

14. *TMWKK*, 84.

15. Ibid., 14.

Chapter 2: The Black Panther of the Veld

1. Doyle, *Great Boer War, 2.*
2. Facts and figures for the Boer battles are drawn from Farwell, *Great Anglo-Boer War;* Griffith, *Thank God We Kept the Flag Flying;* Holmes, *Little Field-Marshal;* Kruger, *Good-bye Dolly Gray;* and Pakenham, *Boer War.*
3. *TMWKK,* 96.
4. Ibid., 99.
5. Farwell, *Great Anglo-Boer War,* 324–25; Pakenham, *Boer War,* 260; Amery, *Times History,* 1:74.
6. Burnham, *Taking Chances,* 19–21; *Spotlight,* 27 May 1955, 10–11.
7. *TMWKK,* 99.
8. Duquesne, "Autobiographical Letter."
9. Ibid.
10. *TMWKK,* 99; Holmes, *Little Field-Marshal,* 109–10.
11. *TMWKK,* 103–6; Wood, "True Story of Duquesne," 10–11.
12. *TMWKK,* 108–9.
13. Farwell, *Great Anglo-Boer War,* 324–25; Pakenham, *Boer War,* 267.
14. *TMWKK,* 119–20; "Writers and Their Work," 285.
15. Tunney, *Throttled,* 221, 223.
16. *TMWKK,* 120.
17. Cloete, *Rags of Glory,* 457.
18. Ralph, *Towards Pretoria,* 55, 56.
19. *TMWKK,* 126.
20. *New York Sun,* 19 June 1919, 7; *New York Times,* 27 Apr. 1916, 5; *Boston Sunday Herald,* 31 Aug. 1931, 5.
21. Duquesne, letter to Linding, 9 May 1951 (author's collection).
22. Ibid., 18 Sept. 1953 (author's collection).
23. Burnham, *Taking Chances,* 15.
24. *TMWKK,* 128.
25. Ibid., 136.
26. Ibid., 142.
27. Ibid., 144.

Chapter 3: The Cape Town Plot and Capture

1. Fisher, *Afrikaners,* 172.
2. Ibid., 174.
3. Magnus, *Kitchener,* 185.
4. Ibid.; Farwell, *Great Anglo-Boer War,* 400.
5. Fisher, *Afrikaners,* 174.
6. Magnus, *Kitchener,* 186.
7. Cloete, *Rags of Glory,* 569.
8. Ralph, *Towards Pretoria,* 68–69.
9. Ibid., 69.

10. Ibid., 58.

11. Holt, *Boer War,* 104.

12. Ralph, *Towards Pretoria,* 71.

13. Cloete, *Rags of Glory,* 405.

14. *TMWKK,* 145; West and Lamb, *He Who Sees-in-the-Dark,* 32, Pound, "Is Fritz Duquesne Alive?" 5–6; Rosenthal, *Southern African Dictionary of National Biography,* 107.

15. *TMWKK,* 146.

16. Ibid., 150.

17. Transvaal Archives Depot, ref. no. T16/4/3.

18. *TMWKK,* 171.

Chapter 4: POW in the Enchanted Isles

1. Unless otherwise indicated, material regarding the Boer POWs aboard the *Harlech Castle* and on Bermuda is from Benbow, *Boer Prisoners of War in Bermuda.*

2. Krynauw, *Private Diary;* Blerk, *Op De Bermudas Beland,* 55.

3. Du Quenne letter, Transvaal Archives Depot. Note that he signed the letter du Quenne, rather than Duquenne as in his letter to the prisoners-of-war staff officer in Cape Town. Apparently the man who always reinvented himself could never be quite sure who he was.

4. *TMWKK,* 179–82.

5. *Hampton's Magazine,* Feb. 1909, 285 (citing *Le Petit Bleu* as the Boer organ).

6. *Le Petit Bleu du Matin,* 26 June 1902, 1.

7. *Fortnightly Review,* June 1902, 989.

8. Ibid.

Chapter 5: Peace in South Africa, but No Peace for Fritz

1. Benbow, *Boer Prisoners of War in Bermuda,* 39.

2. Letter to Dorothy S. Meyers from Prof. F. J. du Toit, Dept. of History, University of Pretoria, 25 Apr. 1965 (author's collection). Facts from Louis Botha thesis by Prof. Johan Barnard, Dept. of History, University of South Africa.

3. Blerk, *Op De Bermudas Beland,* 5.

4. Benbow, *Boer Prisoners of War in Bermuda,* 81; Blerk, *Op De Bermudas Beland,* 55.

5. Arthur Pound, author and former *Akron Beacon Journal* managing editor, also noted Fritz's ability to recite: "The classics of English literature are at the tip of his tongue. I have heard him quote cantos of Sir Walter Scott and pages from Shelley without a skip, and with blazing dramatic power." Pound, "Is Fritz Duquesne Alive?" 5.

6. *Le Petit Bleu du Matin,* 26 June 1902, 1; Pound, "Is Fritz Duquesne Alive?" 14; *New York Sun,* 8 June 1919, 7.

7. *TMWKK*, 184, reports that Fritz was imprisoned on Boaz Island. It was one of the many factual errors regarding his life that got compounded over the years.

8. *Fortnightly Review,* June 1902, 994.

9. *TMWKK*, 189; Wortley interview, 1 Sept. 1973; Pound, "Is Fritz Duquesne Alive?" 14.

10. Either genuinely or to suit his own purposes at the time, Fritz never could keep straight either the name of his future father-in-law or his profession. It was either Edward Wortley, Edward J. Wortley, Stuart J. Wortley, or S. S. Wortley. S. S. Wortley was the closest Fritz ever came to being correct. Oddly, Bermuda government records occasionally record him as E. J. Wortley. To his family he was affectionately known as Uncle Sam.

11. *TMWKK*, 187; Tunney, *Throttled,* 220.

12. Wortley birth certificate, General Register Office, Spanish Town, Jamaica, no. AA766.

13. *New York Mirror,* 26 July 1932, 11; Pound, "Is Fritz Duquesne Alive?" 14; quotation from *TMWKK*, 442. Lady Mary Wortley Montagu (no *e,* 1689–1762), an English poet and noted letter writer, was the daughter of Evelyn Pierrepont, marquis of Dorchester and first duke of Kingston. She married Edward Wortley Montagu. Fritz no doubt noticed the coincidence of Kingston (the Jamaican town of Alice's birth), and the name of Lady Mary's husband may explain why Fritz called Alice's father Edward rather than Samuel.

14. Wortley interview, 1 Sept. 1973.

15. *TMWKK*, 191–94; *New York Times,* 27 Apr. 1916, 5.

16. *London Times,* 10 Mar. 1902, 6b.

17. Benbow, *Boer Prisoners of War in Bermuda,* 40.

18. Ibid., 41.

Chapter 6: Escape to *Who's Who*

1. *TMWKK*, 194–204; *New York Times,* 27 Apr. 1916, 5, 2; Benbow, *Boer Prisoners of War in Bermuda,* 37.

2. *New York World,* 18 July 1920, 8.

3. *TMWKK*, 84; *New York Times,* 27 Apr. 1916, 5.

4. *New York Sun,* 8 June 1919, 7.

5. *Bermuda Royal Gazette,* 5 July 1902. Witer is incorrectly called Captain Horton in *TMWKK*, 215.

6. Fritz liked to relate several versions of his escape from Bermuda. Here is a summary of the various facets of his escape tale as they appeared in *TMWKK*, 194–208; Benbow, *Boer Prisoners of War in Bermuda,* 36–39; Pound, "Is Fritz Duquesne Alive?" 14; Wood, "True Story of Duquesne," 10, 11; and *Boston Sunday Herald,* 31 Aug. 1919, 5.

Fritz planned his escape from Tucker's Island with Jan Bopp and Piet Oosterhuysen (or Nicholas du Toit). They were sighted by soldiers just before slipping into a mangrove swamp, and Jan was shot and sank below the water. Piet was shot in the foot. Nevertheless, Fritz and Piet swam for the main island, managing to avoid marauding sharks and patrol boats.

For the next two weeks they lived in the wilderness and swamps on grass, wild onions, and bananas. Dirty, ragged, and their strength nearly gone, they debated returning to the prison camp. A decision was made for them when Piet's foot became gangrenous. One version has it that, by mutual agreement, Fritz dug a grave for Piet, filled it with what provisions they had, and covered him with leaves, leaving him to die. Fritz never saw him again. Another version is that Fritz carried Piet to one of the refuges marked on his map, the winter home of an American maiden of independent means and independent views—obviously a blend of Alice Wortley and Miss Outerbridge. The maiden then took Piet to a hospital. Still another version has Piet swimming back to Tucker's.

In any case, after either "burying" Piet or turning him over to the "American maiden," Fritz lost himself in the city life of Hamilton, waiting for the ship that would take him to America. For the next few weeks he guided American tourists about the island and could often be seen at the bars of the Princess or the New Windsor Hotel. Then he met Vera and finally stowed away aboard the *Margaret*.

7. Sailors who manned the boats knew better and called it the Suicide Fleet. Their job was to hunt down German U-boats in the Atlantic Ocean. *Maggie*'s two masts were cut down flush to the deck; she was painted battleship gray and was run on steam only. The biggest worry of the crew was that they might discover a U-boat and have to drop depth charges. Knowing how slow *Maggie* was in the water, they feared she would never outrun the explosions. They needn't have feared. *Maggie* never fired a shot in anger except near the end of the war, when she became a venereal station for the fleet in the Azores and took care of sailors who were not as careful as they should have been on shore leave. The end came for *Maggie* in 1920, when the navy sold her to an Italian firm that converted old ships into scrap, and she was towed to Genoa and the junk pile. Buranelli, *Maggie of the Suicide Fleet*, 7, 8, 274, 277.

8. *New York Times*, 24 Jan. 1931, 17.

9. *TMWKK*, 21.

10. Benbow, *Boer Prisoners of War in Bermuda*, 82; Houman, letter to Outerbridge, 13 Aug. 1903, Bermuda Archives; biography from James G. Ward, Passaic County Historical Society.

11. *TMWKK*, 219–20.

12. Shriner, *Paterson, New Jersey; Paterson Morning Call*, 6 Oct. 1915, 5; *Paterson Evening News*, 6 Oct. 1915.

13. Houman, letter to Outerbridge, 13 Aug. 1903.

14. Koss, *Pro-Boers*, 67–68, 73.

15. Weightman's editorials were noted for being "luminous and breezy." The fifty-eight-year-old newspaperman was a veteran of the Confederate Army

and had been appointed by President William McKinley to serve as secretary on the Spanish American War Investigation Committee, a post chosen for him, no doubt, in view of his work for the paper as its first foreign correspondent. Weightman had gone to Cuba in 1897 during the prewar print battles between Hearst's New York *Journal,* which advocated war, and the *Post,* which urged moderation. His job had been to determine what was really going on in the island country. But it seems he was flimflammed by the Spanish authorities for two weeks and was incapable of digging out the truth. His conclusion was that the "insurrection [was] a miserable farce." *New York Times,* 19 Feb. 1914, 9.

16. C.O. 37/237 Despatches 1902, August Section, 26 June 1902, Bermuda Archives. Clement Wood gives 2142 as Fritz's prison number; *TMWKK,* 203.

Chapter 7: Colonel Teddy Roosevelt Meets Captain Fritz Duquesne

1. *New York Times,* 5 Oct. 1902, 6.
2. Royle, *Kitchener Enigma,* 195.
3. Leonard, *Who's Who in New York City and State,* 442–43; *TMWKK,* 274.
4. Leonard, *Who's Who in New York City and State,* 442–43.
5. Ibid.
6. Roosevelt, *African Game Trails,* 12.
7. Morison, *Letters of Roosevelt,* no. 4645, 6:978.
8. Hart and Ferleger, *Roosevelt Cyclopedia,* 48.
9. Morison, *Letters of Roosevelt,* 8:956.
10. Bishop, *Roosevelt and His Time,* 122.
11. Morison, *Letters of Roosevelt,* 7:174.
12. *Hampton's Magazine,* Feb. 1909.
13. Morison, *Letters of Roosevelt,* no. 4645, 7:978.
14. Hahn, "My Dear Selous," 93.
15. *TMWKK,* 248. Wood says Fritz was summoned to Roosevelt's home in Oyster Bay for the meeting.
16. *New York Sun,* 24 Oct. 1941.
17. Morison, *Letters of Roosevelt,* 6:1624.
18. *Washington Post,* 26 Jan. 1909; Duquesne, "Hunting African Big Game."
19. *Washington Star,* 26 Jan. 1909. Berryman, of Teddy Bear fame, would win a Pulitzer Prize in 1944 for a cartoon of Teddy's cousin, Franklin D. Roosevelt. Upon Berryman's death in 1949, President Harry Truman described him as a "Washington institution comparable to the Monument." *New York Times,* 12 Dec. 1949, 33.
20. *New York Sun,* 24 Oct. 1941.
21. Roosevelt, *African Game Trails,* editor's note.
22. Edmund Morris (author of *The Rise of Theodore Roosevelt* [1980]), letter to author, 14 Aug. 1991.
23. Duquesne, "Will Roosevelt Return Alive?" 271–72, 274.

24. *New York Times,* 8 Mar. 1909, 1; Pringle, *Roosevelt,* 358.

25. Duquesne, *East Africa, the Wonderland of Roosevelt's Hunt.*

Chapter 8: Hippos to Louisiana and Hippo du Jour

1. *Washington Post,* 2 Mar. 1910, 3.

2. Ibid., 1.

3. Ibid.

4. Roosevelt, *African Game Trails,* editor's note.

5. *Washington Post,* 3 Mar. 1910, 4.

6. Ibid.

7. *Washington Star,* 9 Feb. 1929.

8. *New York Times,* 27 Sept. 1962, 37.

9. Dawson, *Opportunity,* 57; Dawson, "Hunting with Roosevelt," 122.

10. Millais, *Life of Frederick Courtenay Selous,* 268.

11. Roosevelt, *African Game Trails,* 532.

12. Dawson may have forgotten his own mention of Duquesne in an article written for the November 1909 *Hampton's,* "Hunting with Roosevelt in East Africa." In that article (598) he mentioned that it was Duquesne's "Hunting ahead of Roosevelt in East Africa" (which had appeared in the February 1909 *Hampton's,* 144) that first introduced Roosevelt's safari leader, R. J. Cuninghame, to the American public.

13. *Washington Post,* 3 Mar. 1910, 4.

14. Ibid.

15. Ibid.

16. Ibid., 7 Mar. 1910, 4.

17. Ibid., 11 Mar. 1910, 11; 10 Mar. 1910, 9; 7 Mar. 1910, 7.

18. Ibid., 12 Mar. 1910, 7.

19. Dawson's translation for *Bwana Tumbo* was "Mr. Portly Man." Dawson, "Hunting with Roosevelt in East Africa," 595.

20. "A great actor he might perhaps have been if his lot had been cast with the theatre early in life, but instead he has done his acting on a wilder, broader stage, where death is the penalty of a false step or slurred accent. Pound, "Is Fritz Duquesne Alive?" 5.

21. *Washington Star,* 12 Mar. 1910; *Washington Post,* 13 Mar. 1910, 7; *Washington Herald,* 20 Mar. 1910, 7.

22. *Washington Herald,* 21 Mar. 1910, 20.

23. *Washington Post,* 19 Mar. 1910, 2.

24. Ibid., 18 Mar. 1910, 8.

25. *Washington Herald,* 7 Mar. 1910, 18.

26. *Washington Post,* 15 Mar. 1910, 3.

27. *TMWKK,* 361–62.

28. U.S. Congress, *Hearings before the Committee on Agriculture,* 3:325.

29. Burnham, *Taking Chances,* 14.

30. Burnham, "Transplanting African Animals," 311–15.

31. Burnham, *Taking Chances,* 16.

32. Ibid., 14–15.

33. Ibid., 16–17.

34. U.S. Congress, *Hearings before the Committee on Agriculture,* 3:325. Unless otherwise noted, all testimony in this chapter is from the *Congressional Record.*

35. *New York Times,* 20 Sept. 1938, 23.

36. British nutritionist Dr. Magnus Pyke suggested in 1972 that hippo meat, rich in protein, might become a common delicacy on the dinner table. "There could come a day," he said, "when hippo—or at least hippo meat protein mixed with soya—could take the place of our more familiar but increasingly expensive meats." "Someone Hip to Hippo."

37. Burnham, "Transplanting African Animals," 314. Duquesne and Burnham were foresighted in their suggestions for saving from extinction certain wildlife species by importing the animals to similar habitats in America. Fossil Rim Wildlife Center, a three-thousand-acre ranch seventy-five miles southwest of Dallas, Texas, provides a home on the range where the hippo and rhino play, along with oryx, zebra, giraffe, and more than thirty other endangered species of exotic animals. The purpose of the nonprofit center is to save species from extinction and return them to the wild. It is only one of many such projects around the world. Others include the Washington, D.C., Conservation and Research Center of the National Zoological Park in Front Royal, Virginia; the San Diego Wild Animal Park in California; and the New York Zoological Park on St. Catherine's Island off the coast of Georgia.

38. *Washington Post,* 25 Mar. 1910, 11.

39. Ibid., 6.

40. Pound, "Fritz Duquesne: The Sequel," 17–18.

41. *New York Sun,* 7 Apr. 1911.

42. Fritz was right on target with his menu of cuts of meat from exotic African game animals. Only he was about four decades too soon. Czimer Foods, Inc. in Lockport, Illinois, began supplying hotels and restaurants nationwide in 1946 with exotic meats for wild-food gourmets with cuts from lion, hippo, elephant, and giraffe. In 1979 restaurateur John Ascuaga hosted his first Annual Safari Game Feed, of only a few, at his Nugget casino in Sparks, Nevada. Served up buffet-style were lion, ostrich, stingray, and of course hippo. And the world's largest game preserve near Nuevo Laredo, Mexico, experiments with game animals as another source of meat.

Chapter 9: Last Hurrah for the Bull Moose and Gentlemen Adventurers

1. *TMWKK,* 256.

2. Ibid., 258, 410.

3. Letter to author from Helen MacLachlan, Theodore Roosevelt Association, 13 Nov. 1972. Curiously, one of Roosevelt's hunting rifles turned up mys-

teriously in March 1912 in the bankrupt sporting-goods firm of Henry C. Squires Sons in New York City; *New York Times,* 26 Mar. 1912, 8.

4. Wortley interview, 1 Sept. 1973.

5. *TMWKK,* 267.

6. Ibid., 260, 261.

7. Ibid., 261–63.

8. *New York Times,* 23 Aug. 1914.

9. Hoffman, "Camp-Fire: An Account of Fritz Duquesne's Jamaica Trip," 221.

10. Wortley interview, 1 Sept. 1973.

11. *TMWKK,* 261–63.

12. Hoffman, "Camp-Fire: An Account of Fritz Duquesne's Jamaica Trip," 221–22; *New York Times,* 27 Apr. 1916, 5; Tunney, *Throttled,* 220; *New York Sun,* 28 Feb. 1912, 1; Wortley interview, 1 Sept. 1973.

13. Hoffman, "Camp-Fire: An Account of Fritz Duquesne's Jamaica Trip," 221–22.

14. Naturalization petition no. 21934, certificate no. 400139, 18 July 1912.

15. *TMWKK,* 270.

16. *New York Times,* 8 Mar. 1909, 1.

17. Hart, *Roosevelt Encyclopedia,* 58.

18. Jones, *Roosevelt's Rough Riders,* 265.

19. *New York World,* 31 Aug. 1912, 8; Duquesne, "Why Vote for Roosevelt?"

20. S. C. Latta, letter to Theodore Roosevelt, 30 Mar. 1916, Theodore Roosevelt Collection, Harvard College Library.

21. *New York Times,* 3 Nov. 1950, 27.

22. "Adventure: Dean of the Pulps," 23.

23. "No. 1 Pulp," 40, 41.

24. Downs, *Adventurers,* 4.

25. Schorer, *Sinclair Lewis,* 194.

26. "No. 1 Pulp," 40.

27. Hoffman, "Camp-Fire: With a Message from A.S.H."

28. "Adventure: Dean of the Pulps," 23.

29. Hoffman, "Some Real Adventurers."

30. *New Orleans Times-Picayune,* 17 Mar. 1938, 2.

31. *TMWKK,* 242.

32. Schorer, *Sinclair Lewis,* 195; Downs, *Adventurers,* 1.

33. Downs, *Adventurers,* 1.

34. Ibid., 2–3.

35. Ibid., 3; Henry, *Complete Works,* 1:v.

36. Hoffman, "Camp-Fire: Adventurers Club Inaugural Dinner," 220, 221.

37. Peter Beresford Ellis, *The Last Adventurer: The Life of Talbot Mundy* (West Kingston, R.I.: Donald M. Grant, 1984), 39.

38. Downs, *Adventurers,* 9.

39. *New York Times,* 16 Mar. 1913.

40. *TMWKK,* 246–47; Donohoe, letter to author, 16 Mar. 1973.

41. Cutright, *Roosevelt: The Naturalist*, 254; Gardner, *Departing Glory*, 295. He had said much the same thing prior to his African expedition when he wrote an English friend that it was his "last chance for something in the nature of a 'great adventure.'" Gardner, *Departing Glory*, 113.

42. Cutright, *Roosevelt: The Naturalist*, 236.

43. *TMWKK*, 271.

44. Gardner, *Departing Glory*, 292.

45. Tunney, *Throttled*, 231; *Akron Beacon Journal*, 1 July 1941; *TMWKK*, 280, 362; Pound, "Is Fritz Duquesne Alive?" 14; Wood, "True Story of Duquesne," 11.

46. Ashton biography from files of the Explorers Club, New York City.

47. Tunney, *Throttled*, 224.

48. Ibid., 231; *TMWKK*, 271; Hoffman, "Camp-Fire: Captain Duquesne Prepares," 220.

49. Tunney, *Throttled*, 232.

50. Hoffman, "Camp-Fire: Captain Duquesne Prepares," 220.

51. Certificate of naturalization 400139, petition vol. 90, p. 84, pub. vol. 13193, p. 39., 4 Dec. 1913.

Chapter 10: Kaiser Wilhelm Hires Captain Fritz Duquesne

1. Tunney, *Throttled*, 235, 236.

2. *TMWKK*, 277, 351.

3. Jones and Hollister, *German Secret Service in America*, 102.

4. Graves, *Secrets of the German War Office*, 13.

5. *TMWKK*, 283–94; Wood, "True Story of Duquesne," 11.

6. Quigley, "Espionage"; Quigley Jr. interview, 27 July 1973.

7. *New York Times*, 25 May 1932, 11; *TMWKK*, 287; Tunney, *Throttled*, 234.

8. Tunney, *Throttled*, 237, 238.

9. Ibid., 233.

10. Ibid., 181.

11. Fitch, *Traitors Within*, 212.

12. Tunney, *Throttled*, 235.

13. Ibid., 236, photo of document; *TMWKK*, 293, 363.

14. Tunney, *Throttled*, 237, 238.

15. *TMWKK*, 256, 369, 371, 372; *London Daily Mail*, 27 May 1919.

16. Tunney, *Throttled*, 239; *TMWKK*, 294–96.

17. *New York Times*, 27 Apr. 1916, 5.

18. Ibid., 28 Apr. 1916, 22.

19. *New York Tribune*, 8 May 1916, 1; *New York Times*, 8 May 1916, 2; *New York Sun*, 8 May 1916; *TMWKK*, 296–98.

Chapter 11: "Captain Claude Stoughton, at Your Service!"

1. *TMWKK*, 348; Wood, "True Story of Duquesne," 11.

2. Tunney, *Throttled*, 239, 240.

3. Ibid., 240.

4. *TMWKK*, 307–51; McCormick, *Mystery of Lord Kitchener's Death*, 169–71, 175, 206. An additional note refuting Fritz's claim: The *London Daily Express* published an interview on 20 February 1932 with Colonel Norman Thwaites regarding Clement Wood's just-published biography of Fritz, *The Man Who Killed Kitchener*. While serving as English provost-marshal of New York in 1917, Thwaites had met Fritz at the Tombs when he was arrested for masquerading as Captain Claude Stoughton. "Duquesne was a spy [during the war] and a good one from the German point of view, but whatever else he did he certainly could not have had a hand in the loss of the *Hampshire*.... My records show that in June 1916 when the *Hampshire* was sunk, Duquesne was in America."

5. *TMWKK*, 279.

6. According to Dr. Harold A. Lubick of the Orders and Medals Society of America (see appendix C), Germany never awarded an Iron Cross with gold leaves until 1945 (gold oak leaves), nor is there a Diamond Crescent of Turkey. The Grand Cross of the Iron Cross was the award worn only by the kaiser and others. The Turkish Order of Osmania worn by Fritz in photos gives the appearance of a Diamond Crescent. According to Lubick, Fritz apparently combined several decorations either to confuse or to impress, expecting no one to know the difference.

In *TMWKK* (407) Fritz claims several other awards that, though misspelled, have a similarity to those named in appendix C. He identifies the medals as the Order of Nisch-an-i-Osmanie, the Osmanieh, the Star of Osmanieh, and, from Bulgaria, the Star and Cross and the Order of Military Merit.

7. History is unkind to those who are legends in their own lifetimes. In death they achieve the myth of immortality and leave behind a tangled fabric of controversy as to how they died—or did not. T. E. Lawrence was not killed in a motorcycle accident. John F. Kennedy and Elvis Presley are not dead. John Wilkes Booth, Jesse James, Billy the Kid, and Butch Cassidy did not die as history records. They lived for many more years under other names.

And so it was with Lord Horatio Herbert Kitchener. If he was dead, reasoned the British public, where was his body? Rumors were rampant. A submarine picked him out of the North Atlantic waters, and he was a prisoner in Germany. He was in France directing a new offensive against the Germans. He was reported seen in Cairo, Cyprus, Rome, and even Washington. Like King Arthur he was secreted in a cave, waiting to emerge and save England in its direst moment.

Adding to the confusion is the fact that Fritz Duquesne was not the only claimant to the distinction of having caused Kitchener's death. Others were also accused. It was rumored that Kitchener had been deliberately sent to his death by the Admiralty and that little attempt had been made to rescue him or the *Hampshire* crew; that time bombs had been placed aboard by Sinn Feiners in retaliation for Kitchener's recruiting policies in Ireland; that the prime minister had ordered his death; that German Secret Service agents disguised themselves as crew members and blew up the ship; that the British Secret Service engineered the disaster;and so on.

A German spy, Ernst Carl (Gelrichsheimer), told a story as fanciful as Duquesne's in his autobiography, *One against England*, 177–93. Masquerading as a wounded Belgian army officer named Jaggi, Carl organized several members of the Irish Republican Army to assassinate Kitchener for originating the compulsory military service act, which would "strike a hard blow at the Irish freedom movement." (Kitchener only reluctantly agreed to the National Military Service Bill.) Hearing that Kitchener was planning the Russian trip and knowing that he collected antique furniture—in fact his passion was porcelain, not furniture—Carl arranged a meeting with the field marshal, claiming he had some family heirlooms to sell. Kitchener said he wanted to buy the antiques before he left for Russia, thus confirming the rumor. News that the *Hampshire* was being refurbished convinced Carl that it would be used to take Kitchener to Russia. Two Irish sailors, hostile to England, were persuaded to smuggle two time bombs aboard in a bundle of blankets. Carl and two Irish allies took a boat to the small island of S (he does not name it), "one of the outposts of the Orkneys." From an inn named the White Horse they had a wide view of the sea. A little black dot in the distance was the *Hampshire*. After four o'clock the dot began steering a northward course through stormy seas, when "suddenly two pillars of fire shot up." Carl and his two comrades watched the sea close over the *Hampshire*.

8. *TMWKK*, 360, 377; Tunney, *Throttled*, 240, 241.

9. Tunney, *Throttled*, 241; *TMWKK*, 377.

10. Tunney, *Throttled*, 241, 242. Fritz evidently invented a mine of some sort. Otherwise he wouldn't have pursued proof of the invention so diligently. He wrote the Department of Labor in 1930 and 1931 seeking confirmation of his citizenship. He was apparently under the impression that proof of citizenship was necessary regarding copyrights and patents. Ten years later in 1941, while under FBI surveillance, he made a special trip to Washington to ferret out the patents. He was not successful.

11. Tunney, *Throttled*, 242; *TMWKK*, 364, 377.

12. *TMWKK*, 360, 377; Tunney, *Throttled*, 217, 218.

13. *New York Times*, 3 June 1942, 23.

14. *TMWKK*, 360, 361, 377; Tunney, *Throttled*, 219–22.

15. Mildred Wortley, sister-in-law of Alice, Fritz's wife, said she had never heard of Jocelyn. She said Jocelyn was an old Wortley family name. A Reverend Wortley of the Episcopal church named his son Jocelyn. Alice named her son by a second marriage Lyle Jocelyn. Becker interview, 10 Aug. 1974; Wortley interview, 1 Sept. 1973.

16. Tunney, *Throttled*, 242.

17. *Billboard*, 3, 10, 17 Nov. 1917.

18. Ibid., 10, 17 Nov. 1917.

19. *TMWKK*, 354; Tunney, *Throttled*, 217–19, 242–45.

20. Thwaites, *Velvet and Vinegar*, 231.

21. Pond, *Eccentricities of Genius; Dumas, Dictionary of American Biography* (1935), 60.

22. Bim Pond, letter to Linding, 29 Oct. 1959 (author's collection).

23. Tunney, *Throttled*, 243–45.

24. *New York Times*, 4 Nov. 1917, 7.

25. *TMWKK*, 354–56; *New York Times*, 15 Dec. 1917, 14.

26. Jones and Hollister, *German Secret Service in America*, 292.

27. *New York Sun*, 24 Oct. 1941, 1.

Chapter 12: Fraud and the Bomb Squad

1. *New York World*, 18 July 1920, 8.

2. *Adventurer* bulletin, Jan. 1956, 8.

3. Exchange of letters between Case and Roosevelt, Theodore Roosevelt Papers, Library of Congress, reel 394, series 3A, 1917, Aug. 9, 10, 17.

4. Ibid.

5. *New York Times*, 25 Mar. 1962, 89.

6. In the coming years Brophy would investigate two of America's most tragic fires, the 1942 Coconut Grove nightclub fire in Boston and the 1944 Ringling Brothers and Barnum and Bailey Circus fire in Hartford. He also worked on the blaze that destroyed the French luxury liner *Normandie* at her North River pier in New York in 1942. He determined that sabotage was not to blame but negligence of workmen converting the vessel into a troopship. Brophy died in 1962 at the age of eighty-two, still chasing fires for insurance companies as a consultant with his own company, Thomas F. Brophy Associates.

7. Polenberg, *Fighting Faiths*, 59, 56; Tunney, *Throttled; New York Times*, 27 Jan. 1952, 76.

8. Tunney, *Throttled*, 4.

9. Tunney retired from the NYPD in August 1919 after twenty-two years of service. But he never fully retired from police work, operating a detective agency bearing his name until 1946, when he was named police commissioner of Port Washington, a resort village on Long Island. He died in St. Petersburg, Florida, in 1952 at the age of seventy-nine. *New York Times*, 27 Jan. 1952, 76.

10. Tunney, *Throttled*, 3; *New York Times*, 19 Dec. 1923, 15.

11. Goldman, *Living My Life*, 2:610, 611. In December 1919, after serving almost two years in prison, the two anarchists were deported to Russia. Instrumental in engineering their exile was the twenty-four-year-old chief of the Radical Division of the Bureau of Investigation (forerunner of the FBI), J. Edgar Hoover. According to Hoover's biographers, he personally spoke a farewell to Goldman aboard the *Buford*, the ship taking Goldman, Berkman,

and other anarchists to the Soviet Union. But Goldman makes no mention of it in her autobiography.

12. *Adventurer* bulletin, Jan. 1956, 8.

13. Tunney, *Throttled*, 222.

14. Ibid., 218.

15. Ibid., 219.

16. *New York Times*, 27 Jan. 1956, 23; Thwaites, *Velvet and Vinegar*, 230–32.

17. Thwaites must have been wounded in a previous skirmish at Messines, since the principal battle of Messines did not occur until 7 June 1917, and he writes that he did not arrive in New York until 1916; *Velvet and Vinegar*, 119, 131.

18. Ibid., 119.

19. *New York Times*, 18 June 1962, 25; Fowler, *British-American Relations, 1917–1918*, 13; Viereck, *Spreading Germs of Hate*, 130–36.

20. Fowler, *British-American Relations*, 18; *New York Times*, 18 June 1962, 25.

21. Thwaites, *Velvet and Vinegar*, 219.

22. Ibid., 222.

23. As reported in *Billboard*, 29 Dec. 1917, 24, the *Davenport Times* had jumped into the fray regarding soldier frauds when it editorialized:

For their own protection and for the protection of the general public, the United States Government ought to require that all lecturers upon the war who claim to be telling of their personal experiences shall have federal licenses. These licenses should be issued after the man's credentials have been investigated and found to be correct. The plan would shut out not a few romancers who, after cramming war stories from the war front written by others, have gone about pretending to be fresh from the trenches in Europe. . . . [They] should be what they purport to be and not merely clever actors. There should be protection for the people against misinformation and fakers. The others should be shut off from the lecture platform.

Billboard, the bible of show business, took up the defense of freedom of speech in an editorial critical of the Iowa paper: "To charge a license, and thereby putting the utterances of the lyceum and chautauqua platform up for sale, would rob it of its real freedom and power. The freedom of the press, the freedom of the pulpit would soon follow. We are fighting for the freedom of democracy abroad, but let us not sacrifice the good old American freedom of the platform while we are fighting for the rest."

24. Thwaites, *Velvet and Vinegar*, 230.

25. Ibid., 143.

26. Ibid., 230–32.

27. *New York Times*, 15 Dec. 1917, 14; 30 May 1942, 15.

28. Ibid., 15 Dec. 1917.

29. Ibid., 21 Sept. 1945, 21.

30. Ibid., 15 Dec. 1917, 14.

31. Ibid.

Chapter 13: Insanity and Paralysis

1. *Lunacy Commission Report: Court of the General Sessions of the Peace in and for the County of New York. The People of the State of New York against Frederick Fredericks, otherwise called Frederick Joubert Duquesne, otherwise called F. du Cain, otherwise called Captain Claude Stoughton. In the Matter of the Mental Condition of Frederick Fredericks . . . an Alleged Lunatic* (New York, 15 May 1918). Hereafter *Lunacy Commission Report.*

2. Lichtenstein, *A Doctor Studies Crime,* 138; *New York Times,* 15 June 1954, 29.

3. *New York Times,* 3 Dec. 1943, 23.

4. *TMWKK,* 378; Wood, "True Story of Duquesne," 11.

5. *Lunacy Commission Report.*

6. Ibid.

7. Lichtenstein, *A Doctor Studies Crime,* 139, 140.

8. *Lunacy Commission Report.*

9. Lichtenstein, *A Doctor Studies Crime,* 139.

10. Ibid., 140.

11. *TMWKK,* 379.

12. Eckland, "Cops Laughed Last," 6; *New York Times,* 10 Nov. 1918, 18.

13. *New York Times,* 10 Nov. 1918, 18.

14. *New York World,* 16 Dec. 1918, 3.

15. Ibid.

16. Pound, "Is Fritz Duquesne Alive?" 14.

17. Boshoff, "Die Baas," 6.

18. *TMWKK,* 422.

19. Marriage license no. 8475, Genesee County, Michigan, 17 Nov. 1919.

20. Becker interview, 10 Aug. 1974.

21. Wortley interview, 1 Sept. 1973.

22. Herz interview, 28 June 1973; *New York Times,* 16 Aug. 1940, 15.

23. *TMWKK,* 379, 380; Lichtenstein, *A Doctor Studies Crime,* 140.

24. Hays, *City Lawyer,* 192.

25. *New York World,* 27 May 1919, 6.

26. *TMWKK,* 381; *New York Sun,* 8 June 1918, 7; *New York Times,* 28 May 1919, 17.

27. Hays, *City Lawyer,* 193.

28. Linding interview, 12 Sept. 1973.

29. *TMWKK,* 381.

30. *New York Sun,* 20 May 1919, 7.

31. Ibid.

32. *TMWKK,* 388; *New York World,* 28 May 1919; *New York Times,* 28 May 1919, 17; *New York Sun,* 8 June 1919, 7; Cooper, *Bellevue Story,* 208.

33. *TMWKK,* 381–91.

34. Ibid., 392–94.

35. Ibid., 407; *New York Sun,* 12 Oct. 1919.

36. *New York Sun,* 12 June 1919.

37. Ibid.

38. *Los Angeles Evening Herald,* 10 Sept. 1919, 19.

39. *TMWKK,* 337 (circular reproduced and on dust jacket).

40. *New York Sun,* 24 Oct. 1941, 21.

Chapter 14: "A Prize Picaroon If There Ever Was One"

1. *TMWKK,* 397, 398.

2. *New York Sun,* 21 Oct. 1941.

3. *New York Herald Tribune,* 22 Oct. 1941; preliminary social abstract, 13 Feb. 1942, in Bureau of Prisons Notorious Offenders File, record group 129, National Archives (hereafter Notorious Offenders File).

4. *New York Times,* 25 May 1932, 11; Quigley Jr. interview, 27 July 1973.

5. Quigley Jr., phone interview, 13 Aug. 1994.

6. Ibid.

7. *New York Times,* 24 May 1932, 11.

8. Quigley Jr. interview, 27 June 1973.

9. Quigley, "Espionage."

10. *New York Sun,* 23 May 1932, 1.

11. Quigley Jr. interview, 27 June 1973.

12. Ibid.

13. *New York Times,* 27 Oct. 1950, 29.

14. International News Photos Inc. caption, 19 Feb. 1932.

15. *New York Times,* 24 May 1932, 11.

16. Ibid., 25 May 1932, 11.

17. Wood and Fritz met for the first time in Haiti when the adventurer was masquerading as Major Reginald Anson.

18. *New York Times,* 15 Dec. 1954, 31; Hays, *City Lawyer.*

19. Hays, *City Lawyer,* 192.

20. *New York Sun,* 1 June 1932.

21. Hays, *City Lawyer,* 192.

22. *New York Times,* 7 June 1932, 10.

23. Ibid.

24. Ibid., 5 May 1959.

25. Files in the City Magistrate's Court, Fourth District, Borough of Manhattan, 28 June 1932.

26. *New York Sun* clippings file, New York Public Library.

Chapter 15: Wrath, Reds, and Right-Wingers

1. *New York Evening Post,* 21 Feb. 1934.

2. Fritz often became just as confused when discussing facts concerning other people as he did about himself. Years earlier he had credited two other people with inventing the "doping" of animals. In an article for *The Travel*

Magazine ("African Big Game Hunting Made Easy," 384–87, 405–6) he described methods of drugging animals to make them easy targets for amateur African hunters. But he took no credit for devising the scheme. Instead, a white hunter named "Jack" is credited as the originator. In a story for *Hampton's Magazine* concerning "these wonderful creations of nature" Fritz wrote, "The man to whom the honor is due for the idea of using morphine for subduing fear-maddened beasts was one of my business and hunting associates, Koos Marais, a Transvaal physician" ("Trapping Big Game in the Heart of Africa," 252).

3. Spivak, *Man in His Time,* 255; Rollins, *I Find Treason,* 59.

4. *New York Times,* 2 July 1965, 27.

5. Rollins, *I Find Treason,* 9, 10.

6. Ibid., 6; Spivak, *Man in His Time,* 263, 271; Spivak, *Secret Armies,* 75.

7. *New York Times,* 7 Oct. 1959, 43; Steffens, *Autobiography,* 340–42.

8. Emerson, address at Rough Riders reunion in Prescott, Ariz., June 1948, Theodore Roosevelt Collection, Harvard College Library; Emerson, *Pepys's Ghost,* 128–30.

9. *New Masses,* 2 Oct. 1934, 11, 12; Spivak, *Man in His Time,* 265–71.

10. *Los Angeles Times,* 5 Oct. 1981, 26.

11. Spivak, *Man in His Time,* 258.

12. Rollins, *I Find Treason,* 6.

13. Spivak, *Man in His Time,* 271.

14. Ibid.

15. Ibid., 271–75.

16. FBI parole report, file no. 66-1819, 5 Jan. 1942, 5, in Notorious Offenders File.

17. Ibid., 6.

Chapter 16: Colonel Ritter Hires Colonel Duquesne

1. Farago, *Foxes,* 6.

2. Ibid., 8; Whiting, *Canaris,* 33.

3. Ritter, *Deckname,* 23, 24; Whiting, *Canaris,* 33; Paine, *German Military Intelligence in World War II,* 10–12.

4. Ritter, *Deckname;* Farago, *Foxes,* 456; *New York Times,* 30 June 1941, 1; Cook, *The FBI Nobody Knows,* 252.

5. Ritter, *Deckname,* 7; Farago, *Foxes,* 325. In *Foxes,* the most authoritative history of German espionage in the United States prior to its entry into World War II, Farago calls Ritter Rankin, not Renken. As will be seen, there are many discrepancies between *Foxes* and *Deckname.* Much of Farago's information was derived from the papers and diaries of Ritter, his unpublished manuscript, and personal interviews, so it is difficult to understand the inconsistencies as to dates, names, and other details. Both Ritter and Farago made errors in fact.

6. Ritter, *Deckname*, 125–28; Farago, *Foxes*, 38–49; *New York Times*, 10 Sept. 1941, 1.

7. Ritter, *Deckname*, 47.

8. Irmgard Ritter, letters to author, 16 Oct. and 11 Dec. 1988.

9. *New York Times*, 7 Oct. 1937.

10. The date is a matter of dispute. Ritter says he arrived in New York aboard the *Bremen* on 17 October 1937. Farago agrees with this date, saying Ritter left Bremen's port, Bremerhaven, on 11 October and arrived six days later in New York. Farago evidently worked backwards from Ritter's date, allowing six days for the Atlantic crossing. But according to the *New York Times* "Shipping and Mail Schedules," the *Bremen*'s only two New York arrival dates were the 7th and 25th. The present account uses 7 October as Ritter's arrival date because it is the only date that will work with later erroneous dates given by the spy.

11. Ritter, *Deckname*, 74–76; Farago, *Foxes*, 42, 43.

12. The duke and duchess of Windsor were scheduled to be aboard the *Bremen* but had canceled. Nevertheless, their names had not been removed from the passenger manifest, and they were in a place of honor at the top of the list. Ritter must have seen their names and assumed they were aboard. They finally made the voyage in November. *New York Times*, 12 Nov. 1937.

13. Ritter, *Deckname*, 76; Farago, *Foxes*, 43.

14. Farago, *Foxes*, 49; Jones and Hollister, *German Secret Service in America*, 292.

15. Ritter (*Deckname*, 78) said it was the "main" post office on Lexington Avenue. There were two post offices on Lexington in 1937: one at 2089 Lexington in Harlem and one at the train station. Because of its proximity to the Taft, Ritter must have meant the one at the railroad terminal. After almost four decades it would not be surprising for him to be confused, remembering the huge building as also being the main post office (which incidentally was at Eighth Avenue and Thirty-first Street).

16. There was in fact no branch of that bank at Ninetieth Street, so it is unclear which one Ritter was referring to. He could have gone to several close by, perhaps the one at Fifty-seventh Street and Seventh Avenue, not far from the Taft.

17. Ritter, *Deckname*, 79.

18. Farago calls him "Pops" and Heinrich (*Foxes*, 44). Lang calls him Fritz (*New York Times*, 1 Nov. 1941, 17).

19. When copies of the Norden bombsight were found aboard downed German aircraft during the war, it was thought that they had been copied from devices found in shot-down American bombers, even though crew members were ordered to destroy the bombsight if their plane crashed in enemy territory. Although the American military knew that the Norden bombsight had been stolen and was no longer a secret, the charade was perpetuated throughout the war, and the truth was not admitted until years later. Some authorities even claim that the Lang plans were incomplete and useless. But as events de-

veloped, the German version of the Norden bombsight was not placed in bombers until after the September 1940–May 1941 blitz on Great Britain. After that, the Luftwaffe was limited in its bombing raids. (Knightley, *Second Oldest Profession*, 103.)

As late as July 1945, one month before the end of World War II, *Flying,* a leading U.S. aviation magazine, said this about the Norden bombsight:

Since crashed bombers have provided our enemies with the famed Norden bombsight, the armed services have made available to *Flying,* for the first time, detailed photographs and descriptions of this precision instrument.

For years, the Norden was so secret it could hardly be mentioned. It was kept in air conditioned dustproof vaults surrounded by high barbed wire constantly patrolled by guards. When a bombsight was taken to a plane it was always carried by two men wearing service pistols and its canvas cover was never removed until the aircraft was in flight. AAF bombardiers had to swear a solemn oath to guard it with their lives.

They needn't have bothered.

20. Farago, *Foxes,* 45, 48, 49; Ritter, *Deckname,* 123–27; Wighton, *World's Greatest Spies,* 115–17.

21. Wighton, *World's Greatest Spies,* 120; Franklin, *Great Spies,* 122.

22. Ritter, *Deckname,* 84–86. Farago offers a different account of the meeting between the spymaster and the idealist: "He [Ritter] was so overwhelmed by what Lang had turned over that he gave the man 1,500 dollars in crisp new bills, the highest remuneration ever paid by the Abwehr in a lump sum to any of its agents." Farago, *Foxes,* 48.

23. Ritter, *Deckname,* 86.

24. Ibid., 89–91; Farago, *Foxes,* 46.

25. German engineers immediately built a bombsight based on the Lang plans smuggled out of America. Ritter then invited Lang and his wife to Berlin in June 1938 to see the results. As an honored guest of the Third Reich, Lang was personally congratulated by Reich Marshal Hermann Göring, who said the bombsight "was the most important thing in the world." (*New York Times,* 25 Sept. 1941, 27; Sayers and Kahn, *Sabotage,* 27.) Admiral Canaris considered Lang so valuable that he offered him an important position with either the Luftwaffe or an arms firm, whichever he wished. But Mrs. Lang preferred life in America, and Lang regretfully turned down the offer. Despite their treatment as honored guests and the personal congratulations of Göring, Lang and his wife were shabbily treated when they arrived from New York at Cuxhaven, the port of Hamburg. They were segregated from the other passengers and had their baggage minutely searched. When Lang protested, he was threatened with imprisonment in Dachau concentration camp. When allowed to proceed to Berlin, the Langs could bring only the most necessary articles of clothing. So much for Nazi honors!

26. Farago, *Foxes,* 46.

27. *Reliance* information from John P. Eaton, president, Titanic Historical Society, Inc.; *New York Times,* 5 Dec. 1937.

28. Molveau interview, 18 July 1992.

29. Ritter may have considered Fritz "an old and good friend," but he would have been surprised to know Duquesne's opinion of him. According to FBI special agent William Friedemann, who spoke fluent German and who investigated the spy case in 1940, Fritz had no respect for Ritter. "Ritter was a real German," said Friedemann. "Germans considered the Dutch an offshoot of the Aryan race and inferior. Somehow, this was sensed by Duquesne." Friedemann phone interview, 29 Nov. 1974.

30. Ritter wrote that he remembered Duquesne's number He said he looked it up in the phone book, but his search would have been in vain (*Deckname*, 87). In all the years Fritz lived in New York—except for 1905—he always had an unlisted number. Spies, after all, are supposed to be anonymous.
Farago made two errors when he gave Fritz's address at this time as 24 West Seventy-eighth Street. First, he meant Seventy-sixth Street, an address he gives correctly later. Second, Fritz would not be living there for several years. Farago, *Foxes*, 47.

31. *New York Times*, 20 Aug. 1947, 21.

32. Ritter, *Deckname*, 87.

33. *New York Times*, 30 Mar. 1947, 1; 5 Feb. 1945, 15. In *Deckname* Ritter calls Whitman Whitney and Colonel Riggs a commander.

34. *New York Times*, 18 Jan. 1924, 17.

35. Ritter, *Deckname*, 87.

36. Hall phone interview, 27 Sept. 1988.

37. FBI parole report, file no. 66-1819, 5 Jan. 1942, 3, in Notorious Offenders File. FBI agent Raymond F. Newkirk considered her "a damn good American gal" who unfortunately got involved with Fritz (Newkirk phone interview, 9 Nov. 1974). Agent William Friedemann said "she was not pro-German" (Friedemann phone interview, 29 Nov. 1974). Newkirk recalled that prior to her arrest in June 1941, she had just made a sale of some kind of rubber monkey, which was to go on sale that Christmas. He thought it rather hideous. Others must have thought so too. It didn't make much money.

38. Collins, *FBI in Peace and War*, 211; Hoover, "Hitler's Spying Sirens," 92.

39. Collins, *FBI in Peace and War*, 211.

40. Ritter gives Karl Keitel as the name of Duquesne's "confidence man" (*Deckname*, 87, 88). Farago (*Foxes*, 46) discusses a Karl Eitel, number R.2307, a senior agent and chief courier aboard the *Bremen*. After thirty-five years Ritter can be forgiven for confusing Keitel with Eitel. Or perhaps Farago was in error. But according to Farago, Eitel was transferred prior to the Ritter/Duquesne *Treff*. For the sake of clarity, Oskar, Farago's name for Duquesne's "confidence man," is used in this account.

41. When it came to banking money, the Abwehr was consistent with the policies of its World War I predecessors and used the Chase National Bank in Manhattan. Dr. Heinrich Albert, Germany's chief propagandist and commer-

cial attaché in New York from 1914 to 1917, was also the paymaster for his kaiser's spies. Albert's office was in the Hamburg-Amerika Line building at 45 Broadway, not far from 32 Broadway, where Hans Ritter would establish quarters in 1937.

42. Farago, *Foxes*, 327.

Chapter 17: William Sebold Goes to Germany

1. *New York Times*, 9 Sept. 1941, 14; *Frederick Joubert Duquesne, et al., Espionage* (FBI report, 5 May 1953) (hereafter *Duquesne, et al., Espionage*), 1–5; Farago, *War of Wits*, 312–15; Farago, *Foxes*, 322; Ritter, *Deckname*, 162; Gilman, "How G-Men Trapped," *True Detective*, Nov. 1942, 73–75.

2. Gilman, "How G-Men Trapped," *True Detective*, Nov. 1942, 73–75. According to Farago (*Foxes*) and other sources, Sebold was a machine gunner.

3. Debowski according to Farago (*Foxes*, 322), Debrovsky according to Ritter (*Deckname*, 162).

4. Farago, *Foxes*, 322; *Duquesne, et al., Espionage*, 2; Gilman, "How G-Men Trapped," *True Detective*, Nov. 1942, 73–75.

5. *New York Times*, 1 Feb. 1939, 1.

6. Ibid., 10 Feb. 1939, 11.

7. See note 1.

8. *New York Times*, 9 Sept. 1941, 14.

9. Farago, *Foxes*, 296–97.

10. *New York Times*, 9 Sept. 1941, 14; "World of William Sebold," 16; Farago, *Foxes*, 324.

11. *Duquesne, et al., Espionage*.

12. Farago, *Foxes*, 203–4.

13. Ibid., 463.

14. *New York Times*, 9 June 1948, 29.

15. Ibid., 11 Sept. 1941, 27.

16. Foreign Service List, Oct. 1939, National Archives.

17. *New York Times*, 11 Sept. 1941, 27.

18. Ibid.

19. Farago, *Foxes*, 324–25.

20. *Duquesne, et al., Espionage*, 4; Farago, *Foxes*, 326; *New York Times*, 9 Sept. 1941, 14.

21. See also Sterling, "RID Story," chap. 3, "Spy and Counter-Spy," p. 36.

22. Kahn, *Codebreakers*, 529; Hynd, *Passport to Treason*, 174; Ritter, *Deckname*, 151; Whiting, *Canaris*, 102. During World War I in America, the pulp publication *Blue Book Magazine* was utilized to transmit secret messages in a different way. Messages would be written in lemon juice on certain pages, to be revealed when the pages were heated over a candle flame. Beesly, *Codebreakers of Room 40*, 193.

23. Ritter, *Deckname*, 290, 314; Farago, *Foxes*, 540; Whiting, *Canaris*, 96.

24. Oddly, Farago mistakenly gives Sebold's new identity as William G. Sawyer in his two books on World War II espionage; *War of Wits,* 314, and *Foxes,* 325.

25. Farago, *Foxes,* 324.

26. Farago provides a different set of addresses. First, he gives Fritz's home address as the one put to memory, which is incorrect. The Abwehr did not know where the secretive Duquesne lived. As will be seen, the FBI agents searching for that home address would be led on a hounds-and-hare chase through the streets of New York City. Second, whereas 127 East Fifty-fourth Street was Lilly's address in 1940, Farago gives the address where Lilly was living when she was arrested in 1941. Third, he incorrectly places Lang at his new Queens address in Glendale. At this time the Abwehr was not yet aware that Lang had moved from the Ridgewood apartment in Queens, where Ritter had first met him in 1937. Ibid., 324–25.

27. Sayers and Kahn, *Sabotage,* 26.

28. Farago, *Foxes,* 464; Hoover, "Enemy's Masterpiece," 1.

Chapter 18: Harry Sawyer Arrives in America

1. Farago erroneously gives the date as 6 February (*Foxes,* 325).

2. Friedemann phone interview, 29 Nov. 1974.

3. Ibid.

4. *New York Times,* 22 Jan. 1943.

5. Twenty-four other passengers and nine crew members were also killed. Among them was English author Eric Knight, a major in the U.S. Army, whose many books included *The Flying Yorkshireman, This Above All,* and *Lassie Come Home,* the book that launched several television series and many movies about the precocious collie. Also aboard was Morris Lewis, a public relations expert serving as an information specialist in the Office of the Chief of Special Services and the prewar director of the Planned Parenthood Federation. Lewis was the author of the quasi-humorous series of *Short Guides* to Great Britain and other countries for G.I.'s serving abroad.

6. *New York Times,* 7 Sept. 1939, 8; Farago, *War of Wits,* 303.

7. *New York Times,* 7 Sept. 1939, 8.

8. Friedemann phone interview, 29 Nov. 1974.

9. *New York Times,* 21 July 1957, 60.

10. Newkirk phone interview, 9 Nov. 1974.

11. Ibid.

12. Johnson interview, 25 Nov. 1974.

13. "World of William Sebold," 16.

14. Hynd, *Passport to Treason,* 25.

15. Friedemann phone interview, 29 Nov. 1974; Johnson phone interview, 25 Nov. 1974.

16. The Knickerbocker also played a patriotic role during World War I.

Opera tenor Enrico Caruso and Broadway showman George M. Cohan were residents there for years during its days as the "Hotel Triumph." On 9 November 1918, the day of the False Armistice, hundreds of New Yorkers flocked to the Knickerbocker and besieged Caruso to sing the national anthems of the Allies. The tenor boomed out the songs from a flag-bedecked balcony while his wife, Doro, tossed hundreds of flowers to the cheering, flag-waving crowds below. The singer moved to the Vanderbilt when Biddle negotiated the hotel's sale.

17. Dorwart, "Roosevelt-Astor Espionage Ring," 309–22; Cave Brown, "C," 124, 125; Miller, *Spying for America*, 237; Knightley, *Second Oldest Profession*, 211.

18. *New York Times*, 18 June 1962, 25.

19. Johnson phone interview, 25 Nov. 1974.

20. *New York Times*, 13 Sept. 1941, 8.

21. Johnson phone interview, 25 Nov. 1974; Friedemann phone interview, 29 Nov. 1974.

22. Friedemann phone interview, 29 Nov. 1974.

23. Dynamic microphone information from Hal Landaker, Columbia Pictures Television Sound Dept.; Richard H. Topham, Audio Services Corporation, Burbank, California; Shelley Herman.

24. Friedemann phone interview, 29 Nov. 1974.

25. Ibid.

26. Lowenthal, *Federal Bureau of Investigation*, 429.

27. Flanagan, "Nazi 'Spy Ring,'" 2.

28. After training at the Abwehr's Klopstock Pension, espionage students had to pass a test in transmitting fifty to sixty letters—the equivalent of twelve words—per minute. Sebold, like all candidates, was required to send for five minutes on special equipment that produced a graph indicating his touch, speed, and method of sending. After a study of the graph, each student was assigned his sending speed and required thereafter to send all messages at that speed. To assure that he transmitted at this speed, the student underwent further training in sending only. Then another graph was made as a protective measure and filed for later use in comparing messages from the agent. Having on file the agent's individual characteristics was supposed to assure that the transmitter was indeed genuine and not a counterespionage agent. Obviously it was not foolproof, considering Agent Price's success. See Sterling, "RID Story," chap. 5, "Nazi Spies in Latin America," p. 14, and *Spies Use Radio*, p. 63.

29. Farago, *Foxes*, 326.

30. But the Centerport station did not go unnoticed by the professionals whose job was to discover suspicious and unauthorized transmitting stations: the Engineering Division of the Federal Communications Commission, known as the Radio Intelligence Division or RID. George E. Sterling was the chief. During the period of neutrality between 1940 and 1941 before the

United States entered World War II, RID was responsible for the enforcement of radio rules and regulations and international treaties as they pertained to the technical operation of radio stations. RID feared that enemy agents operating in this hemisphere might use radio transmitters, as did the fifth column in Europe. It also was important to keep all channels of communication free of interference.

RID exchanged information with the army and navy during the summer of 1940 about a suspicious station operating in the 14-megacycle band located somewhere in western central New England or New York State. But it was necessary to determine the station's precise location. Navy cryptographers could not solve the code being transmitted, and the FBI gave no indication of having broken it. Within three days RID located the exact house in Centerport with its monitoring equipment. Mr. Ross, monitoring officer in charge of RID's Bayshore (Long Island) station, drove by the house and each time obtained the same result, observing that "the S-29 receiver on the floorboard 'blocked' even with the collapsible antenna all the way with the cap on the antenna socket." Ross also observed that it was the only house in the small village with a visible antenna, one that conceivably could be radiating signals reaching Germany.

RID realized that the station was located in the same village as the one listed as being the location of a secret amateur radio station licensed to the FBI in the spring of 1940. The station had been given the call letters W2NCK for a confidential purpose, and it was believed that there might be a connection between the two. But a letter from the FBI in response to the FCC inquiry led RID to believe otherwise.

Sterling conferred with Mr. Jett, chief engineer of the FCC, and it was decided to notify the FBI that if the bureau had no interest in the station, RID would arrest the operators. Sterling informed Mr. Carson, an FBI supervisor, regarding this decision on 9 December 1940. Carson requested that Sterling not take any action until he heard from him. A short time later, Carson met with Jett and Sterling and informed them that the station was involved in an operation of extreme importance to the FBI regarding counterespionage and requested that the FCC take no action against the perpetrators. See Sterling, "RID Story," chap. 3, "Spy and Counter-Spy," pp. 31, 34, 35.

31. *Duquesne, et al., Espionage,* 5.

32. Gilman, "How G-Men Trapped," *True Detective,* Oct. 1942, 109–10.

33. *New York Times,* 30 June 1941, 3.

34. Kleiss boasted that he had served aboard a German raider responsible for sinking seventeen Allied ships during the Great War. The ship slipped into Newport News, Virginia, for repairs in 1915, and he was interned with the rest of the crew for the duration. When America entered the war he was placed in a Georgia prison camp. Kleiss was referring to the *Kronprinz Wilhelm,* one of Germany's secret raiders, often referred to as "mystery ships." On a raiding cruise of 251 days she sank fourteen ships (not seventeen) and in the early-

evening hours of 10 April ran a British blockade into the neutral Virginia port to avoid being sunk. Gilman, "How G-Men Trapped," *True Detective,* Oct. 1942, 31; Niezychowski, *Cruise of the Kronprinz Wilhelm,* 286, 294.

35. *New York Times,* 30 June 1941, 3.

36. Tully, *FBI's Most Famous Cases,* 146.

37. Trial Docket Cr 38425, FRC container no. 547802, General Services Administration, Federal Records Center, New York.

38. *Look* editors, *Story of the FBI,* 223, 224.

39. Farago, *Foxes,* 301, 302; Gilman, "How G-Men Trapped," *True Detective,* Nov. 1942, 39.

40. *New York Times,* 30 June 1941, 3.

41. Gilman, "How G-Men Trapped," *True Detective,* Oct. 1942, 110.

42. Ibid.

43. Ibid., 112.

44. Ibid., Nov. 1942, 35.

45. Ibid.

46. *New York Times,* 10 Sept. 1941, 1.

47. Ibid., 12 Sept. 1941, 15.

48. A totally different version of the Sebold story is told by William R. Corson in his *Armies of Ignorance* (286–87), even though he cites Farago's *Foxes* (580–83—the wrong pages) as a source. According to Corson, "one of Hoover's best counterespionage agents," Special Agent William King Harvey (who is not mentioned in *Foxes*), "was best remembered by Hoover because of his skill in capturing Nazi spy William Sebold and turning him into an effective double agent." In a footnote Corson relates that the FBI discovered at the end of 1940 that a Nazi radio station operating in Mexico was sending messages to an Abwehr station on Long Island for relay to Germany by Sebold. "When the FBI collapsed the Abwehr network in New York City on June 30 [the correct date was June 29], 1941 . . . [it] could no longer operate effectively. During this operation Harvey played Sebold like a master, getting him not only to convey false information, but to seek out and acquire information which enabled the FBI to identify the Abwehr's sources, contacts and membership." So, contrary to all published evidence yet claiming *Foxes* as a source, Corson's story is that the FBI knew nothing about Sebold until the messages from Mexico were intercepted. Agent Harvey then convinced Sebold to become a double agent.

Chapter 19: "Get Duquesne to Forty-second Street"

1. Almost six years after his imprisonment in January 1942 for espionage, Fritz received a letter from Orval L. DuBois, secretary for the Securities Exchange Bank in Philadelphia. Dated 4 December 1947 and addressed to Frederick Duquesne, U.S. Penitentiary, Leavenworth, Kansas, the letter is rife with black humor:

You became registered as a broker and dealer transacting business on over-the-counter markets on March 23, 1939. . . . [Our] information . . . indicates that you have ceased to do business as a broker or dealer.

Under the circumstances, you are hereby notified that your registration as a broker-dealer will be cancelled . . . unless on or before January 15, 1948, you file a written statement with the Commission to show cause why your registration should not be cancelled on a finding that you are no longer engaged in business as a broker or dealer.

There is no record of a reply. (Notorious Offenders File.)

2. Newkirk phone interview, 12 Nov. 1974.

3. Ibid., 9 Nov. 1974. Unless otherwise noted, all subsequent details in this chapter are from this source.

4. Gilman, "How G-Men Trapped," *True Detective*, Dec. 1942, 72.

Chapter 20: The Rest of the Players

1. Floherty, *Inside the F.B.I.*, 135.

2. *Duquesne, et al., Espionage*, 28.

3. Hoover, "Hitler's Spying Sirens," 41.

4. Floherty, *Inside the F.B.I.*, 36, 137.

5. Collins, *FBI in Peace and War*, 214; *Duquesne, et al., Espionage*.

6. *Duquesne, et al., Espionage*, 28, 29; Gilman, "How G-Men Trapped," *True Detective*, Sept. 1942, 13.

7. *New York Times*, 20 Oct. 1976, 48.

8. Ibid., 19 Mar. 1941; *Newsweek*, 7 July 1941, 14.

9. *New York Times*, 13 Oct. 1942, 25; 16 Mar. 1943, 13.

10. Gilman, "How G-Men Trapped," *True Detective*, Sept. 1942, 12, 13.

11. Farago, *Foxes*, 32.

12. Friedemann phone interview, 29 Nov. 1974.

13. Floherty, *Inside the F.B.I.*, 137; Collins, *FBI in Peace and War*, 214.

14. Gilman, "How G-Men Trapped," *True Detective*, Oct. 1942, 34.

15. Sayers and Kahn, *Sabotage*, 27; Gilman, "How G-Men Trapped," *True Detective*, Sept. 1942, 75.

16. Gilman, "How G-Men Trapped," *True Detective*, Oct. 1942, 100.

17. Ibid., Nov. 1942, 36.

18. Ritter, *Deckname*, 84.

19. Gilman, "How G-Men Trapped," *True Detective*, Nov. 1942, 37.

20. Farago, *Foxes*, 47.

21. *Look* editors, *Story of the FBI*, 225.

22. Gilman, "How G-Men Trapped," *True Detective*, Oct. 1942, 109.

23. Ibid., 35.

24. Sayers and Kahn, *Sabotage*, 29; Gilman, "How G-Men Trapped," *True Detective*, Oct. 1942, 34.

25. Dr. Ralph Hadley Bullard was chairman of the Department of Chemistry of Hobart and William Smith Colleges in Geneva, New York. He had in-

vented an anti–mustard gas compound that made it possible to spray clothing and give complete protection from the poisonous mists of mustard gas, which would otherwise pass through the clothing and cause severe burns and blisters. News of the compound was released by the wire services on 5 January 1939 (*Syracuse Herald*, 5 Jan. 1939), thus announcing the discovery to the Germans. Bullard served as a full commander and technical aide to the director of the Naval Research Laboratory at Anacostia during the war and retired from the U.S. Naval Reserve in 1958 with the rank of captain. He died 2 November 1961, with death attributed to a recurring respiratory ailment caused by years of inhalation of poisonous gases in laboratory research. He was buried at Arlington National Cemetery. (Hobart and William Smith Colleges News Bureau releases, 2–3 Nov. 1961.)

26. *New York Herald Tribune*, 17 Sept. 1941; Warrant of Commitment, Trial Docket Cr 38425, FRC container no. 547802, General Services Administration, Federal Records Center, New York.

27. Gilman, "How G-Men Trapped," *True Detective*, Oct. 1942, 35.

28. Ibid., 110.

29. Johnson phone interview, 25 Nov. 1974.

30. *New York Sun*, 16 Sept. 1941.

31. Gilman, "How G-Men Trapped," *True Detective*, Nov. 1942, 100.

Chapter 21: "You're under Arrest, Fritz"

1. Farago, *Foxes*, 327; Toledano, *J. Edgar Hoover*, 194.

2. Gilman, "How G-Men Trapped," *True Detective*, Nov. 1942, 36.

3. Ibid., 97.

4. Ibid., 98, 99.

5. Friedemann phone interview, 29 Nov. 1974.

6. Ibid.

7. Hynd, *Passport to Treason*, 173.

8. Farago, *Foxes*, 326.

9. FBI photo, *Justitia*, Jan. 1963, 111; Tully, *FBI's Most Famous Cases*, 149.

10. Tully, *FBI's Most Famous Cases*, 135.

11. Hynd, *Passport to Treason*, 93; Gilman, "How G-Men Trapped," *True Detective*, Dec. 1942, 38.

12. Farago, *Foxes*, 328, 329 (Farago wrongly attributes the scoop to Fritz); *New York Times*, 4 Oct. 1941, 7.

13. Riess, *Total Espionage*, 14.

14. Johnson phone interview, 25 Nov. 1974.

15. "Greatest Spy Roundup in U.S. History," *Life*, 14 July 1941, 25.

16. *Los Angeles Times*, 30 June 1941, 2.

17. Friedemann phone interview, 29 Nov. 1974. All information pertaining to Fritz's office meeting with Sawyer is from the FBI special agents involved and the following sources: *Los Angeles Examiner*, 18 Sept. 1941; *New York Her-*

ald-Tribune, 18 Sept. 1941, 1; *New York News,* 18 Sept. 1941, 1; *New York Sun,* 17 Sept. 1941, 1, and 23 Oct. 1941, 1; *New York Times,* 18 Sept. 1941, 13; Gilman, "How G-Men Trapped," *True Detective,* Dec. 1942, 70.

18. Friedemann phone interview, 29 Nov. 1974.

19. Newkirk phone interview, 12 Nov. 1974.

20. Ibid.; *New York Sun,* 18 Sept. 1941, 1.

21. Newkirk phone interview, 9 Nov. 1974.

22. Ibid.

23. *New York Sun,* 18 Sept. 1941, 1.

24. *New York Times,* 30 June 1941, 1; *Time,* 4 June 1956, 67.

25. *New York Times,* 30 June 1941, 3.

26. Ibid.; *New York Herald-Tribune,* 30 June 1941, 1; "Spies!" *Time,* 7 July 1941; Riess, *Total Espionage,* 288.

27. Floherty, *Inside the F.B.I.,* 142.

28. *New York Times,* 30 June 1941, 3.

29. Collins, *FBI in Peace and War,* 217.

30. Friedemann phone interview, 29 Nov. 1974.

31. Newkirk phone interview, 9 Nov. 1974.

32. Farago, *Foxes,* 458.

33. Ibid., 460–63.

34. Ritter, *Deckname,* chap. 23.

35. *Look* editors, *Story of the FBI,* 223, 224.

36. Ibid., 225.

37. Ritter, *Deckname,* 292.

38. *New York Times,* 30 June 1941, 3.

Chapter 22: Bombshells in the Courtroom and Fireworks from Fritz

1. *House on 92nd Street,* last reel; *Army-Navy Screen Magazine,* no. 42, reel 1, record group 3, accession 2355, National Archives; *New York Sun,* 30 June 1941, 1; Gilman, "How G-Men Trapped," *True Detective,* Dec. 1942, 36, 37; *New York Times,* 1 July 1941, 1.

2. Gilman, "How G-Men Trapped," *True Detective,* Dec. 1942, 4.

3. Herz interview, 28 June 1973.

4. *New York Times,* 6 Mar. 1962, 35.

5. Herz interview, 28 June 1973.

6. Ibid.

7. Ibid.; *New York Times,* 4 Sept. 1941, 4.

8. Herz interview, 28 June 1973; *New York Times,* 2 Oct. 1941, 18.

9. Herz interview, 28 June 1973.

10. Ibid.

11. Friedemann phone interview, 29 Nov. 1974.

12. *New York Times,* 4 Sept. 1941, 4.

13. Duquesne, letter to Herman Linding, 29 Dec. 1941 (author's collection).

14. *New York Times,* 9 Sept. 1941, 1.

15. Herz interview, 28 June 1973.

16. *New York Times,* 9 Sept. 1941, 14.

17. Ibid.

18. Ibid.

19. *New York Times,* 11 Sept. 1941, 27.

20. Ibid.

21. Johnson phone interview, 25 Nov. 1974.

22. Ibid.

23. *New York Sun,* 18 Sept. 1941.

24. Herz interview, 28 June 1973.

25. Newkirk phone interview, 9 Nov. 1974.

26. Ibid.; Friedemann phone interview, 29 Nov. 1974.

27. *New York Sun,* 21 Oct. 1941, 1.

28. Ibid., 22 Oct. 1941, 1.

29. *New York Times,* 22 Oct. 1941, 46.

30. *New York Sun,* 21 Oct. 1941, 1.

31. *New York Times,* 22 Oct. 1941, 46.

32. *New York Sun,* 21 Oct. 1941, 1.

33. Ibid., 22 Oct. 1941, 1.

34. *Los Angeles Examiner,* 23 Oct. 1941; *New York Times,* 23 Oct. 1941, 11.

35. *New York Sun,* 22 Oct. 1941, 1.

36. Newkirk interview, 9 Nov. 1974.

37. *New York Sun,* 22 Oct. 1941, 1.

38. *New York Times,* 23 Oct. 1941, 1.

39. *New York Sun,* 23 Oct. 1941, 1.

40. *Los Angeles Times,* 23 Oct. 1941; *New York Herald-Tribune,* 24 Oct. 1941; *New York Times,* 24 Oct. 1941, 7.

41. *Los Angeles Times,* 24 Oct. 1941.

42. *New York Sun,* 23, 24 Oct. 1941; *New York Herald-Tribune,* 24 Oct. 1941.

43. *New York Times,* 24 Oct. 1941, 7.

44. *New York Sun,* 23, 24 Oct. 1941; *New York Times,* 24 Oct. 1941.

45. *Los Angeles Examiner,* 24 Oct. 1941.

46. *New York Times,* 31 Oct. 1941, 20.

47. Herz interview, 28 June 1973.

48. *New York Times,* 11 Dec. 1941, 4; 12 Dec. 1941, 1.

49. Ibid., 12 Dec. 1941, 1.

50. Ibid., 13 Dec. 1941, 1.

51. Tully, *FBI's Most Famous Cases,* 130.

52. Duquesne, letter to Herman Linding, 29 Dec. 1941 (author's collection).

53. *New York Times,* 3 Jan. 1942, 1.

54. Friedemann phone interview, 29 Nov. 1974.

55. *New York Times,* 3 Jan. 1942, 1.

56. Friedemann phone interview, 29 Nov. 1974.

57. Ibid.

58. Hynd, *Passport to Treason,* 306.

59. Gilman, "How G-Men Trapped," *True Detective,* Dec. 1942, 72; Friedemann phone interview, 29 Nov. 1974.

Chapter 23: No Escape for 5051-H

1. All information pertaining to Fritz Duquesne's incarceration at the
United States Penitentiary in Leavenworth, Kansas, and at the Medical Center
for Federal Prisoners in Springfield, Missouri, has been obtained from the Notorious Offenders File. It includes special progress reports, psychiatric and
medical summaries, memorandums, letters, and legal appeals.

2. Transvaal Archives Depot, ref. no. T16/4/3.

3. Parole information from Department of Justice, Bureau of Prisons, Norman A. Carlson, director, 15 Mar. 1976.

4. Herz interview, 28 June 1973.

Chapter 24: Last Adventure for the Black Panther of the Veld

1. Duquesne, letter to Linding, 9 May 1951 (author's collection).

2. Notification of release, form no. 279, Medical Center for Federal Prisoners, Springfield, Missouri, 19 Sept. 1954, in Notorious Offenders File.

3. Linding, letter to author, 2 July 1972.

4. Darlow Johnson, supervisor, classification and parole, letter to E. Fred
Sweet, chief U.S. probation officer, Southern District of New York, 11 Oct. 1954,
in Notorious Offenders File.

5. Ibid.; Sweet and Evelyn Panella, U.S. probation officer, letter to Johnson,
28 Sept. 1954, in Notorious Offenders File.

6. Duquesne, letter to Linding, 25 Jan. 1955 (author's collection).

7. Ibid., 10 July 1955.

8. Ibid.

9. Ibid., 14 July 1955.

10. Ibid., undated.

11. Bim Pond, letter to Linding, 29 Oct. 1959 (author's collection).

12. *Adventurer* bulletin, Jan. 1956, 7–9.

13. Ibid., 8, 9.

14. Cloete, letter to author, 16 Jan. 1973 (author's collection).

15. *New York Times,* 26 May 1956, 7.

16. Linding, letter to author, 2 July 1972; Mulholland phone interview, 11
Nov. 1972.

17. Boshoff, "Die Baas," 7.

18. Mulholland phone interview, 15 Jan. 1995.

19. *Wilkes-Barre Times-Ledger, Evening News, Record,* 8 May 1974.

20. Boshoff, "Die Baas," 7.

Bibliography

Partial List of the Published Writings of Fritz Duquesne

Articles
"African Big Game Hunting Made Easy." *The Travel Magazine* 15 (May 1910).
"Autobiographical Letter." *Adventure* 2 (Dec. 1913).
"The Fighting Dwarfs of the Congo." *Adventure* 4 (June 1912).
"A Fire-Hunt at Kivu." *Adventure* 7 (Dec. 1913).
"Hunting African Big Game." *Field and Stream* (Aug. 1909).
"Hunting ahead of Roosevelt in East Africa." *Hampton's Magazine* 22, nos. 2 and 3 (Feb. and Mar. 1909).
"The Man-Eaters of M'Wembi." *Adventure* 1 (Jan. 1911).
"Sekokoeni's Raid." *Adventure* 1 (Dec. 1910).
"Shooting a Big Elephant." *Washington Post*, 24 Jan. 1909, 3:1. [Un-bylined excerpt from *Hampton's Magazine*, Feb. 1909.]
"Tracking the Man-Killer." *Everybody's Magazine* 24 (Mar. 1911).
"Trapping Big Game in the Heart of Africa." *Hampton's Magazine* 23 (Aug. 1909).
"When the Rain Was Red." *Adventure* 2 (Sept. 1911).
"Will Roosevelt Return Alive?" *The Travel Magazine* 15 (Mar. 1910).

Novels
Cossack Life. Published in *Le Petit Bleu du Matin.*
Lost in the Bush. Published in South Africa.
The Spectacles of War. Published in South Africa.

Plays
The Harlequin King. Copyright listing only in Library of Congress. Destroyed in periodic cleaning of shelves.
Perdu. Published in Brussels.
The Yankee Amazon. Copyright listing only in Library of Congress. Destroyed in periodic cleaning of shelves.

Other

East Africa, the Wonderland of Roosevelt's Hunt: A Lecture by Captain Fritz Duquesne—Soldier, Hunter, Author. 1909. Lecture brochure, Theodore Roosevelt Collection, Harvard College Library.

"Why Vote for Roosevelt?" By A Democrat. 1912. Political pamphlet, Library of Congress.

Books

Akron Directory. 1914.

American Biographical Directory, District of Columbia: Concise Biographies of Its Prominent and Representative Contemporary Citizens and Valuable Statistical Data, 1908–09. Washington, D.C.: Potomac, 1908.

Amery, L. S., ed. *The Times History of the War in South Africa, 1899–1902.* Vols. 1–7. London: Sampson, Low, Marston, 1900–1909.

Amos, James E. *Theodore Roosevelt: Hero to His Valet.* New York: John Day, 1927.

Andrew, Christopher. *Her Majesty's Secret Service: The Making of the British Intelligence Community.* New York: Viking, 1986.

Aston, George. *Secret Service.* New York: Cosmopolitan, 1930.

Baedeker, Karl. *Northern Germany, as Far as the Bavarian and Austrian Frontiers: Handbook for Travellers.* New York: Charles Scribner's Sons, 1904.

———, ed. *The United States, with an Excursion into Mexico.* New York: Charles Scribner's Sons, 1899.

Bartz, Carl. *The Downfall of the German Secret Service.* London: William Kimber, 1956.

Beesly, Patrick. *The Codebreakers of Room 40: British Naval Intelligence, 1914–18.* New York: Harcourt Brace Jovanovich, 1982.

Behlmer, Rudy, ed. *Memo from Darryl F. Zanuck: The Golden Years at Twentieth Century–Fox.* New York: Grove, 1993.

Benbow, Colin H. *Boer Prisoners of War in Bermuda.* Devonshire, Bermuda: Bermuda College, 1994.

Bennett, James V. *I Chose Prison.* New York: Alfred Knopf, 1970.

Benton, Joel. *Memories of the Twilight Club.* New York: Broadway, 1910.

Bernstorff, Count Johann-Heinrich. *Memoirs.* Translated from the German by Eric Sutton. New York: Random House, 1936.

Bishop, Joseph Bucklin. *Theodore Roosevelt and His Time Shown in His Own Letters.* Vol. 2. New York: Charles Scribner's Sons, 1920.

Blackburn, Douglas, and W. Waithman Caddell. *Secret Service in South Africa.* London: Cassell, 1911.

Bleiler, Richard J. *The* Adventure Magazine *Index.* Vols. 1 and 2. Mercer Island, Wash.: Starmont House, 1991.

Blerk, J. A. van. *Op De Bermudas Beland.* Cape Town: A. A. Belkema, 1949.

Bodry-Sanders, Penelope. *Carl Akeley: Africa's Collector, Africa's Savior.* New York: Paragon House, 1991.

Bonner, M. G. *The Real Book about Crime Detection.* Garden City, N.Y.: Doubleday, 1957.

Braynard, Frank, and William H. Miller. *Fifty Famous Liners.* New York: W. W. Norton, 1982.

———. *Fifty Famous Liners 2.* New York: W. W. Norton, 1985.

Breuer, William. *Hitler's Undercover War: The Nazi Espionage Invasion of the U.S.A.* New York: St. Martin's, 1989.

Brissaud, Andre. Canaris. *The Biography of Admiral Canaris, Chief of German Military Intelligence in the Second World War.* Translated and edited by Ian Colvin. New York: Grosset and Dunlap, 1974.

———. *The Nazi Secret Service.* Translated from the French by Milton Waldman. New York: W. W. Norton, 1974.

Buranelli, Prosper. *Maggie of the Suicide Fleet, as Written from the Log of Raymond D. Borden, U.S.N.R.* Garden City, N.Y.: Doubleday, Doran, 1930.

Buranelli, Vincent, and Nan Buranelli. *Spy/Counterspy: An Encyclopedia of Espionage.* New York: McGraw-Hill, 1982.

Burke, John. *Duet in Diamonds: The Flamboyant Saga of Lillian Russell and Diamond Jim Brady in America's Gilded Age.* New York: G. P. Putnam's Sons, 1972.

Burnham, Frederick. *Scouting on Two Continents.* Elicited and arranged by Mary Nixon Everett. Garden City, N.Y.: Doubleday, Page, 1926.

———. *Taking Chances.* Elicited and arranged by Mary Nixon Everett. Los Angeles: Haynes, 1944.

Caldwell, Theodore C., ed. *The Anglo-Boer War: Why Was It Fought? Who Was Responsible?* Problems in European Civilization series. Boston: D. C. Heath, Feb. 1965.

Cameron, Kenneth M. *Into Africa: The Story of the East African Safari.* London: Constable, 1990.

Carl, Ernst. *One against England: The Death of Lord Kitchener and the Plot against the British Fleet.* New York: E. P. Dutton, 1935.

Carlson, John Roy. *The Plotters.* New York: E. P. Dutton, 1946.

———. *Under Cover.* New York: E. P. Dutton, 1943.

Casey, William. *The Secret War against Hitler.* Washington, D.C.: Regnery Gateway, 1979.

Cave Brown, Anthony. *"C": The Secret Life of Sir Stewart Graham Menzies, Spymaster to Winston Churchill.* New York: Macmillan, 1987.

———. *The Last Hero: Wild Bill Donovan.* New York: Times Books, 1982.

Chapple, Joe Mitchell. *Favorite Heart Throbs of Famous People.* New York: Grosset and Dunlap, 1929.

Chenery, William L., ed. *The University Club: Yesterday and Today.* New York: University Club, 1955.

Churchill, Allen. *The Great White Way: A Re-creation of Broadway's Golden Era of Theatrical Entertainment.* New York: E. P. Dutton, 1962.

———. *Park Row.* New York: Rinehart, 1958.

Churchill, Winston S. *The Second World War.* Vol. 1, *The Gathering Storm.* Boston: Houghton Mifflin, 1948.

City of Cape Town Official Guide. Cape Town: R. Beerman, 1954.

Clammer, David. *The Zulu War.* Newton Abbot, Devon: David and Charles, 1973.

Clark, William Bell. *When the U-Boats Came to America.* Boston: Little, Brown, 1929.

Cloete, Stuart. *Rags of Glory.* Garden City, N.Y.: Doubleday, 1963.

Collier, Joy. *Portrait of Cape Town.* London: Longmans, 1961.

Collins, Frederick L. *The FBI in Peace and War.* G. P. Putnam's Sons, 1943.

Colvin, Ian. *Master Spy: The Incredible Story of Admiral William Canaris, Who, While Hitler's Chief of Intelligence, Was a Secret Ally of the British.* New York: McGraw-Hill, 1951.

Cook, Fred J. *The FBI Nobody Knows.* New York: Macmillan, 1964.

Cooper, Page. *The Bellevue Story.* New York: Thomas Y. Crowell, 1948.

Corson, William R. *The Armies of Ignorance: The Rise of the American Intelligence Empire.* New York: Dial Press/James Whale, 1977.

Courtney, Charles, with Tom Johnson. *Unlocking Adventure.* New York: Whitlesey House, 1942.

Creel, George. *Rebel at Large: Recollections of Fifty Crowded Years.* New York: G. P. Putnam's Sons, 1947.

Creswicke, Louis. *South Africa and the Transvaal War.* Vols. 1–6. Edinburgh: T. C. and E. C. Jack, 1901.

Cutright, Paul Russell. *Theodore Roosevelt: The Making of a Conservationist.* Urbana and Chicago: University of Illinois Press, 1985.

———. *Theodore Roosevelt: The Naturalist.* New York: Harper and Brothers, 1956.

Davies, R.E.G. *Pan Am: An Airline and Its Aircraft.* New York: Orion, 1987.

Dawson, Warrington. *Opportunity and Theodore Roosevelt.* Chicago: Honest Truth, 1924.

Deacon, Richard. *A History of the British Secret Service.* New York: Taplinger, 1969.

DeArment, Robert K. *Bat Masterson: The Man and the Legend.* Norman: University of Oklahoma Press, 1979.

De Kock, W. J., ed. *Dictionary of South African Biography.* Vol. 1. Pretoria: Nasionale Boekhanel Bbk., for National Council for Social Research, Department of Higher Education, 1968.

Demaris, Ovid. *The Director: An Oral Biography of J. Edgar Hoover.* New York: Harper's Magazine, 1975.

De Villiers, C. C., and C. Pama. *Geslagsregister van die Ou Kaapse Families: Genealogies of Old South African Families.* Vol. I, *A–K.* Cape Town: Balkema, 1966.

Diamond, Sander A. *The Nazi Movement in the U.S, 1924–1941.* Ithaca: Cornell University Press, 1974.

Dos Passos, John. *Mr. Wilson's War.* Garden City, N.Y.: Doubleday, 1962.

Downey, Farfax. *Portrait of an Era as Drawn by C. D. Gibson.* New York: Charles Scribner's Sons, 1936.

Downs, Mike. *The Adventurers: A History of the Adventurers Club of New York.* New York: Adventurers Club, 1965.

Doyle, Arthur Conan. *The Great Boer War.* Cape Town–Johannesburg: C. Struik, 1976.

Drinnon, Richard. *Rebel in Paradise: A Biography of Emma Goldman.* Chicago: University of Chicago Press, 1961.

Dupuy, R. Ernest, and Trevor N. Dupuy. *The Encyclopedia of Military History from 3500 B.C. to the Present*. New York: Harper and Row, 1986.

Elite Catalogue of Clubs for 1890–91: The Annual Club Book of New York and Vicinity. New York: Club Publishing Company, 1890.

Emerson, Barbara. *Leopold II of the Belgians, King of Colonialism*. New York: St. Martin's, 1979.

Emerson, Edwin, Jr. *Pepys's Ghost*. Boston: Richard G. Badger, 1900.

"Erratic." *Bermuda: Generally Compiled from Extracts of a "Year's Diary."* Bermuda: Royal Gazette, 1893.

Esher, Reginald. *The Tragedy of Lord Kitchener*. London: John Murray, 1922.

Explorers Club, Members of the. *Through Hell and High Water*. New York: Robert M. McBride, 1941.

Farago, Ladislas. *The Game of the Foxes: The Untold Story of German Espionage in the United States and Great Britain during World War II*. New York: David McKay, 1971.

———. *War of Wits: The Anatomy of Espionage and Intelligence*. New York: Funk and Wagnalls, 1954.

Farwell, Byron. *The Great Anglo-Boer War*. New York: Harper and Row, 1976.

Federal Writers' Project of the Works Progress Administration in New York City. *The WPA Guide to New York City: The Federal Writers' Project Guide to 1930s New York*. New York: Pantheon, 1939. Rpt. 1982.

Fielding, Raymond. *The March of Time, 1935–1951*. New York: Oxford University Press, 1978.

Fisher, John. *The Afrikaners*. London: Cassell, 1969.

Fitch, Herbert T. *Traitors Within: The Adventures of Detective Inspector Herbert T. Fitch*. London: Hurst and Blackett, 1933.

Floherty, John J. *Inside the F.B.I.* Philadelphia: J. B. Lippincott, 1943.

Fowler, William B. *British-American Relations, 1917–1918: The Role of Sir William Wiseman*. Princeton, N.J.: Princeton University Press, 1969.

Franklin, Charles. *The Great Spies*. New York: Hart, 1967.

Gardner, Joseph L. *Departing Glory: Theodore Roosevelt as Ex-President*. New York: Charles Scribner's Sons, 1973.

Gibbs, Peter. *Death of the Last Republic: The Story of the Anglo-Boer War*. London: Frederick Muller, 1957.

Goldman, Emma. *Living My Life*. Vol. 2. New York: Alfred A. Knopf, 1931.

Gordon-Brown, A., ed. *The South and East African Year Book and Guide*. London: Sampson, Low, Marston, 1949.

Goulart, Ron. *Cheap Thrills: An Informal History of the Pulp Magazines*. New Rochelle, N.Y.: Arlington House, 1972.

Graves, Armgaard, with Edward Lyell Fox. *The Secrets of the German War Office*. New York: McBride, Nast, 1914.

Great Britain War Office, Intelligence Division. *Boer Army List*. Cape Town: Intelligence Office, 1902.

Griffith, Kenneth. *Thank God We Kept the Flag Flying: The Siege and Relief of Ladysmith, 1899–1900*. New York: Viking, 1974.

Gross, Alexander. *The Complete Guide to New York City: Manhattan and Bronx*. New York: "Geographia" Map Company and Interborough News Company, 1940.

Hagedorn, Hermann. *The Roosevelt Family of Sagamore Hill.* New York: Macmillan, 1954.

Halacy, Dan. *The Master Spy.* New York: McGraw-Hill, 1968.

Hart, Albert Bushnell, and Herbert Ronald Ferleger, eds. *Theodore Roosevelt Cyclopedia.* New York: Roosevelt Memorial Association, 1941.

Hays, Arthur Garfield. *City Lawyer: The Autobiography of a Law Practice.* New York: Simon and Schuster, 1942.

Henry, O. *Complete Works.* Vol. 1. Foreword by Harry Hansen. Garden City, N.Y.: Doubleday, 1953.

Hersey, Harold Brainerd. *Pulpwood Editor: The Fabulous World of the Thriller Magazines Revealed by a Veteran Editor and Publisher.* New York: Frederick A. Stokes, 1937.

Herwig, Holger H., and Neil M. Hayman. *Biographical Dictionary of World War I.* Westport, Conn.: Greenwood, 1982.

Hilton, Stanley E. *Hitler's Secret War in South America, 1939–1945: German Military Espionage and Allied Counterespionage in Brazil.* Baton Rouge: Louisiana State University Press, 1981.

Hohne, Heinz. *Canaris.* Translated from the German by J. Maxwell Brownjohn. Garden City, N.Y.: Doubleday, 1979.

Holmes, Richard. *The Little Field-Marshal: Sir John French.* London: Jonathan Cape, 1981.

Holt, Edgar. *The Boer War.* London: Putnam, 1958.

Hoyt, Edwin P. *Teddy Roosevelt in Africa.* New York: Duell, Sloan, and Pearce, 1986.

Hynd, Alan. *Passport to Treason: The Inside Story of Spies in America.* New York: National Travel Club, 1943.

Irwin, Will. *The Making of a Reporter.* New York: G. P. Putnam's Sons, 1942.

Irwin, Will, and Thomas M. Johnson. *What You Should Know about Spies and Saboteurs.* New York: W. W. Norton, 1943.

Jackson, Stanley. *Caruso.* New York: Stein and Day, 1972.

Jones, John Price, and Paul Merrick Hollister. *The German Secret Service in America.* Boston: Small, Maynard, 1918.

Jones, Virgil Carrington. *Roosevelt's Rough Riders.* Garden City, N.Y.: Doubleday, 1971.

Jong, Louis de. *The German Fifth Column in the Second World War.* Translated from the Dutch by C. M. Geyl. Chicago: University of Chicago Press, 1956.

Kahn, David. *The Codebreakers: The Story of Secret Writing.* New York: Macmillan, 1967.

———. *Hitler's Spies: German Military Intelligence in World War II.* New York: Macmillan, 1978.

Keller, Allan. *The Spanish-American War: A Compact History.* New York: Hawthorn, 1969.

Kennedy, David M. *Over Here: The First World War and American Society.* New York: Oxford University Press, 1980.

Kludas, Arnold. *Great Passenger Ships of the World.* Wellingborough: Patrick Stephens. Vol. 1, *1858–1912* (1985). Vol. 2, *1913–1923* (1984). Vol. 3, *1924–1935* (1984).

Knightley, Phillip. *The Second Oldest Profession: Spies and Spying in the Twentieth Century.* London: Andre Deutsch, 1986.

Koeves, Tibor. *Satan in Top Hat: The Biography of Franz von Papen.* New York: Alliance, 1941.

Konig, Captain Paul. *Voyage of the Deutschland: The First Merchant Submarine.* New York: Hearst's International Library, 1917.

Koss, Stephen, ed. *The Pro-Boers: The Anatomy of an Antiwar Movement.* Chicago: University of Chicago Press, 1973.

Kruger, Paul. *Die President en Ek.* Cape Town: Tafelberg, 1971.

Kruger, Rayne. *Good-bye Dolly Gray: The Story of the Boer War.* Philadelphia: J. B. Lippincott, 1980.

Landau, Henry. *The Enemy Within: The Inside Story of German Sabotage in America.* New York: G. P. Putnam's Sons, 1937.

Langford, Gerald. *The Richard Harding Davis Years: A Biography of a Mother and Son.* New York: Holt, Rinehart, and Winston, 1961.

Lavine, Harold. *Fifth Column in America.* New York: Doubleday, Doran, 1940.

Lee, Emanoel. *To the Bitter End: A Photographic History of the Boer War, 1899–1902.* New York: Viking, 1985.

Leonard, John W. *Who's Who in New York City and State: A Biographical Dictionary of Contemporaries.* New York: L. R. Hamersly, 1905, 1907, 1909.

Leverkuehn, Paul. *German Military Intelligence.* London: Weidenfeld and Nicolson, 1954.

Lichtenstein, Perry M. *A Doctor Studies Crime.* New York: D. Van Nostrand, 1934.

Lipschutz, Mark R., and R. Kent Rasmussen. *Dictionary of African Historical Biography.* Chicago: Aldine, 1978.

Litvag, Irving. *The Master of Sunnybank: A Biography of Albert Payson Terhune.* New York: Harper and Row, 1977.

Lloyd's Register of American Yachts for 1903–1904. New York: Lloyd's Register of Shipping.

Look, editors of. *Movie Lot to Beachhead: The Motion Picture Goes to War and Prepares for the Future.* Garden City, N.Y.: Doubleday, Doran, 1945.

———. *The Story of the FBI: The Official Picture History of the Federal Bureau of Investigation.* New York: E. P. Dutton, 1947.

Lowenthal, Max. *The Federal Bureau of Investigation.* New York: Harcourt Brace Jovanovich, 1950.

McCabe, James D., Jr. *New York by Sunlight and Gaslight: A Work Descriptive of the Great American Metropolis.* Philadelphia: Hubbard Brothers, 1882.

McCormick, Donald. *The Mystery of Lord Kitchener's Death.* London: Putnam, 1959.

McKelway, St. Clair. *True Tales from the Annals of Crime and Rascality.* New York: Random House, 1950.

Magnus, Philip. *Kitchener: Portrait of an Imperialist.* New York: E. P. Dutton, 1959.

Malone, Dumas, ed. *Dictionary of American Biography.* Vol. 15. New York: Charles Scribner's Sons, 1935.

Maltin, Leonard. *The Great Movie Shorts.* New York: Bonanza, 1972.

Manchester, William. *The Arms of Krupp, 1587–1968.* Boston: Little, Brown, 1968.

Manhattan Address Telephone Directory. Various years.

Manhattan Telephone Directory. Various years.

Martin, A. C. *The Concentration Camps, 1900–1902: Facts, Figures, and Fables.* Foreword by Arthur Keppel-Jones. Cape Town: Howard Timmings, 1957.

Martindale-Hubbell Law Directory. Summit, N.J.: Martindale-Hubbell, 1971.

Miers, Earl Schenck. *The Story of the F.B.I.* New York: Grosset and Dunlap, 1965.

Millais, J. G. *Life of Frederick Courtenay Selous, D.S.O.* London: Longmans, Green, 1919.

Miller, Nathan. *Spying for America: The Hidden History of U.S. Intelligence.* New York: Paragon House, 1989.

Milton, Joyce. *The Yellow Kids: Foreign Correspondents in the Heyday of Yellow Journalism.* New York: Harper and Row, 1989.

Mitchell, Edward P. *Memoirs of an Editor: Fifty Years of American Journalism.* New York: Charles Scribner's Sons, 1924.

Mock, James R., and Cedric Larson. *Words That Won the War: The Story of the Committee on Public Information, 1917–1919.* Princeton, N.J.: Princeton University Press, 1939.

Montgomery Hyde, H. *The Quiet Canadian: The Secret Service Story of Sir William Stephenson.* London: Hamish Hamilton, 1962.

———. *Room 3603: The Story of the British Intelligence Center in New York during World War II.* New York: Farrar, Straus, 1963.

———. *Secret Intelligence Agent.* New York: St. Martin's, 1982.

Morison, Elting E., ed. *The Letters of Theodore Roosevelt.* Cambridge, Mass.: Harvard University Press. Vol. 6, *The Big Stick, 1907–1909* (1952). Vol. 7, *The Days of Armageddon, 1909–1914* (1954). Vol. 8, *The Days of Armageddon, 1914–1919* (1954).

Morris, Donald R. *The Washing of the Spears: A History of the Zulu Nation under Shaka and Its Fall in the Zulu War of 1879.* New York: Simon and Schuster, 1965.

Morton, H. V. *In Search of South Africa.* New York: Dodd, Mead, 1948.

Nash, Jay Robert. *Bloodletters and Badmen: A Narrative Encyclopedia of American Criminals from the Pilgrims to the Present.* New York: M. Evans, J. B. Lippincott, 1973.

———. *Citizen Hoover: A Critical Study of the Life and Times of J. Edgar Hoover and His FBI.* Chicago: Nelson-Hall, 1972.

———. *Darkest Hours: A Narrative Encyclopedia of Worldwide Disasters from Ancient Times to the Present.* Chicago: Nelson-Hall, 1976.

New York Times Obituaries Index. New York: New York Times. Vol. 1, *1858–1968* (1970). Vol. 2, *1969–1978* (1980).

Niezychowski, Alfred von. *The Cruise of the Kronprinz Wilhelm.* Garden City, N.Y.: Doubleday, Doran, 1929.

Nolen, Barbara, ed. *Spies, Spies, Spies.* New York: Franklin Watts, 1965.

O'Brien, Frank M. *The Story of the Sun: New York, 1833–1928.* New York: D. Appleton, 1928.

O'Reilly, Kenneth. *Hoover and the Un-Americans: The FBI, HUAC, and the Red Menace.* Philadelphia: Temple University Press, 1983.

O'Toole, G.J.A. *The Encyclopedia of American Intelligence and Espionage, from the Revolutionary War to the Present.* New York: Facts-on-File, 1988.

Otto, J. C. *Die Konsentrasie Kampe.* Cape Town: Nasional Boeckhandel, n.d.

Paine, Lauran. *German Military Intelligence in World War II: The Abwehr.* New York: Stein and Day, 1984.

Pakenham, Thomas. *The Boer War.* New York: Random House, 1979.

Papen, Franz von. *Memoirs.* Translated by Brian Connell. New York: E. P. Dutton, 1953.

Parish, James Robert, and Michael R. Pitts. *The Great Spy Pictures.* Edited by T. Allan Taylor. Metuchen, N.J.: Scarecrow, 1974.

Pilpel, Robert H. *To the Honor of the Fleet.* New York: Atheneum, 1979.

Pinchot, Gifford. *Breaking New Ground.* New York: Harcourt, Brace, 1947.

Polenberg, Richard. *Fighting Faiths: The Abrams Case, the Supreme Court, and Free Speech.* New York: Viking, 1987.

Pond, J. B. *Eccentricities of Genius: Memories of Famous Men and Women of the Platform and Stage.* New York: G. W. Dillingham, 1900.

Popov, Dusko. *Spy/Counterspy.* New York: Grosset and Dunlap, 1974.

Powers, Richard Gid. *Secrecy and Power: The Life of J. Edgar Hoover.* New York: Free Press, 1987.

Pringle, Henry F. *Theodore Roosevelt: A Biography.* New York: Harcourt, Brace, 1931.

Quigley, Martin S., ed. *First Century of Film.* New York: Quigley, 1995.

R. L. Polk and Co.'s Trow General Directory of New York City: Embracing the Boroughs of Manhattan and the Bronx. New York: R. L. Polk, 1902–17, 1931–41.

Ralph, Julian. *Towards Pretoria: A Record of the War between Britain and Boer to the Relief of Kimberley.* New York: Frederick A. Stokes, 1900.

Rawls, Walton. *Wake up America! World War I and the American Poster.* New York: Abbeville, 1988.

Reitz, Denys. *Commando: A Boer Journal of the Boer War.* New York: Charles Boni, 1930.

Reynolds, Quentin. *The F.B.I.* New York: Random House, 1954.

———. *I, Willie Sutton.* New York: Farrar, Straus, and Young, 1953.

Rider, Fremont, ed. *Rider's New York City: A Guide-Book for Travellers.* New York: Henry Holt, 1916, 1923.

Riess, Curt. *High Stakes: A Story of Strange People and Happenings.* New York: G. P. Putnam's Sons, 1942. [A novel based on the work of the several different spy rings operating in New York City in 1940–41, with several references to Fritz Duquesne and William Sebold.]

———. *Total Espionage.* New York: G. P. Putnam's Sons, 1941.

Rintelen, Captain [Franz Rintelen von Kleist]. *The Dark Invader: Wartime Reminiscences of a German Naval Intelligence Officer.* New York: Macmillan, 1933.

Ritter, Nikolaus. *Deckname Dr. Rantzau: Die Aufzeichnungen des Nickolaus Ritter, Offizier im Geheimen Nachrichtendienst.* Hamburg: Hoffmann und Campe, 1972.

Roberts, Chalmers. *The Washington Post: The First 100 Years.* Boston: Houghton Mifflin, 1977.

Robson, John, ed. *Baird's Manual of American College Fraternities.* Menasha, Wisc.: Baird's Manual Foundation, 1977.

Rollins, Richard. *I Find Treason: The Story of an American Anti-Nazi Agent.* New York: William Morrow, 1941.

Rondon, Cândido Mariano da Silva. *Lectures Delivered by Colonel Candido Mariano da Silva, on the Roosevelt-Rondon Scientific Expedition and the Telegraph Line Commission.* New York: Greenwood, 1969.

Roosevelt, Theodore. *African Game Trails: An Account of the African Wanderings of an American Hunter-Naturalist.* Editor's note by Peter Hathaway Capstick. New York: St. Martin's, 1988.

———. *The Rough Riders.* New York: Charles Scribner's Sons, 1899.

———. *Through the Brazilian Wilderness.* New York: Charles Scribner's Sons, 1914.

Rosenthal, Eric. *Southern African Dictionary of National Biography.* London: Warne, 1966.

Rotogravure Album of New York. 1910.

Rout, Leslie B., Jr., and John F. Bratzel. *The Shadow War: German Espionage and United States Counterespionage in Latin America during World War II.* Frederick, Md.: University Publications of America, 1986.

Royle, Trevor. *The Kitchener Enigma.* London: Michael Joseph, 1985.

Russell, Francis, and the editors of Time-Life Books. *The Secret War.* Alexandria, Va.: Time-Life Books, 1981.

Salmaggi, Cesare, and Alfredo Pallavisini, comps. *2194 Days of War: An Illustrated Chronology of the Second World War.* New York: Gallery Books, 1979.

Sampson, Philip J.. *The Capture of De Wet: The South African Rebellion, 1914.* London: Edward Arnold, 1915.

Sands, Frederick, and Sven Broman. *The Divine Garbo.* New York: Grosset and Dunlap, 1979.

Sayers, Michael, and Albert E. Kahn. *The Plot against the Peace: A Warning to the Nation.* New York: Harper and Row, 1945.

———. *Sabotage! The Secret War against America.* New York: Harper and Brothers, 1942.

Schorer, Mark. *Sinclair Lewis: An American Life.* New York: McGraw-Hill, 1961.

Server, Lee. *Danger Is My Business: An Illustrated History of the Fabulous Pulp Magazines.* San Francisco: Chronicle Books, 1993.

Sheean, Vincent. *Dorothy and Red.* Boston: Houghton Mifflin, 1963.

Shirer, William L. *The Rise and Fall of the Third Reich: A History of Nazi Germany.* New York: Simon and Schuster, 1960.

Shriner, Charles Anthony. *Paterson, New Jersey: Its Advantages for Manufacturing and Residence, Its Industries, Prominent Men, Banks, Schools, Churches, Etc.* Paterson: Board of Trade, 1890.

Siemens, Georg. *History of the House of Siemens.* Vol. 2. New York: Arno, 1977.

Silver, Alain, and Elizabeth Ward, eds. *Film Noir: An Encyclopedic Reference to the American Style.* Woodstock, N.Y.: Overlook, 1988.

Silver, Nathan. *Lost New York.* Boston: Houghton Mifflin, 1967.

Sinclair, David. *Dynasty: The Astors and Their Times.* New York: Beaufort, 1984.

Skaggs, William H. *German Conspiracies in America: From an American Point of View by an American.* London: T. Fisher Unwin 1915.

Small, H. B., and John J. Bushell. *The Handbook of Bermuda: Bushell's Handbook, History, Guide, Directory, and Compendium of Information on the Islands of Bermuda, Hamilton, and Paget.* Bermuda: Bushell's Handbook and General Printing Office, 1899.

Spivak, John L. *America Faces the Barricades.* New York: Covici Friede, 1935.

———. *A Man in His Time.* New York: Horizon, 1967.

———. *Secret Armies: The New Techniques of Nazi Warfare.* New York: Modern Age, 1939.

Steenkamp, E. *Helkampe.* Johannesburg: Voortrekker Pers, 1941.

Steffens, Lincoln. *Autobiography.* New York: Harcourt, Brace, and World, 1958.

Steinhauer, Gustave. *Steinhauer, the Kaiser's Master Spy: The Story as Told by Himself.* Edited by S. T. Felstead. New York: D. Appleton, 1931.

Sterling, George E. *Spies Use Radio: The Radio Intelligence Division in WWII.* Vol. 5 of *The AWA Review.* Holcomb, N.Y.: Antique Wireless Association, Aug. 1990.

Stevenson, William. *A Man Called Intrepid: The Secret War.* New York: Harcourt Brace Jovanovich, 1976.

Stieber, Wilhelm J.C.E. *The Chancellor's Spy: The Revelations of the Chief of Bismarck's Secret Service.* Translated from the German by Jan Van Heurck. New York: Grove, 1979.

Story of Germiston. Germiston: Publicity Association, 1966.

Strother, French. *Fighting Germany's Spies.* Garden City, N.Y.: Doubleday, Page, 1918.

Swanberg, W. A. *Pulitzer.* New York: Charles Scribner's Sons, 1967.

Taylor, John C. *German Warships of World War I.* Garden City, N.Y.: Doubleday, 1970.

Terblanche, A. *Emily Hobhouse.* Johannesburg: A.P.B. Bookstore, 1948.

Terhune, Albert Payson. *To the Best of My Memory.* New York: Harper and Brothers, 1930.

Thomas, Lately. *Delmonico's: A Century of Pleasure.* Boston: Houghton Mifflin, 1967.

Thomas, Lowell. *Rolling Stone: The Life and Adventures of Arthur Radclyffe Dugmore.* Garden City, N.Y.: Doubleday, Doran, 1931.

Thomas, Tony, and Aubrey Solomon. *The Films of 20th Century–Fox: A Pictorial History.* Secaucus, N.J.: Citadel, 1979.

Thomson, S. J. *The Transvaal Burgher Camps, South Africa.* Allahabad: Pioneer Press, 1904.

Thwaites, Norman. *Velvet and Vinegar.* London: Grayson and Grayson, 1932.

Toland, John. *The Dillinger Days.* New York: Random House, 1963.

Toledano, Ralph de. *J. Edgar Hoover: The Man in His Time.* New Rochelle, N.Y.: Arlington House, 1973.

Trager, James, ed. *The People's Chronology: A Year-by-Year Record of Human Events from Prehistory to the Present.* New York: Holt, Rinehart, and Winston, 1979.

Tully, Andrew. *The FBI's Most Famous Cases*. New York: William Morrow, 1965.

Tunney, Thomas J., as told to Paul Merrick Hollister. *Throttled! The Detection of the German and Anarchist Bomb Plotters*. Boston: Small, Maynard, 1919.

Turner, William W. *Hoover's FBI: The Men and the Myth*. Los Angeles: Sherbourne, 1970.

Ungar, Sanford J. *FBI*. Boston: Little, Brown, 1976.

U.S. Congress. *Hearings before the Committee on Agriculture during the Second Session of the Sixty-first Congress*. Vol. 3, *Hearings on Miscellaneous Bills. (H.R. 23261) Importation of Wild and Domestic Animals*. Washington, D.C.. Government Printing Office, 1910.

Viereck, George Sylvester. *The Hapless Boers*. Translated from the Dutch by Eugen Vroom [Viereck]. Scotch Plains, N.J.: Flanders Hall, 1940. [Dedication: Dedicated to Colonel Fritz Duquesne, Undaunted Warrior and Avenger of His Stricken Motherland.]

————. *Spreading Germs of Hate*. New York: Horace Liveright, 1930.

Viljoen, Ben. *My Reminiscences of the Anglo-Boer War*. London: Hood, Douglas, and Howard, 1902.

Walder, David. *The Short Victorious War: The Russo-Japanese Conflict, 1904–1905*. New York: Harper and Row, 1973.

Walker, Alexander. *Garbo: A Portrait*. New York: Macmillan, 1980.

Walker, Stanley. *City Editor*. New York: Frederick A. Stokes, 1934.

Warner, Denis, and Peggy Warner. *The Tide at Sunrise: A History of the Russo-Japanese War, 1904–1905*. New York: Charterhouse, 1974.

Warner, Philip. *Kitchener: The Man behind the Legend*. New York: Atheneum, 1986.

Washington, D.C., City Directory. 1909.

Weber, Harvey A. *Centerport*. Centerport: H. B. Davis, 1990.

Wells, Carveth. *Bermuda in Three Colors*. New York: Robert M. McBride, 1935.

West, James E., and Peter O. Lamb. *He-Who-Sees-in-the-Dark: The Boys' Story of Frederick Burnham, the American Scout*. New York: Brewer, Warren, and Putnam, 1932.

West, Nigel. *MI6: British Secret Intelligence Service Operations, 1909–45*. New York: Random House, 1983.

Wexler, Emma. *Emma Goldman in Exile: From the Russian Revolution to the Spanish Civil War*. Boston: Beacon, 1989.

Weyl, Nathaniel. *The Battle against Disloyalty*. New York: Thomas Y. Crowell, 1951.

Whalen, Richard J. *The Founding Father: The Story of Joseph P. Kennedy*. New York: New American Library, 1964.

Whitehead, Don. *The FBI Story: A Report to the People*. New York: Random House, 1956.

Whiting, Charles. *Canaris*. New York: Ballantine, 1973.

Who Was Who. New York: St. Martin's, various years.

Who Was Who in America. Chicago: Marquis, various years.

Who's Who. New York: St. Martin's, various years.

Who's Who in America. Chicago: Marquis, various years.

Wighton, Charles. *The World's Greatest Spies*. London: Odham's, 1962.

Wighton, Charles, and Gunter Peis. *Hitler's Spies and Saboteurs: Based on the German Secret Service War Diary of General Lahousen*. New York: Henry Holt, 1958.

Wilson, Derek. *The Astors, 1763–1992: Landscape with Millionaires*. New York: St. Martin's, 1993.

Witcover, Jules. *Sabotage at Black Tom: Imperial Germany's Secret War in America, 1914–1917*. Chapel Hill: Algonquin Books of Chapel Hill, 1989.

Wood, Clement. *The Man Who Killed Kitchener: The Life of Fritz Joubert Duquesne, 1879–*. New York: William Faro, 1932.

Zahm, , J. A. (H. J. Mozans). *Through South America's Southland, with an Account of the Roosevelt Scientific Expedition to South America*. New York: D. Appleton, 1916.

Periodicals

"Adventure: Dean of the Pulps Celebrates Its Silver Jubilee." *Newsweek* 6 (26 Oct. 1935).

The Adventurer: Bulletin of the Adventurers Club, Dec. 1955 and Jan. 1956. [Announcement and report on the meeting of 21 Dec. 1955, which featured the last lecture of Fritz Duquesne.]

Barkdoll, Robert. "New Sanctuary: Rare Animals—A Race for Their Lives." *Los Angeles Times*, 11 Apr. 1975.

Billboard, Oct. and Nov. 1917.

"The Bombsight: Here Is the First, Exclusive Description of How the Famed Norden Bombsight Works." *Flying*, July 1945.

Boshoff, Toby. "Die Baas—Spioen van Alle Tye." *Byvoegsel Tot die Burger*, 30 Mar. 1963.

Bratzel, John F., and Leslie B. Rout Jr. "Research Note: Pearl Harbor, Microdots, and J. Edgar Hoover." *American Historical Review* 87 (Dec. 1982).

Burnham, Frederic Russell. "Transplanting African Animals." *The Independent* 68 (10 Feb. 1910).

"Caught in the Act." *Time* 38 (29 Sept. 1941).

Clifford, George. "The FBI's Greatest Cases." *Argosy*, Sept. 1974.

Collins, Frederick L. *Reader's Digest* 41 (Dec. 1942). [Condensed from *Future*, Nov. 1942.]

Culenaere, A. "A Short History of Microphotography (High-Reduction Photography)." *Journal of Forensic Sciences* 4 (Jan. 1959).

Dawson, Warrington. "Hunting with Roosevelt in East Africa." *Hampton's Magazine* 23 (Nov. 1909).

Dorwart, Jeffery M. "The Roosevelt-Astor Espionage Ring." *New York History* 62 (July 1981).

Eckland, Edward. "The Cops Laughed Last at the Crook Who Fooled Them for 13 Years." *New York Mirror* Sunday Magazine section, 26 June 1932.

Elwes, K. W. "The Boer Prisoners in Bermuda." *Fortnightly Review*, n.s., 71 (June 1902).

Flanagan, Keriann. "Nazi 'Spy Ring' Rediscovered in Centerport." *Long Islander*, 1 Aug. 1991.

Gaskill, Gordon. "South Africa's Joke on Hitler." *American Magazine* 134 (Sept. 1941).

Gilman, William. "How G-Men Trapped Hitler's Gestapo." *True Detective* 38 (Sept. 1942); 39 (Oct., Nov., Dec. 1942).

Glanzer, Phil. "Patroling the Airwaves." *American Mercury* 59 (Dec. 1944).

Godfrey, Peter. "The Man Who Hid the Kruger Millions." *Spotlight*, 27 May 1955.

"Greatest Spy Roundup in U.S. History Produces a Great Gallery of Faces." *Life* 11 (14 July 1941).

"Gypping the Gestapo." *Newsweek* 18 (22 Sept. 1941).

Hahn, Emily. "My Dear Selous . . ." *American Heritage* 14 (Apr. 1963).

Hillinger, Charles. "Zebra Steaks: Exotic Game an Alternative Meat Source." *Los Angeles Times*, 31 Oct. 1973.

Hoffman, Arthur Sullivant. "The Camp-Fire: A Meeting Place for Readers, Writers, and Adventurers." *Adventure* 6 (July 1913).

———. "The Camp-Fire: Adventurers Club Inaugural Dinner." *Adventure* 5 (Mar. 1913).

———. "The Camp-Fire: An Account of Fritz Duquesne's Jamaica Trip." *Adventure* 4 (Aug. 1912).

———. "The Camp-Fire: Captain Duquesne Prepares for South America." *Adventure* 6 (Sept. 1913).

———. "The Camp-Fire" [Fritz Duquesne story]. *Adventure* 5 (Nov. 1912).

———. "The Camp-Fire: With a Message from A.S.H." *Adventure* 94 (Nov. 1935).

———. "Some Real Adventurers." *Adventure* 2 (Oct. 1911).

Hoover, J. Edgar. "The Enemy's Masterpiece of Espionage." *Reader's Digest* 48 (Apr. 1946).

———. "The FBI Is on Guard." *Kiwanis Magazine* 14 (Feb. 1943).

———. "Hitler's Spying Sirens." *American Magazine* 138 (Dec. 1944).

———. "The Spy Who Double-Crossed Hitler." *American Magazine* 141 (May 1946).

Hoover, J. Edgar, and Frederick L. Collins. "Hitler's Spies Are Experts." *Collier's* 111 (24 Apr. 1943).

Hoover, J. Edgar, as told to Roderick M. Grant. "Spy Trap." *Popular Mechanics* 80 (Dec. 1943).

Jenkisson, John. "The FBI vs. New York Spies." *New York World-Telegram*, 25 June 1945.

Keens, John. "The Camp-Fire: Rebuttal Letter to Fritz Duquesne Autobiographical Letter." *Adventure* 8 (Oct. 1914).

Key, W. S. "The Boer Prisoners in Bermuda." *Outlook* 70 (15 Feb. 1902).

Kingsley, J. Donald. "Spies and Saboteurs." *Current History* 2 (Aug. 1942).

Krohn, Lewis G. "J.F.K.'s Father Was a Hollywood Wheeler Dealer." *Classic Film Collector*, no. 55 (summer 1977).

"International Spy Story in Centerport." *Long Islander*, 11 Sept. 1941.

Lee, Henry. "Smashing the Biggest Spy Ring." *Coronet* 31 (Dec. 1951).

McKay, Herbert C. "Notes from a Laboratory." *American Photography* 40 (Nov. 1946).

"Milestones." *Time* 67 (4 June 1956).

"Nazi Spies: The FBI Did a Superb Job of Smashing This Gang before It Could Damage U.S. War Effort." *Life* 11 (19 Dec. 1941).

"No. 1 Pulp." *Time* 26 (21 Oct. 1935).

O'Neil, Paul. "The Mystery of Staunton Hill: The Strange Death of Sasha Bruce." *Life* 2 (Jan. 1979).

Pagano, Penny. "Zoos Take on New Role—As Breeders." *Los Angeles Times,* 10 Nov. 1986.

Pelley, William Dudley. "The Camp-Fire: Autobiographical Letter." *Adventure* 11 (Feb. 1916).

Phillips, Cabell. "G-Men of the Airwaves." *New York Times Magazine,* 14 Sept. 1941.

Pound, Arthur. "Fritz Duquesne: The Sequel," *The American Legion Weekly,* 2 Oct. 1925.

———. "Is Fritz Duquesne Alive?" *The American Legion Weekly,* 31 July 1925.

Quigley, Martin S. "Espionage: An Article Devoted to the Gentle Art of Destroying Ships at Sea." *The Loyola '35.* Loyola High School, N.Y., semiannual paper, 1935.

Roraback, Dick. "Gourmet Safari: A Lion in Winter." *Los Angeles Times,* 22 Jan. 1980.

Schlesinger, Toni. "Hungry for Hippo? Lusting for Llama? Try This Exotic Shop." *Us,* 28 Sept. 1979.

Schwartz, Norman. "How to Fox a Flock of Locks." *Cavalier Magazine,* May 1961.

"Secret of Secrets." *Time* 38 (15 Sept. 1941).

Simpich, Frederick. "Hamburg Speaks with Steam Sirens." *National Geographic* 63 (June 1933).

"Some of Our *Adventure* Writers." *Adventure* 9 (Mar. 1915).

"Someone Hip to Hippo May Trip Col. Sanders." *Los Angeles Herald-Examiner,* 11 Sept. 1972.

Sondern, Frederick, Jr. "Catching Spies." *American Mercury* 54 (Feb. 1942).

"South African Hero Dies as Pauper." *Die Brandwag* 20 (8 June 1956).

"Spies." *New York Times Magazine,* 6 July 1941.

"Spies!" *Time* 38 (7 July 1941).

Spivak, John L. "Plotting the American Pogroms." *New Masses* 13 (2, 9, 16 Oct. 1934).

"Spy Crackdown." *Newsweek* 18 (7 July 1941).

"The Spy from S.A." *Justitia* 3 (Apr. 1963).

"Spy Roundup." *Newsweek* 18 (15 Sept. 1941).

Sterling, George E. "The RID Story." *Spark-Gap Times* (Irving, Texas: Old Old Timers Club), various issues. Chap. 3, "Spy and Counter-Spy," no. 17 (Oct. 1963). Chap. 5, "Nazi Spies in Latin America," no. 18 (Dec. 1963).

"Stripes for Spies." *Newsweek* 19 (12 Jan. 1941).

Thorwald, Jurgen. "Die Unsicht Bare Front." *Der Stern,* 1 and 8 Mar. 1953.

"Transition." *Newsweek* 48 (4 June 1956).

Trefousse, Hans L. "Failure of German Intelligence in the United States, 1935–1945." *Mississippi Valley Historical Review,* June 1955.

Van Hoek, Kees. "The Leyds Memoirs." *Dahousie Review* 19 (Apr. 1939).
Warren, Bill. "The 50 Fathom Nightmare." *Adventures for Men,* Apr. 1959.
Weir, Frank H. "From the Files of the FBI." *Philadelphia Inquirer,* 1956. [Six-part syndicated series.]
Whitehouse, A.G.J. "Spies? Phooey!" *Popular Aviation* 23 (Nov. 1938).
Wighton, Charles, and Gunter Peis. "The Untold Spy Plot to Sabotage America." *Action for Men,* June 1959.
Wood, Clement. "The True Story of Duquesne, Boer Soldier of Fortune, Arch Enemy of the British Empire." *New York Mirror* Sunday Magazine section, 3 July 1932.
"The World of William Sebold." *Time* 38 (22 Sept. 1941).
"Writers and Their Work." *Hampton's Magazine* 22 (Feb. 1909).

Author's Letters and Interviews

Appel, Charles A., Jr. FBI handwriting expert assigned to Duquesne case. Letter, 15 June 1973.
Becker, Jocelyn W. Son of Alice Wortley Duquesne Becker. 10 Aug. 1974.
Carroll, Leo G. Portrayed character based on Duquesne in 1945 film *The House on 92nd Street*. Several interviews in 1962.
Cloete, Stuart. South African novelist on same program at Adventurers Club in 1956 with Duquesne. Letter, 16 Jan. 1973.
Dath, P., Major General. Commandant, Ecole Royale Militaire. Letter, 2 June 1972.
Donohoe, Al. Adventurers Club member at same time as Duquesne. Letter, 16 Mar. 1973.
Friedemann, William G. FBI special agent assigned to Duquesne case. Letter, 8 May 1973. Telephone, 29 Nov. 1974.
Giorgio, Herbert P. Defense lawyer for Hermann Lang. Telephone, 29 June 1973.
Hall, John. Registrar, Southern Methodist University. Telephone, 27 Sept. 1988.
Hasso, Signe. Actress in 1945 film *The House on 92nd Street*. Several interviews in 1975, 1977.
Herz, George W. Defense lawyer for Hermann Lang. Interview, 28 June 1973.
Johnson, Richard L. FBI special agent assigned to Duquesne case. Letter, 14 June 1973. Telephone, 25 Nov. 1974.
Linding, Lillian. Close friend of Duquesne. Letters, 2 July, 19 Aug. 1972, 4 Apr. 1973. Telephone, 12 Sept. 1973.
Molveau, Claude A. Friend of Hans Ritter and Else Weustenfeld. Interview, 18 July 1992.
Mulholland, Colonel Mitchell J. Friend of Lillian Linding's, distributed Fritz's ashes at sea, has Fritz's medals. Telephone, 11 Nov. 1972, 15 Jan. 1995.
Newkirk, Raymond F. FBI special agent assigned to Duquesne case. Letters, 9 Mar., 21 May 1974. Telephone, 9, 12 Nov. 1974.
Nolan, Lloyd. Portrayed FBI inspector in 1945 film *The House on 92nd Street*. Several interviews in 1966, 1978, 1983.
Quigley, Martin, Jr. Quigley Publishing Co., Inc. A teen-age friend of

Duquesne's. Letter, 18 May 1973. Interview, 27 July 1973. Telephone, 13 Aug. 1994.
Ritter, Mrs. Irmgard. Letters, 22 Sept., 16 Oct., 12 Dec. 1988, 20 Dec. 1990.
Ritter, Nikolaus. Letter, 13 Feb. 1973.
Winsten, Archer. *New York Sun* reporter who interviewed Duquesne in 1934. Telephone, 1 Sept. 1973.
Wortley, Mildred Una Greenidge. Sister-in-law of Fritz Duquesne. Interview, 1 Sept. 1973.

Archival Material

Despatches C.O. 37/237 August Section, 26 June 1902, Bermuda Archives.
Emerson, Edwin. Address at Rough Riders reunion, Prescott, Ariz., June 1948, Theodore Roosevelt Collection, Harvard College Library.
Krynauw, J.D.T. Private Diary: P.O.W. aboard the *Harlech Castle* and at Bermuda. Unpublished, Transvaal Archives Depot, Pretoria.
Roosevelt, Theodore. Appointment Book: reel 432, series 11, 1906–9 Index. Theodore Roosevelt Papers, Library of Congress.
———. Exchange of letters with Frederick T. Case: reel 394, series 3A, 1917, Aug. 9, 10, 17. Theodore Roosevelt Papers, Library of Congress.
———. Letters in Theodore Roosevelt Collection, Harvard College Library.
Trial Docket Cr. 38425, FRC container no. 547802, General Services Administration, Federal Records Center, New York.
United States Department of Justice, Bureau of Prisons. Notorious Offenders File, record group 129, National Archives.

Film

Army-Navy Screen Magazine: A Pictorial Report from All Fronts for the Armed Forces Only, no. 42, reel 1, record group 3, accession 2355, National Archives.
Booth, Charles. *Now It Can Be Told (The House on 92nd Street).* Story outline no. 2261. 20th Century–Fox Film Corporation. Original copy date 10 Nov. 1945.
"The F.B.I. Front." *The March of Time,* vol. 9, issue 1 (Sept. 1942).
The House on 92nd Street. Film, 20th Century–Fox, 1945.
Monks, John, Jr. *Now It Can Be Told (The House on 92nd Street).* Revised final script no. 2261.8. 20th Century–Fox Film Corporation. 16 Apr. 1945.
"Patrolling the Ether." Episode of *Crime Does Not Pay* series. Metro-Goldwyn-Mayer, 1942.

Index

ABOUT THE AUTHOR

Art Ronnie is a retired television and movie publicist who has worked for all the major networks and studios. From 1956 to 1966 he worked for the *Los Angeles Herald-Express* and *Herald-Examiner* as a reporter, columnist, and book reviewer. He also served in the Army Signal Corps as a telephone lineman and in the Naval Air Reserve as an aircraft mechanic.

Ronnie is the author of *Locklear: The Man Who Walked on Wings,* a biography of barnstorming pilot and silent-movie star Ormer Locklear. A native of Los Angeles, he now lives in Altadena, California.

The NAVAL INSTITUTE PRESS is the book-publishing arm of the U.S. Naval Institute, a private, nonprofit society for sea service professionals and others who share an interest in naval and maritime affairs. Established in 1873 at the U.S. Naval Academy in Annapolis, Maryland, where its offices remain, today the Naval Institute has more than 100,000 members worldwide.

Members of the Naval Institute receive the influential monthly magazine *Proceedings* and discounts on fine nautical prints, ship and aircraft photos, and subscriptions to the bimonthly *Naval History* magazine. They also have access to the transcripts of the Institute's Oral History Program and get discounted admission to any of the Institute-sponsored seminars offered around the country.

The Naval Institute's book-publishing program, begun in 1898 with basic guides to naval practices, has broadened its scope in recent years to include books of more general interest. Now the Naval Institute Press publishes more than seventy titles each year, ranging from how-to books on boating and navigation to battle histories, biographies, ship and aircraft guides, and novels. Institute members receive discounts on the Press's nearly 400 books in print.

Full-time students are eligible for special half-price membership rates. Life memberships are also available.

For a free catalog describing Naval Institute Press books currently available, and for further information about U.S. Naval Institute membership, please write to:

Membership & Communications Department
U.S. Naval Institute
118 Maryland Avenue
Annapolis, Maryland 21402-5035

Or call, toll free, (800) 233-USNI.